*The French Enlightenment and the Jews*

ARTHUR HERTZBERG

# The French Enlightenment and the Jews

## The Origins of Modern Anti-Semitism

COLUMBIA UNIVERSITY PRESS • NEW YORK

Columbia University Press
New York   Oxford
Copyright © 1968, 1990 Columbia University Press
All rights reserved

Library of Congress Cataloging-in-Publication Data

Hertzberg, Arthur.
The French Enlightenment and the Jews : the origins of modern
anti-Semitism / Arthur Hertzberg.
p.    cm.
Includes bibliographical references (p.
Includes index.
ISBN 0-231-07385-2
1. Jews—France—History—18th century.
2. Jews—France—Social conditions.
3. Enlightenment—France.
4. Antisemitism—France—History—18th century.
5. France—Ethnic relations.
I. Title.
DS135.F82H4    1990
944′.004924—dc20    90-1853
CIP

∞

Printed in the United States of America

p  10 9 8 7 6 5 4 3 2 1

# To the Memory of My Mother

צל״ח

א״מ הרבנית נחמה שפרה בת ר׳ משולם הי״ד

ששבקה חיים לכל חי ביום י״א טבת תשכ״ח

ולא הניחה כמותה

להאי שופרא דבלי בעפרא קא בכינא

שלי ושלכם שלה הוא

# Contents

# Preface

With interruptions, the work that has gone into this book spread over more than a decade. During these years I have been helped generously by a number of institutions and individuals. The librarians and staffs of the Jewish Theological Seminary of America, Columbia University, the Bibliothèque nationale in Paris, the British Museum, and the Jewish National Library in Jerusalem all deserve my most grateful appreciation.

Of the many friends in the scholarly world who have aided me at one point or another, I must single out a few for special thanks. On some of the larger problems of this book I have talked repeatedly with Professor Joseph L. Blau. My younger friend, Paul Weissman, spent one summer as my research assistant and argued with me about some of the issues raised in this book. Mr. Zosa Szajkowski, the most ardent of contemporary researchers in Franco-Jewish history, has given me advice, especially in the economic field, and I have benefited from the wide learning of Professor Jeffrey Kaplow in French political and economic history. It goes without saying that none of these scholars are responsible for either my conclusions or my errors.

On the technical side, for taking down the original draft of the book on the typewriter and for repeated retypings of the manuscript, I am indebted to the concern and devotion of the several secretaries who have worked with me: Anne Bischoff, Francine Sager, and Margo Silverman. In the editing stage, the manuscript was greatly improved by the sound judgment of the copy editor, Elizabeth Brown, and by the wisdom and very personal interest of

my editor and good friend at the Columbia University Press, Henry
Wiggins.

Throughout all the stages of my work I have benefited from the
guidance and criticism of the greatest of contemporary Jewish historians, Professor Salo W. Baron, whose student I have had the
privilege of being. His personal friendship and concern, and that
of his wife, Jeannette, helped to sustain me in this large task of
research and writing. From beginning to end the work of this book
involved the collaboration, concern, and forbearance of my wife,
Phyllis. She helped in both the research and the preparation of the
manuscript, and she and our daughters, Linda and Susan, managed
to live with a busy and often burdened author with great grace
and understanding.

This book is about the origins of the Emancipation of the Jews
and the sources of modern anti-Semitism. The inception of this
study was obviously motivated by more than historical curiosity,
for the meaning of the Emancipation and the nature and roots of
contemporary anti-Semitism have remained for two centuries great
questions for Jews and for the larger society which has both accepted and attacked them. This book is being published in the
hope that what it has to say about French society and French
Jews, on the way to the Revolution, may have living relevance.

ARTHUR HERTZBERG

*December 6, 1967*

*The French Enlightenment and the Jews*

# Abbreviations

The following abbreviations have been used in the footnotes and in the bibliography:

AIF    *Archives israélites de France*

ASEJ    *Annuaire de la société des études juives*

HJ    *Historia Judaica*

HUCA    *Hebrew Union College Annual*

JQR    *Jewish Quarterly Review*

JSS    *Jewish Social Studies*

MGWJ    *Monatsschrift für die Geschichte und Wissenschaft des Judentums*

PAJHS    *Publication of the American Jewish Historical Society*

PAAJR    *Publication of the American Academy for Jewish Research*

REJ    *Revue des études juives*

RHB    *Revue historique de Bordeaux*

SBB    *Studies in Bibliography and Booklore*

## ·•§ I §•·

## Introduction

On January 28, 1790, the makers of the French Revolution decreed that all those who were "known in France by the name of Portuguese, Spanish, and Avignonnais Jews" should henceforth enjoy "the rights" of active citizens. Between three and four thousand individuals were thus given equality. Most of these people resided in the southwestern corner of the country, primarily in the cities of Bordeaux and Bayonne. The great majority were Sephardim, that is, Jews who remembered pridefully that their forebears had once lived in the Iberian Peninsula.

Twenty months later, on September 27, 1791, after much debate and many delays, all the rest of the Jews of France were emancipated.[1] This second decree applied to some thirty thousand individuals,[2] who with few exceptions lived on the northeastern border, in Alsace, in the city of Metz and the villages nearby, and in the duchy of Lorraine. These Jews were Ashkenazim: they were among the heirs of those religious and cultural forms that had been fashioned by the Diaspora in central Europe. At the beginning of the Revolution there were some individuals of great wealth among them, and even a small handful of semi-Westernized intellectuals. On the whole, however, this community was much poorer than the Sephardim; it was culturally more foreign and it was much more hated by its gentile neighbors. Nonetheless, by the middle of September, 1791, the parliament that had made the Revolution could no longer avoid granting equality to the Ashkenazim too.

[1] Halphen, *Recueil des lois*, pp. 1–2, 9–10.
[2] Anchel, *Napoléon et les Juifs*, pp. 1–2.

Earlier that month the first French constitution had been adopted. The famous declaration of the "rights of man and of the citizen," which had been proclaimed during the exalted days of the summer of 1789, was now affirmed as the basic law of the realm. The continued exclusion of the Jews of eastern France from full participation in the country's political, economic, and social life had become untenable, for this charter of liberty contained the proviso that "no one may be disturbed in his opinions, and especially not in his religion, provided that their outward expressions do not trouble public order as established by law." Nonetheless, various objections continued to be voiced at the crucial session of Tuesday, September 27, 1791. Duport, a liberal former deputy of the nobility of Paris, reminded the *Assemblée* that to hold such anti-Jewish views was equivalent to doing battle against the constitution itself.[3] The motion to emancipate the Jews then passed. For the first time in the modern history of the West all the Jews within the borders of a European state were united with all of its other citizens as equals before the law.

With these events of 1790 and 1791 in France a new era in Jewish history began. The armies of the Revolution took "liberty, equality, and fraternity" with them beyond the borders of France. Under the dictatorship and empire of Napoleon, Jews continued to be given equality as a matter of course wherever his power extended. The restoration of the Bourbons to the throne of France left the emancipation of the Jews in France itself untouched. In Italy and Germany, where the laws imposed by the French were indeed reversed after the collapse of Bonaparte, at least the memory of equality remained. All over Europe, even during the period of political reaction between 1815 and 1848, Jewish opinion was dominated by two convictions: what had happened in France was now immediately possible elsewhere in Europe; it had to happen in every country because it was an inevitable corollary of the emerging liberal-secular political order to which the future belonged.

These hopes seemed to be on the road to realization in the middle years of the nineteenth century. In the various states of central Europe the Jews achieved legal emancipation after 1848.

---

[3] Halphen, *Recueil des lois*, p. 229; see also Chapter X.

On paper, this principle was extended as far as the Balkans in 1878, when the Congress of Berlin made a guarantee of equality for Jews a pre-condition for giving Rumania its independence. None of these achievements came easily for there was considerable opposition everywhere, even in the midst of a supposedly progressive century. The largest Jewish community in Europe, that of the Russian empire, continued to suffer increasing persecution. Nonetheless, even there the leaders of "enlightened" Jewish opinion believed that further acculturation by Jews and the inevitable growth of liberalism in the gentile majority would bring freedom.

During the nineteenth century the major Jewish efforts for complete integration into European society were led by middle-class elements. A minority group existed (and it became ever more prominent towards the end of the century) which doubted that equality could be achieved within the bourgeois and capitalist order. Jewish socialists of all varieties, however, were even more certain than the Jewish liberals that total emancipation was inevitable as part of the coming social revolution. None believed that the European left could ever develop any serious tendency towards anti-Semitism.

Both bourgeois and socialist Jews were, of course, aware that opposition to the Emancipation was not vanishing. They had to find ways of understanding this phenomenon, that is, of explaining why anti-Semitism was continuing into a supposedly progressive era. Their favorite explanation was "time lag": clericalist, counter-revolutionary, and Christian medievalist elements had persisted into the new age, but they would inevitably die away. Jews could understand their enmity, for anti-Semitism was conceived as the last gasp of those who had either not yet entered the modern age or who had refused to enter it. Jews expected, however, that the secularized, educated, politically liberal or left-wing elements, the heirs of the Enlightenment and of the French Revolution, would be their friends.

Not all of them were. On the contrary, some of the most advanced circles in Europe of the nineteenth century were quite impatient with Jews and even hated them. In their discomfort Jewish liberals and socialists devised several explanations. Some of the

criticism was accepted as reasonable. As a matter of fact, many
Jews were refusing to acculturate themselves completely. Jewish
liberals agreed with their gentile peers that cultural foreignness and
religious apartness were blocking the way to a glorious future both
for the Jews and for the whole of society. Among the socialists the
great outcry was that the Jews, in their traditional economic pursuits as middlemen, were "unproductive." Here, too, Jewish socialists joined with their gentile peers in finding merit in the criticism: Jews should, indeed, reorganize their economy so as to make,
supposedly, a more worthwhile contribution to production. Jewish
liberals and socialists could thus agree with the milder critics of
their people. Nonetheless, they could not avoid recognizing that
some of the politically most advanced gentiles had, at very least,
a particular nastiness in their tone when they talked of Jews. Here
again the concept of time lag was invoked. It was argued that even
great men such as Voltaire and Proudhon could not completely free
themselves of their earliest Christian upbringings. Their angers
were explained, however, as unfortunate personal idiosyncrasies,
which had no bearing on the essential content or thrust of the
progressive ideas they had helped to fashion.

A great turning came in the last decades of the nineteenth century. In the very midst of a wave of pogroms in Russia in 1881 a
young Jewish "enlightener," Moshe Leib Lilienblum, sat cowering
in hiding in Odessa. He wrote in his diary that he had, of course,
known that there had been pogroms before, yet this pogrom transformed him from a believer in assimilation to a passionate Zionist.
What made the crucial difference was the sight of young high school
and university students, the best educated and most politically advanced groups in Russia, among the makers of the pogroms.[4] This
theme was crucial to the pamphlet written by another "enlightened"
Jew from Odessa, Leo Pinsker. He, too, turned Zionist and preached
the doctrine of Jewish *Auto-Emancipation* (the title of his essay),
a Zionist solution to the Jewish problem.

For a number of decades only the Zionists cast any serious doubt
on the meaning of the historic events in France in 1790 and 1791.
They agreed with the believers in the Emancipation that modern

[4] Hertzberg, *The Zionist Idea*, p. 174.

anti-Semitism was nourished emotionally and historically by the
older passions of Christian theology and medieval Jew-hatred. What
was new in the Zionist outlook was that Pinsker and Theodor Herzl,
the central figure of modern Zionism, both independently recognized that modern anti-Semitism was more than just the result of a
time lag; its contemporary version was held to be a new, secular,
and continuing phenomenon. It was endemic among large elements
of the most modern groups within European society, not because
such people had as yet failed to free themselves of the remains of
medievalism, but because they had a new, contemporary reason for
being the enemies of the Jews. It was the hatred that any people
have for aliens in their midst.[5]

The Zionist explanation of anti-Semitism was radical. Unlike the
liberal and socialist theories it did not downgrade the importance of
contemporary Jew-hatred. Nonetheless, this theory too made anti-
Semitism "normal" and to some degree even rationalized it. Pinsker
and Herzl were both liberal nationalists. They shared in the reigning hopes of their day for a world order that would be a concert
of national cultures, expressing themselves through sovereign states.
Such cultures had a right to prefer complete internal unity, and
anti-Semitism could thus be understood as the undertow of the
wave of the future. The sane thing that the Jews could do would be
to normalize their existence by reconstituting themselves as a nation.
They would thus enter the larger society of mankind in the only
way in which this was possible.

Even in his darkest moments Herzl believed that the emancipation of the Jews of Europe was irreversible. He never doubted that
the events which had begun in Paris in 1790 and 1791 represented
a radical break with the European past. The Zionists, too, were convinced that a commitment had been made at that historic moment
by the bearers of modern European culture and the leaders of its
social advance to find some mode of including the Jews within the
polity of Europe.

The era of Western history that began with the French Revolution ended in Auschwitz. The emancipation of the Jews was re-

[5] *Ibid.*, pp. 45–51, where there is more extended comment on this point, and
pp. 209, 218–20, for Herzl's own remarks in the text of *The Jewish State.*

straight
Jabotinsky

versed in the most horrendous way. For a short while after 1945 the reigning explanation of the Nazi phenomenon was psychological: this demonic anti-Semitism had arisen from the depths of the most emotionally disturbed element in Europe.[6] This first attempt at explanation has now been overwhelmed by the evidence that has been mounted against it. Adolf Hitler was undoubtedly mad, but the millions who responded to his hatred of Jews cannot be called insane in any conventional sense of individual psychosis. For that matter, the notion that a mass madness in Europe in the twentieth century expressed itself at its most murderous by choosing to attack the Jews requires explanation in itself. What created such a pre-disposition? Why was the emancipation of the Jews that part of the liberal order which was destroyed most easily and effectively?

Hannah Arendt confronted these questions in the years immediately after World War II from the perspective of an historian.[7] Her explanation had the signal merit of applying systematically, with a richness of understanding all her own, the Zionist insight that modern anti-Semitism was a contemporary, secular phenomenon and not a revival of medieval Christian Jew-hatred. Various aspects of Arendt's complicated and subtle analysis must, however, be qualified or even largely rejected. For example, she has exaggerated the role of the court Jews in the formation of the European nation states in the seventeenth and eighteenth centuries. The fashioning of the French state was the paradigm of that entire historic process. Jews played no role of any consequence there; during the last century of the "old order" the French monarchy was largely financed by foreign Protestant bankers.

A more fundamental issue is raised by the factor she has identified as being primary in the creation of modern anti-Semitism. In the nineteenth century the European nation states, as their economies were becoming national, were ever less disposed to allow the Jews any significant enclave that they could keep as their own. In Arendt's view modern anti-Semites attacked the Jews because their wealth was no longer related to the kind of real power that the court

---

[6] This thesis underlay the massive five volumes, *Studies in Prejudice,* ed. Horkheimer and Flowerman, which were begun towards the end of World War II and appeared in 1950.

[7] Arendt, *The Origins of Totalitarianism;* see especially pp. 3–53.

Jews had once held. Ideological anti-Semitism had thus crystallized in the last third of the nineteenth century to announce that society could and should now dispense with the Jews. But is it conceivable that the enormous power of this hate was bred in a few short decades? Did the new anti-Semitism of the nineteenth century really arise, essentially, out of the contemporary historic situation?

One of the announced purposes of the Emancipation had been to normalize the economy of the Jew so that no particular pursuit, not even moneylending, should be the Jew's own preserve. As this normalization was happening, what predisposed their enemies both to exaggerate, wildly, the economic power of the Jews as it was in fact declining, and concurrently to adjudge the Jews to be even physically redundant because their power had indeed declined? As moralist, Hannah Arendt was eager to avoid the notion of an eternal anti-Semitism because the image of an overwhelming historical force can be used all too easily by individuals and by whole generations to disclaim moral responsibility. Nevertheless, Arendt's assertion that modern anti-Semitism is entirely new is not true to the facts. Medieval impulses towards hatred of Jews remained much more powerful in the new age of post-Christian ideology than she has suggested. More fundamentally, the secularity that she has identified as the new note in modern anti-Semitism did not arise for the first time in the nineteenth century. This Jew-hatred had old antecedents, even older ones than the Christian anti-Semitism it both used and replaced; its power came from the fact that it was a revival of one of the oldest European traditions.

Modern, secular anti-Semitism was fashioned not as a reaction to the Enlightenment and the Revolution, but within the Enlightenment and Revolution themselves. Some of the greatest of the founders of the liberal era modernized and secularized anti-Semitism too. In this new form they gave it fresh and powerful roots by connecting this version of Jew-hatred with ancient pagan traditions. The action of the French Revolution in emancipating the Jews was thus no simple triumph of liberalism over darkness. The immediate context of this declaration and the sources out of which it arose were complicated and not of one piece.

The processes that were at work in France itself were also acting in the seventeenth and eighteenth centuries elsewhere in central and western Europe, but a new understanding of the situation in France is, nonetheless, of crucial importance. The French Jewish community in the eighteenth century was a kind of microcosm of all the others. It contained representative elements of both the major Euro-Jewish traditions, the Sephardi and the Ashkenazi; the political and economic history of these Jews was typical of what was happening at that time elsewhere in western and central Europe. More important, in the eighteenth century, the "century of Voltaire," France dominated the spiritual life of the West. The forces in French thought and politics that created the Revolution were the impulses for most of the important developments in all of Europe in the next century. It is in the land in which the emancipation of the Jews began that we must search for some clues with which to explain not only its successes but also its failure. What appears from this new study is that the events of 1790 and 1791 were surrounded, on every level, with ambiguities and ambivalences.

Among the Jews themselves the communal leadership fought almost to the very end to maintain and even to strengthen the internal autonomous structure of the Jewish community and their control of it. The "price" for equality, the ending of all formal separatism on the part of the Jews, was not paid easily and as a matter of course. The leaders of Jewry were thus in considerable conflict with their best friends among the gentiles, who believed almost unanimously that the complete regeneration of the mass of Jews required the end of their autonomy and their complete assimilation into French society.

More important ambivalences appeared in French opinion itself. Those who voted for the decrees were, indeed, the heirs of newer ideas about tolerance, but they represented very different ideas as well. Each of these several "schools" was, in its turn, divided about the Jewish question.

Even the Church was divided, though here the pro-Jewish elements were very small indeed. The older Christian hatred of the Jews continued to dominate both the clergy and the faithful in France throughout the eighteenth century and into the next. Nonetheless, the most important figure in the debates about the Jews was a parish priest in eastern France, Henri Grégoire. He had received his earliest education from Jansenists who had become millenarians. There can be no doubt that much of his fervor for the emancipation of the Jews derived from a religious semi-underground that was at least a century old in France. It had proposed kinder treatment of the Jews as a preamble to their conversion.

More secular elements were also not of one mind. The whole process of the piecemeal readmission of Jews to France after 1500 had been rooted in mercantilist considerations, that is, in the idea that by allowing at least some Jews into the country France would increase its international trade. By the middle of the eighteenth century both royal administrators and theoretical economists were leaning ever more to the new doctrines that favored free economic competition within the country. The "free traders" were becoming friendlier to Jewish peddlers and illegal store keepers, whom they regarded as representing economic progress. Colbert in the seventeenth century consistently tried to protect large-scale Jewish entrepreneurs; Turgot towards the end of the reign of Louis XVI fought to destroy the guilds, and as one corollary of this effort he wanted to bring Jewish traders and artisans into the mainstream of the economy. These two greatest innovators among French statesmen of the "old order" were also the most important lineal ancestors of the decrees of 1790 and 1791, but their ideas did not easily prevail.[8] Both older and newer outlooks were arrayed against them. Smaller businessmen with whom Jews competed and especially peasants of eastern France, who were traditionally the debtors of innumerable petty Jewish moneylenders, remained anti-Semites after the Revolution, as before it. They continued to use medieval rhetoric but in the last decades of the *ancien régime* they were given new theoretical justification for their hatred. Physiocratic economists arose to deny that any of the traditional Jewish trades were economically useful. One of the leaders of the left during the French

[8] On mercantilism, enlightened absolutism, and the general movement towards the end of medieval corporatism and the creation of the modern state as the sources of the emancipation of the Jews, see Baron, "Newer Approaches to Jewish Emancipation," *Diogenes*, No. 29, pp. 56–81.

Revolution, a deputy from Alsace named Jean François Rewbell, fought bitterly against the emancipation of the Jews; he derived many of his arguments from the physiocrats.

The most crucial and fateful ambivalence about Jews was present among the *philosophes,* the leaders of new thought in the eighteenth century. It has been well known, from his own time to this day, that Voltaire personally disliked Jews quite intensely, and this has generally been explained as an accidental and secondary phenomenon. Voltaire was supposed to have been reflecting both some personal unfortunate experiences with Jews and his incapacity as an individual to free himself from his earliest Christian education. The attacks that he and some of his leading associates mounted on Jews and Judaism were supposedly part of the process by which he was attempting to dethrone Christianity, and they were not meant to lessen the ultimate claims of Jews upon equal regard in the new world that enlightened men were envisaging. A rereading of all the evidence, however, proves beyond any shadow of a doubt that in the discussions of the several decades before the Revolution Voltaire was consistently understood on all sides to be the enemy of the Jews of the present as well as of those of the past. His writings were the great arsenal of anti-Jewish arguments for those enemies of the Jews who wanted to sound contemporary. The "enlightened" friends of the Jews invariably quoted from Montesquieu and did battle with Voltaire.

Voltaire's own views cannot be explained, or rather explained away, in such fashion as to defend a view of the Enlightenment as ultimately completely tolerant. An analysis of everything that Voltaire wrote about Jews throughout his life establishes the proposition that he is the major link in Western intellectual history between the anti-Semitism of classic paganism and the modern age. In his favorite pose of Cicero reborn he ruled the Jew to be outside society and to be hopelessly alien even to the future age of enlightened men.

These ambivalences within the Enlightenment have had large consequences. Jacobin anti-Semites used Voltaire's rhetoric and that of the physiocrats. In the early decades of the nineteenth century some of the greatest figures of European socialism, men like Proudhon and Fourier and even Karl Marx, found reason for doubting or denying entirely that the Jews could be readily included in their socialist vision. Most such arguments derived quite consciously from the same sources. The Christian idea that the religion of the Jews and their rejection of Christianity made them an alien element was still strong in Europe. It had now been reinforced by the pagan cultural argument that the Jews were by the very nature of their own culture and even by their biological inheritance an unassimilable element. It had become possible for religious and anti-religious factions to agree that the emancipation of the Jews could not be realized and that it was dangerous to the European majority.

The sources of the Emancipation are to be found most immediately in the France of the "old order," which the Revolution destroyed. The roots of modern Jew-hatred are to be found there too. Both the hopeful and the tragic elements in modern Jewish history descend directly from the way the Jewish question was defined in France on its way to the Revolution.

## ❧ I I ❧

## The Beginning of the Resettlement

Marie de Medicis was the last ruler of France to apply to the question of the Jews the purely medieval conception that the state existed to be the servant of the Christian faith. Acting as queen-regent for her son, Louis XIII, she issued a decree in 1615 expelling all Jews from the kingdom on the ground that they were "sworn enemies of the Christian religion." Nonetheless, the queen's personal physician, Elijah de Montalto, and his family and retinue were left undisturbed. The queen and Montalto had first met when he visited Paris in 1606. He was then still discreet, at least in public, about his Judaism, but when Marie called Montalto from Italy to her service in 1610 he made it a condition of his acceptance that he be allowed to practice his religion openly at her court. Indeed, when Montalto died in 1616, Marie took great trouble to have his body embalmed and sent to Amsterdam for burial in the Jewish cemetery there.[1]

[1] Malvezin, *Histoire des Juifs à Bordeaux*, p. 122. A bizarre circle which included cabalists supposedly formed around Montalto in Paris. These were years of religious ferment in France and Judaism was involved, if only as an accusation or an epithet. The *parlement* of Paris asked on September 1, 1614, for the expulsion of "Jews, atheists, and anabaptists and others who were professing religions which were not tolerated by royal decrees." In 1615 there was a scandal of large proportions, when an Italian priest, Cosmo Ruger, refused the sacraments on his deathbed. The greatest scandal of all in the court of the queen-regent Marie de Medicis was in 1617, when her favorite, the Italian adventurer Concino Concini, and his wife Leonora Galigai fell from power and were put to death. Galigai was suspected, no doubt correctly, of practicing magic; she was also accused, probably without foundation, of Judaizing. See Poliakov, *Histoire de l'antisémitisme, du Christ au juif du cours*, pp. 194–97; for the pamphlet literature occasioned by the Concini affair, see Szajkowski, *Franco-Judaica*, Nos. 1572–73. During Montalto's first visit to Paris he had

The decree of 1615 had no practical effect. The year before the marranos in Bordeaux had been suspected of Judaizing, but they were able to convince the authorities that this was not so. As "Christians" they avoided the expulsion ordered by the regent.[2] The escapees from Spain and Portugal were to remain marranos in France until the last years of the seventeenth century. The medieval political ideal was still too powerful an influence in Catholic France for them to be able to abjure their baptisms in public. The crucial changes were to come in the later years of the seventeenth century, during the reign of Louis XIV.

The king's own mind was a battleground, in which two political conceptions fought each other. Generally the modern, secularist idea of *raison d'état* won, but, especially as he grew older, he wanted to believe that he really was "his most Christian majesty" and "the oldest son of the Church."[3] He veered between the influence of the very pious Madame de Maintenon, who had great power even before she became Louis XIV's morganatic wife in 1684, and the very different pressures that were exerted by his greatest minister, Colbert. Madame de Maintenon continued in the spirit of Marie de Medicis. Her pithiest criticism of Colbert was that he "thinks only of his finances and almost never of his religion."[4] The king himself believed that it was, ultimately, his duty to establish the complete religious unity of France. He did repress Protestantism in 1685 when he revoked the Edict of Nantes. In the next fifteen years some 300,000 Huguenots, one of the most useful segments in the economy of France, emigrated, to the great harm of French commerce.[5] Louis XIV was convinced that he ought also to expel the Jews from the country at a convenient time, and he was sure

---

treated Galigai, successfully, and she had recommended him to her childhood friend, the queen. This connection was used against Galigai in her trial, as evidence that she was a Judaizer. On Montalto's career in general, see Friedenwald, *The Jews and Medicine*, II, 468–96. Montalto did not take money on the Sabbath for any of his medical services but he did feel constrained to travel to court on that day. He defended that practice in a *responsum* that he wrote in Hebrew; this document has been published by Roth, "Elie Montalto et sa consultation sur le sabbat," *REJ*, XCIV, 113–36.

[2] Malvezin, p. 121.

[3] Sée, *Les idées politiques en France au XVIIᵉ siècle*, p. 139.

[4] Quoted in Cole, *Colbert and a Century of French Mercantilism*, p. 300.

[5] Mathorez, *Les étrangers en France*, I, 55.

that it was relatively easy to do. Despite his ever-increasing religious orthodoxy, that moment never came. On the contrary, during the very years after 1684 in which Louis XIV was personally practicing a most punctilious form of the Catholic faith, his government was permitting the marranos in southwestern France to throw off every vestige of their Christian disguise. Christians of Jewish descent were coming over from Portugal and Spain regularly to Bordeaux and Bayonne, where they were circumcised and lived openly as Jews.[6]

What had wrought the change? By what process, for that matter, had Jews reappeared in France in the sixteenth century, despite their complete exclusion during the Middle Ages?

After the final expulsion of the Jews from France in 1394, they had indeed ceased to exist in law anywhere within the borders of the kingdom. In the years 1481–86, as the Provence was being reincorporated into France, the Jews were expelled from that region too.[7] Some of the descendants of the medieval Franco-Jewish community continued to live as marranos in various places, especially in Paris. There the grandchildren of the earlier Jewish settlers, even though they had long abandoned all vestiges of Judaism, inhabited the old Jewish neighborhood, and engaged for the most part in the "Jewish" trade in old clothes. This trade figured in a notorious murder in 1652. The guild of old clothes dealers mobbed a young man and killed him for calling them "the synagogue" when they marched by in procession.[8] Nonetheless, despite such remnants of Jewish life, and of anti-Semitism, the expulsion put an effective end to the organized Jewish community of medieval France.

Jews never did return in any appreciable degree to the core territory of French rule, the places from which they had been banished by the decree of 1394, until after the Revolution. Even in the nineteenth century the movement into the heartland of France was very slow. Around 1300, as tax records prove, the Jews of France had been living in its center.[9] Five centuries later, in 1808, the first

[6] Szajkowski, "Population Problems," *PAAJR*, XXVII, 83–105; Cirot, *Recherches*, pp. 176–78.

[7] Baron, *A Social and Religious History of the Jews*, X, 91.

[8] Anchel, "The Early History of the Jewish Quarters in Paris," *JSS*, II, 45–60, and especially 56–58.

[9] Nahon, "Contribution à l'histoire des Juifs," *REJ*, CXXI, 58–80, and especially pp. 81–82 for the map of places inhabited by Jews in the years 1285–1306, which is given as an appendix to that study.

complete census of the newly emancipated Jewish community was taken. Even then, after some years of freedom to move as they wished, Jews had made only the barest beginnings of a real presence in the center of France. The overwhelming majority still continued to live on the borders, in the regions to which they had first come after 1500.[10]

What made it possible for Jews to reenter France? In the first place, the resettlement began not with avowed Jews but with marranos, who were fleeing from the Iberian Peninsula. Not all of these people, despite their Jewish ancestry, necessarily became crypto-Jews upon their arrival in the more relaxed atmosphere of France. Some, such as the family of Montaigne, intermarried with French Christians and ceased to be connected with the community.[11] Others retained their identity as part of the community of "Portuguese merchants, known as new Christians," but even among them we cannot be sure that all were really marranos. No doubt some of these people themselves were not sure of what they were. The important intellectual figure Isaac de la Peyrère, for example, was a native of Bordeaux who was almost certainly of Jewish blood; he was in turn a Protestant and a Catholic and his theology contained both Christian and Jewish elements. When he died in 1676, supposedly as a professing Catholic, he refused the last rites of the Church.[12] The religious ambiguities that were so prevalent among these marranos and demi-marranos were not entirely out of character with the temper of southwestern France in the seventeenth century. This region was then the scene of much Protestant propaganda and influence; refugees from the Inquisition whose religion was not the orthodox Catholic kind were, there and at that time, not a complete anomaly.

Jews actually began to reappear in Bordeaux in the aftermath of war. After the French conquered that city from the English in 1454

[10] Archives Nationales de France, *Dénombrement de la population juive, 1808*, F19–11023. There were, for example, only two Jewish families in Blois, three individuals in Le Havre, and only sixty-seven in Lyons. This census has been studied by Posener, "Les Juifs sous le premier empire," *REJ*, XCIII, 192–214; XCIV, 157–66.

[11] Friedenwald, "Montaigne's Relation to Judaism and the Jews," *JQR*, XXXI, 141–48.

[12] Schoeps, *Philosemitismus im Barock*, p. 8. For discussion of Peyrère's theology, see Chapter III.

commerce had languished. Many inhabitants had chosen to leave with the English and a plague in 1473 had further decreased the population. Under these circumstances Louis XI issued a decree in 1474 inviting all foreigners, excluding the recent foreign masters of the city, to settle freely in Bordeaux.[13] Concurrently the situation of the Jews was worsening across the border in Spain and Portugal. The final expulsions from Spain in 1492 and from Portugal in 1497 had involved not only thousands of avowed Jews, who could not ask for admission to France, but also many marranos, who found it safer to emigrate. A few crypto-Jews had appeared in Bordeaux almost immediately after the English left and more arrived after 1500.

The most illustrious of the first families of Jewish origin to live in Bordeaux was the Govea clan. It was headed by two brothers, André and Antoine. They were the founders of the *Collège de Guyenne*, where they taught, among others, Michel de Montaigne. André Govea enjoyed numerous ecclesiastical benefices and held a doctorate in theology. There is no evidence that he himself was a marrano, but he used his influence in the royal court to obtain the first legal charter for the crypto-Jews in Bordeaux and the surrounding province. In August, 1550, Henry II issued *lettres patentes* according the most liberal kind of permission to "the merchants and other Portuguese called new Christians" to settle freely in France with their families and retainers and to conduct all types of business on the basis of complete equality with the king's native subjects.[14] This was the beginning of the political history of Sephardi Jews in France.

This decree was not easily accepted by Bordeaux, the major and key community in which the marranos were settling. The *parlement* of Paris registered the royal act quite promptly in December of the year in which it was issued but there was no comparable action by the *parlement* of Bordeaux. The number of "new Christians" in that city and elsewhere in the region continued to increase, however, and inevitably commercial jealousies, as well as suspicions that these

---

[13] Malvezin, *Histoire des Juifs à Bordeaux*, p. 90.

[14] *Ibid.*, pp. 98–107; Léon, *Histoire des Juifs de Bayonne*, p. 18. The text of this decree is to be found in full in E. Ginsburger, *Les statuts juridiques*, pp. 1–4.

"new Christians" were indeed Jews, brought the matter of their status to a head in 1574. After litigation the *parlement* of Bordeaux forbade any molestation of the Spanish and Portuguese merchants residing in that city. The contention of their lawyer that they were good Catholics was accepted and perhaps even believed. Later that year Henry III reaffirmed their privileges in two decrees, one addressed to the *parlement* of Bordeaux and the other to the *grand sénéchal* of Guienne. These decrees, along with the earlier one of 1550, which they reaffirmed and strengthened, were finally registered by the *parlement* of Bordeaux in 1580.[15] It should be remembered that in the law of the *ancien régime* a royal decree was not valid in any specific province without such registration by its *parlement*.

There was one further quarrel that involved these marranos before the end of the sixteenth century. During the siege of Bordeaux by the Spanish in 1596–97 the local populace feared that this community of "Spanish and Portuguese merchants" would betray the town. By decree of the *parlement* in January, 1597, those who had resided in Bordeaux more than ten years were moved in from the walls to the center of town and all the more recent inhabitants were expelled to Peyrehorade, Bidache, and Bayonne. The arrival of the crypto-Jews in these border towns soon aroused commercial jealousy. Under the pretext of fear that these "Spanish" were a dangerous element on the frontier, a decree was elicited from Henry IV in 1602 enjoining them to leave the region of Bayonne, but this act was never carried out. The expulsion from Bordeaux thus marked the beginning of modern Jewish communal history in Bayonne and the surrounding villages.[16]

[15] Malvezin, pp. 109–11; Léon, p. 19; E. Ginsburger, p. 5.
[16] This account follows Malvezin, *Histoire des Juifs à Bordeaux*, pp. 113–14. Léon, *Histoire des Juifs de Bayonne*, p. 19, accounted for the decree of January, 1597, differently; it was not an act forced by the external enemies of the community, but it was requested by the older Jewish inhabitants themselves, to defend their commercial interests against newer Jewish arrivals. This account is possible.

See also E. Ginsburger, "Les Juifs de Peyrehorade," *REJ*, CIII, 35–69, where he maintained that the first proven trace of Jews in that town dates from 1600, although it is possible that Jews were there earlier. In the brief introduction to his collection of documents concerning Bayonne, Ginsburger asserted that the Jewish community of Bayonne began in the thirteenth century and implied

On the eastern border France reacquired Jews, openly professing their religion, beginning in the 1560s by a different process. Bit by bit in the course of the sixteenth and seventeenth centuries pieces of territory in Alsace and Lorraine, through war and treaty, were taken over from the domain of the German empire. In law the French crown usually accepted upon itself all of the obligations that had formerly belonged to the emperor when these lands were under German rule. It is too simple to say that avowed Jews thus reappeared under French rule because they were present as a legacy from German rule. This was indeed true in many cases, and especially in the parts of Alsace that Louis XIV acquired in 1648 in the Peace of Westphalia. When France conquered Metz in 1552, however, there seem to have been no Jews in the city. The first several families were formally permitted to settle there some years later by the French military governor in order to provide credit both to the ruined bourgeois of the city and to the military garrison. This was the first occasion after 1394 that the French power admitted Jews, as such, to one of its territories.[17]

Nevertheless, even this action represented no reversal of the policy of expulsion. It was possible to admit Jews to Metz without affecting the legal situation in the rest of France because of the patchwork nature of the French state. To the very end of the *ancien régime* France was not administratively united. There were many separate political and economic arrangements for various of the

---

that its French Jewish founding families were still Jews as marranos when the Spanish and Portuguese marranos began to arrive there. He dated the beginning of this new migration in the fifteenth century (*Les statuts juridiques,* p. 1). In this pamphlet, which was prepared for defensive reasons during the Nazi occupation of France, he adduced no evidence for these assertions. Since the purpose of the work was to maintain the great age of the Jewish settlement in France, historical exaggeration was both likely and pardonable. Ginsburger clearly misstated the numbers involved. He maintained that there were from 800 to 1,000 Jewish families in the Bayonne region around 1600. This number was indeed given in one source, the decree of Henry IV in 1602, ordering the Jews to move inland from Bayonne during the war with Spain. As Ginsburger certainly knew, those numbers were very much exaggerated. Jewish population in Bayonne never reached 400 families at any point before 1789. A census in June, 1718, showed 100 families (Léon, p. 22). The figure in Henry IV's decree represented either the inadvertent adding of a zero or exaggeration by the complainants in Bayonne. Bordeaux, which was always the larger community, had only from 50 to 60 Jewish families in 1609 (Malvezin, p. 118).

[17] Clément, *La condition des Juifs,* pp. 20–21.

larger regions, and even for individual provinces or much smaller areas. This was all the more true of the lands on the eastern border, which were ruled as occupied territory until the Revolution. This region was in the control of the Ministry of War, and the military necessities of the garrison were the paramount concern of the crown. Special arrangements of purely local extent, including the admission of Jews or the permission for them to remain, were thus all the more possible in places which were kept separate from the core territory of France.[18]

The admission of marranos in the region of Bordeaux in the seventeenth century and beyond was always an arrangement that depended directly on the royal will. There were other forces at work on the eastern border of the country. Innumerable *seigneuries* and municipalities jealously guarded the right to admit Jews to their domains by their own choice. They found in this a source of quick income, in the large charges they could impose for the *droit d'acception,* and a constant advantage to their exchequers, through the long list of other taxes that were added as "carrying charges" for the right to live, to raise children and have them marry, and to do business. The numbers involved by the end of the seventeenth century were still negligible. In all of France in the year 1700 there were not five thousand Jews. These small groups were, however, there to stay.

The process of settling is clearest in Metz. The decree of 1615 to expel all the Jews from France had been issued in the name of Louis XIII. Yet seventeen years later the now adult king confirmed the privileges of the Jews of Metz. The reasons were, however, the same as those that had motivated the Marshal de Vieilleville in 1567 to give the first several families permission to stay in Metz: the military garrison required credit and provisions.

The scene was still largely medieval in 1657 when Louis XIV came to Metz on the morrow of his personal victory at the siege of Montmédy, but some newer elements now appeared. A few days after his arrival the king himself, for the first time in the history of the French monarchy, came in great pomp to visit a synagogue.

[18] Szajkowski, *Economic Status,* pp. 20–21; Hoffman, *L'Alsace,* I, 3, 421. Strasbourg, the commercial center of the province, opposed a project as late as 1785 to integrate Alsace into France because it feared harm to its commerce.

Two days later, after some back and forth, the rabbi and two lay leaders went as a delegation to be received in audience by the chancellor, the Count de Brienne. The rabbi at that time was Moshe Cohen Narol, who wrote a description of that scene. De Brienne's opening question was terrifying; Louis XIV wanted to know why Narol had come to Metz to exercise the function of rabbi without royal permission. Narol was so frightened that he could not answer. De Brienne then hastened to assure Narol that, despite the king's slight displeasure, he was well disposed to the Jews. On that very day Louis XIV reconfirmed the privileges of the Jews of Metz; he added one significant new provision, by giving the Jews the right to deal in all forms of merchandise.[19]

In 1670 Raphael Lévy was condemned to death in Metz on the medieval ground that he had stolen and murdered a Christian child. This case became famous, not the least because Richard Simon, who was then the leading biblical scholar in France, wrote a pamphlet in defense of Lévy.[20] The condemned man was not saved. This accusation did not, however, have the result that had been all too usual in the past ages. There was no pogrom and no decree of expulsion of the entire Jewish community. Jewish population continued to grow in Metz in the next years and, more in actual fact than by formal permission, the commerce of the Jews greatly increased. By the end of the seventeenth century the Jewish population had grown to 1,200, by far the largest group in France. At that moment there were roughly 2,500 Jews in all of Alsace, and perhaps 500 each in Bordeaux and Bayonne.

In 1697 the intendants of France were asked to write a set of secret memoranda for the education of the Duke of Bourgogne, who was then heir apparent to his grandfather, Louis XIV. The royal representative in Alsace at the time, Turgot, wrote approvingly of the Jews in his area. Speaking specifically of the Jews of Metz, Turgot found that they were better businessmen than their gentile competitors. He noted that they surmounted obstacles put in their

---

[19] Frankel, "Eine historische Notiz," *MGWJ*, 44–47.

[20] Simon's volume was actually a short pamphlet that appeared in two editions under two separate titles: *Juifs de Metz* and *Factum* (Szajkowski, *Franco-Judaica*, Nos. 1419–20). Lévy had been burned alive on January 17, 1670; Simon was replying to the continuing attack on his supposed "accomplices" and on the Jews in Metz in general.

way by the authorities "either by corrupting the vigilance and honesty of the officials or by evading them through fraud." Turgot found this to be an advantage to himself as governor of a recently annexed territory, for he badly needed horses for the cavalry and he could obtain them in sufficient numbers only from the Jews who were smuggling them in from Germany. Turgot had no doubt as to why the merchants of Metz fought the Jews: the Jews sold at lower prices and got merchandise sooner. Hence, Turgot added, the gentile merchants were in conflict not only with the Jews, but with the state, for "they only want them expelled to protect their own parochial interest, even though it is to the interest of the state to keep them in Metz." The country was almost always at war and, at very least, the services of the Jews remained necessary as provisioners of the armies. Their rights and privileges, including internal self-government and the right to inherit property, had to be maintained. To be sure, the Jews were in the law of France neither subjects nor aliens but, in Turgot's word, a *"singularité."* What he emphasized was the usefulness of this *singularité* to the crown and the continuing basis in *raison d'état* for maintaining it.[21]

This was the language of modern, secular French statecraft. Its ultimate roots were deep in the Middle Ages, when the theory of the independence of the Gallican church and state from Rome was first defined. It had made its appearance around 1300 in the course of a struggle between Philippe le Bel and Boniface VIII over the king's desire to appoint his own clergy without reference to the pope. The king's partisans in that debate went so far as to argue that the royal power was based not only on the king's religious status as one anointed, but also on the existence of human societies as natural fact.[22] The more immediate source of these political ideas was in the theorists of the sixteenth century, who had attempted to solve the critical political problem that had been caused by the Reformation. The unity of the state had been shattered by the wars of religion, and the most advanced minds in France struggled to define a principle in the name of which peace could be made. These thinkers, the school of the *politiques*, proposed the image of a state

[21] Clément, *La condition des Juifs*, pp. 39–41.
[22] Lagarde, *La naissance de l'esprit laïque*, I, 199.

that would regard the religion of each of its citizens as a private matter. Not all of these men were pro-Jewish, for many, including some of the Huguenots among them, argued for the toleration only of Christians.[23]

The greatest political thinker in France in the closing decades of the sixteenth century, Jean Bodin, understood completely the implications of the contemporary attempt to make civil peace between Catholics and Protestants, and it was Bodin who was the most widely read and revered in the next century as the "new Aristotle" of politics. In 1576, four years after the massacre of the Protestants on the night of the feast of St. Bartholomew, Bodin published *Les six livres de la république.* The Jews were not mentioned directly in this work. It was, however, the first book to envisage a secular constitutional state ruled by law and dedicated to the well-being of all its inhabitants. Bodin solved the religious problem not as a Christian but as one of the precursors of Deism. He did not imagine a state for Christians of all persuasions, but one that would be equally hospitable to all kinds of religious opinions and would totally forbid any kind of religious coercion.[24]

Bodin was not alone in these views, even in his own time. Charles Gravelle, one of the major figures among the *politiques,* drew comparable conclusions from comparable premises. The state should not be endangered by massacres and civil wars, and even Jews therefore should be tolerated. He added that "the example of the popes should be followed, for they have tolerated the Jews, even though this is, formally, contrary to the Christian religion. . . . It would be better to leave the Jews to the judgment of God and to work to bring them to salvation by good doctrine and pious argument, since no one should be constrained by force in matters of belief." [25]

The major heir of these views in the next century was Colbert, the greatest of the ministers of Louis XIV. During the years of his ministry Colbert's instructions on the subject of the Jews were con-

---

[23] Jardeni, "The Attitude to the Jews," *Zion,* XXVIII, 70–85.

[24] Meinecke, *Machiavellism,* pp. 56–64; Franklin, *Jean Bodin,* p. 79. For discussion of Bodin's views of religion and his relationship to Judaism see Chapter III.

[25] Gravelle, *Politiques royales,* p. 225.

tradictory. Sometimes he spoke of the scandal to religion of allowing any freedom to the Jews, but the idea that dominated his outlook was that they were to be tolerated insofar as they contributed to the economic life of France. The Christian theme was always clearly the result of his bowing to Louis XIV; the more secularist outlook was just as clearly his own, for it was a natural outgrowth of the mercantilist conception of statecraft for which he is most famous.

In 1683 Colbert expressed serious concern over a case of sacrilege against the sacraments that had supposedly been committed by a Jewish couple in Bordeaux. Nonetheless, he added, "His Majesty knows it would be dangerous to punish this crime with rigor, because the general expulsion of all the Jews would be an inevitable result; since commerce is almost entirely in the hands of people like these, His Majesty knows that such a general exodus from the kingdom would be dangerous; nonetheless, one cannot permit such profanation to continue." Colbert, therefore, advised the intendant in Bordeaux not to admit any more Jews and to start reducing the number who were there, so that by gradual means the Jews might be entirely expelled without hurting commerce.[26] Two years earlier Colbert had written to the intendant in Aix. The king was already of the opinion that he could and ultimately ought to chase all the Jews out of France. Nonetheless, Colbert added, "Commercial jealousies always move the merchants to want to expel the Jews. You must, however, rise above such pressures, which are based on parochial interests, in order to make a reasoned judgment: is the commerce that the Jews carry on, through the ties that they have in all parts of the world with others of their sect, of such nature that it brings advantage to the state; what is that advantage; could the same commerce be carried on by Frenchmen if the Jews were expelled?"[27] Ten years earlier, in 1673, Colbert had dealt with the question of the presence of Jews in Marseilles less ambiguously:

There is nothing as advantageous for the general estate of commerce as the increase of the number of those engaging in it. What might not be of advantage to the particular inhabitants of Marseilles is of great importance to the kingdom as a whole. The establishment of the Jews has never been forbidden by commercial considerations, because

[26] Clément (ed.), *Lettres, instructions et mémoires de Colbert*, VI, 188–89.
[27] *Ibid.*, p. 159.

business generally increases wherever they are, but only by religion. Since, at this moment, commerce is the only issue, there is no reason to pay any attention to the arguments which have been advanced to you against the Jews.[28]

Perhaps the most characteristic instruction by Colbert on the subject of the Jews was the letter that he wrote on May 23, 1671, to the governor of the French islands in America. Here he was stating his own policy, when the growing Christian orthodoxy of Louis XIV was not yet so powerful. Colbert had been informed that the Jews in Martinique and the other French-American islands were contributing in an important way to agriculture. He therefore ordered in the name of the king that the Jews "should enjoy the same privileges as all of the other inhabitants of those islands and that they should be allowed complete liberty of conscience, although necessary precautions should be taken that the exercise of their religion should not cause any scandal to Catholics." [29]

Colbert was fighting a largely losing battle in the last decade or so of his life. Within days after his death in 1683 a special decree ordered the Jews out of all the French islands. Two years later, in 1685, the first paragraph of the *Code Noir* for the regulation of the Negroes repeated the ban on Jews. The Jewish businessmen in Marseilles whom Colbert tried to protect were nonetheless expelled.[30] Local interests and religious prejudices, the very forces against which he was contending, did prevail. Nevertheless, despite the revocation of the Edict of Nantes, his outlook was the one that determined the future.

With regard to the Jews, the greatest single change before the Revolution took place very shortly after Colbert's death, as the immediate result of a decree that was conceived in his mercantilist spirit. In order to stimulate commerce his brother, Colbert de Croissy, who was then the secretary of state for foreign affairs, issued two decrees in 1686 and 1687 inviting all foreigners, "of whatever quality, condition, or religion that they might be," to trade in France. They could henceforth enter and leave the country without a passport; they were required only to declare their business to the judges in the localities to which their affairs called them. These

---

[28] *Ibid.*, II, 679.      [29] *Ibid.*, III, 522–23.
[30] See Chapter V for the details of this battle.

THE BEGINNING OF THE RESETTLEMENT

decrees were not intended for the Jews, certainly not for those already resident in France as marranos, for the royal power was decreeing the expulsion of the Jews from its American islands at the very same time, but the meaning of the acts was clear: the French state had taken an important step towards becoming officially indifferent to the religion of those who brought it commercial advantages.[31] These acts were, therefore, the signal for the Jews of Bordeaux and Bayonne to drop their Christian practices.

In the very nature of the situation no formal contemporary declarations are recorded. So many individual acts of public acknowledgment of their Judaism follow immediately after 1686, however, that there can be no doubt that this date marked the turning point. That very year the Jews in Bordeaux ceased presenting their newly born infants for baptism. Marriages, though, continued to be celebrated in churches for another quarter of a century, until 1711. Even thereafter, although there is no longer any mention of the priest's giving his "*bénédiction nuptiale*," as late as 1753 some Jewish marriages were registered on the books of the parishes in which the parties resided. Another sign of the Bordeaux Jews' increasing public avowal of their Judaism is the beginning of a series of public conversions of Jews, the first of which took place in 1695.[32] In Bayonne the language of the running battle between the city and the Jews

[31] Mathorez, *Les étrangers*, II, 303. A. Cahen, "Les Juifs dans les colonies," *REJ*, IV, 129.

[32] Francia de Beaufleury, *Histoire de l'établissement*, p. 24. Beaufleury is a pseudonym for Louis Francia, a descendant of a prominent family long established in Bordeaux. His book was based in part on family memories and it is a prime source. The registers of the parishes in Bordeaux within which Jews lived substantiate that baptisms ceased among them in the decade 1690–1700; see Cirot, *Recherches*, pp. 171–72. The Catholic clergy began to keep *état civil* registers for birth, marriage, and death after 1539. The sole exceptions were the Protestants and Jews of eastern France, where both groups had legal standing. Increasingly in the eighteenth century the Sephardim of southern France were recognized in their own *état civil*. In addition to the *Ketubah*, the Hebrew marriage contract, their marriages were often registered as notarial acts. (See Bethencourt, "Le trésor des Juifs Sephardim," *REJ*, XXVI, 240–41.) An official Jewish marriage register for the *nation* as a whole was not kept until 1774 (Cirot, p. 164). This register and others containing births beginning in 1738 and deaths from 1739 are in the Archives Municipales of Bordeaux. The keeping of such registers was ordered by the ruling body of the *nation* on December 7, 1738 (*Registre*, No. 85; the *Registre* is the minute book of the Sephardim of Bordeaux, 1710–87; it is in the Archive de la Gironde in Bordeaux).

changed about the same time. Throughout the seventeenth century the complaints of Bayonne against its marranos always spoke of them correctly as "marchands Portugais." In 1691 the reference is to "Juifs Portugais." When de Vancy, the historian of the Duke of Anjou, visited Bayonne in 1701 he told as a matter of course of the existence of the Jews in St. Esprit.[33]

The process of coming out of hiding as Jews spanned a period of some forty years, but the crucial events took place mostly in the decade 1690–1700. They involved three kinds of changes: in relations with the king, in arrangements with the local civic authorities, and within the organization of the Jewish community. In Bordeaux itself a quarrel began between the Jewish community and the royal power in 1697; it was a battle about taxes. In law the Jews, in the guise of "marchands Portugais," were clearly right: their status, based on the *lettres patentes* of 1550, entitled them to be regarded as subjects of the king. Nonetheless, after three years of argument they were made to pay a special tax of 21,000 livres, which was imposed under the authority of a decree taxing foreigners who had settled in France since 1600.[34]

In relation to the civic authorities there had been a period in the seventeenth century when a number of the Portuguese, who were then still marranos, had been accepted individually as bourgeois of the city. This status involved them in such onerous civic duties as accepting the office of treasurer of the local poorhouse (which was at that time, of course, being run by the Church). The treasurers were personally responsible for the perennial and large deficit. In 1693 the city of Bordeaux needed money with which to free itself, by a one-time payment, of certain medieval royal taxes. The *nation* was corporately taxed 11,000 livres for this purpose, in the form of a "loan." In turn, its representatives successfully negotiated an agreement with the city to turn over the income from this loan to the poorhouse, on condition that all the Portuguese would henceforth be free of the burden of ever being its treasurer.[35]

This settlement perforce implied that the *nation* would, in the

[33] Léon, *Histoire des Juifs de Bayonne*, p. 35.

[34] Malvezin, *Histoire des Juifs à Bordeaux*, p. 135.

[35] Detcheverry, *Histoire des Israélites de Bordeaux*, pp. 70–71. Malvezin, *Histoire des Juifs à Bordeaux*, pp. 133–34; Cirot, *Recherches*, pp. 30–31.

future, take care of its own poor and that it would not avail itself of the facility in the name of St. André that was open to all. Six years later, in 1699, the Jews of Bordeaux raised a capital of exactly the same amount, 11,000 livres, by voluntary subscription to buy *rentes* (annuities) from the state; this investment formed the basic sum for the support of their own poor. On that very day (April 28) the *Sedaca* (charity fund) was organized and Léon Peixotto was named syndic to receive these funds.[36] He was the first head of the organization that grew, within several decades, to be the government of the entire Jewish community. It existed in that form until the Revolution.

That the establishment of the *Sedaca* meant the open acknowledgment of their Judaism cannot be doubted. Soon thereafter, in 1706, during the political troubles that marked the very last years of the reign of Louis XIV, a patriotic service was held by the Jews of Bordeaux. They received permission from the authorities to print the text of this service in French translation and to distribute it.[37] By 1710, the year in which the existing minute book of the *Sedaca* began, this body had become publicly engaged in running a kosher abattoir and a bakeshop for matzot, and both of these establishments were even being rented out to entrepreneurs.[38] At the same time the practice of Judaism in St. Esprit became at least as open. In the period between 1707 and 1715 the civic authorities of Bayonne frequently reiterated the injunctions, which obviously were unheeded, to force the Jews to keep their shops open on Jewish holidays and the Sabbath and not to do business on Christian holidays and on Sunday.[39]

During this period local interests in Bayonne were thus fighting

[36] Malvezin, p. 136; Cirot, pp. 26–30. The *Registre* itself, although it begins only in 1710, contains evidence that the *Sedaca* is older. There are three references in it to older minute books, which are lost: Nos. 3, 27, and 29.

[37] Malvezin, *Histoire des Juifs à Bordeaux*, p. 222. No copy of this service is known to exist.

[38] *Registre*, No. 5. Indeed, control of these ritual facilities was being used as a matter of course from the very beginning against those who did not pay their assessment to the *Sedaca*, by refusing them kosher meat and matzot (No. 7). See also Chapter VII.

[39] Léon, *Histoire des Juifs de Bayonne*, pp. 46–47. A letter written in 1707 by a local dignitary in Bayonne to an official in Bordeaux complained of the "exercice presque publique de leur religion" by the Jews in their suburb of St. Esprit.

very hard against the Jews; to a lesser degree this was true in Bordeaux, too. What made it possible for the Sephardim to cease being
marranos was the support of the royal power. In 1686 the controller-
general wrote to the intendant in Bordeaux to forbid a local suggestion that the Jews should be expelled: "Such a notion should be
approached with even greater reserve and caution, because commerce, having now been greatly affected by the fact the Huguenots
are leaving, might be ruined entirely, were we to move too overtly
against the Jews." [40] In 1710 the governor of Bayonne was willing
to permit the Jews, de facto, an undisguised synagogue on the
ground that it would gain for him "the friendship of the Jews" so
that he could borrow money from them quite freely. Clearly economic considerations were paramount in permitting the marranos
of the sixteenth and seventeenth centuries to come to the surface as
Jews after two centuries of living clandestinely.[41] As we have seen,
comparable reasons were being given at that time by Turgot, the
intendant in Alsace, for tacitly permitting the Jews of Metz to illegally broaden their commerce. Precedents, local interests, and religious prejudices were taking second place to the practical needs
of the state.

Before Colbert, all the Jews might still have been expelled from
France; after him this was seldom proposed even by their enemies.
Colbert had secularized the question of the Jews in French statesmanship. The issue had been transformed and the process that led
to the events of 1790 and 1791 had begun.

[40] Anchel, *Les Juifs de France*, p. 135.
[41] Léon, *Histoire des Juifs de Bayonne*, p. 32.

# ᥅᥆ III ᥊᥆

## *Colbert, Spinoza, Bossuet, and Bayle*

In the intellectual realm as well as in the political, the century that
led to the Revolution began with Colbert. Here the connection is
less clear than in the field of statecraft, for two reasons. Colbert was
himself no intellectual. He was not personally involved, even in-
directly, in the renewed philosophical debate about the worth of
Judaism and the Jews that began in his time. In the second place,
French statesmen in the next century almost all followed Colbert in
being pro-Jewish. His influence was clear and it was universally
acknowledged. There was never at any point, however, such near
unanimity among the *philosophes*. On the contrary, throughout the
eighteenth century an important anti-Jewish element could always
be found among the new thinkers, even as they were arguing for
tolerance for all opinions. Intellectuals were capable of making distinctions of the sort that did not occur to men of affairs.

Nevertheless, a crucial change in thinking about Jews took place
in the age of Colbert. This was a period of considerable freedom,
which Colbert had encouraged; he had invited to France not only
artisans and entrepreneurs but also scholars and scientists. In 1670
the *Theological-Political Tractate,* Spinoza's revolutionary work on
the Bible, appeared in Latin and copies began to find their way to
Paris. Eight years later the book appeared in French translation, and
the leaders of thought in France became all the more aware of his
shocking criticism of the Bible.[1] To be sure the book was banned—

[1] Three separate editions of the French translation (the text is identical) appeared in 1678, in Leyden, Amsterdam, and Cologne. The titles given by the
various publishers differed, the most interesting being *Treatise Concerning the
Superstitious Ceremonies of Both the Ancient and the Modern Jews.*

but "everybody" had a copy. In the intellectual atmosphere of Colbert's Paris Spinoza's heresies could not be answered merely by suppressing his work or by reasserting the orthodox faith. The appearance of the *Tractate* forced a serious debate about the trustworthiness of the Bible as history and about the importance of the ancient Jews. Other, more immediate questions, such as the truth of any or all religions and the worth of contemporary Jews and Judaism inevitably arose as corollary issues. These matters were now discussed on all sides. Even the apologists of orthodoxy, if they hoped to be taken seriously, had to use the tools of historical and philological learning.

The crucial turn in the 1670s was that the debate about the Bible and the Jews, both ancient and modern, was essentially secularized. This took place in Colbert's own lifetime, in immediate reaction to Spinoza. Indeed, most of the men who debated the issue were either Colbert's appointees or his pensioners.[2] This was very nearly true even of Spinoza. His heretical views were well known to his hosts in 1673 when he was invited to Utrecht to the headquarters of the French army, which was then invading Holland. Spinoza was offered a pension (which he refused) on behalf of Louis XIV, whose chief minister Colbert then was.[3] By 1700 the reverberations of Spinoza's work in the age of which Colbert was a chief architect had been so profound and diverse that the main outlines of all the newer views of Jews and Judaism which were to dominate the next century were already defined.

A discussion of the French Enlightenment and the Jews must however begin with two important caveats. In the first place, the newer ideas about Jews and Judaism that appeared in France at the end of the seventeenth century and thereafter cannot all be attributed to Spinoza. Secondly, the older medieval Christian prejudices persisted in an important way throughout the century of the Enlightenment, and beyond it. Let us consider these two points in order.

[2] On Colbert as a patron of literature, the arts, and sciences, see Cole, *Colbert and a Century of French Mercantilism*, II, 318–19.
[3] Vernière, *Spinoza et la pensée française*, pp. 20–21. The French military commander who offered the pension, the prince de Condé, had previously protected Isaac de la Peyrère.

Before the last years of the seventeenth century, and certainly before the debate initiated by Spinoza, newer ideas about the Bible and the Jews, both ancient and modern, had appeared sporadically in France. Earlier French thinking had announced religious relativism almost a century before Spinoza. Pierre Charron, one of the founders of French skepticism, had pronounced all religions to be "strange and repugnant to common sense" in his *De la sagesse*, which had appeared in 1601, two years before his death. Men acquire their religions not by revelation but by the accident of birth, he said; "we are circumcised or baptized Jews, Mohammedans, or Christians before we know that we are men; our religion is not of our own choice." [4] This was, indeed, an attack on revealed religion, but it represented no particular and special assault on Judaism.

Jean Bodin had defined a similar view some years earlier in his political work (*Six livres de la république*), in which he had pleaded for tolerance in the name of *raison d'état*. Bodin also wrote a major work on religious philosophy, the *Heptaplomeres*. This book was not published in his lifetime, but it was quite widely known in manuscript, indeed widely enough known so that it was causing scandal even a century later to minds as enlightened as that of Leibniz. It is in the form of a dialogue among seven men, each of whom represented a different religious view: Catholic, Lutheran, Calvinist, Jew, Mohammedan, pagan, and rationalist philosopher. All seven agreed on religious and ethical fundamentals that were Deistic; the Jew was the best characterized of the septet. He was presented as a man of great ability and character, and he dominated the discussion. Bodin was an outspoken partisan of tolerance, who believed that even heathens should be tolerated by the state, and, a fortiori, the Jews. He was bold enough to assert that persecution of the Jews was not rooted in religious ideals, but that these had been used as rationalizations of the rapacity of princes. Bodin believed that the Jews had served as civilizing agents in all the lands of their dispersion, and that their persistence in the Diaspora was a sign not of God's anger but of his favor. Into the mouth of the

[4] Charron, *De la sagesse*, p. 327. Rousseau's only important statement about Jews derived consciously and directly from this passage by Charron (see *Emile*, ed. Masson, pp. 369–75).

Jew of his dialogue Bodin put opinions as bold as the following: Christian dogmas such as the virgin birth and the divinity of Christ are false; original sin is an inconceivable doctrine; the Mass is idolatry; the Christian laws are so stringent as to be impossible of fulfillment; what is morally useful and true in the Gospels is borrowed from Judaism. It is far from certain that Bodin himself agreed with all of these opinions, but for a Christian writer to state them at all, in any context, was something that would not happen again for more than a century. Bodin himself clearly did believe in the ideas that he had the Lutheran voice at the end of the dialogue. That figure, who usually appeared in the text as a fanatic, concluded the discussion with a plea for universal tolerance.[5] Bodin was thus even less of a source than Charron for an uncomplimentary estimate of Judaism and its founders, the biblical Jews.

The most notable contemporary enemy in France, among the theologians, of Christian orthodoxy was Isaac de la Peyrère. In his *Du rappel des Juifs* (1643) Peyrère maintained that the Jews would be given equality among the nations once they were converted to Christianity, through concession in dogma. Once this happened they would be restored to Zion, in the temporal sphere. Peyrère went much further, theologically, in a later work that appeared in Latin in 1655, his *Systema theologicum ex preadamitarum hypothesi*. He argued that the Book of Genesis is about the origin of the Jews, who descended from Adam. All other men came from pre-Adamite stock. There were, therefore, two human families and two theologies, each proper to its own human type. Christ was the Messiah for all men, but the Jews—the descendants of Adam—were still waiting for theirs. The point of this rather weird theology was to suggest that there was a true natural religion which was anterior to both Judaism and Christianity.[6]

Peyrère was one of the founders of biblical criticism. He asserted that the Pentateuch, even though it was of Mosaic origin, had been

---

[5] The question of Bodin's possible Jewish ancestry remains open. On Bodin and Judaism, see Guttman, "Über Jean Bodin," *MGWJ*, XLIX, 315–48, 459–89; and Jardeni, "The Attitude to the Jews," *Zion*, XXVIII, 82–84. The *Heptaplomeres* was first printed in part in 1841 and in full in 1857.

[6] On Peyrère, see Strauss, *Spinoza's Critique of Religion*, pp. 64–85, and Schoeps, *Philosemitismus im Barock*, pp. 3–17.

edited and arranged by someone else later. This view was so well known (his *Systema theologicum* had gone through five editions in one year, 1655) that Spinoza was regarded by some of his enemies as merely a rehasher of Peyrère's heresies, but there was a crucial difference between Peyrère and Spinoza. To Peyrère the Jews were even more important in the divine history of mankind than an orthodox reading of the New Testament would suggest; Spinoza was to be understood to say that they were no more than other men —and that in the past they had been less. The more skeptical, relativistic, native French tradition was to be inherited by Montesquieu in the next century. The mainstream of the Enlightenment would use Spinoza, generally without acknowledging the debt, as the arsenal for attacks on the Bible.

To turn to the other question, the older, medieval anti-Semitism: it is most important to recognize that the new thinking that had begun in the 1670s and 1680s had not, even a hundred years later, conquered the majority even of educated Frenchmen. Education remained Catholic and every child in France was therefore taught that the Jews were Christ-killers who deserved their exile and low estate. This medievalist Jew-hatred inevitably colored the feelings even of those who later rejected the Christian faith from which it sprang, but this was a subjective influence that cannot always be proved. There is much objective evidence that religious anti-Semitism continued to have large power into the very era of the Revolution.

In Bayonne in 1622 Catherine de Fernandes was seen to take communion in the church frequented by the "Portuguese merchants" and then to spit it out in her handkerchief. She was summarily burned alive for blasphemy by an enraged mob.[7] Two other cases already mentioned are germane here. In Paris the dealers in old clothes, who were generally thought to be of Jewish extraction and were even suspected of being marranos, murdered a young man for shouting these accusations at them when they marched by in procession at their annual feast day in 1652. This incident was the occasion of the publication of a number of anti-Jewish pamphlets. Some of these attacks went to the length of suggesting that the Jews

[7] Léon, *Histoire des Juifs à Bayonne*, pp. 26–29.

had perpetrated another ritual murder.[8] That the charge of ritual murder continued to be believed in France is clear from the condemnation of Raphael Lévy in Metz in 1670 for the supposed murder of a Christian child. The story of this case was retold, along with other such canards, in a book about alleged Jewish ritual murderers; this volume was first published in 1737 and was republished without any substantial change as late as 1775.[9] This libel continued to be spread in France, even though it was well known there that the Vatican itself had condemned the accusations of ritual murder as a baseless libel in 1763.

The famous Jean Calas, the Protestant for whom Voltaire fought, was not the only victim of religious fanaticism in the 1760s. At the beginning of the decade two Jews were condemned to death in Nancy for desecrating sacred hosts and one of them was actually executed.[10] Arthur Young undoubtedly reported correctly towards the end of that decade that the religion of the upper classes and of the educated in France was Deism, on the way to materialism [11]

---

[8] Szajkowski, *Franco-Judaica*, Nos. 1395–1413, is a list of the pamphlet literature occasioned by this incident; for an account of the affair see Lévi, "L'affaire bourgeois (1652)," *REJ*, XXVII, 180–206.

[9] Pitaval, *Causes célèbres et intéressantes*, La Haye edition of 1745, XX, 238–361; the title of this section is "Juifs condamnés pour un crime énorme qui révolte l'humanité." In addition to an account of the case of Raphael Lévy this section included a summary of Jewish religious practice, which derived from Richard Simon's translation into French of Leon de Modena's summary (see fn. 24). Pitaval believed, in orthodox Christian fashion, that the Jews had been God's chosen people, but they had forfeited that dignity by rejecting and hating Jesus; hence they were punished by the destruction of the Temple and the exile in the year 70. (See Chapter VIII for comparable Christian orthodox views in the eighteenth century.) Pitaval had no doubt that Jews did murder Christian children, as part of their religious practice in preparation for Passover (pp. 344–45). Raphael Lévy's "murder" of a Christian boy was enough to give one "an idea of their execrable character, which is a horror to nature itself" (p. 242). The most saddening passage in the book describes the death of Raphael Lévy. At the stake the condemned man said that he would not beg God to forgive him for the crime for which he had been sentenced. Pitaval adds this anti-Semitic gloss: "This proved to many people that the Jews regarded the stealing of Christian children as religious acts and they did not believe that they were offensive to God" (p. 267). Pitaval himself died in 1743; before his death twenty volumes of his collection of legal cases had appeared (Paris, 1734–43). The work was rewritten and made popular again by François Richer and published in twenty-two volumes (Amsterdam, 1773–92).

[10] Godechot, "Deux procès de sorcellerie et de sacrilège à Nancy au XVIII⁰ siècle," *REJ*, LXXXIX, 86–97.

[11] Young, *Letters concerning the Present State of the French Nation*, p. 152.

—but on their deathbeds most of the freethinkers and libertines of the day were still being reconciled to the Christianity of their youth. Ideas were changing in a very dramatic way, but the changes must be understood in a context of large and persisting influence of the older notions and emotions.

The orthodox theological attitudes about the Jews appeared not only in catechisms and popular prejudices; they were a theme on which the two major antagonists among French theologians of the seventeenth century, Pascal and Bossuet, could agree. Pascal's attitude towards Jews descended directly from St. Augustine, and from the medieval collection of "proof texts" from Jewish sources against Judaism, the *Pugio fidei* by Raymond Martin, which was republished in Paris in 1651. Pascal repeated the age-old Christian view that the Jews had rejected and crucified Jesus; that their dispersion is proof of his divinity because it is merited punishment; and that both the persistence and the persistent misery of the Jews were a theological necessity: "The Jews should be miserable, because they have crucified Him." Christianity is superior to Judaism because the Jews are deficient in the love of God and in spiritual quality. On the other hand, Pascal was no Marcionite heretic. Judaism is indeed a divine religion, he said, and Christianity is therefore all the more divine because it has the valid revelation of the Old Testament. Pascal was constrained to believe that until Jesus appeared Israel in the flesh was the divinely appointed center of human history. He bolstered this view by consciously following Josephus in asserting that the Jews had taught law to the Greeks and the Romans and that the Jews were the oldest people of all.[12] He wrote in full awareness of the ancient denigration of Judaism by Apion, whom Josephus had been refuting.

Unlike Pascal, Bossuet seems to have had some connection with Jews through his direct involvements with the city of Metz. He had served there as a canon from 1654 to 1659. He was aware of its Jewish community and he reported on the great impact that the appearance of Shabbetai Zvi, the most famous of the false messiahs, had made there. Bossuet wrote that this sudden and wild enthu-

[12] On the relationship between Pascal and Raymond Martin, see Hay, *The Prejudices of Pascal*, p. 89; for Pascal's views on the Jews and Judaism, see *Pensées*, ed. Giraud, Nos. 571, 601, 619, 620, 638, 675, and especially 640.

siasm was but further evidence of the seditious nature of Jews, which had been their unchanging character from ancient times to the present. He was even touched somewhat by the contemporary interest of Christian Hebraists in rabbinic literature; he invoked the authority of Jewish precedents from these sources to validate the ritual of prayers for the dead as an inheritance by the Church from Judaism.[13]

Bossuet spoke about Jews from the same orthodox Christian perspective as Pascal: the Jews who have persisted since the appearance of Jesus are being punished for rejecting and crucifying the Messiah. This "monstrous people" had once been the happiest of all nations, but it was now pursued by a curse; it was the object of "the hatred of the whole world." The present misery of the Jews was therefore theologically ordained and nothing need be done about it. They will eventually be redeemed by divine grace, when their eyes will be opened and their punishment will be at an end, but "meanwhile they remain the laughingstock of all peoples and the object of their aversion." [14] Bossuet was equally orthodox in his approach to the ancient Jews, for he devoted his major work, the *Universal History,* to defend the Bible. It was a true record for it was the word of God, and the ancient past described in the Old Testament was crucial to all mankind for it was the story of His initial revelation. These sentiments were the clichés of orthodoxy, but Bossuet was making these assertions in a new situation. He wrote to Pope Innocent XI on March 6, 1679, to explain why the *Universal History* had been prepared for publication at that time, with the addition of new material to the original manuscript. It was necessary to establish "truth as always victorious" and to "confound heresies." His newest labors had been to explain the laws and customs of the leading ancient peoples, from Egyptians to Greeks and Romans, and to define their fatal flaws and errors.[15]

[13] The relationship of Bossuet to Metz Jewry was discussed, on the basis of remarks by Bossuet in the twelfth chapter of his *Discours sur l'histoire universelle,* by A. Cahen, "Le rabbinat de Metz," *REJ,* VII, 226. For Bossuet's citation of rabbinic precedent, see S. Reinach, "De l'origine des prières pour les morts," *REJ,* IV, 161–73.

[14] Bossuet, *Discours,* ed. Gasté, II, 105–106.

[15] *Ibid.,* preface to Volume I. As he told the pope in this letter, the earliest version of his work had been prepared in manuscript as part of Bossuet's labors

Bossuet never mentioned Spinoza, but he is known to have read him thoroughly, and this was his answer to the arch-heretic.[16] Spinoza's *Tractate* had been the first book to analyze the Bible systematically as if it were an ancient secular text in Latin or Greek. Miracles had been denied and the ancient Jews had been dethroned as the bearers of unique, divinely revealed truth. Spinoza had gone even further, to the assertion that the laws of Moses had been written for a people of the lowest estate. They were but recently slaves and they had brought all the superstitions of Egypt, but only some of the high culture, with them from bondage.[17] There could be no doubt for Spinoza, therefore, that any valid history had to deny utterly the centrality of the biblical experience. Modern criticism of religion had thus announced as its first result a negative, down-grading estimate of the ancient Jews. Bossuet answered by attacking the most advanced of the non-biblical ancient peoples, especially the Egyptians and the Greeks and Romans, as terribly debased in religion. He replied to the inconsistencies that Spinoza had pointed out in the biblical text by stating flatly that Moses had foreseen all the laws that future ages might require because he was enlightened by the spirit of God.

It is unfair to Spinoza not to see that his own views were not far removed from those of Bodin, Charron, and even the skeptical substratum of Peyrère's outlook. Spinoza had replaced the revealed truths and miracles of the Bible with religious truth that was avail-

---

as tutor to the dauphin, the crown prince of Louis XIV. The book actually first appeared in print at the beginning of 1681.

[16] Vernière follows Hazard in citing the contemporary testament of the journal of the Abbé Ledieu that Bossuet regarded it as his main task to provide an original Christian apologetic in answer to the new arguments of the most contemporary atheists *(Spinoza* p. 149).

[17] When the Jews came out of Egypt, "they were entirely unfit to frame a wise code of laws and to keep the sovereign power vested in the community; they were all uncultivated and sunk in a wretched slavery" (Chapter V of the *Theological-Political Tractate;* see *The Chief Works of Benedict de Spinoza,* tr. Elwes, I, 75). Indeed, Spinoza continued in Chapter XVII, the laws of the Jews were given to them by an angry God, who instituted these laws as part of his vengeance for the sin of the golden calf: "God's object at that time was not the safety of the Jews but vengeance. I am greatly astonished that the celestial mind was so inflamed with anger that it ordained laws, for the sake of punishment" *(ibid.,* p. 233). Since Spinoza did not believe in revelation, what he was saying, in transparent language, was that the Jews had constructed a nasty code of laws for themselves.

able to all men, through the use of reason. An argument for the
equality of all men flowed naturally from this premise. In his own
person Spinoza was the first modern adumbration of the Jew who
had risen above "the narrow prejudices of his tribe" and had therefore become "worthy" of the world of advanced culture. Some "enlighteners" in the next century were to cite him as example in pro-
Jewish argument, even though Spinoza's philosophy remained sufficiently scandalous throughout the eighteenth century that he was
more often mentioned in negative connections and attacked for his
heresies by both Christians and Jews. Most important, Spinoza cannot fairly be charged with having launched single-handedly an
attack on the Bible in the name of the superiority of the Greeks.
That argument was an inevitable result of the revival of classic
learning in general. The assertion that Jewish customs and ideas
descended from the Egyptians had been made independently of
Spinoza in the works of the English Deists, Herbert of Cherbury
and John Spencer. In the early decades of the eighteenth century
Anthony Collins argued the superiority of Epicurus over the New
Testament and of the Greco-Roman philosophers, in general, over
the Jewish priests. He called the Jews "such an illiterate, barbarous,
and ridiculous people," "cross-grained brutes" with whom God had
to deal by using "craft rather than reason." Another contemporary,
Matthew Tindal, attacked the biblical revelation in all its aspects.[18]
His constant theme was to contrast natural religion with the superstition and barbarity of the Jews. A somewhat younger contemporary, Peter Annet, followed directly after Pierre Bayle in lambasting
David, to whose sins he devoted an entire volume. D'Holbach trans-

[18] On the relationship between the English Deists and the *philosophes* of the
eighteenth century, on the Jewish question, see, in general, Torrey, *Voltaire and
the English Deists,* and Ettinger, "Jews and Judaism," *Zion,* XXIX, 182–207.
The quotations from Collins in the text are from his *Discourse on Freethinking,*
pp. 129, 157. For Tindal, see his *Christianity as Old as the Creation;* he attacked the Jews for their murderousness in destroying the Canaanites, in the
name of God (pp. 83–84), and he continued harping on this theme (pp. 245–
47). It is now generally accepted that Peter Annet was the author of the
anonymous *David, the History of the Man after God's Own Heart.* This volume
elicited a reply, in book form, from Chandler, *A Critical History of the Life of
David.* It was made clear on the title page that Chandler knew he was refuting
arguments that were not original with the author of *David,* for Chandler wrote
that he was refuting "the chief objections of Mr. Bayle and others against the
character of this prince."

lated that volume into French, but Voltaire himself did not need Annet.[19] He had written a short early drama, clearly under the direct inspiration of Bayle, devoted to that theme. Voltaire's biblical criticism, especially after 1760, owed something to his study of Spinoza, but Bayle and the English Deists were the crucial sources of Voltaire's arguments against the Bible.

Despite all these qualifying remarks, it must be remembered that the controversy in France about the cultural stature of the Bible began not with the Deists but with Spinoza, whatever Spinoza himself might have intended. It was his work and not theirs that first introduced a considerable contempt for biblical Jews into "enlightened" French opinion. This is the way the English Deists themselves had read his strictures on the Bible. The *Theological-Political Tractate* was used as an arsenal in France in the early decades of the eighteenth century for all sorts of attacks on the Bible.[20] The question of the worth of the modern Jews became immediately a part of the discussion. Two ideas of the Enlightenment about history, and there were roots of both in Spinoza, were involved. The new thinking in general lacked historical sense, and yet it arose to cure men of their past, of their history.[21] Any secular

[19] The first edition of d'Holbach's anonymous translation of *David, ou l'histoire de l'homme selon le coeur de Dieu* contained, anonymously, Voltaire's *Saul.* For the date of its composition, 1763, see Voltaire, *Oeuvres complètes,* ed. Moland, L, 494 (unless otherwise noted, subsequent citations from Voltaire will be from this edition).

[20] See the remarks of Vernière (*Spinoza,* pp. 218–19) on the *Theological-Political Tractate* as the "sole doctrinal work which could provide the bases in reason for the new philosophy" before 1700. On the influence of Spinoza on the English Deists and the new thought in France about the Bible, see *ibid.,* pp. 334–85. Vernière is very defensive of Spinoza, arguing that he had a far greater respect for the biblical Judaism than his followers attributed to him. The citations from Spinoza in fn. 17 tend to prove the contrary. For an interpretation of Spinoza's views that depicts him as a supremely self-conscious radical enemy of the Bible, see Strauss, *Spinoza's Critique of Religion,* pp. 251–58. For our present purpose, this question does not have to be resolved, for there is no doubt that Spinoza was read in the eighteenth century as a prime source of contempt for the Bible.

[21] The best discussion of the question of the relationship of the thought of the eighteenth century to history is by Cassirer, *The Philosophy of the Enlightenment,* pp. 197–233. The central dilemma, which Cassirer found especially manifest in Voltaire's *Essai sur les moeurs,* was the conflict between the belief in progress, of which history was the record, and the conviction that human nature has never changed (pp. 218–19). For Spinoza the Jews were part of universal human nature, and they could attain to universal reason by sloughing

estimate of biblical Jews tended to become an evaluation of the existing ones as well; perforce the question arose whether the influence of this past was a curable disease—and there were various opinions.

Spinoza, the Jew, thus influenced his direct disciples, or those who thought they were, in anti-Jewish directions; his impact on Christian theologians was to push them towards exaggerating the virtues of the ancient Hebrews. So, the major work of Pierre Daniel Huet, the bishop of Avranches, appeared in 1679 as an avowed refutation of Spinoza. This work, the *Demonstratio evangelica,* defended the Mosaic authorship of the Bible by answering Spinoza's arguments point by point. Huet was emphatic in asserting that the legislators of pagan antiquity had learned from Moses. There was in Huet the beginnings of a kinder view of contemporary Jews. He had met Menasseh ben Israel in Amsterdam in 1653 and had discussed religion with him at length. Huet often referred with pride to these encounters as the crucial event in his intellectual development.[22]

The most significant attempt to reckon with Spinoza was made by Richard Simon. He accepted the critical approach, and his own work, the *Histoire critique de Vieux Testament,* ranks with the *Theological-Political Tractate* as one of the foundations of modern biblical criticism. What was in Simon's own heart of hearts remains in some doubt. Perhaps he was, indeed, a radical skeptic who disguised his views. Bossuet found the book so dangerous that he had it suppressed; he saw the negative implications for faith of Simon's view that Moses was not the sole author of the Scripture. Simon's own view of himself was that he was an opponent of Spinoza's conclusions and a defender of the essentials of the faith. The Old Testament had, indeed, been organized by scribes, using earlier

---

off the accidents of their history. It was, however, possible for "enlightened" anti-Semites to attribute to Jews a primal and continuing nature of their own, which was impervious to progress; see Chapters IX and X.

[22] Tschirnhaus wrote to Spinoza from Paris in 1676 that Huet was preparing a refutation of the *Theological-Political Tractate.* In his memoirs Huet wrote of his encounter with Menasseh ben Israel that "the result of these long and profound movements within my soul was the work which I published much later under the title *Demonstratio evangelica*" (Vernière, *Spinoza,* pp. 126–27). Voltaire knew the work of Huet, both in its own right and as it figured, in order to be refuted and ridiculed, in the writings of John Toland (Torrey, *Voltaire and the English Deists,* p. 20).

works, but the scribes were as much divinely inspired as the primary authors of the books of the Bible.[23] The ancient Jews were as important to Simon as to Bossuet—and Simon, even though there is some evidence of later disenchantment, felt at least a psychological connection between his respect for biblical Jews and the responsibility he undertook in the case of Raphael Lévy to defend contemporary ones. He did more in that work than to defend one unfortunate Jew's reputation; he used the occasion to defend the Talmud, in general, against calumny. Perhaps his most lasting contribution to raising respect for modern Jews and Judaism in France was his translation from the Italian, in 1674, of Leon de Modena's *Historia degli riti hebraici*. This statement by a rabbi of the main outlines of contemporary Judaism was to have great and positive influence on such writers as Calmet, and on all the other abbés who were to write on the Bible in the eighteenth century.[24]

In the very few years around 1680 when the issues raised by Spinoza were being debated with him by the theologians, one other book appeared in defense of the ancient Jews. It was written by a close associate of Bossuet, the Abbé Claude Fleury. His *Les moeurs des Israélites* was the single most widely known book on ancient Judaism to appear in France before the Revolution; it was reprinted in various forms at least sixty times in the eighteenth century. In it a major new theme of the seventeenth century, primitivism, was linked to the question of Jews and Judaism. In Fleury's view Christianity was but a further, more general expression of this vision. He asserted that the true Jews had accepted the new dispensation, for which their whole history was a preparation, and that the era of the primitive Church had been the happiest and most perfect in human history.

[23] Simon, *Histoire critique,* p. 55. The first edition, which Bossuet suppressed, appeared in Paris in 1678. That Simon later changed his mind about Jews is apparent from one of his letters: "I confess to you that I did not know the Jews well enough when I gave to the public in our language a small book by Leon de Modena. In the light of what I have learned afterwards through my contacts with several of them, I spoke of this miserable people in too complimentary a fashion in my preface. All of them hate us mortally" (Simon, *Lettres choisies,* I, 235).

[24] The French title of this work was *Cérémonies et coutumes qui s'exercent aujourd'hui parmi les Juifs.* There were seven editions of this work by 1710; see Szajkowski, *Franco-Judaica,* No. 1587.

Fleury even defended the dietary laws of the Jews as a reasonable regulation: these laws curbed the passions and thus contributed to the natural life. To be sure, the Jews did not understand the truth of the Trinity and they did have a tendency toward idolatry, but the life that had been lived according to the faith of the Old Testament represented the most perfect estate that man could reach before Jesus appeared. He had no doubt that the ancient Jews were much superior to the Greeks and Romans and to all the other ancient people: "They knew true religion, which is the foundation of morality." Certain results followed from this identification of the perfect primitive society with biblical antiquity. Fleury himself concluded his volume by bemoaning the estrangement of the modern Jews from agriculture, which had been the chief pursuit of their biblical ancestors, and their entry into the crass occupations of trade and usury: "Thus the Jews forgot the greatness and the nobility of God's law, and they turned to low and petty things." The corrupt Jews of the present were, of course, not to be equated with the true ancient Israelites.[25]

In Fleury's argument the groundwork was being laid for the notion that the way to regenerate the modern Jew and return him to the true biblical faith, the Christianity of the time of its origin, was to make him take up agriculture. Even at their fairest, Fleury and the writers who descend from him, such as Voltaire's favorite target, Calmet, were opposed to talmudic Judaism. The primitivist glorification of the biblical era was thus counterposed, in their version of the history of Judaism, to the age of the Talmud, which included the present. The notion was thus created in the eighteenth century that a biblically oriented, reasonable (non-talmudic), and pastoral, or at least economically regenerated, Jewish society was the kind of Judaism that the world could respect. These notions, created

[25] Fleury, *Les moeurs des Israélites et des Chrétiens*, pp. 1, 2, 7–12, 50, 60, 72, 99, 131, 153; for the various editions of this work, see Szajkowski, *Franco-Judaica*, Nos. 1589, 1598. The orthodox side of Fleury's views on the Jews appeared in the catechism that he framed. This work was much studied in France for the next two centuries and appeared in seventy-two separate editions. Here Fleury repeated the conventional notions that Jerusalem was destroyed as punishment for the death of Jesus and that the Jews remained in exile and would continue in the state of misery until the end of time as punishment for their crime of rejecting him (Poliakov, *Histoire de l'antisémitisme, du Christ au Juifs du cour*, p. 200).

by French abbés, were to have great impact not only in French opinion, but also, as we shall see, on the "enlightened" Jews in the eighteenth century.

The connection of primitivism with the Jew gave birth to another idea early in the eighteenth century. As is well known, the perfect primitive society was identified by many in the age of exploration and discovery with Indian societies in the New World or with the various Oriental cultures in Asia, which were increasingly coming into the consciousness of Europe. Early in the eighteenth century the Jew was pressed into service as a wise man from outside of Europe, superior in that role to a Persian or Chinese "sage" because his religion was the ancestor of the Christian faith and his history had kept him in closest relationship with European events. Judaism was imagined, at least at its purest, as the highest form of a reasonable Deism. In this use, neither the Jew of antiquity nor the one really existing in the present was depicted or considered. An abstraction was coming into view, the first definition of the "resident alien" in the West, who by his very standing apart is the source of critical wisdom. This Jew was respected precisely because he was to be not himself, but a figure made over to suit the perfect world of some advanced theory.

In the religious debates of the 1670s the New Testament had been discussed with great caution even by so radical a figure as Spinoza, yet it was inevitable that the subject would have to be confronted head on. This was still inconceivable in France, but the atmosphere was more free in Holland, where Catholics and several kinds of Protestants were then arguing with each other, and with Spinozists. The first overt attack on the New Testament ever written by a Jew in a Western language was published there in 1687. Its author was Isaac Orobio de Castro, who had already appeared on the literary scene as an avowed opponent of Spinoza's philosophy. Orobio was an ex-marrano who had been born in Braganza in 1620. By profession he was a physician. After falling afoul of the Inquisition he went into exile. Orobio found his way to Amsterdam where he made public avowal of his Judaism. He died there in 1687, immediately after the publication of his critique of Christianity. The book appeared in the name of the man with whom he was debating, the Arminian Dutch theologian, Philipp van Limborch. It was a dialogue entitled *De veritate religionis christianae: amica collatio cum eriditio Judaeo*.[26] Limborch advanced the classic, orthodox Christian arguments for the truth of the New Testament, revolving around the theme that Jesus was indeed the Messiah who had been foretold in the Old Testament. Orobio denied all the "proof texts" on the basis of a Jewish biblical exegesis. Though Orobio did not know the Talmud, or make use of it in the debate, he was, as he had proved in his arguments against Spinoza, a believing Jew. Perhaps the most important point that he had made in the book was Orobio's assertion that the advent of the Christian Messiah had not changed the world. Men do not love each other more, nor are the Christians more spiritual than other people, even though they claim to be.[27]

Orobio's work was known in the eighteenth century. It was the prime source of the kind of argumentation against Christianity that used Jewish criticism to demolish the dominant religion. More important, the very existence of Orobio, who had been raised a Christian, who knew Christianity extremely well and who had nonetheless rejected it, was a paradigm for men like Voltaire and d'Holbach. The latter translated Orobio into French.[28] Even though

[26] On Orobio see "Don Balthasar Isaak Orobio de Castro," *MGWJ*, XVI, 321–30. The author of this article, signed with the initial G, was Heinrich Graetz. The only work published in Orobio's own name appeared in Amsterdam in 1689. It was the *Certamen philosophicum propugnatum veritatis divinae ac naturalis adversus Jo. Bredemburgh*. Here Orobio argued not only against John Bredemburgh, whom he regarded as a semi-disguised atheist, but also against what he considered to be the overt atheism of Spinoza. For a bibliography of other works by Orobio that exist in manuscript, see the introduction to the publication of one of them, *La Observancia de la divina ley de Mosseh* by Moses Bensabat Amzalek. The most recent treatment of the Orobio-Limborch dialogue is in Schoeps, *The Jewish-Christian Argument*, pp. 78–94.

[27] Orobio, *Israel vengé*, p. 67.

[28] The French translation of Orobio appeared in London in 1770 under the title *Israel vengé, ou exposition naturelle des prophéties hébraiques que les Chrétiens appliquent à Jésus, leur prétendu messie*. In his introduction the editor asserts that the basic translation into French had been made by a Jew called Henriquez, and that this unpublished manuscript was the basis for the corrected translation which he was now publishing. That editor has been identified as d'Holbach by Naville in his *Paul Thiry d'Holbach*, p. 417. *Israel vengé* does not actually represent a direct translation of the Orobio-Limborch discussion; it was rather a book written on the basis of Orobio's ideas as advanced in that discussion.

these high priests of the Enlightenment did not like Jews or Judaism, they came closest to identifying with them when they defended Jews like Orobio, who had been persecuted for his faith
by the Inquisition and who was imagined, incorrectly, to be a
rationalist.

Indirect echoes of Spinoza are thus to be found everywhere in
the renewed debate about Jews and Judaism; his most direct influence was on Pierre Bayle. On the question of the Jews, as for so
much else in the history of French thought, the age of the Enlightenment really begins with him. Bayle was an opponent of the
atheism that he found in Spinoza's philosophy, and yet he read and
reread him with the greatest care. Bayle also knew the work of the
early English Deists, and much else besides, for this Huguenot
refugee in Holland was a bachelor who read voraciously, and he
specialized in the works of skeptics and unbelievers. Bayle delivered the first forthright attack on the morality of the Bible in
French, in the famous article on David in his *Dictionnaire*. He
pointed out many inconsistencies in the biblical account of David,
such as Saul's not knowing David when he came to camp during
the battle with the Philistines, even though this story is told in
the Bible after a passage which describes David playing the harp
for Saul. Bayle explained by saying that if such a problem in understanding were to be found in Thucydides or Livy all the critics
would conclude that a copyist had mixed up the pages and had
even lost one or two. "But one must carefully avoid such suspicions
when it is a question of the Bible." Bayle, nonetheless, added a
broad hint of his own opinion by concluding that there were people
(he meant Spinoza, of course) who were bold enough to hold such
views. Bayle attacked David as a traitor, in human terms, for his
activities both in league with and in betrayal of the king of Gath
and as a thief and murderer in the affair of Nabal. His "apology"
for David is that "even the greatest saints have something for which
they need to be forgiven."

Bayle's basic position on the understanding of biblical history
rested on two premises. The Bible itself is subject to moral criticism,
in the name of Deistic morality: "It is important for true religion
that the lives of the believers should be judged by the general

ideas of right and order." As a text of history, the Bible itself tells both good and bad. It does exercise its own moral judgment. The contemporary historian must do likewise, even if his judgments are not the same and his intelligence makes a different construction of the history told in the Bible: "In a dictionary it is not permissible to imitate the panegyrists, who emphasize only the good; one must behave like a historian and report both the good and the bad; this is precisely what the Bible itself did." [29]

Bayle's negative estimate of the biblical Jews led directly to the anti-Judaism of the Enlightenment, but there was another side to his influence and to that of Spinoza: they had posed the question of the Jews as a proper subject for rational, non-theological investigation. Both Bayle and Spinoza had concentrated on the biblical Jews, but it was inevitable that theology would soon be eschewed in relation to the post-biblical Jews, as well. In the second place, Spinoza and Bayle had both strongly urged complete religious toleration. As we have seen, in the sixteenth century the beginnings of the Catholic-Protestant confrontation had evoked such ideas in France in Bodin, Charron, and Gravelle. Renewed persecution in France a century later again evoked such currents, in much stronger form. The Huguenot refugees and those who felt for their sufferings were at the center of this propaganda. Most of it emanated from Holland. Henri Basnage, a Huguenot who had fled there in 1683 two years before the revocation of the Edict of Nantes, published an important essay in 1684 in which he maintained on theological grounds that tolerance was owed to all those who erred in good faith. John Locke was in Holland in those years (he moved there in 1683); the "first draft" of his famous *Letter concerning Toleration* was a personal letter he wrote to his friend Limborch, under the impact of the suffering of the Huguenots. Bayle himself had been moved comparably to write an impassioned plea in 1686 for complete religious toleration even of Jews, Moslems, and freethinkers.[30] In this atmosphere it was possible to take a new look at the post-biblical Jews.

[29] Bayle, *Dictionnaire historique et critique*, V, 400–18.
[30] Henri Basnage's views on tolerance appeared in a pamphlet he published in Rotterdam in 1684 entitled *Tolérance des religions*. The views that he expressed were an important influence on Pierre Bayle's plea for tolerance in his

In 1706 Jacques Basnage, the brother of Henri, published his most important work, *Histoire des Juifs, depuis Jésus Christ jusqu'à présent*, the first history of modern Jews ever written. Basnage was a believing Christian who wrote, at the beginning of his work, that "merely by looking at the present misery of the Jewish people one is convinced that God is angry with it, an anger it deserves because of the sin of blindness which made it reject Him." [31]

The merit of Basnage's work is that he was willing to give the Jews a hearing on their own terms. In the introduction to the second edition of his history, Basnage related with some pride that the Jews had been accepting of his work because he had been an impartial historian: "I have included the Jews' own arguments and defenses. I have recounted events in all their injustice, violence, and persecution. I have followed the example of the most exact historians by writing without prejudice, blindness, or partisanship and without any regard for persons." [32] Basnage praised himself for paying special attention to talmudic literature and its commentaries, and he even attacked the former marrano, Orobio de Castro, and other recent writers for not being sufficiently aware of talmudic opinion.[33] Basnage's personal bows towards Christian orthodoxy may have been real rather than pretended, but his work helped effect a crucial change: the question of contemporary Jewry and Judaism was ceasing to be a theological issue and it was becoming an argument about history.

In a little more than thirty years most of what the next century would find to say about Jews had thus been sketched out, at least

---

*Commentaire philosophique*. In this connection, see Meyer, "The Attitude of the Enlightenment towards the Jew," *Studies on Voltaire*, XXVI, 1172. Locke's views on religious toleration were published in Latin in 1689 and translated almost immediately into Dutch, French, and English: "If solemn assemblies, observations of festivals, public worship be permitted to the Presbyterians, Independents, Anabaptists, Arminians, Quakers, and others, with the same liberty. Nay, if we may openly speak the truth, and as becomes one man to another, neither Pagan nor Mahometan, nor Jew, ought to be excluded from the civil rights of the commonwealth because of his religion" (Locke, *A Letter concerning Toleration*, ed. Gough, p. 170). For some recent discussion of the relationship between Locke's view on toleration and the thought of the eighteenth century, see Lamprecht, *The Moral and Political Philosophy of John Locke*, pp. 153–61, and Cobban, *In Search of Humanity*, pp. 55–67.

[31] Jacques Basnage de Beauval, *Histoire des Juifs*, I, 5.
[32] *Ibid*., p. xl.          [33] *Ibid*., p. xlvii.

in premise. This was the generation that Paul Hazard has characterized as the one of transition, when all the old certainties were disappearing in a great, many-sided "crisis of the European conscience." [34] As all questions were being reopened the Jewish question too was being redefined in new, secular forms.

After 1700 French opinion and statesmanship were themselves not static. To be sure, the question of the Jews was never, not even in the 1770s and 1780s, of dominant importance in France or, for that matter, elsewhere in Europe. This issue was to become a major storm center only in the nineteenth century. Nevertheless, the new, "enlightened" era of the eighteenth century was considerably involved in discussing the Jews. Within this nascent modern age the estate of the Jews in France was changing for the better. To understand the roots of their emancipation by the Revolution we must now describe, in turn, the history of the Jews in France and the changing relationship of France to its Jews in the century before 1789.

[34] This was both the theme and title of Hazard's famous work, *La crise de la conscience européene* (*1680–1715*). This book has been translated into English under the title *The European Mind: The Critical Years* (*1680–1715*).

## ✌ IV ✍

## *The Century That Led to the Revolution*

The "political history" of the Jews in France in the eighteenth century was, in itself, of minor importance. The determining factors were in the realms of economics and ideas, in the changing French economy, and in the new intellectual atmosphere. By and large until the Revolution formal political arrangements lagged behind the rights that were really being exercised by Jews. This situation changed somewhat only in the last decade or so before 1789. Before then the decrees of the French crown, with little exception, merely acceded to what the Jews had already fashioned extra-legally. The new turning in the Revolution was that its political acts of emancipation opened fresh possibilities for Jews that they had not yet created for themselves.

The laggard nature of French jurisprudence regarding the Jews in the eighteenth century is clear in a number of areas. Even the favored Sephardim had fewer rights in law than in practice; they continued lobbying for formal recognition of existing, de facto arrangements. To deal first with politics: the Jews were increasingly visible in southwestern France in the first years of the eighteenth century. They were publicly avowing their Judaism, their commerce was increasing, and their numbers were growing.

With the death of Louis XIV there ensued the eight-year period of the Regency, until Louis XV attained his majority at the age of thirteen early in 1723. The finances of France had been left in a disastrous state and royal officials immediately began to cast about for ways of finding new revenue. In 1718 and for a number of years thereafter the controller-general of finances, Leblanc, pressed the royal representatives in Bordeaux on several occasions with regard to the Jews. He wanted to expel those who were not "useful" and to impose new taxes on the rest. The Sephardim were eager for the expulsion of Jews from Avignon and elsewhere, who had come to the city without any legal permission, but at that moment they were still trying to protect the rights of even poor Sephardim. De Courson, the sub-intendant in Bordeaux, followed the usual path of royal administrators and defended the Sephardim staunchly. He praised their services in lending vast sums, without interest, to the city of Bordeaux during the famines of 1709, 1710, 1712; in 1715 the Portuguese Jews had upheld the credit of the city during a great economic crash.[1]

The most dangerous attack on the Sephardim at that moment was not, however, Leblanc's desire to tax them more heavily. A royal representative of intermediate rank in Bordeaux, de Pressigny, argued vehemently that the Jews from Spain and Portugal in that city had no right at all to the protection of the ancient *lettres patentes*. He claimed that they were all newcomers and, more important, that the decrees which had been issued in favor of the "new Christians" could not be enjoyed by avowed Jews.[2] The Sephardim had to turn this corner or their basic position would always remain tenuous. We know rather little about how this was done, for their contemporary communal minutes in Bordeaux contain no information. The struggle culminated in the early months of 1723, at the propitious moment when Louis XV was becoming king in his own right. They were granted new *lettres patentes* in June, 1723, confirming their privileges. The cost of this act was the large sum of 110,000 livres, paid in honor of "the joyous event of His Majesty's coronation." For the first time ever these Jews were formally recognized as such in this decree. The text specified that the royal act was being issued "at the request of the Jews of the provinces of Bordeaux and Auch, known and received into the kingdom under the title of Portuguese, or new Christians."[3] The ancient rights issued to the marranos were unmistakably being

[1] Malvezin, *Histoire des Juifs à Bordeaux,* pp. 172–74; Detcheverry, *Histoire des Israélites de Bordeaux,* p. 72.

[2] Schwab, "Documents," *REJ,* XI, 145.

[3] The full text of this decree is reprinted in Léon, *Histoire des Juifs de Bayonne,* pp. 41–43; it is listed in Szajkowski, *Franco-Judaica,* No. 243.

transferred to the "Portuguese, Jewish, and Spanish nation." What they already were in fact had now been recognized in law.

A second case in point is the major and continuing battle in Bordeaux from 1722 to 1762, involving the Jews who had come there from Avignon.[4] Local commerce in the Papal States had long been insufficient to support its Jewish population; either as peddlers or as migrants, Jews from Avignon had to spread out. By 1722 their presence was noticeable enough in Bordeaux for the local textile merchants to have elicited a royal decree of expulsion against them. This decree was never carried out. It did, however, result in the taking of a census, which showed that there were then twenty-one families from Avignon in Bordeaux. Almost all had arrived after 1700 and were engaged in brokerage and mostly in the trade in old clothes.

The objective of these newcomers was self-evident, to obtain the legal right to stay in the city. The Portuguese Jews were very careful in every one of their actions to deny that there was any relationship between them and the Avignonnais. They thus refused in 1724 to help a representative from Avignon to bring certain natives of that city to trial for taxes that these men owed back home. In the view of the leaders of the Portuguese Jews, "the Jews from Avignon have never been part of the Portuguese community. . . . It is our purpose and to our self-interest to take no part in the quarrels of these Avignonnais . . . for whatever pertains to them is for us a foreign affair, in which we do not want to be involved in any way." [5] In 1730 the Avignonnais attempted to share in the rights granted the Portuguese under the *lettres patentes* of 1723 by paying the royal treasury 4,000 livres, which sum was, as they were later to argue, proportionately greater than the 110,000 livres given by the Portuguese. This action at that time was defensive in character; it was probably related to a drive initiated that year by the leaders of the Portuguese *nation*, with official sanction, to drive out the "large numbers of vagabonds who are arriving in town every day." [6]

[4] A detailed account of this largely economic battle is to be found in Chapter V.

[5] *Registre*, No. 33 (deliberation of December 31, 1724).

[6] Detcheverry, *Histoire des Israélites de Bordeaux*, p. 76, and Cirot, *Recherches*, p. 62. *Registre*, No. 48, is the record of an unusual action taken early that year; all the taxpayers of the *nation* were called together to impose sanctions in order to get the *annuel* for the support of the poor paid. Clearly this

The money paid by the Avignonnais was to no avail, for the battle against them continued, and the presumption that they were at best merely tolerated remained. Despite many decrees and several expulsions the Jews from Avignon remained in Bordeaux and the region in the 1740s and 1750s. In May, 1759, the six leading families of this group were issued a royal charter addressed to them as "Jews, or new Christians from Avignon resident in Bordeaux." They were finally granted their request for very broad commercial rights equal to those of the Sephardim; they now had the legal right to do what they had been doing illegally for many years.[7]

In Alsace the situation was even more laggard. To the very last years of the *ancien régime* the Jews were limited by law to the few pursuits that had first been permitted them. Everything else was forbidden and it remained forbidden until the Revolution.

Early in the century, from 1715 to 1717, Alsatian Jewry was engaged in battle with economic interests in a number of cities, led by some of the merchants of Strasbourg. What was proposed by their enemies was a strict limitation of Jewish commerce in Alsace to the three pursuits originally permitted by imperial decrees in the fifteenth and sixteenth centuries—the trades in old clothes, cattle, and moneylending. After two years of complicated debate, including the disavowal by the official leaders of the Jewish community of one set of requests that had been submitted to the king on their behalf by a group headed by Isaiah Brunsvick, a formal petition was presented in 1716.[8] This document stated a number of reasons supporting the notion that Jews ought to have broad rights and security in the province. If Jewish commerce were limited there would be considerable loss of tax revenue to the crown. The Jews offered to enter the guilds of merchants and

burden was increasing at that time. On April 12, 1730, the intendant, Claude de Boucher, acceded to a request by the leaders of the Sephardim to carry out their taxing decrees and their expulsions of "vagabonds" by use of his police (MS in JTS).

[7] This decree is No. 266 in Szajkowski, *Franco-Judaica;* for more extended discussions of the economic implications of the activities of the Jews from Avignon in Bordeaux and elsewhere see Chapter V.

[8] Hoffman, *L'Alsace,* IV, 365–70; the *mémoire* is reprinted in full in Szajkowski, *Economic History,* pp. 146–49; a copy of the original is in JTS, *Pour les Juifs établis en Alsace.*

artisans and do business subject to controls of these bodies "in every respect which would not contravene the law of Moses." They supported this "offer" by the argument that, if their proposal were accepted, there would henceforth be no question of the business probity of the Jews, for their commerce would be regularized. A fixed place of business would remove all temptation to sharp practice.

The other major argument advanced in this *mémoire* was economic: "The more merchants there are in a province, the richer it is, the better able it is to pay taxes." The Jews observed further that there were almost no merchants in Alsace, outside of Strasbourg, except themselves. To limit Jewish commercial activity would therefore be tantamount to raising the prices of what was bought; it would also lower the price of the grain that was sold by the people of Alsace for they would be constrained to do all their selling in Strasbourg at additional cost in transportation. Without Jewish competition the merchants of Strasbourg would become monopolists in every area and could control prices to their advantage.

The Jews therefore made the following requests: the right of residence for women from outside the province who married into resident families; a restriction against foreign Jews' coming to live in Alsace without express permission from either the king or an individual *seigneur;* complete economic equality, and especially the right to keep shops publicly; the right to own and build houses for themselves, as an exception to the general prohibition against owning any real estate whatsoever; permission to farm both royal and *seigneural* taxes without restriction. In sum, the Jews wanted to get away from their usual pursuits, especially that of moneylending, into the whole spectrum of business. The only aspect of Alsatian production that remained unmentioned was farming, for the obvious reason that at this relatively early date, before even a single Jew had been given any form of personal naturalization in eastern France, such a request was unthinkable.

This request failed in its entirety, for the *Conseil de Dedans* ruled on November 30, 1716, affirming all the old restrictions against the Jews even to the extent of not permitting them to build or buy a house without express royal permission. In law the situation was to remain the same for the next fifty years, even as the Jews did illegally broaden their trade.

## Battles with the Guilds

To understand the politics of the Jews in France after the middle of the eighteenth century it is necessary to recognize the crucial distinction between those of Bordeaux and all the rest. The dominant families in Bordeaux wanted, essentially, to be confirmed in what they had. All the rest, including not only those of eastern France but also their fellow Sephardim in Bayonne, wanted laws that would allow them to leave what they had for new opportunities. The difference between these two situations was, as we shall see below, economic: Bordeaux was getting ever richer by being the chief colonial port for the French empire; elsewhere the Jews had to fight for position in petty commerce under much more straitened circumstances. In the last decades of the old order a new political idea was being defined, and it was immediately applied to the discussion of the Jewish question: law could regenerate men.

One of the discomforts for the Jews of Bordeaux was the situation in the colonies. It had changed after 1717 with the entry of the house of David Gradis into the colonial trade. The few Jews in the American islands now had behind them the influence of a house that very soon had five major trading posts in various places in the area, often staffed by members of the Gradis family. The intendant of Bordeaux was charged with supervising and granting the passports of those embarking for the islands. Such passports were freely given to French Jews, especially after the issuance of the *lettres patentes* of 1723.[9] On the other hand, the king had ordered the expulsion of all Jews from Louisiana in March, 1724.[10] The small handfuls in the Caribbean continued to be tolerated there, although there was an attempt in the 1760s by the Count d'Estaing,

[9] A. Cahen, "Les Juifs de la Martinique au XVIIᵉ siècle," *REJ*, II, 121, 137; Maupassant, "Un grand armateur," *RHB*, VI, 181.

[10] A. Cahen, "Les Juifs dans les colonies," *REJ*, V, 69. There were, nonetheless, stray Jews in Louisiana in the middle of the century; see Nasatir and Shpall, "The Texel Affair," *PAJHS*, LIII, 3–43.

the governor general of the islands, to make them pay large sums to stay and, when they finally protested, he tried to expel them. Attempts to apply the *droit d'aubaine* (the law that the estate of deceased foreigners belonged to the crown) to Sephardim from Bordeaux were annoying, especially since two early cases involved the estates of members of the Gradis family who had died while on commercial journeys to the colonies. After protracted litigation both sets of heirs won; it was held that Sephardim were *régnicoles* in France, and this judgment was consistently confirmed thereafter.[11]

These were victories, but quite unsatisfactory ones. To continue to be tacitly tolerated, or to have to fight protracted suits against the *droit d'aubaine,* was quite different from being treated as equals. This was all the more galling and hampering since the house of Gradis had been the contractor in the 1760s for provisioning the French troops in the islands and had been the major supplier of Canada during the Seven Years' War.[12] Jacob Rodrigues Péreire, who was then the agent in Paris of the Sephardim of Bordeaux, therefore, appealed for complete Jewish equality in the French colonies in a *mémoire* which he, to all intents, attached in 1776 to his efforts for new *lettres patentes* confirming and broadening the privileges of the Sephardim at the beginning of the reign of Louis XVI. This specific effort failed, despite ministerial feeling that "the edict of 1685 [expelling Jews from the colonies] may appear too harsh for contemporary manners."[13]

A more immediate and more pervasive reason for renewed discussion of the rights of the Jews involved the guilds. A royal decree in March, 1767, caused this question to be raised in all parts of France. Under this act the commercial monopoly of the guilds was loosened by the creation of four new *brevets* in each *corps de maîtrise,* wherever such existed, and making these new places freely

[11] The story of d'Estaing and the Jews was told at length by Cahen on the basis of documents in the archives of the ministry of marine: *REJ,* IV, 24–48; V, 69–79. Regarding the *droit d'aubaine* see Malvezin, *Histoire des Juifs à Bordeaux,* pp. 228–30, and Szajkowski, "The Jewish Status," *HJ,* XIX, 147–61. See also, in general, A. Cahen, "Les Juifs dans les colonies," *REJ,* IV, 127–45, 237–48.

[12] For the relationship between the Gradis family and Canada, see Chapter V.

[13] A. Cahen, "Les Juifs dans les colonies," *REJ,* V, 90.

available to foreigners. For a very brief moment it seemed that this act would be interpreted as applying to Jews, for three were given *brevets de maîtrise* in Sarreguemines by a decree dated September 16, 1768, and two others in Phaltzbourg on December 12 of the same year. Six more were given the same privilege in Sarrelouis, in the region of Metz, but the merchants and butchers of the town opposed the grant before the *parlement* of Metz; their contention was that the Jews could never become *régnicoles* in France and that the *brevet* was a form of naturalization.[14] Comparable arguments were advanced by the city of Bayonne against two Jews who tried under this decree to enter the guild of drapers. The most significant battle took place in Paris, where five Jews from Avignon did succeed in acquiring *brevets* in 1767 and in holding on to them for seven years, while a bitter fight went on between them and both the guilds and the *parlement* of Paris.[15]

Most of the arguments that were to mark the next several decades of debate about the Jewish question, into the period of the Revolution, appeared in these battles. The Jews in Sarrelouis appealed over the head of the *parlement* of Metz to the *Conseil d'Etat* in Paris, charging the local organ with prejudice. In their brief the Jews maintained that they were *régnicoles* and different from any other subjects of the crown only by religion. Their chief argument, however, was that the royal decree itself had recognized the need to increase the wealth of the country by adding to its population and business activity; what better way could there be to achieve these objectives than by a kind of internal immigration, the opening of every area of commercial life to a people particularly gifted with genius for commerce, the Jews? This was, essentially, the argument of the Alsatian Jewish brief of 1716, that the Jews were economically useful to the country.

This case for allowing the Jews *brevets* was made quite differently in a more interesting and important brief from the same region. Three Jews from Metz, Moses May, his son-in-law, Godechaux Spire Lévy, and his grandson, Abraham Spire Lévy, had applied for *brevets* in Thionville but were opposed by the municipality and the

---

[14] *Requête au roi*, pp. 16–17 (in JTS).
[15] See below in this chapter.

local merchants.[16] The case was argued before the *parlement* of Nancy by a young lawyer making his maiden appearance, Pierre Louis Lacretelle.[17] Here was the very first appearance, in a formal pleading, of a full-blown *philosophe* basing himself entirely on the new outlook and applying it in a broad and unprecedented way to the Jews.

Lacretelle paid little attention to the whole question of legal precedent. Unlike the author of the brief from Sarrelouis, he did not involve himself in the history of the status of the Jews in France. He merely repeated, in almost the same language, its central argument, that the Jews in eastern France, having been legally admitted, are *régnicoles:* unlike foreigners, they inherit from each other; their goods are not confiscated at death; they are not required to put up collateral of solvency when they are involved in a lawsuit. If the Jews are *régnicoles,* the easier conditions of acquiring *brevets* now extended to all natives of France should apply to them; if they were truly foreigners, then they should have this privilege along with all others now being welcomed to the country. But, Lacretelle exclaimed, they must be one or the other, "else we are excluding them from the human race."

The other favorite argument of pro-Jewish documents before that of Lacretelle, about the economic advantages to be gained by the state and society by extending the rights of Jews, was barely mentioned. Lacretelle admitted that the new decrees of 1767 were silent about the Jews and that no definite command to admit them to *brevets* could be derived from them, but neither was this expressly prohibited. The real burden of his impassioned presentation was that the very silence of this progressive economic legislation offered

[16] Moses May was the founder, in 1764, of the first Jewish press in Metz. The story is told in Chapter VI. At this point in May's life he had gone bankrupt and was no longer living in France. The press was being continued by his son-in-law, who had finally obtained royal permission to print in his own name in 1775. Spire's printing activity was limited and clearly not remunerative. Evidently the attempt of the two of them to establish themselves in Thionville represented the hope to reunite the family and recoup its fortunes.

[17] Lacretelle was born in Metz in 1751 and knew its Jewish community well. For a biographical notice, see the preface by André Spire to his edition of *Plaidoyer.* There is some doubt as to the date of the argument before the *parlement* of Nancy. It was either 1775, the date given on the title page of the first edition of the *Plaidoyer,* or, less probably, 1777, the date given in the second edition of 1823.

the court an opportunity to take the first step in a great, humanitarian revolutionary task, the regeneration of the Jews, through granting them equality: "Reason has raised its radiant head in our century. . . . It is everywhere attacking the laws it did not enact." Hence courts, which are charged with the sacred trust of safeguarding the public weal, must move away from inflexible severity to creative compassion. A proper policy must aim at decreasing the faults of the Jews and increasing their virtues. There can be only one policy: "Let us open our cities to them and allow them to spread out in our countryside; let us receive them, if not as compatriots, at least as men." [18]

The quarrel over *brevets* for Jews, however, foreshadowed a situation that was to become ever more evident in the next two decades: not even all the partisans of the Enlightenment would be on the side of the Jew. The most important and most vehement battle took place in Paris, where the largest number of new *brevets,* seventy-two in all, had been created. This meant that each of its guilds, organized in a body as the *Six Corps,* now had to admit twelve new masters including the most hated competitors of all, the Jews. These guilds reacted immediately by going to law and by publishing their arguments.[19]

Their opening brief repeated the standard, older charges about Jewish chicanery, but some newer notions were present that derived from more modern sources. The authors of this statement maintained that contemporary philosophy, which was defending the Jews against their persecutors in the past, was in effect maligning the sovereigns who had done the persecuting. Clearly, they said, the Jews must have been guilty of all the crimes, such as poisoning the wells, of which they had been accused in medieval France. Their chicanery today is such that wherever they are admitted they ruin commerce. Whatever rights the Jews have in Metz are very narrow ones, those appropriate to a people held in servitude. In Bordeaux,

[18] *Ibid.,* pp. 4, 13, 14, 17, 24, 27, 28–32.
[19] The pamphlet by the *Six Corps* was entitled *Requête des marchands et negociants de Paris contre l'admission des Juifs.* It was reprinted in 1790 at the height of the debate about legal equality for the Jews, as were some of the replies to it. For the battle of the Jews with the *Six Corps* see Monin, "Les Juifs de Paris," *REJ,* XXIII, 85–98.

despite the arguments that their agent in Paris, Péreire, had been advancing, the Jews had been admitted not as Jews, but as Christians. The Sephardim were guilty, therefore, of double apostasy, since they had left, in turn, both Judaism and Christianity. In principle the rights of strangers in France are based on the theory of the international fraternity of people of equal status ("kings are brothers"). The Jews are different because they have no sovereignty; therefore they can have no real basis for fraternity with other nations. To admit the Jews into society is to admit subversives. On the economic side, in an early echo of physiocratic thinking, it was argued that the Jews had contributed nothing to production and that their total activity was obnoxious and harmful because it was centered in exchange and usury.

It seems curious, at first glance, that Péreire entered this battle between five Jews from Avignon and the guilds of Paris. As we shall see later, he had spent almost twenty years fighting the Avignonnais on behalf of the Sephardim, and there was little likelihood that he would feel the need to rise to their defense. Two other issues, of the largest importance to the Sephardim, were at stake however. Their right to be in France as Jews was again in question on the basis of precedents; Péreire had to invoke again the language of the *lettres patentes* of 1723, in which the Portuguese were recognized and accepted as avowed Jews.[20] There was an even more discomforting note in the attack: the uncomplimentary discussion of the history of the Jews in earlier centuries in France. Such remarks were not new. They had been made before and they would be made again in many anti-Jewish briefs in the eighteenth century, but the charges of the *Six Corps* rested not on the authority of church historians but of the most modern "enlightened" writers.

The key name was Charles Jean François Hénault. He was a fig-

[20] Péreire published a broadsheet (*Lettre circulaire*) dated September 4, 1767, in answer to a brief of the *Six Corps*, which chiefly called attention to a collection of *lettres patentes* in favor of the Portuguese that he had published in 1765. An anonymous letter dated the next day made the embarrassing point that Péreire had himself downgraded the Jews from Avignon in this publication in 1765, thus proving part of the "case" of the *Six Corps* about the demerits of the Jews. Péreire answered on September 30, 1767, in a *Seconde lettre circulaire*, that he had also said something about the virtues of Jews other than the Sephardim (on this point, see Chapter VI); he reiterated that the legal precedents in favor of the Portuguese were undeniable.

ure of considerable consequence: a president in the *parlement* of
Paris, a friend of the queen and very close to the Duke of Choiseul
(Etienne François de Choiseul, the all-powerful foreign minister
of the king from 1758 to 1770, was a friend and protector of both
the leading Sephardi and the leading Ashkenazi figures, David
Gradis and Cerf Berr). Hénault was intimately connected with
Voltaire and he was himself a distinguished historian. His chrono-
logical summary of the history of France until the death of Louis
XIV had first appeared in 1744 and it was to go through eight editions before Hénault's death in 1770.[21] In the earliest versions of this
work some of the medieval calumnies against Jews, such as the tale
that the trusted doctor Sedecias had poisoned Charles the Bald, had
been repeated as fact; Hénault had also denied that the Sephardim
had any right to be in France, except as Christians.[22] Jews occupied
very few lines and even less attention in Hénault's large work, yet
Péreire felt that he, in particular, had to be answered. Hénault's
book was accepted on all sides as scrupulously exact and objective
history by a reasonable and unprejudiced mind. He had pronounced
in the name of the best modern learning that the Jews had themselves to blame for at least some of their troubles and that their
legal right to be in France was shady.

Péreire, therefore, published in 1765 a collection of royal *lettres
patentes* in favor of the Jews, in direct answer to Hénault.[23] In the
battle of broadsheets and counter-broadsheets that began in September, 1767, after the appearance of the brief of the *Six Corps*,
Péreire reminded the guilds of Paris that Hénault had corrected
himself in the next edition of his work. He had, indeed, to the degree of omitting all references to the Jews in France after 1550. For
the earlier years Hénault had gone out of his way to condemn the
several medieval expulsions of the Jews as devices to rob them, but
he did leave in the tale of Sedecias and Charles the Bald, and he

[21] See the biography of Hénault: Perey, *Le Président Hénault*, especially pp.
251–68.
[22] This is stated in Péreire's *Seconde lettre circulaire*. The earliest edition
of Hénault's work in question that I have seen, the *Abrégé chronologique*, is
the one of 1768, i.e., an edition corrected in the light of Péreire's criticism.
[23] This was the *Recueil de lettres patentes*. Except for an introduction sketch-
ing the history of the Sephardim in France, this pamphlet is almost identical
with *Recueil de lettres patentes*, which was printed in Paris in 1753, almost
certainly by Péreire; see also Szajkowski, *Franco-Judaica*, Nos. 237, 239.

passed on without any comment, for or against, the story that the Jews had been accused of poisoning the wells in 1320.[24] More than a little thus remained of the attitude that the Jews and their medieval oppressors were both equally unworthy of the regard of modern, civilized men.

Such an "objective" judgment was all the more damaging because it was not argued or even stated, so much as assumed. The answers of the Sephardim to the attacks and the sneers were quite pat in the 1760s. Along with their own tailored versions of the royal precedents in their favor, the Portuguese Jews praised themselves, with considerable success and even with some truth. Their leading families were in international trade, which depended on credit, and they could fairly claim a reputation for honesty at least equal to that of their Christian peers. Isaac de Pinto had argued in his letters to Richelieu and Voltaire in 1762[25] and Péreire had repeated in 1765 that the Sephardim were different and that all the charges that could be leveled with some truth against other Jews did not apply to them. Moreover, both men were quite consciously in their own persons living proof of the assimilation of the Sephardim to French culture and manners. But what were other Jews to do? How could they counter an assault such as that by the *Six Corps,* which derived much of its bite from its very contemporaneity?

Those under immediate attack, the Jews from Avignon, did not dare argue that they possessed an unblemished reputation for commercial honor. They had been extending their peddling and retail

[24] *Abrégé,* years 875 and 1320. On the other hand, Hénault condemned the expulsion of the Jews by Philip II in 1180 (a mistake for 1182) as "an unjust action which was contrary to natural law and therefore to religion." The expulsion in 1391 (a mistake for 1394) was characterized as "a disgraceful but customary tactic resulting from an incompetent fiscal policy" of the government. A comparable tension between pro-Jewish and anti-Jewish motifs, more weighted against the Jews, was present in another contemporary historian, Nicholas Lenglet du Fresnay. He told of their expulsion by Philip II as a "meritorious action," for the Jews had "afflicted and ruined the subjects of the king by their exorbitant usuries" and they "had been convicted of many other crimes." The Jews were readmitted in 1196 by paying the king a great sum "which they well knew how to regain" by their usuries. Fresnay did not, however, quite believe the tale of the poisoning of wells by Jews, but he did state as fact that Sedecias had poisoned Charles the Bald. (See *Plan de l'histoire,* II, 50, 61–62, 161; see also the edition of 1778, II, 133, 203.)

[25] The interchanges between Pinto and Voltaire are discussed in detail in Chapters VI and IX.

commerce in France for a century in defiance of innumerable laws and ordinances, and at least some of them were indeed notoriously guilty of shady dealings.[26] They were, no doubt, no worse than their competitors, even among lawful merchants in the guilds, but falls from grace by Jews were doubly visible and well remembered.

The defense of these Jews from Avignon was undertaken in 1767 by their leading intellectual figure in Paris at that moment, Bernard de Valabrègue.[27] He was living in the city in the employ of the royal library as its expert for Hebrew, and he served his immediate Jewish compatriots as a kind of lay rabbi. Valabrègue wrote a pamphlet anonymously, in the pose of an English lord, in rebuttal of the brief of the *Six Corps*. Like Péreire, he denied the medieval allegations against Jews and he cited the royal *lettres patentes* in their behalf, including the very recent decrees of May, 1759, in favor of the Jews from Avignon in Bordeaux, but this was not central to his case. His essential argument was cast in a different mode. Following some earlier remarks by Pinto, Valabrègue admitted that the Jews had some criminals among them, just as every other group did. Whatever was wrong with the Jews, he maintained, was not their fault. It had been caused by the gentile majority, which had excluded them from almost every economic pursuit. To admit Jews to full commercial liberty was not to increase subversion; it was rather the only possible cure of their ills. Enlightened statesmen and even popes had always made it their policy not to "protect" society against the Jews but to add benefits to the state by protecting them from their enemies. Has not the reign of philosophy begun, Valabrègue exclaimed? Was it appropriate for philosophy to find new reasons for keeping Jews in misery in the name of the good of society, or should the new age proceed to its proper task, one congenial to its true genius, of regenerating them through wise laws? The main theme of the pro-Jewish arguments of the next three decades, of the kind that Lacretelle was to utter again in eastern France some years later, had now been clearly announced.

[26] See the discussion of the commerce of the Avignonnais and the Ashkenazim in Chapter V.

[27] J.B.D.V.S.J.D.R. [Israel Bernard de Valabrègue], *Lettre ou réflexions d'un milord.*

Nine years of battle brought two conclusions in 1776: the Sephardim succeeded in getting a broadening of their privileges, and all the rest finally lost the battle to enter the guilds. In June, 1776, Louis XVI decreed that "Spanish and Portuguese Jews known by the name of Portuguese merchants and new Christians" were to be given complete commercial freedom in France. This formula, written by Péreire, very carefully picked up every version of their identity in the earlier decrees and affirmed that the rights granted applied in their quality as Jews. The arguments that Péreire advanced in the body of this decree for granting such rights were their commercial usefulness, their international contacts, the new branches of commerce they brought to France, and their productivity as sources of tax revenue. These Jews were, therefore, given the right to live "according to their custom" anywhere in France, and it was ordered that they be treated on a par with "our other subjects, born in our kingdom and known as such." This was Péreire's climactic achievement.[28]

Let us note the reasoning: the richest and most advanced group of Jews were being confirmed in very broad rights because of their demonstrated usefulness to the state. That the state had political and human obligations to the Jews had been argued by Valabrègue

[28] Malvezin, *Histoire des Juifs à Bordeaux*, pp. 255–57; this action was so important to the Portuguese of Bordeaux that the *Sedaca* used 6,690 livres, the endowment of the *Talmud Thora*, to pay its costs (*Registre*, No. 444) and it gave Péreire a gift of 2,400 livres in recognition of his achievement (*ibid.*, No. 455). For this decree really to apply everywhere in French territory it had to be accepted by the various *parlements*. There was no trouble about Bordeaux, where it was registered in March, 1777; the *Conseil du Cap*, the *parlement* of the island colonies, registered the decree in 1782, thus finally putting an end at least to the arguments about *aubaine* involving Sephardim from mainland France. The *parlement* of Paris was immovable, for its acceptance of this act would regularize the status of the half-tolerated but legally non-existent Jewish group in the capital. On the other hand, this decree did initiate a dispersal into new places in France. Under it, for example, one Isaac Léon moved to Blaye in 1777 and, after a two-year fight, he forced that city to allow him to celebrate the circumcision of his son there. This process of moving into new areas did not occur in a straight line, for after 1776 there were still many expulsions of Jewish merchants, both Sephardi and Avignonnais, from various places. It seems clear, however, that the free spread of the Sephardim anywhere in France as commercial equals was well under way at the end of the *ancien régime*. This process, of course, was far slower than what it would be when the Revolution ended all exclusions (La Rochelle, *Péreire*, pp. 389–91).

and Lacretelle—and the argument had failed. Nonetheless, the granting of these new *lettres patentes* to the Sephardim had a direct relationship to the rising new spirit.

## The Role of Turgot

A very famous name was involved in the political improvements the Jews were gaining: Anne-Robert Jacques Turgot. He had come to power in 1774 as director of finances for the new young king, Louis XVI. His appointment was hailed by the "enlightened" as the dawn of the victory of reason and humanity in the affairs of the French state. This chorus of praise and hope increased a few months later when Turgot succeeded in bringing Charles Guillaume Lamoignon de Malesherbes into office as minister of the royal household. Turgot was already widely known both as a reformer (for his work as intendant in Limoges from 1760 to 1774) and as a writer who belonged to the new age of economic and political thought. Malesherbes was one of the rare new thinkers among the hereditary class of French magistrates; he had served as treasurer of the famous *Encyclopédie* of Diderot and d'Alembert, the *chef d'oeuvre* of the French Enlightenment. Turgot dealt very little with the "Jewish question" during his twenty months in office; his ministry, as a whole, failed.[29] Nonetheless the larger battles that he fought were the crucial last political preamble during the "old order" to the emancipation of the Jews by the Revolution.

The legacy of Colbert to his successors in the royal administration had been the policy that all rich foreigners, who brought commercial advantage to France, should be admitted. He was keenly aware that the French economy was stagnant, that it was outclassed by both Holland and England, and that these two dominant powers owed something of their economic strength to their hospitality to Jews. What had flowed from such premises was the notion that "useful" Jews, such as bankers, merchants, and large-scale international traders, were accepted. On the other hand, for Colbert the

---

[29] On Turgot's life and career, see Dakin, *Turgot and the Ancien Régime in France,* and Sée, *L'évolution de la pensée politique en France au XVIII<sup>e</sup> siècle,* pp. 225–47.

function of the Jews was, like that of any other foreigner, to add economic value in those areas which were not controlled by guilds or by feudal rights. The crafts and agriculture were reserved by Colbert for true Frenchmen. One of his main labors had been to refashion the guilds and to institute the strictest kind of regulation of production.[30] The force of this second idea was weakening in the century after Colbert's death; Turgot tried and, in the short run, failed to make an end of it.

Mercantilist opinions had persisted in the circle of royal administrators into the middle of the eighteenth century; they continued to dominate the decisions of the central government. So, when the Jews of Avignon in Bordeaux were fighting for the right to stay in the city, they could attain this permission at first only by agreeing to leave the trade in silk and drapery, which brought them into competition with local guilds, for occupations in which Jews, in the mercantilist view, could "usefully" engage—the sea trade and banking. The briefs of the Avignonnais about the virtue of free competition in silk did not convince the *Conseil d'Etat* in the 1740s and 1750s because the royal government was still primarily Colbertian in economic approach, but opinions were changing.[31]

In the course of the century, ideas about free trade were becoming an ever greater influence in the governing circle, and this too affected the Jewish question. Royal administrators were generally protective of the merchants at fairs, many of whom were Jews, because the intendants wanted to add an element of competition. In this use the Jew was not merely adding dimensions to the economy of France that had not previously existed; he was now a tool for the refashioning of the older economic structure. In 1741 the controller-general of finances wrote a circular letter to all the intendants asking them, in all their various provinces, about the commerce of the Jews. All twenty-five who responded answered unanimously that the Jews should not be excluded from the fairs and the markets because they served a useful function in keeping down prices, which would otherwise be artificially high because of the monopolistic

[30] Lodge, *Sully, Colbert and Turgot*, p. 153; Heckscher, *Mercantilism*, II, 305–307.
[31] See Chapter V.

practices of the guilds.[32] In the same spirit the Marshal de Coigny, the military commander in Alsace, wrote to the intendant of that province in 1756:

It seems to me that the Jews have busied themselves in some aspects of commerce which are very often useful. During the war I have gotten help through them which I could not otherwise have had without their extended connections and their industriousness. I suspect that the commerce of the Jews in the province and their influence on the fairs and markets are increasing business; to halt their activity would be dangerous. Indeed, the commerce of the Jews is causing Christians to emulate them, and this is surely useful.[33]

De Coigny had thus moved beyond the traditional view of the military commanders in eastern France, which was to support the Jews primarily as necessary to the provisioning of the armies, to an appreciation of the economic value of competition in trade.

The settled view of responsible statesmen in the middle of the eighteenth century was, therefore, that in reasonable numbers the Jews were useful. Jews appealed to older mercantilist interests because of their large-scale international business and credit enterprises; Jewish traders helped the newer tendency towards creating competition in local retail trade.

There was one French economist at that time who applied these economic notions, and some newer ones, to the Jewish question in a systematic way. He was Ange Goudar, who published in 1756 a lengthy analysis of the economic situation of France. Goudar was pointedly aware, as Colbert had been before him, that the great competitors of France—England and Holland—were aided by the presence of Jews in their economies. Unlike Colbert, who thought that the total amount of commerce in the world was fixed, Goudar's economic vision was expansionist. He was not fearful of what Jewish competition might do, because "in industry, as in the intellectual realm, production can increase infinitely." As a free trader Goudar held that the Jews would help by increasing production and the

[32] The Bureau of Commerce consulted thirty intendants by a circulating letter dated March 10, 1741. No new action resulted; another letter was issued after the poll instructing the intendants to leave things as they were, de facto, that is, not to interfere with the liberty that "Jews had always had" to trade at fairs. See Wolfson, "Le Bureau de commerce," *REJ*, LXI, 224–57.

[33] Hoffman, *L'Alsace*, IV, 371–72.

demand for goods. In his view France needed Jews more than any other country in the world; it was a strong state with a large population and the vitalizing effect of the Jews on its commerce could bring it only advantages. He suggested, as well, that the occupation of the Jews should be normalized by bringing them into primary production. A large state would not endanger itself by giving the Jews such enlarged opportunities. Many of them might remain in their traditional occupations of middlemen, but economic redistribution would ensure that Jews would not dominate any specific part of the economy.[34] Goudar thus adduced Colbertian, free-trade, and productionist reasons for giving the Jews economic freedom. He pressed all of the current economic ideas into the service of this cause.

The doctrines of free trade had already found their way into the highest councils of the royal government a few years before. Vincent de Gournay had become the director of the Bureau of Commerce in 1751; he wanted to end the older practices of bounties, restrictions, and protection. In those years the nascent school of physiocratic economists, led by François Quesnay, were becoming partisans of free trade; in their view the best way to help agriculture was through the free movement of raw materials. Both Gournay and Quesnay influenced Turgot in the direction of free enterprise.

For their own purposes the Jews had been arguing for free trade in many pleadings for at least a century. As we have seen, they had been supported by an increasing number of statesmen, royal officials, and economic theorists. Nonetheless there was some element of time lag even in these liberal approaches to the Jewish question. Contemporary economists such as Goudar tended to take the view, in general, that any new energies would be of benefit to a state; potential immigrants did not have to establish in advance their credentials as economic innovators. The only point at which Goudar's argument became rather narrowly Colbertian was in his consideration of the Jews. Goudar then went to great lengths to establish that increased economic opportunity for Jews would be useful to society in very specific and definable ways. This was certainly the flavor of the declarations of even the most pro-Jewish royal officials. The presumption continued to color their views that the rights of

[34] Goudar, *Les Intérêts de la France,* I, 365–72.

Jews depended on obvious proofs that they were indeed useful to the state. This was the outlook to which Péreire appealed in his campaign for new *lettres patentes* for the Sephardim. Even though this act was not issued until several weeks after Turgot's fall, it was during the twenty months that Turgot was in power that Péreire had won the battle. He would not have prevailed so completely, however, if Turgot had been merely a man of the past or even merely a free-trader. Like Colbert, Turgot appreciated the contributions of rich grand entrepreneurs to the economy; even more than the royal administrators of his own day, he was a partisan of free trade. Turgot's ultimate motivations, though, were not economic but humanitarian.

As soon as Turgot came to power the ritual of the impending coronation of the new king was very much a public issue. There was a traditional passage in the oath that Louis XVI was to take in which he promised to extirpate heretics. Clerical pamphleteers were arguing with great vehemence that it was the young king's bounden duty to take this oath and to follow its precepts. Turgot wrote the king a secret *mémoire* in which he urged that the traditional passage be omitted. In a typical compromise, at his coronation Louis XVI chose not to change the formula but he mumbled it inaudibly. The immediate cause of the debate about the coronation oath was the ongoing agitation to give rights to Protestants. They did not get any new rights as a result of this debate. Turgot published his state paper on the subject of the oath in 1778, after his fall, and it helped form public opinion.[35] His associate in office, Malesherbes, was the minister responsible for giving the Protestants civil status in 1787; as we shall see in the concluding chapter, it was Malesherbes who then linked that action with the need to reconsider the situation of the Jews.

This connection was made by Turgot at the very beginning of the debate, in 1775. In the early months of his ministry Turgot had collected statistics to show that the revocation of the Edict of Nantes had had disastrous effects on the economy of France. At the dawn of a new reign the Protestants had submitted a *mémoire* to the royal administration in which they had argued, in a manner that would have appealed to Colbert, that if religious toleration were allowed

[35] Dakin, *Turgot*, pp. 217–21.

hundreds of wealthy refugee merchants and industrialists would return and thus add to the economic strength of France. At that very moment Péreire was emphasizing the economic importance of the great Sephardi business houses as the crucial reason for giving wider rights for the Jews of Bordeaux. By endorsing the Protestant *mémoire* Turgot knew, like Colbert a century before, that the same economic arguments applied to both groups. Turgot's climactic argument against the coronation oath was not, however, based on economic utility but on the principle of the broadest toleration: all religions, without exception, should be permitted by the French crown, as long as they were not harmful to public order.

The bitterest battle of Turgot's ministry, which he won for a moment but whose victory was abortive and led directly to his fall, was his fight to abolish the guilds. In his argument to the king he maintained that their complete destruction would, by creating liberty of production, lower prices and attract workmen and capitalists from abroad; it was a fundamental step to the regeneration of France. The guilds, led by the *Six Corps* of Paris, resisted with all their might and the *parlement* of Paris refused to register the decree. Louis XVI forced its acceptance on March 12, 1776, but two months later, to the day, both Turgot and his only ministerial supporter, Malesherbes, were dismissed from office. In the course of this battle Turgot had become directly involved in the question of Jews. The five Jews who had bought entry into the guilds of Paris had lost their suit in 1774, but Turgot reversed this ruling in 1775. This was only a temporary victory, for the guilds were restored after his fall. The restored guilds were, however, never quite the same as they had been before Turgot. One thing happened that was significant, even in law: the newly recreated *corps* in Paris were no longer organized as religious brotherhoods, only as secular economic associations. The five Jews from Avignon who had bought masters' places in the guild of mercers were not, to be sure, admitted to that association when it was restored, but the ultimate result of this battle was a partial breakthrough: they did succeed in retaining the right to trade openly in Paris.[36]

[36] Dakin, pp. 231–51; on the Jewish aspects of this battle, see Monin, "Les Juifs de Paris à la fin de l'ancien régime," *REJ*, XXII, 85–98; the decree of 1777 granting the five Avignonnais Jews the right to trade is listed in Szajkowski, *Franco-Judaica*, No. 14.

Even in this strictly economic realm of the battle with the guilds, Turgot's basic motivations were ideological and moral. His dominant value was not the state but the individual. He declared very early in his career, in essays published in 1753 and 1754, why he had rejected *raison d'état* as the ultimate value: "Governors have been much too prone to offer up the happiness of individuals to the supposed right of society. One forgets that society is made for individuals, that it is created only in order to protect the rights of all men by guaranteeing that they honor the duties they owe each other." For Turgot, freedom of religion was not merely a device for attracting useful new economic forces to France; it was a moral value of the highest importance, "for the state does not have the right to exclude from its concern those who follow their own conscience and refuse to submit to its laws about religion." Economic liberty itself was more than a tool for increasing the power of the state; it was a necessary pre-condition for realizing the happiness of the individual. The right of work, Turgot wrote in 1776 in the decree abolishing the guilds, "is the first, the most sacred, and the most inalienable of all rights." The state was thus more than an umpire, beyond the sectarian and economic battles, to which it was indifferent. It had the positive task of creating the well-being of all its citizens.[37]

Turgot was an eclectic and not a systematic thinker, but in this he was all the more typical of the bulk of the "enlighteners" who were to make the Revolution. Side by side with his religious relativism and the notion of extending tolerance to all there existed in Turgot's mind the conviction that the religion of nature was the best of all and that a society organized around it would be the most united and secure. Such an idea opened the door to the intolerances that were perpetrated in the name of the religion of reason in the early years of the Revolution. In the mind of Turgot, and of many of his contemporaries, however, the clash between the relativism they derived from Montesquieu and the absolutism of Voltaire was not yet felt. A decent, contemporary attitude meant that one believed in the regeneration of all men through the freedom to be themselves. Turgot and men of his stamp did not doubt that this

[37] Schelle, *Oeuvres de Turgot*, I, 387, 424; see also Sée, *L'évolution de la pensée politique*, pp. 227, 232.

applied to Jews, too, and that it had immediate bearing in 1776 on the most "French" group among them, the Sephardim.

The more radical effort, to regenerate the Ashkenazim as one corollary of the abolition of the guilds, failed, as several of Colbert's pro-Jewish acts had failed a century before, but, again like Colbert's work, Turgot's ministry announced the future. In the years that were to follow until 1789, and beyond, all the older antipathetic views of the Jews figured in the debates, but the new, humanitarian ideas that influenced Turgot had penetrated beyond the pamphleteers to the minutes of royal officials. For example, in 1781 the *Conseil d'Etat* was contemplating a new code for the Jews of Alsace and it asked the opinion of the intendant in Bordeaux, Dupré de Saint-Maur. He wrote in July that with regard to all the Jews of his region, both Sephardim and Avignonnais, "there was nothing more to be said that did not apply as well to Catholics and Protestants of comparable estate." In September a subordinate of his, the sub-delegate Capmartin, wrote even more pointedly in praise of the Sephardim. He was completely persuaded that they were honest in business and that they behaved "in society as good citizens." The Jews of Bordeaux could not be put on the same plane as those of Alsace "for they deserved special regard." The Gradis family in particular had been of great service to the state. These views of Capmartin were almost verbatim the kind of thing that the Sephardim had been saying about themselves through Péreire and Pinto. Capmartin's superior, Dupré de Saint-Maur, added a note of his own to this very letter before sending it forward to Paris: "Although there is a great difference between these Jews and those of Alsace, both are equally human beings. Treat them in the same way and their characters and habits will be the same." [38]

The "Jewish question" in its newest form had now been defined as an object for political action: not what could the Jew do for the state but what ought and could the state do for and with the Jew.

## The Physiocrats

The immediate political background of the acts of emancipation by the Revolution was in an eclectic blend of ideas very much like

[38] Cirot, "Les Juifs et l'opinion," *RHB*, XXI, 164–65.

those of Lacretelle and Turgot: some Jews had already proved that they were honest men; the rest could be directed to honest work, preferably in physical labor; enlightened men could not ultimately exclude the Jews from society. This mood prevailed among the moderate majority at the beginning of the Revolution, but more doctrinaire, negative views of the Jewish question had already appeared in France among the most advanced economic thinkers. The ground had been laid for regarding the existing Jew, even at his best, as an economic parasite and for doubting that he could ever be regenerated.

These attitudes were rooted in the thought of the physiocrats. They had arisen during the period of the Seven Years' War, when both the economy and the credit of France had declined disastrously. The way was open for new economic doctrines as the old ways had obviously failed. Since the founders of the physiocratic school, François Quesnay and the elder Mirabeau (Victor de Riquetti), did not discuss the Jews directly in any of their writings, the immediate relationship of their thought to the Jewish question has not been apparent. It is nevertheless true that a debate about the economic utility of Jews, in the light of the physiocratic principles, was provoked immediately as their view appeared in print. In 1760 Quesnay and Mirabeau published together an essay that was occasioned by the fiscal difficulties of the French state, their *Théorie de l'impôt*. In this short essay they argued that the way to restore the credit of France was through a single tax on land, for agricultural production is the source of all values. They took a dim view of both commercial and industrial mercantilism and of the whole system that obtained in France of many taxes and tariffs.[39]

The ideas of the physiocrats had immediate influence on men of affairs. At the end of the war the various *parlements* of France were sent a royal questionnaire about financial reform. The *parlement* of Provence, which had in the past fought for the guilds, replied by pleading for free trade. It was opposed to monopoly of any kind, and it spoke for an economic policy that would attract foreigners to France. Its position was rooted in three ideas: that wealth is the product of land and manufacture; that a large population was

[39] *Théorie de l'impôt* and *Philosophie rurale,* both published anonymously; see also Weulersse, *Le mouvement physiocratique,* I, 78–79.

needed, especially of independent farmers; and that the enemies of a healthy economy were the financiers, and especially the tax farmers. There were some local reasons in Provence for the position that was taken by its *parlement*, but these views were shared by a significant number of other such bodies at that time.[40]

These newer economic ideas implied a new way of thinking about the question of the Jews. Mercantilism's most useful Jews, who were essentially bankers and international traders, began to come into disrepute as the social utility of financiers in general was being questioned. The case of Cerf Berr is instructive. In defending themselves against his entry into Strasbourg, even though he was armed with royal permission, the local authorities questioned his worth to France. He himself countered, in part, as we shall see, by beginning to engage in manufacturing and by buying feudal land, on which he seems to have made an abortive attempt to settle some poor Jews. Cerf Berr's response to the newer ideas of social utility was to try to change the image of himself into that of at least a part-time manufacturer and land owner.

In the light of the newer ideas the question of poor Jews also looked different. The attempts at exclusion continued and were even increased, but it became ever clearer, at least in France, that this was a hopeless solution. No one had any doubt that Jewish petty traders and small-scale moneylenders were economically obnoxious. Two antithetical positions thus arose, although they were often held by the same thinker. One attitude was that the state needed to engage actively in moving these Jews to economically productive occupations, to manufacturing and to working the land. The state would thus increase its own wealth. Such thinking came to expression in Joseph II's Edict of Toleration in Austria in 1782 and Louis XVI's decree of 1784 for the reordering of the life of the Jews of Alsace (although both these decrees were greatly influenced still by older ideas about limiting Jewish population). On the other hand, there was fear that any new economic role for the Jews would dangerously increase their power.

There can be little doubt that the crucial implications of physio-

[40] Beik, *A Judgment of the Old Regime,* pp. 30, 64–68; see especially his lengthy analysis of the economic views of the *parlement* of Provence, pp. 93–200.

cratic thought for the Jews were seen immediately by Isaac de
Pinto, the Dutch Jewish intellectual who is most famous for his
debate with Voltaire about toleration for Jews. The trigger mecha-
nism for the writing of his major work on economics, the *Traité de la
circulation et du credit*,[41] was the appearance of the Quesnay-Mirabeau essay. Pinto began his work during his stay in Paris in 1761,
in immediate refutation of the economic theories advanced by the
physiocrats. He was moved to continue his work by the appearance
in 1763 of the important Quesnay-Mirabeau volume on economics,
the *Philosophie rurale*.[42] There is something Aesopian in Pinto's approach, yet there can be little doubt that he had "Jewish" motivations, as well as those of an economic theorist in general. He
defended credit and circulation as the basic forms of economic endeavor against what he termed "the frenzy of the soil." It was
obvious to Pinto, and to everybody else, that the Jews had an out-
size stake in European credit operations. He was himself a typical
eighteenth-century Jewish banker. To defend the economic role of
credit meant, to a considerable degree, to defend the Jews. That the
Jews were a central issue to Pinto when he wrote his *Traité* is made
more likely by another point that he made: a static economy freezes
society as a whole; the dynamism of commercial activity makes it
possible for outsiders to rise. In the second half of the eighteenth
century, who needed new economic forms and a new open society
more than the Jews? Pinto mentioned Jews directly only at the end
of his book, where he took great pains to argue, quite speciously,
that the Bible permits the taking of fair interest in all situations.[43]
Nonetheless, he served the Jewish cause far more fundamentally
than any overt defender could have. Pinto rooted the case for regarding the Jews, bankers, brokers, speculators, and traders, as they
actually were at the time, in a general economic theory of exchange.

Even though he did not know it as he was writing, Pinto was not

[41] Pinto's work was published in Amsterdam in 1771; on internal evidence,
it was finished some years before.

[42] *Traité*, preface, p. v; see p. 134, where Pinto refuted the views advanced
in *Théorie de l'impôt*, and pp. 207–209, for his direct answer to *La philosophie
rurale*.

[43] *Traité*, p. 211. Pinto especially attacked Voltaire here for spreading the
"false and calumnious" notion that the Bible permitted Jews to take usury
from non-Jews.

alone at that moment. The far greater Turgot was responding in very much the same way to the work of Quesnay and Mirabeau. Turgot's most important essay, the *Réflexions sur la formation et la distribution des richesses*, was written, like Pinto's *Traité*, in reaction to the most doctrinaire statements made in the early 1760s by the founders of the physiocratic school. Turgot agreed with the physiocrats that the basis of the entire economy was agricultural endeavor and that all other forms of economic activity were valid insofar as they were ultimately of service to the health of agriculture. Turgot was, however, emphatic in insisting that land was not the only form of capital and that even the lending of money at interest was a valid endeavor if the borrowers were willing to use the loans directly in farm production, manufacturing, or even commercial speculation.[44] Within such an economic theory even stock market speculators could be accommodated, as Pinto was to do, though Turgot himself did not go quite that far.

An overt defense of the Jews, on economic grounds, was attempted some years later, less ably and more eclectically, by Christian Wilhelm Dohm in his plea for the Jews. Dohm was a mercantilist and a free trader, and he imagined the Jews as a useful economic element in the light of the kind of general principles that had appealed to enlightened French royal administrators in the middle of the century. Dohm did not defend the existing Jew in the way that Pinto had. Something of the influence of the physiocratic thinking, which Pinto had condemned, was present in Dohm, despite his mercantilist stand. He envisaged an economic policy by the state that would shift the Jews away from trade and towards the crafts and agriculture.[45] The notion was thus becoming ever more pervasive that larger economic opportunity for the Jew in his traditional function as middleman was not the answer to the Jewish question.

All of the economists of change had to face one stubborn issue: economic freedom might enable the Jew to achieve positions which

[44] Dakin, *Turgot*, pp. 287–95.
[45] Dohm, *Réforme politique*, pp. 147–52. It has been argued in a monograph that Dohm's opinions of the Jews derived from his economic views in general. He was opposed to the contempt in which the physiocrats held commerce; he could, therefore, not agree that the Jews were economically useless. See Rapoport, *Christian Wilhelm Dohm, passim*.

they thought that no state could, for its own safety, allow outsiders to control. The more generous spirits, such as Dohm and Mirabeau, answered this objection by saying that economic regeneration would make the Jews into honest men, good citizens, and indissoluble parts of society. Others, such as the Alsatian anti-Semites, Hell and Foissac, held that no society could afford to allow real economic power to Jews, for they were an international element without roots in any particular country. Nevertheless no one except Pinto could imagine that the Jews should be allowed to go on as they had. In their traditional occupations they were regarded on all sides as clearly unproductive. But what was to be done with the Jew in a new economy? Should he be made productive where he was? Or should he be put to work in some ghetto of his own? The answers were vague.

Such ambiguities marked the work of numerous French writers who discussed conditions in Poland in the eighteenth century. They unanimously agreed that the country could not continue to allow the Jews to be its merchant class and that the only possible solution to the Jewish question in Poland was to make the Jews become farmers.[46] The proto-socialist Mably went further in his study of the Polish question. He insisted that the Jews, as the overwhelming majority of the bourgeoisie of Poland, were the real masters of the country. The Poles must therefore nationalize their economy by taking over all of its roles from the Jews, "who have nothing to gain if you are prosperous and nothing to lose if you are ruined." Mably did recognize that the Jews themselves were in an unfortunate situation. Nevertheless he thought that they could not be either trusted or regarded as having a real stake in Poland until they became land owners. Industry and business are not occupations that are rooted in any particular soil, even though they are of the utmost necessity. Those who engage in them are not, by nature of their role, indissolubly part of the community. Mably made it very clear that his essential proposal for Poland was that it so organize its economy that the Jews should not participate in it in any important way. The health of Poland required that all roles be played by Poles.[47]

[46] See Frydman [Szajkowski], "French Notices of Jews," *The Jews in France*, ed. Tcherikower, I, 16–32.

[47] Mably, *Du gouvernement et des lois de la Pologne, Oeuvres*, VIII, 38.

Mably's suggestion that the Jews be put on uncultivated land meant, essentially, that he wanted to remove them from the economic arena.

It was not accidental that Pinto, with his excellent antennae for the Jewish implications of the new economic theories, argued in his *Traité* against the enthusiasm of the physiocrats for a largely agricultural image of France. He cited Poland to prove how little such an economic structure produced.[48] Here was the most agricultural country in Europe, and it was no accident that its economy was the most debased. Pinto knew as well as Mably that the Jews were crucial in providing what credit there was in Poland, but Pinto thought far better of their enterprise.

On the eve of the Revolution, a half century of economic discussion had resulted in one crucial ambiguity: it was agreed on all sides that the Jew needed to be moved to new economic pursuits. Their friends thought that this would solve the Jewish problem, but their enemies were maintaining that even the economic regeneration of the Jew could not transform him into an unquestioned member of society. This issue was at least in debate, but no one was arguing seriously against the premise that Pinto had tried to demolish, that the Jew as he actually existed was economically obnoxious. Hatred of financiers and emphasis on the peasant and artisan laid the groundwork, together, for Jacobin anti-Semitism. This debate was to continue in the nineteenth century between the anti-Semitic proponents of primary production and those who saw the virtue of exchange as a real economic value. The issues that had first been joined as early as 1761 by Pinto with Quesnay and Mirabeau were to have a fateful history.

In the short run of the 1770s and 1780s, however, the anti-Jewish use of physiocratic premises was the work of a minority. Majority opinion among the "enlightened" held that economic change among the Jews was possible and desirable. Part of the evidence was in the changes that had actually been occurring in the course of the eighteenth century.

[48] Pinto, *Traité,* pp. 138, 219.

## ❧ V ❧

# *From Mercantilism to Free Trade*

More than half a century ago Werner Sombart pronounced the Jews to have been the founders of modern capitalism. In his construction, the expulsion of the Jews from Spain in 1492 had been a radical turning point in the history of the West as a whole. These exiles, who spread almost immediately to the major centers of Europe and the Mediterranean basin, had brought with them both their so-called Jewish capacity for commerce and large liquid capital. Wherever they went they were the pioneers in creating new forms of economic enterprise, which replaced the older, static, medieval economy. Since the essence of European history in the eighteenth and nineteenth centuries was the rise of the bourgeoisie to power, "Jewish capitalism" was the impulse for the remaking not only of the economic but also the political structure of Europe.[1] From the logic of Sombart's thesis, it followed that the new age that had emancipated the Jews was actually an era they had themselves created. Europe, therefore, had not admitted the Jews to equality: the Jews had created a new Europe in the spirit of their "Oriental" nature, and that Europe had had no choice but to accept its authors.

This theory derived from sources as diverse as Hegel, Marx, Gobineau, and Max Weber, as well as from some overt anti-Semites such as Drumont. Much of Sombart's argument was rooted in theories of race and is now thoroughly discredited. However, one aspect of his work remains important. It is the question of the relationship of the Jews and capitalism. Did the Jews indeed create modern capitalism and, through it, the new age of the nineteenth

[1] Sombart, *Die Juden, passim.*

century, or were they created by it? Were the marranos who fled from Spain really the sole, or even the dominant, creators of modern capitalist enterprises in their new homes? Was their commercial importance in Amsterdam, London, Venice, Hamburg, and Bordeaux so great as to justify Sombart's contention?

Since the appearance of his book a considerable amount of research has been done on the history of these various Jewish communities. The results of the investigations have, without exception, been the same: the role of the Jews in creating the new European economy was everywhere of more significance than their numbers, but it was nowhere predominant. The Jews did not create the more mobile economy that was coming into being in Europe after the seventeenth century; they were, rather, the beneficiaries of new trends. Some Jews did, indeed, bring large capital with them from the Iberian Peninsula, especially in the sixteenth and seventeenth centuries, and this wealth, together with their commercial contacts and activities, was their passport to a variety of places. Generally, however, wherever these Jews were admitted such action was part of a process in which doors were being opened at that time in certain places to all kinds of foreigners. Both their friends and their enemies tended vastly to exaggerate the largeness of the Jews' role in international trade in cities such as Amsterdam, Hamburg, and Bordeaux.[2]

Sombart was quite taken with the Sephardim of Bordeaux and he made much of the several declarations by royal officials towards the end of the seventeenth century that the Jews there were indispensable to its commerce.[3] A critical evaluation of the relevant facts establishes the contrary, that Dutch, Irish, German, and other for-

[2] Bloom's study of Amsterdam came to the conclusion that the Jews there were important but not economically dominant, or even in the lead; see his *Economic Activities*, pp. 219–25. The economic role of the Jews in London was comparable. It was estimated that they represented one-twelfth of the trade of the kingdom, yet they were completely eclipsed by the English goldsmith-bankers and they played no part in the evolution of English banking (Roth, *A History of the Jews in England*, pp. 193, 283). An elaborate recent study of the Sephardim in Hamburg (another of Sombart's favorite examples) concluded that they neither created nor dominated Hamburg's international trade, as it began to develop in the latter years of the sixteenth century (Kellenbenz, *Sephardim an der unteren Elbe*, pp. 452–62).

[3] Sombart, *Die Juden*, p. 21.

eigners were far more important then and later to the international trade of Bordeaux than the Jews.[4] The arrival of the Jews on the scene, and especially the permission for them to come up from underground and avow their Judaism, was a corollary of the secular economic outlook of mercantilism. The expansion of the Jews in the rest of France was favored by a general movement towards free trade in the eighteenth century.

In the economic history of France as a whole the eighteenth century began under the star of mercantilism. Despite defeats in the wars of the eighteenth century, and the temporary harm that came to French international trade as a result, the over-all trend of French sea trade was to double and redouble. The value of the foreign trade of the port of Bordeaux rose from nothing towards the end of the seventeenth century to a trade of 250 million livres with the Antilles alone in 1782. The colonial trade of France as a whole was then four times that amount.[5] Trade, especially international trade, and not domestic production, provided the element of growth in the French economy in the last century of the *ancien régime*. Economic leadership was shifting from the guilds to a high bourgeoisie of commercial capitalists: financiers, tax farmers, bankers, and *négociants*—men of business who were not tied to a specific pursuit but who engaged in general trade, and especially in import-export.[6]

The most remarkable social mobility in French society in the eighteenth century occurred among these groups. The typical mode of social ascent was through success in business. Very few families stayed in commerce for three generations, for the new rich bought noble lands, or married into the nobility, or bought offices. The exceptions were the Protestants and the Jews. They could not enter the nobility, not even the parliamentary nobility, because of their

---

[4] There were Dutch business houses in Bordeaux, as well as in La Rochelle and Nantes, early in the seventeenth century (Mathorez, *Les étrangers*, II, 249–61).

[5] Sée, *Histoire économique*, p. 330.

[6] Soboul, *La France à la veille de la Révolution*, pp. 17,79. For a general outline of French economic history from Colbert to 1789, see, in addition to Soboul, Clough, *France, A History of National Economics, 1789–1939*), pp. 19–30; *idem* and Cole, *Economic History of Europe*, pp. 283–85, 318–43; on the physiocrats and the movement of economic thought and practice after the middle of the century, see pp. 356–81.

religion, and the richest, therefore, remained in business throughout the century. More important, the fields of activity of large-scale businessmen were largely new to France. They were therefore outside the older economic structure, which was entirely in the hands of native Frenchmen.[7]

These newer economic stirrings tended increasingly to break the hold of the guilds. This was happening in two ways. The independent artisan, producing in his own workshop on a small scale and selling his product, was under increasing attack from new forms of production. In Lyon, for example, most of those who in theory were masters in the guilds were actually working on raw materials supplied to them by large-scale entrepreneurs in silk. The textile industry came to represent in the eighteenth century over half of all the industrial production in France and a large part of its export trade. As the century wore on, the mode of production was increasingly changing under the cover of the older guild forms in an ever greater segment of the economy. There was, therefore, large scope for new people, who had no legal right to be in production. They entered the field by providing the raw material for masters who belonged to the guilds; there were other, complicated arrangements, by which members of the guilds dummied for the newer capitalists or even worked as their direct employees. Inevitably this trend gave rise to many lawsuits, as guilds fought against the new men, but the movement of the economy was against the older order.[8]

The guild system was under attack from another direction. In theory, the right to sell, in those locations where the guilds existed, was reserved for its members. Fairs, generally on a semi-annual basis, had existed for centuries in France and had served as a kind of safety valve. On these occasions, merchants from the outside who were not in the guilds could come for the duration of the fair and sell. Quarrels between the local merchants and the *forains* were endemic because the latter were constantly attempting to remain

[7] Soboul, *La France à la veille de la Révolution*, p. 75; Mathorez, *Les étrangers*, I, 97–98, 136.

[8] Soboul, *La France à la veille de la Révolution*, pp. 26–34. The domestic consumption of textiles was rising, because of a rising population, and the export trade doubled between the period of the Regency and the eve of the Revolution.

behind after the fair was over; or to peddle on the way to the fair, in the hinterland; or to find a way of keeping a store permanently, de facto, in places where they were forbidden by law. In the eighteenth century the commerce of the fairs rose remarkably.[9] It was to the advantage of the buyers that there be free competition. In those places where *parlements* were dominated by land owners, as in Bordeaux, they tended to take the part of the visiting sellers against the local guilds.[10] In the myriad arguments that marked the eighteenth century, the royal government veered from one side to the other but, as we have seen, by the middle of the century it had largely moved in the direction of freedom of commerce.

The chronic need of the state for money made bankers particularly useful to it. In France these were usually foreigners, like Necker, who was Swiss, or the earlier figure, Law, who was a Scotsman. Capitalists who were willing to take the risk of purveying to the army, the navy, and the colonies were encouraged and cultivated.[11] They were needed, for the banking system of France was the scandal of advanced economic thinking in Europe in the eighteenth century. It was held accountable for the fact that the potentially greatest power in Europe was outclassed by Holland and England, which had smaller populations and fewer natural resources.[12]

The movement in France in the eighteenth century was therefore in a direction away from a static economy of fixed status towards

[9] The commerce of the fair at Beaucaire (in which the Jews participated in an important way) rose from 14,000,000 livres in 1750 to 41,000,000 in 1788 (*ibid.*, pp. 317–19). The figure for the fair at Caen is 2,500,000 in 1715 and 41,000,000 in 1781 (*ibid.*, p. 22). This estimate is contrary to that of Sée (*Economic and Social Conditions*, p. 142), who held that the fairs were declining.

[10] Lheritier, *L'intendant Tourny*, II, 57.

[11] Sée, *Economic and Social Conditions*, pp. 303–306.

[12] Pinto argued this point over and over again in his *Traité;* see especially p. 90, where he maintained that its bad banking system was the reason why France was not achieving the potential of its power. There were no banks of emission in France before the Revolution except one, the Caisse d'Escompte, created in 1776. Most French banking in the eighteenth century consisted of credit facilities related to business, i.e., banks which granted short-term credits to buyers by paying their bills in cash and then waiting for them to pay, with interest, when they had sold the goods (Soboul, *La France à la veille de la Révolution*, p. 21). The large-scale credits that the state needed could hardly come from such sources. On foreign bankers in France see also Mathorez, *Les étrangers*, I, 99.

a more mobile and open one. The greatest single fact was the colonial trade, which required new forms of enterprise. International trade, as it grew in importance, could not be run under guild control. Internal commerce and production were increasingly breaking the old bonds, and the state itself had to look outside the structure of the older French society for support. This is a picture of an economy on the rise. On the other hand, there is evidence that large segments of the nobility were being impoverished and that, by the end of the century, the peasants were increasingly being reduced to a rural proletariat. Some were indeed buying their own land parcels, and a case can be made for the proposition that the Jewish moneylenders in eastern France provided indispensable credit for those peasants who were striving to become independent. Nonetheless, in an age in which the new men were becoming richer, the older orders were all losing ground. The peasant in particular was suffering, because any bad harvest meant that his noble overlords took more proportionately from him in taxes. The peasant, in turn, had to buy grain at higher prices to feed himself, generally with money that he borrowed. He also had to borrow money with which to pay his feudal dues or, sometimes, to buy the land on which he was working. The men who lent the peasant this money incurred his envy and his enmity, and in eastern France the lenders were Jews.[13]

Since the Jew could not own land anywhere, or belong to any guild, his economic career had to be made in the newer avenues of enterprise. Increasingly, the Jew legitimized himself under those decrees that favored all of the emerging economic pursuits, or the liberalization of access to older forms of endeavor. He stretched these new possibilities as far as he could. One of the oldest elements in Europe thus largely became typical new men of the eighteenth century. This does not mean that the Jews, who were small in number, perhaps 40,000 in a population of some 20,000,000, were of profound economic importance or that they were decisive in any aspect of eighteenth-century French economy. The Jews were, however, a significant barometer of the changes that were taking place

[13] Soboul, pp. 97–129. Landless peasants, many of them reduced to begging, were increasing in the eighteenth century; in 1790 the rural proletariat was estimated at 40 per cent of all the peasants, which means that this group numbered at least eight million people.

in France as a whole, and they were of course far more visible **than** their number suggests.

Essentially there were three orders of Jewish economic endeavor, and each was related to a larger concern within the French economy. The emphasis in Bordeaux in the eighteenth century was on the colonial trade because that city, beginning with the activity of Colbert, had become the major port for the trade with the French possessions in America and its islands. The primarily agricultural territories in eastern France served as an *entrepôt* for trade between Switzerland and the Lowlands, and they remained throughout the century a border area over which wars were consistently fought. The troops stationed on the border needed to be provisioned; peasants were constantly in need of loans, both to tide them over bad years and to help them buy their lands; smuggling, especially of gold and coins, was a "recognized" profession in a border area, in which the profusion of tolls under the *ancien régime* was particularly complicated. The third element, the Avignonnais, kept coming into France because there was ever less room and fewer opportunities for Jews in the restricted ghettos in the Papal States. They especially collided with the local merchant guilds because they usually began as traders at fairs. From this they spread out to keeping shops illegally and eventually to large-scale trading in silks and textiles.

## The Portuguese of Bordeaux

In Bordeaux as a whole, three kinds of commercial interests existed in the seventeenth and eighteenth centuries. There was the ancient trade in wine, based on the famous and important vineyards of the area. Despite radical changes in the eighteenth century of the character of Bordeaux's economy, the *corps de ville* and the *parlement* of Bordeaux were dominated not by businessmen, or even by the guilds of local merchants, but by the important wine growers. Their policy as sellers was consistently protectionist, so that the market and port of Bordeaux were closed even to the wines of the province of Guienne. As consumers, however, they had no concern with defending the local guilds against outside competition, because it was clearly in their interest to be able to buy what they needed as

cheaply as possible.[14] Hence, as we shall see, in the battle against
the appearance of Avignonnais Jews in Bordeaux, which was fought
by a coalition of the merchant guilds and the Sephardim, the Avignonnais were supported by the local *parlement.*

The second major older interest was that of the merchants. Bordeaux was one of those places in France in which commerce was
organized in the guild system. Some manufacturing had existed as
early as the sixteenth century, and such things as gold and silver
cloth had been sold in Spain and in several northern countries. The
artisans in various fields and the local merchants were all organized
in guilds and these persisted until 1789. These guilds behaved precisely like all others: they fought against any threat to their commercial monopolies. They were represented by the *Jurade,* which
was organized for most of the eighteenth century as an assembly of
130 local notables, who fought consistently for local rights.[15]

The third and most important element in Bordeaux's commerce
was the sea trade—a new industry. In the seventeenth century that
trade was in the hands of foreign ships; towards the end of the period it was carried primarily by four or five hundred ships that
called each year from England, Holland, and the Baltic states.[16]
This situation was altered radically by Colbert, who created Bordeaux as an international port for French-owned ships by inviting
individual foreigners to settle and to establish seafaring enterprises.
Irish, Dutch, Hanseatic, and Jewish entrepreneurs came to Bordeaux.[17] An important Protestant colony also existed in the city.[18]

[14] Lheritier, "La Révolution à Bordeaux de 1789," *RHB,* VIII, 125.

[15] Bachelier, *Histoire du commerce de Bordeaux,* pp. 98–100, 117–19.

[16] *Ibid.,* p. 71. As we have mentioned earlier (Chapter II), in 1699 the
intendants of France wrote memoranda on their various provinces for the
education of the heir to the throne, the Duke of Bourgogne. De Besans, the
intendant of Guienne, wrote that commerce in Bordeaux was least in the hands
of the French and that its largest share was controlled by naturalized foreigners. Some was in the hands of foreigners, who made money and left after a few
years (Francisque-Michel, *Histoire du commerce et de la navigation à Bordeaux,* p. 182).

[17] Each of the various national groups in Bordeaux was organized as a
*nation,* which was represented by a local syndic and by the consul of its place
of origin (Charpentier, *Les relations économiques,* pp. 22–23). The open appearance of a Jewish *nation* in Bordeaux towards the end of the seventeenth
century thus was aided by the creation of a new legal structure for trade by
foreigners.

[18] Leroux, "Histoire externe," *Bulletin de la société de l'histoire du Protas-
tantisme français,* LXVIII, 35–62. Several of the major fortunes in the sea

Indeed to the very end of the *ancien régime* the entire sea trade of Bordeaux and allied trades, like ship-building and marine insurance, were so completely in the hands of descendants of the newcomers that there was not a single French family to be found in these enterprises. In the constant wars of the eighteenth century this trade was of the most profound political and economic importance to the state. The religion of those who carried it on was always irrelevant.

Jews were involved in almost all of the aspects of Bordeaux trade, but not in agriculture. There is no indication that they figure at any point during the *ancien régime* as wine growers, even though their wealthiest ship-owning families, such as the Gradis clan, do appear by the middle of the century as the owners of country houses surrounded by land. Indeed, since the bourgeois of Bordeaux, including some Jews, had the right to possess noble lands, professing Jews could even acquire a title of nobility in this way. There is record that as early as 1720 Joseph Nunes Péreire, who had made his fortune in merchant banking, became, by purchase, the Vicomte de Menaude and the Baron d'Ambès.[19] There was, however, one spe-

---

trade were in Protestant hands. J. J. Bethmann, for example, came to Bordeaux from Frankfurt in 1740 and by 1775 he was the leading *armateur* of the city. The greatest single fortune in Bordeaux on the eve of the Revolution, 15,000,000 livres, belonged to another Protestant, François Bonnaffé. In 1765 the pastor of Bordeaux, Olivier-Desmont, wrote: "This province provides a liberty which the Protestants of France have not known since the revocation of the Edict of Nantes." In regard to the Protestants in Bordeaux, see also Mathorez, *Les étrangers,* I, 97–98, 141, 148; II, 146. In legal theory, after the revocation of the Edict of Nantes, foreign Protestants did still enjoy the right to religious liberty, and the overt practice of that religion in Bordeaux centered on the Dutch and German colonies, to which the local crypto-Protestants attached themselves. In the middle of the eighteenth century there were perhaps as many as 4,000 Protestants in Bordeaux as a whole. On the eve of the Revolution there were 500 large business houses in Bordeaux and almost 100 were in the hands of the Dutch and Germans. The Jewish community, which was numerically more than half as large as the Protestant groups, was represented by perhaps 30 firms in large-scale commerce. Szajkowski (*Autonomy and Communal Jewish Debts,* p. 65) has maintained that the Jews in Bordeaux were treated administratively like one of the local trade corporations. The Jews were known, however, not as a guild but as a *nation,* and it is therefore possible that the paradigm was the way foreign traders were being treated.

[19] Malvezin, *Histoire des Juifs à Bordeaux,* pp. 231–32. It is not quite certain whether Joseph Nunes Péreire exercised the right of ecclesiastical patronage. It is likely that he did not, for the precedent is not mentioned in the quarrel a half-century later over the barony of Picquigny, which was bought, comparably, by the Ashkenazi banker, Leifman Calmer. Jewish

cific "Jewish" element to the wine trade. In orthodox ritual law, wine that is prepared by gentile hands is not fit for Jewish use. The Jewish communities of Europe, therefore, required a source of supply of wine that had been prepared under Jewish supervision. Bordeaux served this function not only for itself, but also for Hamburg, Altona, and Amsterdam. This wine was prepared by Christian vintners, under the supervision of the rabbis of Bordeaux. The Ashkenazim of Hamburg had a supervisor of their own, Ephraim, who lived in Bordeaux in the 1740s; there was controversy between him and the local community because he attempted to operate independently of the local rabbis.[20]

The most important economic function that the Jews performed in Bordeaux was commercial. The marranos who appeared there, especially after 1675, retained family connections with relatives even

---

country homes outside Bordeaux were not unusual. There were such in the Henriques, Coste, Lopes de Paz, Raba, Peixotto, and Gradis families, at very least, and births and deaths are recorded in these places. See Cirot, "Les Juifs et l'opinion," *RHB*, XXI, 126; Szajkowski, *Franco-Judaica*, No. 1285.

[20] A sketchy and inexact account of this affair is to be found in Malvezin, pp. 203–205. The house which produced kosher wine, for which Ephraim worked, was itself not one of the older French concerns. It was created in the late 1730s by Jacob Schröder and Johann Schuyler, German Protestants, who came from Hamburg to Bordeaux in that period (Mathorez, *Les étrangers*, II, 146). The making of kosher wine in Bordeaux is mentioned in the communal minutes of 1719 (*Registre*, Nos. 19, 20). The three *parnassim* (syndics) ruled that the charge for certification by their rabbi of each cask of wine as kosher be 5 livres per tonneau. Any individual on the roll of the poor who worked on kosher wine not under their supervision would be stricken from the rolls. There is record in these minutes of an agreement between the rabbi, Aaron Falcon, and Aaron Sasportes, who was evidently the active supervisor of the production of the wine, that they would divide 4 livres per tonneau between them, and that the fifth would go to the community fund for the poor. The Sephardi reaction in 1752 to Ephraim's attempt to produce wine, with local Jewish workers, at Schröder and Schuyler, was the same: those who would work for him were threatened with exclusion from the poor rolls, as well as religious excommunication, so Ephraim could get no workers (*Registre*, No. 204). The issue seems, at least in part, to have been religious. Upon his arrival as rabbi in Hamburg (in 1749 and not, as Malvezin states, in 1744), Jonathan Eibeschütz forbade the wine supervised by the rabbi of Bordeaux; it is likely that his experience in France, as rabbi in Metz, had convinced him that the Jews of Bordeaux were not pious by his standards. The charge of 5 livres per tonneau also was objected to by the Jews of Hamburg as too high. This matter went to the intendant, who ruled that the Portuguese tax had to be paid and that their supervisor, being acceptable to Amsterdam and London, had to be accepted also in Hamburg.

in Spain and in Portugal. More important still there were strong ties
with London and Amsterdam. Since these two cities, especially the
second, were the great centers of international banking and trade
in the eighteenth century, the accession of such an element to
France was important. An anti-Jewish *mémoire* at the end of the
seventeenth century described the commerce of these Jews as very
"subtle." They dealt, then, in banking and letters of exchange, being
in close connection with many foreign correspondents. They were
accused of pandering to the taste of the French for luxuries by im-
porting jewels and precious stones. In the evidence of this unfriendly account they were also then trading in wool, leather, sugar,
oil, and brazilwood. The force of the argument was that the Jews
were acting primarily as importers and thus "draining the country of
gold." [21]

The Jews thus first made their place in Bordeaux, not through
the sea trade with America, but in the more usual way. They represented international economic connections in a stagnant city within
a depopulated region. Even as late as the middle of the eighteenth
century the overwhelming majority of Jews who were doing well
were not in shipping but in brokerage.[22] The Gradis family, destined
to become the single most important Jewish influence in Bordeaux
sea trade, was still engaged in such pursuits at the end of the seventeenth century. Members of the family did not enter into the trade
with the islands until after 1700, and it was not until 1722 that
David Gradis abandoned all other business to devote himself en-

[21] Anchel, *Les Juifs de France,* pp. 133, 136. On the trade of the Jews of
Bordeaux with Spain and Portugal, see Szajkowski, "Trade Relations of Marranos," *JQR,* L, 69–78. Szajkowski found almost no trace of any commerce with
Spain in the eighteenth century. One possible explanation of the change is that
in that period the Jews of Bordeaux had ceased to be marranos and thus faced
difficulties as Jews in dealing with Spain. It is also possible, and indeed more
likely, that the port of Bordeaux was primarily devoted, after Colbert, to the
overseas trade and that the trade with Spain was conducted in the eighteenth
century by Bayonne. We know that Jews of that city figured prominently in
the Spanish trade in the eighteenth century. (The most recent, very detailed
study, is by Jaupart, "L'Activité commerciale," p. 36.) On the trade of Bayonne,
see below.

[22] A list prepared for the office of the intendant ca. 1737–39 names eleven
brokers in general trade and sixteen brokers in the trade in spirits. There
were no more than three or four Jewish firms of any consequence in the
colonial trade. Cirot, "Les Juifs à Bordeaux," *RHB,* XXXII, 16–19.

tirely to the colonial trade.[23] He engaged in the export of wine, alcohol, flour, and saltbeef to the colonies; his ships brought back to France sugar and indigo.[24]

The firm rose to major importance in the 1740s during the War of the Austrian Succession. Conditions at sea were very risky and the trade with Canada was reduced by British naval action to a trickle. Under these ruinous conditions the freight rate rose to 200 livres per ton. The only house in Bordeaux that was willing to risk provisioning Canada under those circumstances was the Gradis firm. The hazards at sea were even greater for the French during the Seven Years' War, and this was reflected in an even higher freight rate and an even greater reluctance on the part of the sea traders of Bordeaux to risk their ships on the Atlantic. Gradis nonetheless organized the *Société de Canada* in 1748 in partnership with both the intendant and the controller of ships in New France and contracted to provide regular ship service to Quebec for six years. When the *Société* was dissolved in 1756 it had made almost a million livres of profit for the Gradis firm alone.[25]

The important role of the Gradis firm, and of other Jews, in the colonial trade involved them in certain aspects of production. Sugar

[23] The Gradis family has had more written about it than any other in eighteenth-century French Jewry. In the first place, contemporary opinion, both within the Jewish community and outside it, regarded the Jews of Bordeaux in the colonial trade as the apex of Jewish society. An undated manuscript document, but clearly from the early 1790s, in which Bordeaux Jewry answers some questions about itself put by the local authorities, names the Gradis, Raba, and Rodrigues families as the "most remarkable" (Archive de la Gironde, V, 13). The first two were in the sea trade and the third were bankers. In the second place, the Gradises themselves and especially the second David Gradis, who lived through the period of the Revolution, were men of considerable force of personality and culture, who exercised active leadership in the Jewish community. The general accounts of the Gradis family are Gradis, *Notice sur la famille Gradis*, and Graetz's summary of this book of family piety in two articles entitled "Die Familie Gradis," *MGWJ*, XXIV, 447–59; XXV, 78–85. More recently a biography of Abraham Gradis by Maupassant appeared in two versions, in installments in *RHB*, and as a printed volume in Bordeaux in 1919 (the citations below will be from the series of articles). Despite all this writing and quite a number of specialized articles on the Gradis clan we are still in the dark on a number of essentials. Maupassant, who was given access to the family archives, was quite clearly allowed to use selected material only, and no other scholar has as yet had full use of all the Gradis papers in Bordeaux.

[24] Graetz, XXIV, 450; Maupassant, "Un grand armateur," *RHB*, VI, 183.

[25] Graetz, p. 451; Maupassant, pp. 281–96.

was the main import from the French islands, and a refinery in Bordeaux was owned by several of the richest Jews, led by Gradis.[26] More important, the Jewish bankers and sea traders of Bordeaux pioneered in the field of marine insurance, not only for their own ships but for those of gentile houses. This was a new economic pursuit, unencumbered by older legislation and therefore open to Jews.[27] Insurance is a field to which fraud and chicanery are particularly attracted. In one well-known case in the early 1750s members of the Francia family attempted to defraud gentile assurers from Bayonne of 50,000 écus, through a pre-arranged sinking of the ship Vigilant.[28]

David Gradis died in 1751 and the firm was continued by his nephew, Abraham. In 1758 his exports to Canada alone were worth well over 2,000,000 livres. For the entire period of the Seven Years' War (1756–63) his trade with Canada amounted to 9,000,000 livres. There were many losses, for more than half of the ships that he sent out were captured by the English, and he had trouble collecting from the state. Nonetheless, the Gradis house and several collateral branches of the family prospered greatly.[29]

There is evidence that investing in the sea trade, which was an especially speculative enterprise during the dangerous years of the wars of the eighteenth century, was attractive to some members of the nobility. They could engage in this pursuit without endangering their status.[30] Several Parisian nobles invested with David Gradis. No doubt there was an element here, on Gradis' part, of the buying of influence. Such connections were a help in the fight to get contracts with the government and in the often harder battle to be paid. One incident is illustrative. After the worst naval disasters of the Seven Years' War, in 1758, Gradis went to Paris to negotiate for the

[26] Szajkowski, Franco-Judaica, No. 787. In 1790, by contemporary account, there were ten refineries in Bordeaux, doing a trade of 10,000,000 livres annually. There were also seven or eight tobacco factories (Bachelier, Histoire du commerce de Bordeaux, pp. 217–19).

[27] Szajkowski, Franco-Judaica, Nos. 1071–1176.

[28] Cirot, Recherches, pp. 57–8.

[29] Maupassant, "Un grand armateur," RHB, VI, 432–48.

[30] A decree of 1701 had granted permission to nobles to engage in wholesale trade by land and sea, without losing their titles. They were particularly prominent as investors in the sea-trading companies of Bordeaux and Nantes (Soboul, La France à la veille de la Révolution, p. 51).

future. He had not yet been paid very much for his past operations in the provisioning of Canada and he was not disposed to prepare for the next year's expedition until he had some money in hand. Whether and how soon he was to be paid was very much involved in the politics of the French Naval Ministry, and Gradis was attached to the party of the enemies of the Minister of Marine, Le Normant. After intricate in-fighting, Gradis was eventually paid most of what was owed him, but he did not receive the contract for the expedition of the next year even though the influence of his noble friend, Mlle de Beuvron d'Harcourt, who invested with him, was brought to bear on his behalf. Gradis' stance in this affair was that of a considerable figure who was dealing with his equals. He wrote in August of that year to one of the officials involved: ". . . I was forced to accept payment for my services of previous years in letters of credit issued by the treasurer of the colonies. I had never expected to be treated this way, but I have now learnt my lesson." [31]

The Gradis firm was sufficiently important in the provisioning of Canada that, when it fell, Abraham Gradis was one of the witnesses summoned to the royal inquiry in 1762. He was given prior warning by his friend and protector, the Duke of Choiseul, that his papers would be requisitioned. The intendant himself, Boutin, came with great politeness to take these documents, and they did indeed contain some damaging information about the partnership deals that Gradis had made with the two royal officials on the spot in Canada. Choiseul clearly protected Gradis in this affair and there were no negative consequences.[32]

The Gradis firm also had a continuing interest in provisioning the French islands in America. Abraham Gradis was in business partnership in 1753 with the famous Jesuit Antoine Lavalette, who built an empire in Martinique. Gradis himself lost no money in Lavalette's fall, essentially because the debts were guaranteed by Mlle de Beuvron d'Harcourt, but this crash led to at least one important bankruptcy in Marseilles. It was an immediate factor adding to the outcry that led to the suppression of the Jesuit order in

---

[31] Maupassant, "Un grand armateur," *RHB*, VI, 433.
[32] *Ibid*., VII, 124–26.

France.[33] In the last two decades before the Revolution the Gradis firm had a royal contract to provide specie for the French islands in America, which were suffering a money shortage.[34] In the 1770s Abraham Gradis, in the settlement of several debts, became the owner of considerable land in San Domingo and Martinique. Under the *Code Noir* of 1683 Jews could not own property in the colonies, and this decree had been repeated at the beginning of each reign. Nonetheless, *lettres patentes*, dated August 21, 1779, gave special privilege to Gradis.[35]

An interesting sidelight to the whole question of the commerce of the Gradis family is the issue of their involvement in the slave trade. All of the accounts to date have carefully avoided the subject. As is well known, Bordeaux was a major slave port, buying slaves in West Africa for resale in America. We know that other houses in Bordeaux made this trade their primary activity. The house of Gradis seems to have dealt mainly in the shipping of provisions directly to the islands. There can be no doubt, however, that the Gradis firm too had no scruples about the slave trade. In 1748 Abraham Gradis proposed to the royal government that something major be done for the development of the French possessions in Louisiana. His plan envisaged the exporting of 2,000 Negroes a year for five years through the agency of private traders. This live cargo would be bought by the king and sold in Louisiana on the king's behalf at prices that would be fixed by the government. It is quite clear that he saw himself as the entrepreneur, because this was the very year in which he had just begun acting as the royal agent in Canada. The plan came to nothing, but this proposal makes obvious that Gradis regarded the slave trade as normal business.[36] In 1763 Abraham Gradis' friend Choiseul became the Minister of Marine, and Gradis immediately got a contract to provision the French possessions in West Africa. In these transactions Gradis supplied Africa with such commodities as whiskey, gunpowder, knives, and cloth, and he took his payment in slaves, whom he sold in San Domingo for sugar.[37]

---

[33] *Ibid.*, VI, 344–52.     [34] *Ibid.*, pp. 272–82.     [35] *Ibid.*, p. 286.
[36] Marcus, *American Jewry*, pp. 326–27.
[37] Maupassant, "Un grand armateur," *RHB*, VII, 134–35. Maupassant is careful to use the euphemism "merchandise" for the goods that Gradis acquired in West Africa for sale in San Domingo.

The Jewish sea traders of Bordeaux were such a striking phenomenon that they have obscured the fact that even in that city the
great bulk of the Jews were poor and engaged in various petty
occupations. In 1744 the Portuguese community forbade any of its
poor to trade in old clothes.[38] Some of the Portuguese were dummying for Jews from Avignon in Bordeaux,[39] and others were trying
to make a living in the brokerage business or on the bourse, although they had not a sou in capital.[40] All of these pursuits em-
broiled them with various local authorities. It was consistently the
object of the Portuguese leadership to keep their poor out of the
forbidden trades and thus out of trouble.

What was the comparative wealth of the Jews of Bordeaux? It
has often been presumed that their top element was extraordinarily
wealthy relative to the rest of the merchant population. This notion
is simply not true. In the middle of the eighteenth century at least
sixty businessmen were multi-millionaires in Bordeaux.[41] The internal tax rolls of the Jewish community, using the Gradis clan as
a standard, point to the conclusion that, at most, only five or six of
these were Jews.[42] There is other evidence at the end of the century. In 1782, after the defeat of de Grasse in America by the British
fleet, an appeal was made in Bordeaux to collect the funds to purchase another ship. Various bodies and individuals in Bordeaux
quickly subscribed 1,500,000 livres. There is record of the results
of that appeal among the Bordeaux Jewish leaders; their total contribution was only a little more than 60,000 livres.[43]

### Avignonnais and Others in Bordeaux

In the Papal States, the domain ruled by the Church, Jewish commerce had been severely restricted. The burden of taxation kept

[38] *Registre*, No. 110.
[39] Cirot, "Portugais et Avignonnais," *RHB*, XXI, 73. There is even an incident on record of a band of smugglers, consisting of two Portuguese and one
Avignonnais, who were caught in 1742.
[40] Malvezin, *Histoire des Juifs à Bordeaux*, p. 198.
[41] Sée, *Economic and Social Conditions*, p. 151.
[42] There are two complete tax rolls, with the amounts assessed, in the
*Registre*. One is dated April 20, 1746, and it contains the assessments of eighty-
four taxpayers, i.e., all who paid towards the *annuel* for 1747, of 2,400 livres.
The next year twelve more taxpayers were added (No. 140).
[43] *Registre*, No. 505. Charpentier, *Les relations économiques*, p. 140.

rising and an ever larger number felt constrained to seek their fortune elsewhere. These Jews (they were known as "Avignonnais" after the capital of the Papal States) spread out all over southern France, peddling and trading at fairs, especially in dry goods and silk. They had long experience in this field, for, despite innumerable prohibitions, Jews had dominated this trade in the Papal States themselves.[44]

In the eighteenth century Bordeaux was a particularly attractive place to Jews from this region. It was a rich city and it contained a Jewish community with stable rights. By the beginning of the century a few of these Jews from Avignon had settled quietly in Bordeaux, without permission.[45] In 1722 there were twenty-two families, and both their numbers and their activities had come to sufficient public notice so that a decree was issued to expel them. By their own account, as they fought to stay, these families divided evenly between the trade in textiles and that in old clothes. The intendant reported to Paris in his covering letter that these Jews from Avignon were "almost all so poor and miserable that I believe that they are absolutely incapable of paying anything in order to obtain permission to remain in this city."[46] The local merchants, especially the drapers, mercers, silk merchants, and clothes dealers, were opposed to the Avignonnais because they represented competition. The Portuguese leadership disliked them for a variety of reasons: these Avignonnais were taking advantage of privileges that the Portuguese had bought dearly; they were poor, and the Portuguese feared any increase in the numbers of those whom they might have to support; the Portuguese regarded themselves as socially superior; but, most important, the Avignonnais were attempting to carve out a new kind of economic position, that of a Jewish middle class in domestic trade, and this could be achieved only by persistent battle

[44] Mossé, *Histoire des Juifs*, p. 220.

[45] All of the monographs on the history of the Jews in Bordeaux have paid major attention to the struggle between the Portuguese and Avignonnais: Detcheverry, *Histoire des Israélites de Bordeaux*, pp. 74–89; Malvezin, *Histoire des Juifs à Bordeaux*, pp. 188–211; the most detailed account is in Cirot, "Les Juifs de Bordeaux," *RHB*, VII, 353–70; VIII, 22–38, 169–89, 267–75; IX, 22–38, 169–85; X, 23–36, 203–20; XI, 128–42, 200–207; XII, 14–28; XXIX, 209–19; XXXI, 63–75, 119–27. See also Chapter IV.

[46] Cirot, VII, 361. This is a minute by de Boucher to the controller-general of finances.

with local interests. The Portuguese leaders preferred to keep matters quiet, and they therefore joined all the attempts to keep the Jews from Avignon out of Bordeaux, or to reduce their numbers and importance.

This does not mean that the policy of the leadership was followed by all of the Portuguese community. Some Portuguese helped Jews from Avignon weather expulsion, or the threat of expulsion, by dummying for them. Others loaned them money at exorbitant interest.[47] Indeed, after the Avignonnais were finally expelled in 1735 a few Portuguese tried to enter the textile trade, which the Avignonnais had dominated, but these newcomers soon went bankrupt. The Avignonnais also managed to make strong friends among leading Christian personalities. Despite the expulsion of 1735 they were soon drifting back into Bordeaux or coming into the city to trade from country places in the neighborhood. One group of families, the Petits, remained near Bordeaux and were unassailable because they had leased the estates of the Duke of Gramont.[48] In 1737 one of the Avignonnais families, the Dalpugets, were able to secure a testimonial to their high character and commercial usefulness that was signed by a majority of the members of the *parlement* of Bordeaux.[49]

One way or another, the Jews from Avignon managed to remain in Bordeaux and the surrounding area in the next two decades. When they were forbidden to trade in silk and textiles, as a precondition for their right to remain, they attempted banking and the sea trade, using these "legal" endeavors as the cover for their ac-

[47] In an undated brief, in the 1730s, by the merchants of Bordeaux (*Mémoire des marchands boutiquiers de Bordeaux*) it was stated that "the Portuguese Jews of the tribe of Judah, although enemies and separated in organization and sentiment from the Avignonnais . . . furnish them all the money they want [in truth at exorbitant interest] in order to enable them to make their shady deals." See Szajkowski, *Franco-Judaica*, No. 244, and Cirot, "Les Juifs de Bordeaux," *RHB*, XI, 138, 203.

[48] Cirot, VIII, 178. The Petits were not the only ones who continued to trade in or near Bordeaux. The *Conseil d'Etat* repeated its expulsion order on September 9, 1737, for there were still Avignonnais and German Jews peddling in the city. On May 4, 1738, a certain Castille was caught peddling gold, jewelry, and old watches; he was expelled and his goods were confiscated. The general decree of expulsion was reaffirmed on February 28, 1740 (Documents, JTS).

[49] *Certificats;* the copy of this document in the JTS Library contains more than forty names. See also Szajkowski, *Franco-Judaica*, No. 245.

customed pursuits.[50] They spread out into jewelry and all kinds of luxury articles. They were constantly under attack by their enemies, the local merchants, for selling supposedly defective merchandise and stolen goods. A truer charge against them is that these Jews from Avignon pioneered in the introduction into France of calico, which they smuggled in despite the French protective laws against this cheap imported textile.[51] It was also true that the Dalpugets were not above going bankrupt, somewhat fraudulently. In 1750 the *parlement* of Bordeaux forbade a certain Dubillon, who was associated with the Dalpugets, from selling ready-made clothes in the city. This prohibition was reversed by the *Conseil d'Etat*, so that this first venture in selling ready-made clothes on a large scale in France was permitted. The Dalpugets invested heavily in this venture. They were able to do this, so the local merchants asserted, because they had recently made quite a lot of money, with the help of friendly Portuguese Jews, by going bankrupt falsely to the tune of 1,200,000 livres (the largest bankruptcy in the history of the province) and paying their creditors 30 per cent.[52]

Essentially, however, the commerce of these Jews flourished not because they sold bad goods or because they defrauded their suppliers, but because the guild merchants sat home, ordered from factories they never saw, and divided a limited local market. The Avignonnais dealt directly with the sources of production, to which they traveled. They lowered prices and created new demands. They battled everywhere that they could get a foot in the door to increase the outlets for their goods. None of them made large fortunes of the order of those of the leading Portuguese, but they prospered.

In 1730 the corporate wealth of the Avignonnais in Bordeaux was estimated officially at less than 600,000 livres, and the single larg-

[50] Detcheverry, *Histoire des Israélites de Bordeaux*, p. 77; Malvezin, *Histoire des Juifs à Bordeaux*, pp. 195–97; Cirot, "Les Juifs de Bordeaux," *RHB*, IX, 31. The decree by the intendant, de Tourny, of February 16, 1750 (JTS Library) issued at the request of the drapers and silk merchants forbade Jacob and Emanuel Dalpuget to engage in that trade. They were clearly doing exactly that, even though they had agreed not to, as a pre-condition of the right to be in Bordeaux, given them in two decrees the year before.

[51] Cirot, IV, 25. Both these charges, that the Jews sold inferior goods and that they were subverting French textile production by smuggling in calico, date from 1727.

[52] *Ibid.*, II, 200–207.

est fortune was that of Lange Mossé, at 150,000 livres.[53] In 1739 Pudeffer, the sergeant-major of Bordeaux, wrote to the intendant that almost all of the Jews arriving in Bordeaux then, both Portuguese and Avignonnais, were poor.[54] By 1751 Salon Dalpuget, Leon Petit, and David Petit had rented the property of the Duke of Gramont for ten years at 30,000 livres a year. According to their own commercial statement, they were in the sea trade, in sea insurance, and in the selling of silk at many fairs, especially in Bordeaux. They were also supplying the troops in Rochefort. Their capital was worth more than 200,000 livres and they had warehouses of their own in Bordeaux, Brittany, Reims, and Paris. They owed money to suppliers and business correspondents in a dozen places all over France. Jacob and Emanuel Dalpuget, as we can tell from the credits extended to them, were even wealthier.[55]

Most important, these Jews from Avignon were increasingly convincing the government that what they were doing was good for the French economy. In 1734 the current intendant, de Boucher, was noticeably reluctant to expel them. By 1750 the intendant, de Tourny, was convinced that there was no difference between the Jews from Avignon and the Portuguese, and he wanted to deal with each one on his individual merits. In his view the Avignonnais were good for the economy because they were reducing prices. Indeed, he permitted two Avignonnais merchants to sell for three days twice a year, in each of the major towns of the province.[56] In 1757 it was clear that none of the Jews from Avignon had remained in banking and sea trade and that they were all back in their usual pursuits. The Avignonnais admitted this freely but this did not then lead to their expulsion. The renewed controversy resulted in the granting of individual *lettres patentes* to their six leading families, in which they were given commercial liberty equal to that of the Portuguese. In that year de Moraçin, the controller-general of finances, wrote to de Tourny that "it is a matter of principle that the more business-

---

[53] *Ibid.*, VII, 369.    [54] *Ibid.*, VIII, 176.    [55] *Ibid.*, IX, 218–19.

[56] Lheritier, *L'intendant Tourny*, II, 68–82. In 1749 the Bureau of Commerce of Bordeaux advised Tourny that the Dalpugets should be allowed into Bordeaux but forbidden the trade in silk and drapery. Tourny's covering letter to the controller-general made the point that the reason for this opposition was the personal interest of the members of the Bureau, who had invested in these trades ( Cirot, "Les Juifs de Bordeaux," *RHB*, III, 33).

men there are of every kind, the more business increases and is profitable."[57] It was in the name of this theory that the *lettres patentes* of 1759 were finally issued. Those in whose favor this decree appeared paid 60,000 livres for the privilege, so the poor peddlers of thirty or forty years before had come to some substance.[58]

Other Jews were coming into Bordeaux right behind the Avignonnais. A census of the Ashkenazim in Bordeaux in the years 1762–63 listed 129 persons and added that 10 or 12 more were out peddling at the time of the census. Thirty-eight heads of families are described, by name; they were mostly engaged in dealing in junk, in peddling, in a bit of lending money on pledges, or, so this unfriendly account insists, in receiving stolen goods. Ephraim, the hero of the battle about kosher wine, was the most important among them, having been in Bordeaux longest. His children were already brokers, the typical Sephardi trade, and the family was lending money on pledges. This account tells us that all of these "Germans" had arrived in a miserable estate but that they had been rising. It concluded by paying these Jews the grudging compliment that "they live among themselves with much intelligence, and that is the reason why they can hide all their illegalities."[59] The local powers persisted in trying to keep them out. The Portuguese were particularly eager to join this effort, both because such people as the Duke of Richelieu had made the suggestion, and because they had no desire to increase their own burden of supporting more people without means. They had already tried to expel German and Italian Jews in 1744, and they were to repeat the pattern a number of times, notably in 1773, when they declared that the stream of immigration into Bordeaux was continuing.[60] In the next year they

[57] Letter of August 23, 1757 (Cirot, XXIX, 213). The petition by the six Avignonnais families to which this letter refers had argued that they were exactly like the Portuguese Jews and should have the same rights and that freedom of commerce was good for the city. This second point was accepted by the controller-general.

[58] *Ibid.*, pp. 216–17. The six families named in this decree were given the same economic rights as the "marchands Portugais ou Nouveaux Chrétiens."

[59] Anonymous, "Juifs Tudesques et Allemands à Bordeaux, 1762–1763," *Archive historique de la Gironde*, XLVIII, 583–88.

[60] See *Registre*, No. 110, for the expulsion of 1744; for the attempt in 1773, see No. 416; many "Ashkenazim, Italians, and Germans, all of them vagabonds of no settled occupation" have been drifting into the city, and the syndics were authorized to use all the necessary power to expel them. The next entry makes

even fought hard in legal proceedings against Serf Pollac, an Alsatian Jew married to a Portuguese, to get him expelled from the
city.[61] Nonetheless, it can be proved from the records of their charitable endeavors that the Sephardim were helping some German
Jews in the 1780s.[62] Such people kept coming and there was nothing
else to do but help the needy.

## Extending Jewish Commerce

Handfuls of the Sephardim had established themselves in several
places independently of the major communities of Bordeaux and
Bayonne. There had been Jews in the small town of Peyrehorade
as early as 1600. This community, which averaged one hundred
inhabitants, may perhaps have begun with people who came to it directly from the Iberian Peninsula.[63] By the same token, there were
Jews in Nantes almost as early as in Bordeaux and Bayonne, and
there they did come directly. This community was entirely marrano,
and it disappeared in the course of the seventeenth century.[64] During the eighteenth century some Portuguese Jews spread out from
Bordeaux to other places. As we have seen, a few went to the
French islands, and then, quite often, to America.[65]

---

it clear that their attention had been called to this situation by "many authorities"; the name of Richelieu is mentioned. The various attempts in the course
of the century to expel unwanted poor are summarized in Cirot, *Recherches*,
pp. 62–72; see also below in this chapter.

[61] Szajkowski, *Franco-Judaica*, Nos. 270–73. In their brief the syndics of the
Portuguese were venomous enough to use such language as this: "Who would
have believed that a Jew from Alsace, a miserable servant and peddler. . . ."

[62] The evidence is in a file of undated receipts, from the 1780s, for aid from
the Bordeaux *Sedaca* (JTS Library, uncatalogued). Helping others than
Sephardim was the exception however.

[63] E. Ginsburger, "Les Juifs de Peyrehorade," *REJ*, CIII, 35–69. Some of
these Jews were even farmers. Others were drapers and mercers, dealt in cattle
or eggs, or peddled in the countryside. See also Chapter II, fn. 16.

[64] Colbert knew that the Portuguese in Nantes in his time were Jews, but he
protected them. There were perhaps 500 then, but not all were judaizing. In
the eighteenth century Nantes was, along with Bordeaux, the port for American
trade, but there were no known Jews among its sea traders. See Brunschvicq,
"Les Juifs de Nantes," *REJ*, XIV, 126–31; Halgouet, *Nantes*; Szajkowski, "Population Problems," *PAAJR*, XXVII, 99; Bloom, *Economic Activities*, pp. 100–102,
regarding trade of the Spinoza family of Amsterdam with relatives in Nantes.

[65] "Incidents in the Life of Mr. Aaron Soria," *PAJHS*, XXVII, 475–79. Aaron
Soria and his wife were both born in Bordeaux, migrated to San Domingo, and

Some Sephardim moved out into various places in France, and especially in southern France, after the granting of the *lettres patentes* of 1723. This action had assured the rich Sephardim that, in their well-known and by then completely open quality as Jews, they could continue large-scale enterprise in international trade. A few poorer Sephardim immediately used the new decree as the basis for becoming merchants at fairs in the territory of the *parlement* of Dijon. Five such Portuguese Jews convinced that authority in 1724 to issue a formal decree permitting them to trade one month a year everywhere in the province. Six years later three Avignonnais Jews from Bordeaux, following immediately behind the Portuguese, got the same permission. These two decrees opened the way for considerable extension of Jewish traders in southern France, but these new activities also brought the issue to a head before the *Conseil d'Etat*. On February 20, 1731, it ruled that the decree of 1723 had intended to permit Jews to do business only where they were entitled by law to live, the areas of Auch and Bordeaux, and that this decree therefore could not be used as the legal basis for broadening Jewish commercial rights to allow those from Bordeaux or, a fortiori, any other Jews, to trade everywhere freely in France.[66] Nonetheless, this prohibition was a very temporary hindrance, for the spread of Jews continued as before.

Stray Jews of various provenance had been drifting into southern France from the beginning of the seventeenth century. In 1618 a Portuguese Jew, Antonio Lopez Pereira, bought one-quarter of the cargo of the ship *Esperanza*, which was then in the harbor of Mar-

---

came to New York after the revolution on the island. Bordeaux was also a port of transit for Spanish and Portuguese Jews on their way to other places. In the eighteenth century there was both emigration to London of Jews resident in Bordeaux, and transit traffic to that city. During the French Revolution there was some traffic from Bordeaux to the United States (Szajkowski, "Jewish Emigration," *JSS*, XVIII, 118–24). See *Registre*, Nos. 5, 29, for evidence of help being extended by the community to Jews on their way through to Holland.

[66] A copy of the decree of February 20, 1731, in four pages printed in Dijon and containing the registration of this decree in its *parlement*, is in the archives of the Israel Historical Society. This act was careful to distinguish between the five Portuguese, who were termed "residents of Bordeaux," and the three Avignonnais, who were "established in Bordeaux." A broadside version of this act, printed in Montpellier, is described in Szajkowski, *Franco-Judaica*, No. 314.

seilles.[67] In 1667 Joseph Vais Villareal, a Jew from Leghorn, arrived in Marseilles and settled down to do business. With him there came a number of other families, and there were even regular Sabbath services in his home. As we have seen, Colbert tried to convince Marseilles to allow this group to stay, but he failed. A royal order issued in 1682 expelled them. While they were there these Jews had engaged in several forms of trade, the most interesting being the import-export business with the Barbary Coast. Villareal was accused by his enemies of being in secret league with the Algerian and Majorcan corsairs and of selling stolen goods at depreciated prices. Marseilles commercial interests were then particularly angry at the Jews because Jews of Aleppo and Leghorn were underselling French textiles in the Levant.[68]

By the middle of the seventeenth century the most important consistent Jewish migration into southern France, that from the Papal States, had well begun. The *parlement* of Toulouse was already expelling these Jews in 1653. The consuls of Montpellier attempted to protect these Avignonnais merchants against the local interests, but without success.[69] In two decrees in 1680 the *parlement* of Toulouse ordered the Jews to leave the entire jurisdiction, and especially the cities of Nîmes and Montpellier, in which they were to be found "in very great numbers." One of the decrees specifically named such Avignonnais Jews as the Astrucs, Naquets, Perpignans, and Dalpugets, all of which families were to be represented in Bordeaux very soon thereafter. The form of their commerce, which was now forbidden, was to come to Toulouse, Nîmes, Montpellier, and one of the smaller towns in turn, and to settle down in each of them for three months of the year.[70] This expulsion

[67] Bloom, *Economic Activities*, p. 64.

[68] Anchel, *Les Juifs de France*, p. 142; Weyl, "La résidence des Juifs à Marseilles," *REJ*, XVII, 99–106; Bergasse, *Histoire du commerce de Marseilles*, IV, pt. I, 103. There was a further decree by the *parlement* of Provence dated September 20, 1683, forbidding Villareal and the rest to come to Marseilles, or anywhere else in the province. This document (JTS Library) contains an interesting remark about the intendant. He was accused of dragging his feet in executing the royal expulsion order of 1682 "for secret motives known to himself." Can one suspect private instructions from Colbert, in the last months of his life? Regarding Colbert and the Jews of Marseilles, see Chapter II.

[69] S. Kahn, "Les Juifs de Montpellier," *REJ*, XXXIII, 283–85.

[70] There is an eight-page pamphlet, printed in Toulouse in 1680, containing both these decrees. A copy is in the JTS Library; it is identical with Szajkow-

was of little effect. By 1695 the Jews were, even legally, back in the area, with permission to trade all over Languedoc one month in each of the four seasons in "all sorts of merchandise, both old and new." In 1705, indeed, one Jew obtained the right to live in Montpellier during the fairs, and others soon followed him. By 1729 the textile dealers of the city were complaining to the controller-general that the Jews had rented stores and had settled down permanently to trade there. The intendant did not pretend to the controller-general that these Jews had any legal rights in Montpellier. He simply argued that he had been using their presence as a counter-foil to the high prices being charged by the local merchants. An attempt to expel them in 1732 proved ineffective because, as in Bordeaux, local notables were protecting them. A few years later a nobleman, the Marquis de Grave, was not only allowing Jews to trade at fairs in his jurisdiction; he was even lodging them in his castle. In 1740 the intendant of Languedoc wrote to Paris that "if the Jews are excluded [from the fairs of Languedoc] I am sure that this will create a commercial void which will probably cause considerable hardship in the factories." By that point they were selling a considerable amount of the textile production of southern France.[71]

The essence of the battle between the Jews from Avignon and the local commercial interests in Montpellier was that Montpellier was a center for the manufacture of woolens. Its guilds were sensitive to all competition from imported goods. Smuggling across the border between the Papal States and France was a well-established industry and the Jews participated in it. The free fair at Beaucaire was an *entrepôt* for Mediterranean commerce. Avignonnais Jews bought 500,000 livres' worth of silk a year there and sold it in Languedoc in competition with the production of Nîmes. The unsold production of local masters, both in silk and in woolens, was taken at reduced prices by the Jews, who then used these goods to undersell the guilds. They thus created a free market, and even occasionally found local authorities who sided with them against the restrictive practices of the guilds. In 1754, in an unusual action, the authorities

---

ski, *Franco-Judaica*, No. 300. There were also some marranos, of Spanish and Portuguese extraction, in Toulouse, who were condemned to death in 1685 (see Szajkowski, No. 306).

[71] S. Kahn, "Les Juifs de Montpellier," *REJ*, XXXIII, 285–94.

of the city of Toulouse defended the Jews against an attempt by the
local merchants to have them excluded. This dispute went to Paris
in 1755 where the new controller-general, Trudaine, wrote that the
Bureau of Commerce is "today very favorable to everything which
permits the liberty of commerce. It frequently rejects any exclusion
even of the Jews." [72]

The most privileged of Jewish merchants in Languedoc were the
dealers in horses and mules, who came to that province mostly from
Carpentras. There was a general lack of farm animals in France in
the eighteenth century, partly because of a restrictive monopoly in
the hands of a group of Christian merchants. The Jews offered
credit to the peasants, and by 1750 they had come to dominate the
entire trade in farm animals in southern France. So great was the
need for animals that Jews from as far away as Metz came to participate in one branch of this trade, the furnishing of horses for
the provincial garrison. [73]

The need of Languedoc as a whole had created the opportunity
for the spread of Jewish commerce. At the beginning of the century
it was a poor province, which had been particularly disorganized by
the crusade against the Protestants in the Cévennes. The restrictive
practices of the guilds could not succeed there because an increase
in commercial activity was vitally necessary to the region. In 1744
the intendant, Le Nain, wrote to the controller-general that even the
activities of Jewish peddlers and old clothes dealers, the mass of
poor Jews, were of great value in Languedoc. [74]

Jews began to drift into Brittany later and in much smaller numbers. In 1742 the local authorities of Chalon-sur-Saône wrote to
Nantes for information about the Jews. The answer was that there
were no Jews living in Brittany; an occasional peddler came through,
but this was of no commercial importance. [75] As in Languedoc, the

[72] Roubin, "La vie commerciale," REJ, XXXIV, 276–93; see also the discussion in Chapter IV.
[73] Ibid., XXXV, 91–98; see also Bloch, "Un épisode," REJ, XXIV, 272–80.
In this particular incident twenty-two mules which were brought to Montpellier
in 1738 by Jews from Carpentras were confiscated by local authorities, but the
intendant countermanded the confiscation the very next day.
[74] Roubin, "La vie commerciale," REJ, XXXIV, 101–104; XXXVI, 75–100,
and especially 90–93.
[75] The only study of the history of the Jews in Nantes from earliest times to
the Revolution is Brunschvicq, "Les Juifs de Nantes," REJ, XIV, 80–91; XVII,

opening wedge of Jewish commerce was the fairs. The year before this exchange of letters the intendant of the province had ordered the toleration of Jews coming to trade at the local fairs. In 1744 Israel Dalpuget and Moses Petit of Bordeaux were given direct personal permission to engage in such trade. A number of protests, which came from various localities, prove that these Avignonnais took advantage of the situation to do more than they had been permitted. In St. Malo they kept open stores, directly, and in Rennes they did the same through Christian dummies. Dalpuget and Petit managed to stay in business in Brittany until 1766, when they were followed by Jacob Lisbonne and other Portuguese Jews from Bordeaux, and by some from Metz. None of this commerce amounted to very much, and in 1780 all of the few Jews who were resident in Brittany were expelled.[76]

Many of these battles throughout the century kept coming, for ultimate adjudication, to the central government. It was advised by the Bureau of Commerce, which invariably was asked its opinion by the controller-general of finances and by the Council of State. Most cases were decided locally, however, and almost none that came to Paris involved Portuguese Jews or those from eastern France. The rights of each group were sufficiently defined so that economic arguments could be settled for the most part within local jurisdictions. The overwhelming majority of cases involved the Jews from Avignon, and the issues generally revolved around their rights to trade at free fairs. It was well established that all foreign merchants, including Jews, could trade at the free fairs and, despite one flurry in 1717, that remained undoubted. The problem was the trade that fair merchants, and especially Jews, wanted to conduct in smaller places on their way to and from the fairs and, most important, their right to sell in a town one month in each season. Some

123–42; XIX, 294–305. On the letter from Chalon-sur-Saône, see the third section of the Brunschvicq study, p. 295. The decree of expulsion of the Jews in Languedoc in 1717 had been triggered by this community. The local authorities had permitted Jews to trade at its fair. When the case came to the Bureau of Commerce, it held that free fairs meant the freedom of all merchandise and not the freedom of all sellers. See Wolfson, "Le Bureau du Commerce," REJ, LX, 79–81.

[76] Brunschvicq, "Les Juifs en Bretagne," REJ, XXXIII, 88–121; Sée, "Note sur le commerce," REJ, LXXX, 170–81.

of the Avignonnais tried to go further and get formal permission to sell everywhere the goods they bought at fairs.

The restrictive decree of 1731 was, as mentioned above, of little damaging effect. This act was to be invoked as precedent in various battles until the Revolution, but it had no lasting results. For a few years the Jews were less in evidence, but Christians dummied for them. There were a number of interesting cases of noblemen and even of superiors of convents who let Jews trade from their premises and protected them from the guilds and their economic police officers. In the 1730s some of the merchants used their quarrels with Jews to attempt to create new guilds, but the policy of the royal government was against this because it would restrict commerce. By the 1740s the Jews were back in the fairs and the Bureau of Commerce, which for a while had opposed the Jews, was advising that they be allowed to trade in order to restrain the rapacities of the local merchants. Even at the height of the agitation in the 1720s to expel the Avignonnais from Bordeaux, a petition to create a new textile guild in that city as a weapon against these Jews failed. Despite affidavits from manufacturers of textiles in a number of cities stating that the Jews had been coming there to buy bad goods, the Bureau of Commerce refused to be convinced that a new guild should be created.[77]

By the middle of the eighteenth century Jewish retail commerce had spread quite widely in France and had achieved de facto toleration. Why this happened, in terms of the policy of the royal government, is quite clear: it was part of a continuing process of freeing trade from guild control. It is equally clear how the Jews could enlist local support. Once the Jews were settled in a place, all of those local forces that had reason to dislike the town merchants found them to be useful allies or instruments in their battles. The

[77] The relationship between the battle of the Avignonnais for increasing commercial freedom and the decline in royal support for the guilds has been studied at some length by Wolfson, "Le Bureau de Commerce," *REJ*, LX, 73–97; LXI, 88–111, 255–78. One of the favorite ways that Jews had of stretching their trading permission of a month was to follow each other into the major towns so that there was always a drapery shop open in Jewish hands, though not with the same Jew in residence (LX, 85). The drapers, mercers, and silk merchants of Bordeaux tried to get permission to create a guild in 1727, but the Bureau of Commerce denied this request in 1729 (LXI, 267).

question that still needs to be answered is why these Jews from Avignon, rather than the much more numerous poor from the Jewry of eastern France, and the significant poor element from Bordeaux and Bayonne, were the effective bearers of this endeavor. The answer is to be found in a crucial difference in legal and communal structure. Their own community in the Papal States had tried, for the purpose of communal taxation, at least twice to get its authority over Jews who had migrated to France enforced in the French courts. These efforts had failed.[78] The Avignonnais themselves in Bordeaux had attempted in 1722 to be admitted to the Portuguese community, to its tax roll, and thus to its discipline, but they were rebuffed.[79] In the very act, therefore, of crossing the border into France to try to make a living, a Jew from the Papal States became a free agent because his own community could not pursue him, and no established Jewish community wished to accept him. He belonged to no *nation* and no *corporation*. If he did anything to endanger the status of other Jews, as those of Bordeaux felt the Avignonnais were doing, he could not be disciplined; the only recourse the Portuguese had was to try to get him expelled. These marginal individuals were therefore free economic agents, standing outside all earlier legal structures erected for the discipline of Jews. It is not accidental that they played an important role in the eighteenth century in the battle for dynamic and individualistic commerce. The battle of the Jew to exist in France in the eighteenth century was thus both aided by the growing tendency towards free trade and also one of the significant forces that contributed to that process.

[78] Cirot, "Les Juifs de Bordeaux," *RHB*, VII, 355–56. Representatives of the Jews of Avignon attempted in 1717 to collect taxes from the Avignonnais in Bordeaux, and some were imprisoned at their request. The *parlement* of Bordeaux took their part twice, voiding decrees of confiscation on September 26, 1717, and April 10, 1725. There is trace of the second affair in the minutes of the Portuguese (*Registre*, No. 33, the entry of December 31, 1724). The syndics of the Jews in Avignon tried to bring certain expatriates to trial. An emissary from Avignon requested help from the Sephardim, which they emphatically refused, declaring that the affairs of the Avignonnais were totally foreign to them. On appeal in 1726 the *Conseil des Dépêches* upheld the Avignonnais in Bordeaux against their mother community.

[79] Cirot, p. 366.

## The Jews of Bayonne

The more characteristic kind of economic battle of the Jews of France in the eighteenth century was that of a community with some recognized rights, battling to broaden them. It is typified by Bayonne. All of the usual elements were present there. The Jews did have the right to live across the bridge in St. Esprit, but the city itself jealously guarded its ancient privilege to exclude them from even staying overnight. Retail trade in Bayonne was in the hands of guilds, which fought steadily to keep Jews out. Only the wholesale trade and the import-export business were permitted. There were no guilds in St. Esprit, so the situation was different. Jews dominated retail trade in the suburb, and by 1751 they owned 32 of the 230 houses there and rented many of the others.[80]

Three-quarters of the foreign commerce of Bayonne was with Spain, as it was the main port for the Spanish trade. The value of the goods exchanged when commerce was flourishing was between ten and fifteen million livres annually.[81] There were a number of foreign houses established in Bayonne, and at the height of the city's commercial activity the Jews represented some twenty of its eighty major business firms.[82] Essentially what was being exchanged were the wool and gold of Spain for silk, wine, and various manufactured products of France. The difficulty with this commerce was that throughout the second half of the century it was languishing. More and more houses were going out of business because Spain itself was engaging in a protectionist policy. In the squeeze between Spanish tariffs and rising French taxes, the population of Bayonne was consistently dropping, so that its population of 20,000 early in the century decreased to about 10,000 by the 1770s. There was large-scale emigration across the border to San Sebastian and Bilboa.[83]

[80] Léon, *Histoire des Juifs de Bayonne,* p. 58.
[81] Jaupart, *L'activité commerciale,* p. 123.
[82] *Ibid.,* p. 36.
[83] During the 1770s as many as two thousand left Bayonne for Spain. Foreign business houses in Bayonne declined from a high point of twenty-six to only two in 1755 (*ibid.,* p. 148).

The Jews obviously could not emigrate to Spain, so they had to fight in a declining market to make a living. This they could do only by confronting the guilds of Bayonne. Having been admitted in the name of their usefulness to the external commerce of France, the Jews were then forced to fight out a place in its internal trade, and even in production, in order to remain.

In 1691 the Jews were forbidden by a decree of the city of Bayonne to engage in retail trade. In the next year a number of merchants complained to the intendant of the province that retail commerce had left Bayonne for St. Esprit.[84] Bazin, the intendant, decided on January 9, 1692, that the only trade to which the Jews had a right, even in St. Esprit, was the wholesale one, "on the condition that the goods come from foreign countries." [85] This decree was totally ineffective, for the city repeated the prohibition against Jewish retail trade in Bayonne in 1705 and many times thereafter.[86] In 1706 it complained to the king regarding George Cardose and his nephew Isaac, who had bought a house in Bayonne through the good offices of a friendly gentile. Cardose answered that, having been naturalized in France together with all other Portuguese by the *lettres patentes* of 1656, and being himself the third generation born in France, he should at least have the right to own a house in the city of Bayonne for the purpose of using it as his business headquarters. Cardose admitted, however, that as a Jew he could not claim the right to live in Bayonne. The city argued that he could not own any property for any purpose in a place in which he had no right to stay the night. On July 16, 1706, a royal order forbade Cardose to keep the property.[87]

These battles continued. In 1735 another local order was issued to stop Jews from engaging in retail business in Bayonne.[88] In 1742

[84] Document in the Bibliothèque Municipale of Bayonne, Box GG 229, No. 4. This battle was already then of long standing. The mercers of Bayonne had sued in the *parlement* of Bordeaux in 1642 to forbid the Jews to sell in Bayonne (Léon, *Histoire des Juifs de Bayonne*, p. 30).

[85] BM Bayonne, GG 229, No. 6. This order went so far as to forbid the Jews retail trade even in St. Esprit. The real estate owners of St. Esprit took the side of the Jews in this dispute. They had a stake in the welfare of the Jews, who rented houses from them. They added that competition by Jews kept prices down in the area (Léon, pp. 30–31).

[86] BM Bayonne, GG 229, Nos. 8, 17.     [87] *Ibid.*, Nos. 10, 11, 15.
[88] *Ibid.*, No. 21.

a captain of the local garrison accused a Jew named Fonsecqua of selling tobacco on the street "from his pockets," and Fonsecqua was fined.[89] In 1750 Jacob Castro, a broker, pleaded with the city to allow him to sleep over occasionally because he was paralyzed, but the permission was curtly refused.[90] In 1756 the drapers and mercers asked that the Jews be forbidden to compete with them in the retail trade. It is clear that this was no idle complaint, for the next month two Jews were caught selling linen from a semi-concealed store in a widow's house in Bayonne, and two more were found out in the next two months. An undated complaint from this period maintained that linen was the major internal commerce of the city and that the Jews had seized it. The way they operated was to send out agents into the markets to steer strangers to their stores.[91]

All of these various battles occasioned an inquiry by the intendant as to the actual situation of the Jews in St. Esprit. The report that he received, in an undated document from around 1760, gave the following information. There were perhaps four hundred Jewish families in the community (this estimate was almost certainly exaggerated). Many of them had been in France a long time, and some were more recent arrivals. They were involved in all kinds of commerce, including even the trade in codfish and whales (though this last enterprise was a vanishing affair). This report was written by unfriendly hands; its author insisted that even in St. Esprit, where there was no guild structure, the Jews did not choose to engage in production. They were merchants, keeping stores; the wealthier were bankers and wholesale merchants, of whom this inimical account said that "they had little credit and even less honesty." In the peroration, the Jews were accused of seducing their Christian servants; of leaving for Holland, Hamburg, or London when they made money, where they could be Jews in freedom; of changing their names and fleeing for America when they went bankrupt; and —a charge that was constantly repeated, and not only in Bayonne— that the better prices that the Jews offered were based on their sale of shoddier goods and on the offering of false weights and measures.[92] This complaint was denied in a covering letter by the in-

89 *Ibid.*, No. 22.  90 *Ibid.*, No. 23.  91 *Ibid.*, Nos. 25, 26, 27, 29, 32.
92 *Ibid.*, No. 38.

tendant, d'Etigny, who ascribed this accusation to the jealousy of the local merchants.[93]

By around 1760 Jews in Bayonne were beginning to win some battles against the local authorities. In 1759 a Jewish dancing master named Quiros, most of whose pupils resided in Bayonne, did get permission from de Gramont, the military commander of the province, to live in the city despite the opposition of the local authorities.[94] Two years later the battle between the Jews in Bayonne and the city was joined on a broader front. In October the syndics of the Jews took a formal complaint to the authorities of the city, in which they argued that the *lettres patentes* of 1723 and the formal royal recognition of their internal communal statutes in 1756 together represented the acceptance of the Jews of Bayonne as *régnicoles* in France. Individual Jews had already argued this point in 1723, immediately after the first decree was issued. Nine Jewish merchants had attempted to force the registration of their right to do business in Bayonne, but they were refused. It was now a generation later. Under the influence of the drapers' guild a municipal decree was issued on September 25, 1761, in which the city ordered that all stores open without permission should be closed. It was this attack that was being answered by the Jewish community as a whole. The decree was nonetheless enforced.[95]

The battle was joined immediately on another front by those involved in the making of chocolate. The Jews had introduced that skill into Bayonne, having brought it with them from Spain. In 1761 Christians who had learned the trade attempted to form a guild. The intent of this new organization was to create a monopoly and exclude the Jews. The local authorities of Bayonne did confirm the existence of this guild.[96] This action by the city was, however, quite

[93] Léon, *Histoire des Juifs de Bayonne*, pp. 85–86.

[94] *Ibid.*, p. 67; BM Bayonne, GG 229, Nos. 34, 35. The civic authorities of Bayonne tried to pretend in writing to Gramont that he must have given Quiros the permission to live in the city because he was misled into thinking that the dancing master was not a Jew, but Gramont would have none of it.

[95] For the opening guns in this battle, the documents are to be found in BM Bayonne, GG 229, No. 39—the brief of the syndics of the Jews—and in the minutes of the municipality, BB 60, pp. 78, 91.

[96] The first defense by the civic authorities of the right to create the new guild of chocolate-makers is in their answer of November 23, 1761, to the Jewish brief of the month before (BM Bayonne, GG 229, No. 40; BB 60, p.

illegal, for guilds could be created only by royal charter. Moreover, by this point in the eighteenth century the founding of new guilds was contrary to the dominant tendency of the policy of the central government. The provincial intendant's representative in Bayonne, de Moraçin, wrote to the civic authorities of the city in 1763 in this spirit: "I am constrained to tell you that for some time the opinion of the government has been very much in favor of liberty, which it wishes that all art, commerce, and industry should enjoy." [97] After a battle of six years the *parlement* of Bordeaux finally suppressed this guild.[98]

The tensions between the merchants of Bayonne and the Jews continued until the Revolution. The persistent drive of the Jews to move into the city of Bayonne and to get permission to do business there was becoming more intense in the 1760s. There were briefs by the Jews and counter-briefs by their enemies, the authorities of the city. It is clear that the Jews themselves were becoming ever bolder in pressing their claims for wider economic liberty. This happened all over France after 1767 as a result of the decree creating new positions in the guilds and making them freely accessible to purchase by foreigners, but the Jews in Bayonne had already been fighting with unprecedented boldness some years before this happened. A *mémoire* by the city of Bayonne, dated October 29, 1764, contained the pained sentence: "The fathers of the Jews of this generation were quite far from extending their ambitions to the point to which their children are daring to extend them today." [99] The decree of 1767 simply gave the Jews of Bayonne more ammunition with which to fight.

Immediately after the *mémoire* was issued Isaac Frois tried to acquire a *brevet* as a draper under the new decree, as did Aaron Gomes Rabalho on the same day. The city answered both by arguing that only Christian foreigners could apply for this right, not

104). The city formally registered and published the statutes of the guild of the chocolate-makers on November 8, 1762 (BB 60, p. 236).

[97] Léon, *Histoire des Juifs de Bayonne*, p. 70; BM Bayonne, GG 229, No. 43.

[98] Léon, p. 73; BM Bayonne, GG 229, No. 54, for the decree of September 17, 1767. The Jews were joined by the grocers' guild in fighting against the chocolate-makers, for the new guild was against their interests, too.

[99] BM Bayonne, GG 229, No. 44.

Jews.[100] In 1775 the *Conseil d'Etat* validated the right of five Jews
from Avignon resident in Paris to trade freely, despite the opposition
of the guilds. This precedent was used by two Jews of Bayonne,
who maintained that they had paid for *brevets* quite a time before
and that they now wanted permission to use them. The city refused.[101] Two years later the syndics of the Jews forced the authorities in Bayonne to register the *lettres patentes* issued in behalf of
the Sephardim in 1776. The city complied, but it "reserved" its
ancient "right" to exclude Jews from Bayonne proper. The syndics
then took the case to the *parlement* of Bordeaux. From that jurisdiction the case was appealed to the *Conseil d'Etat* in Paris. The
matter dragged on and it was never resolved until the Revolution
made the question academic.[102]

The question of the comparative wealth of the Jews of Bayonne is
not easy to answer. We know that in the 1750s there were about one
thousand Jews in Bayonne, certainly no more than one-fifteenth of
its population, and they were paying roughly one-third of the taxes
of the city.[103] This is quite possible, however, even if the Jews were
poor. On the other hand, there is overwhelming evidence that they
dominated the brokerage trade (not the poorest of pursuits), and
that this was the characteristic Jewish occupation in Bayonne.[104] A
list of the Jews of St. Esprit and their fortunes does exist from the
early years of the Revolution. The fifty-seven richest Jews were
worth, together, 7,500,000 livres, whereas the wealth of the twelve
richest gentiles amounted to 1,290,000 livres.[105] This account rings
true in regard to St. Esprit, which was dominated by Jews. However, the gentile wealth in the area was in the hands of the bourgeois of the city of Bayonne proper, and we have no contemporary
estimate of their worth. It is reasonable to assume that within the
declining economy of Bayonne and St. Esprit the Jews, who had

[100] *Ibid.*, Nos. 52, 53, 54.     [101] *Ibid.*, No. 58.
[102] *Ibid.*, Nos. 61–64. In this controversy the legal fees of the city kept
mounting, and there is some evidence that the city fathers were becoming increasingly tired of the expense of the battle; see also Léon, *Histoire des Juifs
de Bayonne*, pp. 92–108, 130.
[103] *Ibid.*, p. 151.
[104] *Ibid.*, p. 108. The information is a *mémoire* by the city of Bayonne in
1765 in its continuing battle against the extension of Jewish economic rights.
[105] *Ibid.*, pp. 167–69.

no choice but to stay in France, managed to do comparatively better than their gentile competitors.

## Stagnation in Eastern France

The bulk of the Jews of France lived in the eastern border territory, in Metz and Alsace, with a handful in the duchy of Lorraine. Their economic history in the course of the eighteenth century was of a different order from that of the Jews in southeastern France. Their numbers in the region increased markedly, but until 1784 there was not a single change in any major restriction upon their commercial activities, restrictions which had existed at the beginning of the century. The organized communities themselves were ever more impoverished by the burden of taxes and by their responsibilities to the poor.[106] There were rich Jewish bankers and army purveyors in the region throughout the century, and their numbers were perhaps increasing, but the overwhelming majority of the Jews of eastern France were and remained poor. No new economic avenues were becoming available to them, to make possible even the beginnings of an escape from poverty. The traditional Jewish occupations of peddling, selling on credit, and usury, which obtained from Poland to eastern France, were as prominent in Metz as in nearby Clèves in Germany, or in any village in Poland.[107] The patterns of

---

[106] Szajkowski, *Autonomy and Communal Jewish Debts*, pp. 102–109. The council of the Jews of the province kept borrowing money: 24,000 livres in 1775 and 100,000 livres in 1787. These loans were from Christians, but the Council also borrowed from Jews, its major creditor being the leader of the Alsatian Jews, Cerf Berr, to the tune of more than 70,000 livres. See Baron, *The Jewish Community,* II, 247, regarding the mounting debts of the Jewish communities throughout Europe in the eighteenth century.

[107] In Clèves the Jews attempted, quite early, to give up the right to usury in return for access to the guilds. This battle in Clèves of 1664–75 is paralleled by the petition in Alsace in 1717 of comparable content (see Chapter IV). The pervasive rule in many of the localities of Alsace in the eighteenth century, that only the eldest child had the right to marry and live there, is the same as a decree issued by Frederick the Great in 1750 in Clèves. As in eastern France, a few families at the very top of Jewish society were bankers and moneylenders, and they were increasingly becoming part of Western culture, but most Jews in Clèves lived in poverty. They sold old clothes, kept stores illegally in back rooms, peddled, and lent money. A few tried to fight their way into primary production, but there was little Jewish involvement in nascent industry in the second half of the century (Baer, *Das Protokollbuch,* pp. 27, 46–47, 51–52, 66–

Jewish economic activity in eastern France, therefore, show little
that is new in the course of the eighteenth century. The very lack
of change and the persistence of bitter economic hatreds between
Jews and gentiles in a century of increasing intellectual enlightenment and economic liberty made the unchanged situation of the
Jews in eastern France an ever more painful problem, both for the
Jews themselves and for the royal government.

The process by which France acquired Jews on its northeastern
border was described at the outset of this study. To recapitulate,
briefly, the French crown simply replaced, at least at first, the German emperor; the king acquired all of the existing rights and com-
mitments of the sovereign, including those to Jews. Since the region
remained a theater of war it was always heavily garrisoned. If in
Bordeaux mercantilist reasons predominated in the policy of the
state towards the Jews, in eastern France the royal policy was rooted
in military considerations.[108]

There were other consequences of the continuing treatment of
eastern France as occupied territory. In all of Alsace, even as the
differences between the lands conquered before the 1660s (the "old
dominion") and the newer conquests were disappearing, ancient
German precedents remained in force. One of them was the arrangement that the king did not have the sole right to admit, or to refuse
to admit, Jews to his territories. This made it possible for Jews to
spread in the course of the century into many more places by individual arrangement with various local potentates. The increase
in the number of Jews, and in the number of places in which
they lived, did not however mean any increase in their economic
rights. It only meant that the same kind of economy, of peddling,
smuggling, illegal production, insecure shopkeeping, and usury,
spread to more places.

The special status of Alsace was such that its goods were subject

78). As in Alsace, the Jews were given the right to live in the cities of the
duchy in the course of the seventeenth century because of the impoverishment
of the region by war and the needs of the rulers for money. The higher authorities, who had the right to receive Jews, generally protected them against the
cities, which fought their admission (*ibid.*, p. 13).

[108] Hoffman, *L'Alsace*, I, 3; Scheid, "Histoire des Juifs," *REJ*, VIII, 243;
Szajkowski, *Economic Status*, p. 20.

to tariff as foreign merchandise on entering the rest of France, but there were no customs barriers against the commerce of foreign countries. The region was therefore of high importance as an *entrepôt* for commerce moving between Switzerland and Holland. This trade was dominated by the city of Strasbourg, which imported fish, sugar, and oil from Holland and sold these commodities for grain. Belfort was second in importance, buying wool in Saxony and Prussia and reselling it in Switzerland.[109] Both of these cities fought bitterly against Jews because the dominant commercial elements wanted no competition in their international trade. Strasbourg was also a manufacturing center for tobacco, which could be produced there, because the monopolies on that commodity in the rest of France did not apply in the separate legal structure of Alsace. There was some Jewish manufacture of tobacco in the eighteenth century, but it was in Lorraine and not in Alsace until the last few years before the Revolution.[110]

In the course of the seventeenth century the region as a whole had been ruined and depopulated by war. Capital was needed to rebuild it. The peasants in particular needed small loans, either to tide them over bad harvests or to help them buy land.[111] By absolute standards the amount of money available through Jews was not very large. At the very end of the century the worth of all the debts owed to the 20,000 Jews of Alsace was estimated at 9,000,000 livres in one account and 12,000,000 in another.[112] This is less money than

109 Hoffman, pp. 385–404.

110 There were fifty-three tobacco factories in Strasbourg by 1787, employing fifteen hundred or more workers (Hoffman, p. 406). There were no Jews in Strasbourg except Cerf Berr and his establishment. He established factories (a factory?), evidently of tobacco, in the 1780s and employed young Jews. (See M. Ginsburger, "Nancy et Strasbourg," *REJ*, LXXXIX, 83, quoting a document of 1790.) Berr Isaac Berr owned a tobacco factory in the city (Szajkowski, "Occupational Problems," *HJ*, XXI, 124).

111 Hoffman, *L'Alsace*, pp. 3–5; Szajkowski, *Economic Status*, p. 5.

112 Szajkowski, "The Decree of September 28, 1791," *Zion*, XVII, 84–85. The anti-Jewish Alsatian radical, J. F. Rewbell, estimated these debts at 12,000,000 to 15,000,000 livres in a speech at the *Assemblée Nationale* on September 28, 1791. The *Société des Amis de la Constitution* of Strasbourg guessed 9,000,000 in the next year. There is a comparable estimate in a handwritten report, dated September 30, 1790, from Colmar to the *Assemblée Nationale* (JTS Library). This document is anti-Jewish and would, therefore, not err in the direction of underestimating the "usuries of the Jews." It gives the figure of 12,000,000 livres.

the worth of the Gradis family alone at the time, but it made a difference in Alsace. Loans owed to Jews were a major economic and political issue there throughout the eighteenth century and into the nineteenth. It remains a matter of debate as to how large a proportion of the land of eastern France was owned by peasants before the Revolution, but undoubtedly much of the money with which such land was bought was borrowed from Jews.[113]

A considerable amount of economic information about Alsatian Jewry in the eighteenth century can be found in documents reflecting cases that were judged by various rabbinic tribunals, and in marriage contracts and guardianship arrangements that were registered with them. For example, the minutes of the rabbinic court in Niedernai for 1758–59 include a major case involving the bankruptcy of six Alsatian Jews, who were in prison for defaulting on a deal in which they bought cattle in Belfort for 130,000 livres.[114] Innumerable marriage contracts throughout the century involved considerable sums of money. In 1719 Abraham Moch of Haguenau was married to Miriam, the daughter of Moshe Yaffa of Vienna. One of the clauses of the contract obligated the father of the groom to pay 3,000 Reichsthaler to the bride for the cost of her trousseau and travel.[115] In 1782 Raphael Sel, a nephew of Cerf Berr, married a daughter of another Abraham Moch (probably the grandson of the first), and the two families together gave the young couple 24,000 livres.[116] A more modest wedding contract of 1767, involving the daughter of the current rabbi of Haguenau, Eliezer, required each side to put up 1,000 Reichsthaler. Three years later, when the same rabbi married off another daughter, the two families each put up 4,000 livres.[117] Nonetheless, we cannot deduce from such instances that there was any considerable wealth among significant numbers of Alsatian Jews. The business cases that would be judged, or the marriage contracts that would be registered, would tend to represent the larger amounts and the more prominent families. The Cerf Berr and Moch families were at the very top of Jewish wealth and status in eastern France.

[113] Szajkowski, *Economic Status*, pp. 54–57.
[114] MS, JTS Library, decrees of the rabbinic court in Niedernai.
[115] MS, British Museum, Oriental 12333, leaf 19.
[116] *Ibid.*, leaf 32.    [117] *Ibid.*, leaves 36, 51.

In commenting on the census of Alsace in 1732, in which 1,675 Jewish families were found, the intendant wrote that only 50 of them could live without begging or usury.[118] At the beginning of the Revolution, in 1790, two anonymous anti-Jewish pamphleteers attested to the poverty of Alsatian Jews. Most Jews had "fortunes," according to these accounts, of the order of 100 livres, and half were paupers.[119] This picture of overwhelming poverty is proved further by a tax toll for the purposes of assessing the head tax, which exists in an undated manuscript from the middle of the eighteenth century. In Haguenau itself, the source of this document, there were 44 households with sufficient resources to be taxable, and the corporate capital worth of all these families together was about 67,000 livres. For all of Alsace 2,498 households were estimated as having a corporate worth of about 3,000,000 livres.[120] Evaluations for tax rolls were always notoriously low, and the dowries in Haguenau give one the feeling that the Jews of that town had more money than they were admitting. Nonetheless, even in a situation where assets were being concealed, that such low estimates were believable tends to prove that all the Jews of Alsace together were certainly not worth more than the value of their loans at the end of the *ancien régime*. It is possible that there was almost as much money in the hands of the Jews in Bayonne at that time; there was certainly much more in Bordeaux, and both these communities together had a population only one-fifth the size of Alsatian Jewry.

The evidence from smaller places was much more revealing of the nature of Jewish commerce in Alsace. An official list in Mutzig of debts owed to Jews by Christians in 1715 shows not a single one

[118] Weiss, *Geschichte*, p. 59.

[119] Szajkowski, "Occupational Problems," *HJ*, XXI, 123; *idem, Poverty and Social Welfare*, p. 6. There is further corroborating evidence in the report from Colmar of September 30, 1790 (the document in JTS Library cited above). The author wrote as follows: "With the exception of a few individuals who are either more industrious or luckier than the others, this [the Alsatian] part of the Jewish people has constantly been in the grip of misery and of a low estate, which have turned it entirely to trickery and to usury."

[120] MS, British Museum, Or. 12333, leaf 23. The tax accounts for Haguenau given in this document are consonant with those printed in Scheid, "Histoire des Juifs," *REJ*, X, 214–18. A tax roll for 1750 and another for 1760 each shows a gross assessed worth of the value of the Jewish fortunes in Haguenau of over 60,000 livres.

as large as 500 florins; most of them were less than 25 florins.[121] These were debts that were registered and, as was constantly at issue in eastern France throughout the century, the majority of debts owed to Jews were not on public record. There is a series of the legal notices of eighteenth-century Hatten which prove that the handful of Jewish families in that town were peddlers, dealers in cattle, or very small-scale moneylenders.[122] In 1841 a Jew of Lorraine, who was almost a hundred years old, published his memoirs. Conditions there had been the same as in Alsace. He had been born in a village to a father who was a peddler, "as were then almost all the Jews of the province." He was married at eighteen to the daughter of the rabbi of a nearby village. The dowry was 200 livres, and it was raised by collection. He then followed his father into the family "trade." [123]

There were indeed a few unusual Jewish occupations in Alsace in the course of the century. As early as 1749 some Jews rented an iron factory and thus became involved, at least for a while, in primary production.[124] Cerf Berr and the people of his circle prepared for the Emancipation by fighting very hard in the last two decades of the *ancien régime* to get into agriculture and manufacturing.[125] There was a continuing battle with the city of Strasbourg about what business the Jews, who were allowed in the city only by day, would be permitted to transact there. They were always permitted to sell horses quite freely in the market because throughout the century the province suffered a continuing shortage of animals. Especially in years of bad harvest, Strasbourg and other Alsatian cities and towns did not object to the role of the Jews as importers of foodstuffs. Anything beyond that, such as the attempts of Jews to deal in gold, silver, and jewelry, met with repeated decrees of

[121] M. Ginsburger, "Mutzig," *Souvenir et Science*, IV, 12.

[122] *Idem*, "Hatten," *Souvenir et Science*, III, 6–8.

[123] Ben Lévi, "Mémoires d'un colporteur Juif," *AIF*, II, 686–91; III, 459–61.

[124] A consortium was created to rent the iron foundry at Zinsweiler, and it had even had to pay *péage*, as if they were Jews, for the Christian help (Weiss, *Geschichte*, p. 64).

[125] After the decree of July 10, 1784, which invited Jews to establish factories, forges, glassworks, and manufacture of crockery, a few such attempts were made, but it was difficult to get Jewish workers immediately (Pfister, "Les Juifs d'Alsace," *Pages Alsaciennes*, fasc. 40, p. 210). See also Levylier, *La famille Cerf Berr*, I, 22, and above, fn. 110.

prohibition. The classic Jewish trades, worked by the overwhelming majority, remained the sale of livestock, trade in old and used things of all kinds and, above all, moneylending. This was as true of the handful in Lorraine as it was of the majority in Alsace.[126]

In order to defend the Jews against the charge of usury, it has been argued that this commerce represented a relatively small part of the economic activities of the Jews in the province. This was maintained by the Jews themselves in the eighteenth century and it seems proved by lists of debts, in which invariably less than a quarter of the Jews of the communities in question are on the record as moneylenders.[127] The proof is not convincing, however. In the first place, the persistent problem in eastern France was that the bulk of the loans made by Jews were not registered with any governmental authority. Secondly, no Jew in the region ever engaged in only one kind of business. It is clear from a wide variety of legal and business documents that a man might be, and usually was, by turns a merchant, broker, or granter of small loans on the same day. More important, in Alsace as a whole the overwhelming majority of the Jews were very poor. Any list that records some as usurers represents many more who were not recorded. Without a lifetime of very precise research in all the local archives of eastern France, therefore, we cannot settle the question of the exact significance, both positive and negative, of Jewish moneylending in Alsace in the eighteenth century.

It is beyond doubt that in the eighteenth century even the friends of the Jews regarded this trade as Jewish. Almost as vehemently as their enemies, the friends of the Jews consistently maintained that Jewish usury was a scourge, especially to the peasants, and that the health of the region required that it be ended. This was the attitude that Pierre Louis Lacretelle had taken in his defense of the Jews in

[126] Regarding the continuing battle of the Jews with the city of Strasbourg, on the economic aspects of the fight, see the following major monographic discussions: Scheid, *Juifs d'Alsace,* pp. 151–87; Glaser, *Geschichte,* pp. 27–48; Levylier, *passim.* The city of Strasbourg decreed in 1778 that no one should do business with Jews except in the trade in foodstuff and horses. Earlier, in 1700, the city decreed against the smuggling by Jews of gold, silver, pearls, and jewels, which were sold there with the cooperation of various Christians. This decree was repeated often in the course of the century (printed decrees in JTS Library).

[127] Szajkowski, *Economic Status,* p. 96.

the lawyer's brief that he wrote in 1775. In listing the charges that
could fairly be made against them, Lacretelle admitted that the
most important criticism was that "the Jew has a unique passion for
money" and "that, deprived of any resources other than deceit, the
Jew has made a vocation of the art of lying." Lacretelle's defense
was that those characteristics did not reflect the intrinsic nature of
the Jew but that they were created by his situation. Mirabeau took
the same position, and he stated it as a truth beyond any question.
The Jews were indeed guilty of all the crimes of which they were
being reproached, but that was due to their circumstances and not
to their nature.[128] This view recurred in the writings of Guénée,
Dohm, and Grégoire, among others. Since these men were the defenders of the Jews, there can be no doubt that, even by the friendliest contemporary estimates, the Jews of eastern France were heavily involved in usury.

In 1777 the accumulated anger over Jewish usury led to a famous
affair, the battle over the sudden flooding of Alsace with counterfeit
receipts. These documents appeared by the thousands in the hands
of Christian debtors. It soon became clear that a ring was producing
these receipts, under the leadership of F. J. A. Hell, the *bailli* of
Landser, who had had previous brushes with Jews. The "philosophy" behind these activities was expressed in a book he published
anonymously in Frankfurt in 1779 at the height of the affair. He
maintained that, if the receipts were indeed forged, that was nonetheless a smaller evil, necessary to bring about the good of freeing
the Alsatian peasants from the rapacity of the Jews.[129]

The *Counseil Souverain* of Alsace and the royal government were
immediately involved. On the one side were the Jews. There was
some regard for the justice of their cause, but the authorities were
especially fearful of the consequences that would ensue if the Jewish
community were ruined. At least some of the money lent out by
Jews had been borrowed from Christian creditors. Various governmental authorities all had a stake in the ability of the Jews to pay

[128] Lacretelle, *Plaidoyer*, pp. 28–29; Mirabeau, *Sur Moses Mendelssohn*, pp.
70–71, 80–88; *idem, De la monarchie prussienne*, III, 462. See also Chapter X.
[129] This was the climactic argument in Hell, *Observations*, pp. 110–12.
About Hell as a theoretician of Alsatian anti-Semitism, see further in Chapter
IX.

taxes. Less tangibly, the awareness was growing that the Jewish creditors themselves were, for the most part, very poor and miserable. On the other hand, there were pogroms and threat of pogroms in Alsace in 1778, and the atmosphere remained tense thereafter.[130] A series of governmental decrees in effect reduced the total owed to Jews and granted the debtors longer terms of repayment. One important immediate result of this battle was that it raised the Jewish issue before government and public opinion in the sharpest form in the last decade of the *ancien régime*. In direct stages all else that happened in the 1780s was given its immediate impulse by this battle.

## The Jews in Metz

By the end of the century Jewish population in Alsace represented more than half of all the Jews in France. In smaller or larger groups they were to be found in many places, but there was no single Jewish community in the province that was sufficiently large, well established, and economically important to be the acknowledged leader. The most important city of Alsace, Strasbourg, excluded Jews entirely. The leading Jewish community of eastern France was therefore, in economic terms as well as in all other regards, the city of Metz. Jewish population grew by stages from the 3 families admitted in 1565 to some 2,000 people in 1789 in a city of 30,000.[131] In addition, there was a growing Jewish population, especially in the second half of the century, in the region near Metz, the farming country dotted with villages known as the *pays messin*. In the last few decades before 1789, as the right to live in Metz itself became ever harder to obtain, this population grew markedly to perhaps 1,500.[132]

[130] Pfister, *Les Juifs d'Alsace*, pp. 211–12; Rochette, *Histoire des Juifs d'Alsace*, p. 120.

[131] There is a comprehensive article on the economic life of the Jews of Metz in the seventeenth and eighteenth centuries in Anchel, *Les Juifs de France*, pp. 153–212; this ground is covered again in Szajkowski, *Economic Status*, pp. 31–49.

[132] There are MS tax rolls in the JTS Library listing the assessments for the Jews in the *pays messin* in 1772 and in 1785. The first contains 334 names and the second, 386.

The basic occupations of the Jews of Metz were no different from those of Alsace. All the professions and all of the branches of business that were organized in guilds were closed to them by law. Aside from houses in their own ghetto, the Jews could own no real estate. In the course of the seventeenth century they fought out the right to deal in old clothes, in second-hand objects of gold and silver, and in new goods if they were imported from outside Metz. The merchant guilds of the city constantly opposed even this commerce. As late as 1718 they petitioned for a royal decree under which the Jews of Metz would be forced to return to moneylending "at honest interest rates" as their sole occupation. This attempt failed and the Jews remained in possession of the right to engage in this limited trade.[133]

It was an open secret that the Jews were not making their living only in permitted occupations. In the trade in precious metals they certainly did not content themselves with dealing only in second-hand gold and silver objects. Using masters to dummy for them, some Jews tried to enter production. For example, on July 29, 1763, Léon Moyse, who was originally from Hamburg, and Jacob David May, an old-time resident in Metz, were found guilty of surreptitiously manufacturing gold objects, with the connivance of Joseph Manray, a master in the local guild. May was even guilty of owning the tools of the trade. This was a particularly "heinous" crime, for it proved that he had been, or at least intended to be, in manufacturing illegally on a long-term basis. Moyse was banished for three years; Manray was suspended from the guild for a year; and May was warned "to be more circumspect in the future." [134] In 1769 the Conseil d'Etat ordered the syndics of the Jews of Metz to produce a list of all the Jews who were authorized to deal in precious metals and to see to it that such dealers kept a record of all pieces that they imported. A heavy fine was prescribed for all those caught engaging in this trade without authorization, and the local customs officials were authorized to search Jewish homes and businesses in

[133] The summary statement of the economic rights of the Jews in Metz on which all later writers have drawn is to be found in Merlin, Répertoire universel, VI, 256–60. See also Clément, La condition des Juifs, pp. 143–206.

[134] Decree by the parlement of Metz of July 29, 1763, in JTS Library.

order to confiscate all objects not properly registered.[135] These are
but two examples of such incidents almost without number.

The meaning of these battles was that Jews were suspected not
only of illegal production but also, with more than a little justice,
of smuggling. There was trouble throughout the century over their
bringing gold, silver, and jewels illegally into Metz. For that matter,
smuggling in general was quite widespread in eastern France, with
its intricate patchwork of local, ducal, and national boundaries, each
with its customs tolls. The Jews were not the only smugglers, but
they were highly involved, both because very little else was open
to them and because, as peddlers, they traveled. The smuggling of
coins (a pursuit known as *billonage*) from one locality to another,
and especially from Lorraine into France, was a trade in which the
Jews of Metz and of eastern France in general were especially
prominent. The royal authorities were not always opposed to such
activities for this smuggling helped to alleviate the shortage of
specie in the region.[136]

It was to the advantage of the king not to ask precise questions
about Jewish activities in the field of provisioning the armies. France
was constantly at war in the eighteenth century. In almost every
decade some highly placed official of the royal government declared
that it would be impossible to maintain the military on the eastern
border without the Jews. The two main commodities the various
purveyors supplied were horses and grain.[137] The chief source was
Germany, and the Jews had to contend with many regulations there
which forbade such exports, especially in times of scarcity. The
major importance of these Jews to the French government was thus
in their usefulness in conducting a trade that was often frowned
upon at its source.

The provisioners of the armies were at the top of the social and
economic ladder among the Jews of eastern France. Their com-

[135] Decree by the *Conseil d'Etat,* dated April 11, 1769, in JTS Library.
[136] The first decree against smuggling of coins into Alsace was issued by
Jacques de la Grange, the intendant of the province, in 1684. See Szajkowski,
*Franco-Judaica,* No. 1317, and, in general on cases of smuggling and fraud in
the region, Nos. 1317–89; regarding *billonage* from Lorraine, see *idem, Economic Status,* pp. 46–47.
[137] Hoffman, *L'Alsace,* IV, 371–72.

merce was not limited to this one field, for they invested their capital in the import-export of a wide range of commodities, in banking and commercial paper, and even in tax-farming. For example, the authorities of the city of Strasbourg and Cerf Berr had no love for each other. They had fought hard over his right to live in the city, and he was the man who effected the royal decree ending the body tax (*péage*) on Jews who entered the city. Nonetheless, he was the tax farmer who collected this tax for most of the last two decades of its existence.[138]

These economic leaders were not necessarily always Jews who originated in Metz. Because in law the Jews of that city had the most secure status of any group in eastern France, the leading Jewish personalities of the region, regardless of the extent of their economic interests, all in turn secured for themselves formal citizenship in Metz's Jewish community. Samuel Lévy, the most prominent figure at the beginning of the century, was himself a native of Metz.[139] He reached the zenith of his career as the banker and un-

[138] The first Jew to farm this tax was Moshe Belin in 1745, for nine years. Cerf Berr appeared in this connection for the first time in 1769 (Scheid, *Juifs d'Alsace*, pp. 185–86). The battle of Cerf Berr with the Lehman family in Bischheim was occasioned by their attempt to outbid him in 1781 for this franchise (M. Ginsburger, "Les familles Lehman et Cerf Berr," *REJ*, LIX, 106–30). This quarrel was settled by the rabbinic tribunal of Niedernai in 1783. A fascinating sidelight is the attack of Reb Leima (Lehman) on David Sinzheim, the brother-in-law of Cerf Berr, who was the rabbi in Bischheim and who was later to be a key figure at the Napoleonic Sanhedrin and to become the first chief rabbi of France. Leima wrote that Sinzheim was indeed more versed than himself in "books of apostasy and heresy and books of gentile culture which, God save us, I know not even by name."

[139] Lévy was a stepson of Glückel of Hameln, the most famous Jewish woman memoirist of her time. The whole of Lévy's career is described in M. Ginsburger, "Samuel Lévi," *REJ*, LXV, 274–300; LXVI, 111–33, 263–84; LXVII, 82–117, 262–87; LXVIII, 84–109; for Lévy's Paris years, see L. Kahn, *Les Juifs de Paris au dix-huitième siècle*, pp. 75–80. Lévy's connection with Leopold of Lorraine began in 1708. Needing money, the duke admitted five Jewish bankers from Metz into Nancy: Samuel and Solomon Lévy, Jacob Schwab, Isaiah Lambert, and Moses Alcan. In 1709, Lévy bought grain in Trèves for the duke. A main activity of these Jewish bankers was to export coin and specie illegally from France to Nancy. The intendant of Alsace ordered these Jews home to Metz under threat of permanently excluding them from the city. Lévy seemed to have escaped the rigor of this decree by promising to spy for France. In a few short years his activities in Nancy made a fortune for the ducal mint. In 1715 Leopold named him formally the head of all the finances of Lorraine. The financial bureau of the duchy refused to administer the oath of office to him because he was a Jew, so he occupied the

official finance minister of the Duke of Lorraine. Before that he had
become through family influence the rabbi of Upper Alsace. Many
Jews of Metz invested with him in Lorraine, and his bankruptcy in
1717 cost them more than a million livres. This typical court Jew
ended his career in debtors' prison in the Bastille, where he was
put by his Christian enemies. The leading Jewish family of Lorraine
in the second half of the eighteenth century was that of Jacob Berr
of Nancy. In addition to their formal permission to live in Lorraine,
the Berrs also secured for themselves the right of Jewish residence
in Metz.[140] In part, the motives for such actions by these wealthy
families were religious, for citizenship within Metz's Jewry safe-
guarded burial rights in the Jewish cemetery in the city, but some of
the motives were economic. A Jew of Metz was, in the strictest
legal theory, the only Jew of France in the eighteenth century
whose right to be there permanently as a Jew (and not as a new
Christian) was unquestioned. In that city the right of residence had
been conferred by the king and not, as elsewhere in the region, by
local potentates who kept claiming the right to expel Jews if they
wished, after having admitted them. Metz was thus both the religious and cultural center and the economic base of the Jewish oligarchy of the entire region.

For the bulk of the Jews of Metz petty trading of all kinds was
the major economic pursuit. Jews kept stores publicly in the Jewish
quarter, in theory only in used goods. They employed people to
stand in front of their places of business to steer customers their
way. Battles inevitably occurred between the steerers, so the Jewish
community regulated their activity. Many Jews resided in Metz and
peddled in the surrounding territory. On the intermediate rung of
the economic ladder there were Jewish businessmen who were ex-

post without formality. A bankruptcy in Frankfurt soon led to his ruin. Lévy
was ousted from office in 1716 and his bankruptcy represented the loss of three
million livres in all. (See also Aron, "Le duc de Lorraine Léopold et les
Israélites," REJ, XXXIV, 107–16; on the negative attitude of the French government to the activities of Jews from Metz in Lorraine, see the documents
given by Szajkowski, Economic Status, pp. 141–44.)

[140] In 1761 Ittele, the widow of Isaac Berr, who had been the head of all
the Jews of Lorraine, asked for a reduction on the taxes she paid as a non-
resident citizen of Metz's Jewish community. She was refused (Metz, Pinkas,
35b). For the comparable action of Cerf Berr and the Halphen family of Nancy
in securing citizenship in Metz, see Chapter VII.

panding their trade beyond the borders of Metz. The papers of such a middle-range Jewish merchant, Alexander Hess, still exist. In the 1760s he was offering commercial credit to both Jews and gentiles, including the discounting of notes and the buying of due bills. His trade extended to all the cities of the region, and to Bâle and Paris.[141] In 1772 a case was judged in the rabbinic court of Metz involving a dispute among the members of a consortium that had successfully bid in Paris for the contract to supply the armies in Lorraine and the Trois Evêchés. The principals involved were Alexander Hess, as the minor partner, along with two of the wealthiest Jews of the region—Hertz Halphen, a banker in Lorraine, and Seligman Wittersheim, a son-in-law of the military purveyor Moshe Belin, who had succeeded his father-in-law as the head of the family.[142]

A community of bankers, some of them connected with foreign merchants; dealers in hides and jewels; miscellaneous businessmen; even a few artisans; and poor peddlers making up fully two-thirds of the whole—this is the picture that the Jews of Metz tried to give of themselves in a *mémoire* they addressed to the *Etats Généraux* in 1789.[143] All this was true, but it was only a half truth because it avoided the issue of their role in usury. In the sixteenth and seventeenth centuries, the interest rate permitted to Jews fluctuated, from more than 20 per cent in the early years to 12 per cent in the middle of the seventeenth century. In a decree of 1669 this rate was fixed at 5½ per cent but it is clear that this official rate was never kept.[144] Several attempts were made during the eighteenth century to require that loan contracts between Jews and Christians be registered

[141] Business papers in JTS Library, in Yiddish, Hebrew, and French. This collection also contains a business journal, fifty-one leaves in French, for the years 1751 to 1755 of Jacob Marig (?), "garçon Juif," which reflects a comparable commerce.

[142] MS of two folio volumes in the Library of the Jewish Scientific Institute (YIVO), containing the decisions of the rabbinic court of Metz between 1771 and 1789, I, 19b.

[143] *Mémoire particulier pour la communauté des Juifs établis à Metz*, pp. 10–11. This text, a pamphlet of thirty pages, is undated, but it was composed in 1789 as an address to the gathering which was to make the Revolution. It is signed by Goudchau Mayer Cahen and Louis Wolff, the deputies of the Metz Jews in Paris, and it was written by Isaiah Berr Bing.

[144] Clément, *La condition des Juifs*, pp. 173–92.

with notaries. There was such a decree in 1733, repeating several
earlier ones, but they all remained dead letters. It is even clear on
the face of the decree of 1733 that those who wrote it were aware
that official contracts at the legal rate of interest would almost inevitably be accompanied by private side agreements providing for
greater returns.[145]

Jews lent money not only to soldiers and officers of the military
garrisons, but also to local merchants and to the peasants of the
surrounding region. The most dangerous part of this trade was the
lending of money to minors. This was forbidden several times in
the minute book of the Metz community, at the latest in 1761 and
1786, on the ground that such actions endangered the entire community. In 1786 the announcement included the reasoning that the
relatives of these young people, who generally were cadets of the
military garrison, belonged to influential families and that helping to
contribute to the ruin of such youths was increasing anti-Semitism
in important quarters. On that occasion, the syndics of Metz Jewry
went to the head of the garrison for a list of debts owed by soldiers
under his command, and they promised to force the creditors to
accept repayment without any interest at all.[146]

It is true that no record has yet been found of even a single
charge brought in Metz against individual Jewish creditors for sharp
practices. This has been used to help make a case for the economic
usefulness of Jewish moneylending and to downgrade the role of
usury in the economy of the Jews in Metz.[147] That the conduct of
the Jews in this trade was not completely irreproachable is proved
by repeated entries, such as those just quoted, in the minute book
of the Jewish community itself, regulating and punishing transgres-
sions. No cases came to public court in large part because moneylending was so sensitive and important to the Jewish economy that
the community as a whole could not allow abuses in this commerce.

There can be no doubt that moneylending and petty banking

[145] The Jews petitioned against the decree of 1733, the main purpose of
which was to make them register their loans with notaries. This action had
some effect, because a royal decree in September of that year suspended the
execution of the earlier action, but this second decree was never published. In
reality, the situation remained one in which some loans were formally registered
and almost all small loans were not (*ibid.*, pp. 210–13).

[146] *Pinkas,* 7a, 136a-b.          [147] Szajkowski, *Economic Status,* p. 100.

remained the prime pursuit of the mass of the Jews of Metz throughout the *ancien régime*. There was not a single Jewish will recorded in Metz after 1750, regardless of whether the amount is small or large, in which debts owed to the deceased did not take the most prominent place. This assertion is based on more evidence than that of the comparatively few wills that were entered in the communal minutes. The decisions of the rabbinic court of Metz between 1771 and 1789 are more instructive, for 1,500 cases involving every class of Metz's Jews were recorded and many of them concerned wills. The estate of Leib Chambrai, settled between 1772 and 1775, is quite typical. It consisted mostly of loans, at varying degrees of interest, but never higher than 10 per cent. However, there was one revealing entry: the largest single loan, of 274 livres, was divided between what the debtor owed "by contract" (the amount as officially registered) and what he owed by "manuscript," which I take to mean by a side agreement to pay higher interest. This was a relatively small estate, of some 7,000 livres.[148] The estate of Seligman Wittersheim, however, was very large, of almost half a million livres. Most of it was in loans, although Wittersheim also did business in wood and candles and he was even a shareholder in river barges. In the accounting of this estate there were loans listed in two categories: "assured" and "mediocre." [149] A man such as Wittersheim was hardly likely to make petty loans, for that business was left to people such as Chambrai. All the levels of such enterprise were included in a complaint made against the Jews of Metz in 1745, in which it was specified that "their business is mostly to make money on their capital by moneylending and by discounting bills." [150]

How rich were the Jews of Metz and of the surrounding countryside? All of the evidence points in the direction of a community that was polarizing in the last decades of the eighteenth century. Wills and marriage contracts prove that some of the rich were very rich indeed.[151] On the other hand, the poor were becoming not

[148] YIVO MS, II, 8a.       [149] *Pinkas*, 119a.
[150] Anonymous MS in JTS Library.
[151] In 1750 the Metz community ruled that no wedding would be permitted in the city unless the dowry of the bride was at least 2,400 livres, lest the young couple immediately become a public charge (*Pinkas*, 4b). Especially

merely more numerous but also poorer. On various occasions, and increasingly in the second half of the century, the communal authorities of Metz complained of their difficulty in collecting the necessary taxes, and they tried to keep more poor from coming to the community. Because of such measures Metz's Jewish population actually declined in the last decades of the century.[152] Nonetheless the charity bill kept rising, so that in the middle of the century it was more than 6,000 livres a year.[153] This means that a Jewish community of less than 500 families was spending 15 livres a year per family, or, more realistically, something over 20 livres a year for those families who were not self-supporting. There is equally revealing evidence from the election procedure of the Metz community. Its electors were organized in three orders. There never was any trouble finding enough to fill the places of the rich and poor, but there was often a problem about those of the middle order.[154] The oligarchy at the top, consisting of army provisioners and bankers, remained remarkably stable and there were always enough people worth something like 600 livres, for the lowest order, but the middle was disintegrating.

The minutes of the Metz community prove that the situation was worsening in the 1780s. In 1780 a new set of communal regulations was promulgated because "taxes and imposts keep increasing" and "the members of the community are ever poorer." More people were coming in from the outside illegally and competing with the older settlers. The community itself, therefore, raised the cost of acquiring the right to live in Metz to the prohibitive figure of 10,000 crowns. It enacted stringent measures aimed at reducing the local population. This decree was so strict that it was repealed in a

---

in the families of the oligarchs, there are a number of dowries in the *Pinkas* for far greater amounts.

[152] Anchel, *Les Juifs de France*, pp. 165–67. See also *Pinkas*, 37b, 67b, 85b, 92a, among many entries through the years.

[153] There is an undated, but clearly mid-eighteenth-century, MS in JTS Library representing a few leaves from the expense book of the Metz charity accounts. To the beginning of Ab (i.e., in ten months) 5,191 livres were spent.

[154] *Pinkas*, 57a, the entry for the election of 1765. In 1780 there was talk for the first time of having representatives of the poorest elements take part in the actual administration of the community if there would not be enough from the two highest orders (*ibid.*, 112b).

few months. The next year all of those who received incomes from
the community, either in the form of salaries or as the beneficiaries
of trusts, were cut between 10 and 40 per cent. In 1782 there was
a sad decision by the rabbis that the traditional charity box for the
Holy Land might now be used to support families of social standing
who were newly impoverished; their numbers were mounting. In
1783 the aid that was extended to poor Jewish wayfarers was cut
and nothing at all would henceforth be given to their children.[155]

There is no known list of the entire Jewish population of Metz
containing an assessment of its capital worth. We do have such a
list for the *pays messin,* the surrounding countryside, which contained almost as large a population as Metz itself. In a manuscript
tax list of 1772, out of 334 taxpayers who were assessed, 185 were
listed as having no net worth whatsoever and only 31 Jews had
capital of more than 5,000 livres. All these figures represent a
corporate wealth of about 750,000 livres.[156] In Metz itself we know
that at the beginning of the century all of the loans then owed to
the Jews amounted to less than 1,000,000 livres. It was at very least
three times that amount by 1789. This is consonant with the growth
in population during the period.[157] It seems a fair guess that the
corporate wealth of Metz's Jewry was between six and nine million
livres.

This assumption is corroborated by tax documents. The tax *pour
l'industrie* was assessed at the rate of 24 sous for each head of household, with 24 sous in addition for each 1,000 florins (a florin was
worth 2 livres in Alsace at the time) of capital worth. In the second
half of the century the total of that tax in Metz ran at an average of
7,000 livres per year and the amount was rising, but very slowly,
between 1765 and 1789. Extrapolating from this figure again pro-
duces an estimate of 6 to 9 million livres as the corporate wealth of
the Jews of Metz.[158] This is further confirmed by a tax list of
Metz's Jewry for the year 1792–93. On it were entered the assessments of 590 individuals, representing all those who contributed to

[155] *Ibid.,* 110b, 120a, 122a, 127b.    [156] MS in JTS Library.
[157] There were 1,200 Jews in Metz in 1699; the number had risen to 3,000
in 1789 (Anchel, *Les Juifs de France,* pp. 154–57).
[158] Clément, *La condition des Juifs,* pp. 118–19.

a tax assessed on their total capital worth. The amount collected was 61,573 livres. This tax was imposed at the rate of 1 per cent of total worth; we therefore arrive at the figure of something over 6,000,000 livres.[159]

This estimate of the corporate wealth of the Jews of Metz is consonant with the one given above for the whole of Alsatian Jewry. Together these figures establish beyond reasonable doubt the proposition that the Jews of the region were poor. Nonetheless it must be reemphasized that there was some great Jewish wealth, of the order of several of the fortunes in Bordeaux, in the hands of Yiddish-speaking Jews of eastern France. The acknowledged leader in the last generation of the *ancien régime*, Cerf Berr, was rich enough to establish a charitable foundation in 1786 in his home town of Bischheim and to finance it with a grant of 75,000 livres. This represented part of the value of the landed property of Tomblaine, which he had succeeded in buying through Christian intermediaries despite the opposition of the city of Strasbourg.[160] Cerf Berr was, as we have seen, a semi-honorary syndic of Metz's Jews. He was actively the head of all the Jews of Alsace, and he kept lending its communal organization money with which to pay its ever-mounting debts. When that body needed 100,000 livres in 1784, Cerf Berr lent it three-quarters of the amount.[161] In 1783 the Cerf Berr family had business establishments and a number of employees in various places in Alsace, Lorraine, the Trois Evêchés, and Bourgogne.[162] Just before the Revolution, and in the wake of the royal

[159] MS, JTS Library, No. 01565. This tax list is interpreted by Szajkowski (*Autonomy and Communal Jewish Debts*, p. 127) as representing a tax of one thousandth of the total capital of the taxpayers, and he thus derives a figure of 60,000,000 livres as the corporate wealth of the Jews of Metz, as represented by self-estimate. This interpretation is manifestly impossible because it results in the assumption that the average wealth of the Jewish families of Metz exceeded 100,000 livres each. This flies in the face of everything else we know about the economic situation of that Jewish community.

[160] M. Ginsburger, "Une fondation de Cerf Berr," *REJ*, LXXVI, 47–57.

[161] Szajkowski, *Autonomy and Communal Jewish Debts*, p. 109.

[162] A report of July 15, 1783, by Cerf Berr's son Marx Berr, accounted to the authorities of the city of Strasbourg for the whole of the family's commercial activities. It is printed in M. Ginsburger, *Cerfberr et son époque*, p. 30. Despite the spread of Cerf Berr's business activities into various areas, his principal role remained that of an army contractor. A royal decree of May 31,

decree of July, 1784, reordering the situation of Alsatian Jewry, two of Cerf Berr's sons owned a cloth factory in Nancy, which employed thirty or forty children, and at the beginning of the Revolution there was another such establishment at Tomblaine.[163] It has even been said, on doubtful evidence, that at that time Cerf Berr was trying to settle some Jews on the land.[164]

When the Royal Society of Metz announced as its prize essay subject in 1785 the question of "How to Make the Jews Happy and Useful," that language aptly reflected the economic conditions of the overwhelming bulk of the Jews of Metz and of the whole region. Their occupations were unsettled, hazardous, or non-existent, so that useful work needed to be found for them. Everyone knew that these people were poor and unhappy. The success of a small rich element acted only to accentuate the misery of the Jewish poor. Above all, Jew-hatred remained endemic in Alsace. In 1789 all of the deputies of the province, from the extreme right to the extreme left, opposed the emancipation of the Jews on economic grounds for the most part, and in this they faithfully reflected public opinion.[165]

---

1776, abolished the system of private contracting in provisioning of the army, but an exception was made for Cerf Berr; he remained the purveyor of the army in Alsace-Lorraine. This is stated in a document issued by Cerf Berr himself in his battle with the city of Strasbourg for his right to settle there permanently (see *Mémoire justificatif pour le sieur Cerf Berr*, pp. 2–5). At the end of 1785 Cerf Berr divided his enterprises; he announced that he himself would henceforth devote himself entirely to provisioning the armies and that his sons and sons-in-law would engage in banking, general commerce, and the commission business (see the announcement of *Cerf Berr et Cie* in JTS).

[163] Godechot, "Les Juifs de Nancy," *REJ*, LXXXVI, p. 4.

[164] M. Ginsburger, *Cerf Berr et son temps*, p. 7. This is a pamphlet representing a radio address and it contains no supporting documentation. In 1777 Cerf Berr did attempt to buy 3,000 acres of forest in Haguenau and convert it into arable land. He offered to pay 400,000 livres and 8 livres an acre annual rent for this land. The offer was not accepted, but it seems likely that Cerf Berr made it at the time with a view to converting some Jews into farmers. (See Szajkowski, "Occupational Problems of Jewish Emancipation in France," *HJ*, XXI, 120, and Levylier, *La famille Cerf Berr*, I, 22.)

[165] Scheid, the first historian of the Jews of Alsace, concluded that "at the end of the *ancien régime* neither the laws nor the people were more liberal in Alsace" ("Histoire des Juifs," *REJ*, X, 211). This was also the view of Reuss in his two studies of the question of anti-Semitism during the Revolution: "Documents nouveaux," *REJ*, LIX, 248–76, and "L'anti-sémitisme," *REJ*, LXVIII, 246–63.

## The Jews of Paris

The only other major Jewish community in France in the eighteenth century was in Paris. The first small group of Jews drifted
into the city from Metz, with passports allowing them to conduct
short-run business with various government agencies. When the
widowed Glückel of Hameln came to Metz to be remarried, she
found that her son-in-law, Moshe Krumbach, was in Paris on business.[166] The earliest known list of Jews to be found in the police
archives of the city was compiled in August of 1715, in the month
when Louis XIV lay dying. It contained seventeen names.[167] There
was evidently some stirring then about the question of the residence
of Jews in the city. The finances of France at the beginning of the
Regency were in a very bad state. The start of a new reign was,
in general, a propitious moment for requesting new arrangements.
At that moment a group of Jews (one would guess that they were
bankers from Metz) were reputed to have offered "many millions
of livres" for the right to live permanently in Paris and to have a
synagogue. The offer was rejected by the regent.[168]

By 1789 there were perhaps five hundred Jews in the city. This
community was, in its composition, a microcosm of all the Jews of
France, since it contained elements representing eastern France,
the Sephardim of Bordeaux and Bayonne, the Jews from Avignon,
and individuals from all over Europe, including London, Amsterdam, Germany, and even Poland. All of the rich army and marine
purveyors spent long periods in Paris on business. As we have seen
Gradis was there often. Cerf Berr was well known in the city and he
was even presented to Louis XVI, in an incident which has been
retold by his decendants with some seemingly legendary additions.[169]

[166] *Zichronot Glückel*, tr. Rabinowitz, pp. 127–28.
[167] L. Kahn, *Les Juifs de Paris au dix-huitième siècle*, p. 1; Anchel, "The
Early History of the Jewish Quarters in Paris," *JSS*, II, 45–60.
[168] The tale of such an offer got as far as London in 1716. The Sephardim
of that city drafted a letter of inquiry (Roth, "La prétendue réadmission," *REJ*,
XCIV, 193–95. This story was repeated in the eighteenth century by Gayot de
Pitaval, *Causes célèbres et intéressantes*, XX, 364. The account of this incident
seems wildly exaggerated.
[169] Levylier, *La famille Cerf Berr*, I, 25.

In the eighteenth century Paris was, of course, the greatest city in Europe. All kinds of people were attracted to it. There is record of Jewish adventurers, especially of those who came to it to be converted, and sometimes reconverted, in order to be supported by the pious Christian foundations that existed for such purposes.[170] The famous Azulai came twice to visit, both to raise money for the academies of the Holy Land and to visit the royal library.[171] This institution employed a succession of several scholarly Jews as its experts in Hebrew, and at least two of these men generally regarded as the intellectual leaders of the Jewish community.[172] The first professing Jew to enter the general learned world of France, Jacob Rodrigues Péreire, came to Paris in 1749 to demonstrate his new technique for teaching deaf-mutes, and he remained there till the end of his days as the representative in Paris of all the French Sephardim.[173]

In the course of the eighteenth century the court nobility centered in Paris was always in need of money. The speculation introduced into France by John Law had been a leveler of class distinctions since all elements of society, including the nobility, bought his shares. When the crash came in 1720 many ruined individuals needed loans and the Jews who could provide them were valuable to impoverished Parisian nobles, then and later. This trade earned such individuals influential protectors who occasionally intervened against attempts by the police to expel Jews from the city.[174]

---

[170] L. Kahn, Les Juifs de Paris au dix-huitième siècle, pp. 114–32. This represents a whole chapter of Kahn's book, in which he gathered together some of the stories of the forty converts who are mentioned in the police archives between 1718 and 1772. Many of these people were frank enough to give as their reason for conversion the desire for a job, a military commission, or the right to live in Paris.

[171] Azulai was in Paris in the summer of 1755 and in the winter of 1777–78. See his famous travel diary: Maagal Tov, pp. 34, 119–24.

[172] Szajkowski, "Secular Private Libraries," Kirjath Sefer, XXXV, 497–98.

[173] See Chapter VII; see also his death notice (he died on September 15, 1780) in Hildenfinger, Documents, p. 247.

[174] Solomon Lévy was among those who were recorded as receiving gold and jewelry which was pawned after the crash of Law. One Jewish moneylender, Nathan de Morhange, lent money to a personage as highly placed as the dauphine (L. Kahn, Les Juifs de Paris au dix-huitième siècle, pp. 61–65). Solomon Lévy had a stormy career. He was a brother of Samuel Lévy, and he had been part of the consortium of Metz Jewish bankers that had gone to Nancy in 1708 to serve Leopold of Lorraine. After Samuel Lévy went bank-

The bulk of the Jews of Paris were, however, poor shopkeepers, peddlers, or workmen. The death records of the Jews of Paris during the eighteenth century were registered with the lieutenant-general of the police, whose office supervised these illegal residents. A large number of individuals were listed merely as businessmen. Many of these people were from Avignon, by way of Bordeaux, and they were primarily engaged in their traditional trade in silks and textiles. There were two Jews from Bayonne engaged in making chocolate, and there were also Jewish jewelers, painters, engravers, designers, embroiderers, and shoemakers.[175]

The very tenuousness of Jewish existence in Paris tended to create the paradox of Jewish commercial freedom. Since all pursuits were equally illegal, the Jews had no reason for avoiding one more than the other. Even before the Revolution, therefore, the handful of Jews in Paris had pioneered for those who were to spread out later into an ever wider variety of endeavors.

The small Jewish community in Paris was ever more secure, de facto, after the middle of the century. The pretense that no Jew was a permanent resident in the city was ending. In the last decade

rupt, Solomon came to Paris. There is a police record that in 1727 he was still in Paris and talking of converting to the Catholic faith. The police reported that this was a trick, because at that very time Lévy was celebrating Passover in the company of other Jews (*ibid.*, pp. 105–106).

A curious sidelight on the careers of both Lévy and Voltaire is to be found in the letter that Voltaire wrote to Cardinal Dubois on May 28, 1722. Voltaire was here acting the part of an informer; he was attempting to ingratiate himself with the authorities by accusing Lévy of being a spy for Austria, using "the facility which the Jews have for being admitted and expelled everywhere." According to Voltaire, Lévy had served both as an army provisioner and as a spy for France for a number of years (these were the years when his brother Samuel was playing a dubious role in Lorraine). Now, in 1722, according to Voltaire, Solomon Lévy was spying for the emperor of Austria, for "a Jew belongs to no land other than the one where he makes money; can he not just as easily betray the king for the emperor as the emperor for the king?" The text of Voltaire's letter is in *Correspondence*, I, 146–47. This particular denunciation seemed to have no immediate effect; it neither hurt Solomon Lévy nor helped Voltaire. The act itself and the rhetoric of the denunciation add no luster to Voltaire, but for once there was probably some truth in a charge he made against a Jew. Both the Lévy brothers seemed, indeed, to have been playing complicated and dangerous games. See also fn. 139 above.

[175] An analysis of the death records, as given in Hildenfinger, *Documents*, yields the fact that fifty-three of the deceased are simply listed as businessmen. These represented every Jewish community in France and a scattering of foreign countries.

of the *ancien régime* three Jewish cemeteries were bought in Paris to replace an undignified and semi-clandestine burial place that had been used for decades. One was purchased by Péreire for the Portuguese and the other by Cerf Berr for the Jews of eastern France. This happened because negotiations for joint action by all sections of the Jewish community, under the leadership of the banker and army purveyor, Liefman Calmer, had broken down. He remained in possession of the ground that he had personally bought for that purpose, but no one used it. Calmer was thus rebuffed when he attempted to become the undisputed leader of the Jews of Paris.[176]

Calmer had some important claims to the status to which he aspired. He had been born in Hanover in 1711 and had made his fortune in Holland. He came to Paris in 1769 and was immediately given personal *lettres patentes,* which naturalized him in France, undoubtedly as reward for his activities in provisioning the French armies. In 1774 he bought the barony of Picquigny and the *vidamé* d'Amiens. This purchase cost him 1,500,000 livres, but it was much more expensive than that for it was the occasion for a bitter and protracted lawsuit, attended, as we shall see later, by an envenomed public debate. One of the rights that pertained to the property was that of conferring two ecclesiastical benefices, subject to investiture by the Bishop of Amiens. The bishop refused to confirm Calmer's appointments on the ground that a Jew had no right to nominate priests to any office. In 1779 Calmer resold much of his domain to the king's brother, the Count d'Artois (later Charles X), but the suit continued and it dragged on even after his death in 1784. The family of Calmer lost at least an additional 1,000,000 livres in paying the feudal dues for their barony and in pursuing the quarrel, which ended only when the whole question became irrelevant due to the Revolution.[177]

On the eve of the Revolution, a century of economic change had produced some important results for the forty thousand Jews who were then living under the French crown. A number of men of

[176] Regarding the difficulties over the cemeteries, see Hildenfinger, *Documents,* pp. 16–24.
[177] Loeb, "Un baron Juif français," *AIF,* XLVI, 188–90, 196–98.

large affairs, such as Calmer in Paris, Cerf Berr in Alsace, and Gradis in Bordeaux were an accepted part of the economic scene. None of these three was as wealthy as some of the great financiers, tax farmers, and international traders of Paris and Bordeaux, but they had at least penetrated the lower reaches of the very top of the high bourgeoisie. Being Jews, they were, of course, more visible than any three Christians of comparable means and importance. This does not mean that either popular anti-Semitism or advanced economic opinion were accepting of such rich Jews. In the 1780s, however, this economic echelon seemed secure.

The French economy as a whole had been changing in the eighteenth century in the direction of a national economy of commerce, international trade, and production. Its objectives were now different from the medieval economic purposes, which had centered on the self-efficiency of small units, and there thus was much more scope for even the Jews. *Raison d'état* and mercantilism had introduced the Jews into France. Free trade and laisser faire had broadened their economic opportunities. The Jews who took advantage of the new situations were largely the Sephardim and those who had come to France from the Papal States. These were, however, a minority of the Jewish population in France. The large majority were Ashkenazim in eastern France, where both the older economy and the older hatreds persisted unabated into the era of the Revolution and beyond. On the economic evidence alone it makes perfect sense that the Sephardim and Avignonnais were emancipated first and with relatively little difficulty in the early months of the Revolution and that the really bitter battle of more than two years revolved around the Ashkenazim. The economy of Bordeaux had been consciously constructed in the eighteenth century to parallel and compete with contemporary London and Amsterdam, the most advanced centers in the world and, not incidentally, the cities in which Jews were then the most accepted. At that time the economy of eastern France was no more advanced than that of contemporary Poland. The position of the Jew in Metz was the same as in Vilna; so were the attitudes towards him.

# The Culture of the Jews

In the last decades before the Revolution all the friends of the Jews
wanted them to give up their old ways. Some intimated that Westernization was a pre-condition for freedom, and others emphasized
that more liberal laws would encourage the necessary changes in
Jewish religion, culture, and customs. Did Westernization precede
the Emancipation, or did the cultural assimilation of the Jews take
place only after the Revolution? What, in general, was the role of
inner, Jewish cultural factors in leading towards the Emancipation?
The essence of the answers to these questions is that enough acculturation had already taken place after the middle of the eighteenth century, especially among the Sephardim, to act as an argument for equality. Among the Ashkenazim the overwhelming mass
was culturally and religiously untouched by any of the new trends
until after 1789, but a small handful of "enlightened" young men
appeared in the last few years before the Revolution. These figures
played a considerable role in the fight for Jewish emancipation.

In the course of the eighteenth century all parts of the Jewish
community became, to varying degrees, at home in the French
language. One community, indeed, the Jews from the Papal States,
had had a long relationship to the Provençal dialect. It had developed its own version of that language, and some literary activity
in Judeo-Provençal had been going on since the fourteenth century.[1] A play in Provençal entitled *Queen Esther* appeared in

[1] Szajkowski, *The Language of the Jews, passim.* See especially pp. 14–15
regarding Judeo-Provençal as the spoken language of these Jews until 1789.
A rhymed romance in Provençal, *Esther,* by the Jewish doctor Crescas de
Cayalar is one of the major early works in the language (*ibid.,* p. 9). Much religious poetry was written by Jews for inclusion in services of the Comtadin

Carpentras in 1739. This work was a literary version of the Purim theatricals that were traditional there as elsewhere in the Jewish world.[2] Several Jews from the Papal States made contributions to "enlightened" Jewish literature in the second half of the century, for the step from their dialect to literary French was not a great one.[3]

At the other end of the spectrum, in eastern France, the linguistic and cultural world of its Jews remained, even into the Revolutionary era, Yiddish and Hebrew. The dominant language of these border provinces was German rather than French. Nevertheless the handful who engaged in large-scale enterprises that had connections to major centers of the French interior needed to acquire French. This was particularly true of those businessmen who dealt with the royal government and other authorities, such as the Duke of Lorraine. There is evidence that as early as 1700 French was in use within the Jewish community itself on state occasions. In that year the widowed Glückel of Hameln was married in Metz to Moshe Lévy, the lay head of Metz Jewry. One week after the wedding Glückel received a formal visit of congratulations from the leaders of the community. These people, of course, usually spoke Yiddish but Glückel tells: "I wanted very much, then, to know French, to be able to respond to each of the well-wishers directly; my husband acted as the interpreter." In 1744 the Jews of Metz were ordered to produce for the use of the appellate courts a summary of their own traditional civil law. They prepared such material in French under the guidance of the chief rabbi at the time, Jonathan Eibeschütz (he himself seems to have known no French) and submitted it in manuscript to the *parlement* of Metz.[4]

---

rite. This literature has been studied by no less a personage than the last emperor of Brazil: Don Pedro II d'Alcantara, *Poésies hebraico-provençales.*

[2] Szajkowski, *Franco-Judaica*, No. 1687: *La Reine Esther. Tragediou en vers et en cinq actes. à la lengou vulgari. compousadou à la manière dei Juifs de Carpentras, à la Haye* (Carpentras, 1739).

[3] French was not in great use within the Comtat Venaissin until it was annexed to France. Nonetheless there is record of the confiscation in Carpentras in 1743 from the home of Jacob Lunel of a manuscript, written in French, against Christianity; see Szajkowski, "Documents Dealing with the 'Four Communities' in the 18th Century," *The Jews in France*, II, 304.

[4] *Zichronot Glückel* (tr. Rabinowitz), p. 128. The summary of Jewish civil law was edited for the Metz *parlement* on the basis of the material supplied by

Nevertheless, Jews of eastern France really did not know French well until after 1789. The handful of Jewish intellectuals and pamphleteers who appeared in the 1770s in that region wrote badly, and sometimes even ungrammatically. All of the French used in print by Jews in eastern France before 1789 was directly related to economic or Jewish interests. There is not a single figure from that region who entered the wider French culture before the beginning of the nineteenth century.

What there was of Jewish writing in French on general themes before 1789 came from the Sephardim. The earliest minutes of the community in Bordeaux were written in Spanish. For a few years, in the second decade of the century, Spanish and French appeared indiscriminately in the minute book, but French was used almost invariably afterwards, except for a few religious decisions or communal regulations.[5] The ruling oligarchy, which consisted of men of international business affairs, was increasingly comfortable in French.[6] Spanish lived on as the spoken language of many, if not most, of the Jews of Bordeaux and Bayonne throughout the century, especially since these communities were regularly acquiring new immigrants from the Iberian Peninsula.[7] On the other hand, as these families continued into the second and third generation of native-born, rich Jews, their culture became increasingly that of the majority.

A number of Sephardim who were converts to Christianity entered the world of French learning in the eighteenth century and earlier,[8] but the first practicing Jew to become a figure of some

the Jews by a Christian lawyer, Nicholas François Lançon. The book that he edited appeared in 1786, after his death; see *Recueil des lois*. This volume was not printed until after Lançon's death. The communal and legal significance of this translation is discussed in Chapter VII.

[5] French became the usual language in the *Registre* of Bordeaux in 1719.

[6] See in the biography of Abraham Gradis by Jean de Maupassant, the remarks on his culture and outlook: *RHB*, VII, 334–45. His style of life was thoroughly high bourgeois, with close personal and social connections with clergy and nobility. Gradis was one of the sixteen friends of the Duke of Richelieu who put up the money for the reconstructed theater in Bordeaux after 1772. Nonetheless, he was still a sufficiently traditional Jew not to travel on the Sabbath.

[7] Cirot, *Recherches*, pp. 3–20; see Chapter V.

[8] J. B. Silva, the physician of Louis XV, was born a Jew in Bordeaux (Szajkowski, *Franco-Judaica*, XXI). Jacques Cardozo was another Jew of Bordeaux

consequence in the intellectual circles of Paris was Jacob Rodrigues
Péreire. He appeared before the Royal Academy of Sciences on
June 11, 1749, accompanied by a young man who had been a deaf-
mute at birth. Péreire had taught him to speak, read, write, and
even to understand some grammar. Péreire had begun to teach this
pupil in Normandy in 1746 and after a few months he had presented him to the Academy at Caen. His method of instruction was
based on a manual alphabet, which he had learned in Spain but
had perfected further. The Academy in Paris was most impressed;
it endorsed his work with enthusiasm. Péreire was so confident of
his techniques that he agreed to take pupils without any payment
in advance. He guaranteed that he could teach basic language skills
for everyday use in fifteen months.[9]

Péreire's position in the learned world of Paris gave him a certain
entreé into society, of which his compatriots in Bordeaux soon made
use. As their political agent in Paris he was consistently lobbying
to protect their rights and to increase them.[10] This work involved
him in a certain amount of quasi-literary endeavor in writing propaganda for the cause of the Sephardim. Péreire himself was directly
responsible for printing two collections of the *lettres patentes*
which had been issued since 1550 in behalf of the Portuguese Jews
in France.[11]

---

who converted, and he too had an important career in medicine, first in
Bordeaux and later in Paris. As a Christian, Cardozo was admitted to the
medical guild in Bordeaux. His wife was a Francia, and in 1748 she
appeared in the minutes of the Bordeaux Jewish community in disagreement
with the taxes its leaders has assessed on her. The decision was that since,
as the widow of a member, she belonged to the medical guild (this despite
the fact that she had remained a Jew), she was to pay her royal taxes, the
*capitation* and the *dixième,* to the medical guild and all the rest to the Jewish
community (*Registre,* No. 161).

[9] Péreire announced his method for teaching deaf-mutes in an eight-page
pamphlet: *Mémoire que M. J. R. Péreire a lu dans la séance de L'Academie
Royale des Sciences du 11 Juin 1749.* The approbation of the commission
of the Academy, which is printed at the end, is laudatory without reservation: one cannot "encourage Mr. Péreire too much to cultivate and to perfect
his methods."

[10] Péreire was hired as the agent of the Jews of Bordeaux in Paris in 1756,
with a life pension of 400 livres a year (*Registre* No. 248a). This pension was
doubled in 1762 (*ibid.,* No. 301).

[11] See Chapter IV for Péreire's debate with Hénault and the *Six Corps*
of Paris.

His professional activities as teacher of deaf-mutes and as political agent of his brethren in Paris were not the sole causes for Péreire's literary work. Especially after the middle of the eighteenth century, all of the various Jewish communities of France organized special religious services on patriotic occasions, and they were in the habit of printing these services with suitable translations. In the early years of the eighteenth century prayers for these observances in Bordeaux were translated not into French but into Spanish. In 1744 Péreire appeared as the first translator anywhere in France of such a service into French. He did this many times thereafter both for the Sephardim in Bordeaux and for those who lived in Paris.[12] The purpose of such publications was, of course, to emphasize the patriotism of the Jews, and Péreire's excellent French was useful.

Péreire was, indeed, a considerable linguist. Towards the end of his life, in 1779, he published the first part of a projected large work, a method for learning, together, the thirteen principal languages of Europe. In this work he showed considerable familiarity with several European cultures. Péreire knew Spanish, English, and German well, and he seems to have had fair knowledge also of Swedish, Russian, and Polish.[13]

The most important Jewish literary figure who wrote in French before the Revolution, Isaac de Pinto, also made his debut in print with a pamphlet in defense of his people. This was the first version of his *Apologie,* which appeared in 1762. The fame of Pinto's *Apologie* has tended to obscure the importance of his considerable body of writing on economics, politics, and contemporary cultural questions. He was perhaps born in Bordeaux,[14] although he lived mostly

[12] Szajkowski, *Franco-Judaica,* Nos. 1665, 1667, 1668, 1672, 1673, 1675; see also Chapter VII.

[13] *Observations;* this was a small book marked "first part of the first volume," but no more appeared, since Péreire died soon after. His announced intention was to publish a work in installments to teach a basic reading knowledge of all the thirteen languages. The purpose of putting the first part into print was to ask for subscribers for the whole series.

[14] There is some question about both Pinto's birth date and the place of his birth. In the only biography that has ever been written, his birth date is given as 1717 and the place as Amsterdam (Wijler, *Isaac de Pinto,* p. 3). On the other hand Kayserling, in his standard bibliography of writings in Spanish by Jews, gives the date as 1715 and the place as Bordeaux (*Biblioteca española,* p. 91).

in Holland. Pinto spent time in both France and England, and he knew many of the major intellectual figures of the day. He seems to have been regarded in the literary world as a bit of a crank. Nonetheless, he left a considerable body of work and, at least as an economist, he was far ahead of his time.

Pinto's first work was published in 1748 in Portuguese. It was a pamphlet on the ancient political constitution of the biblical Jews.[15] We know of nothing else of his in print until the 1760s, when he began to write exclusively in French. His debut in that language was the famous pamphlet defending the Jews, but he turned after that to other, general subjects. In 1763 Pinto wrote a short essay explaining the operation of the speculative market in English bonds, with special emphasis on how to speculate on margin. Pinto was aware that many of these speculators could never afford to pick up their options and that such activities were, therefore, often quite ruinous to some. Nonetheless, he maintained that a continuing market in bonds was good for the economy and for the state. It satisfied the passion for gambling; it gave people a place to invest their money; above all, the market in securities was the place where cash was available when the state needed it.[16]

Pinto wrote a comparable short essay on the tax system of Holland. The basic forms of taxation there were of three kinds: direct taxes on houses and land; on grain, wine, and beer, at the source; and on the shares of the East and West Indies companies, since these shares had been regarded for a century as real property in Holland and were taxed as such. The essential purpose of Pinto's essay was to denounce this third tax: "Such a tax runs counter to the true principles of credit. Public funds should never be taxed. This is contrary to the principles of good faith and of credit, which is the basis of the power of the state." The taxing of securities lessens their value and it is particularly harmful in a falling market.

---

[15] The book, which I have not seen, is listed in Kayserling as *Reflexoens politicas, tocante a constitucão de Nacão Judaica; exposecão de estada de suas finances, causo dos atrosos, a desordens que se experimentao a meyos de os prevenir* (Amsterdam, 5508–1748).

[16] *Tableau ou exposé de ce qu'on appelle le commerce, ou plutôt le jeu d'actions, en Hollande.* This pamphlet is printed in the back of his *Traité* of 1771, pp. 291–312. Pinto tells in a footnote that this essay was written in 1763, but there is no evidence that it was published separately at that time.

Here Pinto argued that securities are not the same kind of capital as land, although he was to argue the contrary, for a different purpose, in his major treatise on economics. The purpose of his discussion in this essay was to plead for complete freedom for stock operations. That remained a consistent theme because Pinto believed that the stock market was both the creator of capital and the source of prosperity. Pinto suggested taxation on foodstuffs in place of taxation of stocks. Any increase in stock market operations increases circulation and the consumption of goods. Circulation is the nerve of the whole economic enterprise.[17]

Pinto seems to have published his first essay on economics by 1762 (I could not find this first edition), the very year in which he began his controversy with Voltaire on the Jewish question. It was "An Essay on Luxury," which appeared also in English translation in London in 1766. Pinto took an intermediate view between those who regarded luxury as the main force that makes society strive for greatness and those moralists who denounced luxury as the ruin of society. This was, of course, a typical subject of the time, as the glittering life of nobles and great merchants was both widely envied and widely denounced. Pinto's position was conventional. He regarded luxury as good if it were based on real production for the majority of the population and not on inequality. States are destroyed when the burdens that are put on one part of society are unfair. If wealth is distributed with too great inequality, government is inevitably corrupt. Pinto was particularly acute in his comments on the situation of France in his day. He pointed out that the ruling class in France was living in luxury, in the capital, without any real functions either in government or in business. They were therefore useless and bored, and they debased the standards of society and of civic virtue. The rich should live on their estates and actually manage them; otherwise, their luxury would be a threat to social stability.

Pinto's image of the rest of the social structure was not too far different from English and American contemporary respect for the

---

[17] *Méthode dont on se sert en Hollande pour faire la perception des taxes, et des impôts sur les biens fonds: et comment on en verse le provenu dans la caisse de l'état*, in *Traité*, pp. 313–20.

honest yeoman and the local artisan as the backbone of society. The majority should work the land, and there should be rural and small-town manufacturers, among whom some men of property would arise, providing a bridge between the classes. In such a society fortunes would be acquired honorably; they would arise out of useful economic endeavors. Pinto knew that this vision he was holding out derived from the writings of the literary greats of the age: "What elevation, what love of virtue, of order, of humanity do not the compositions of a Corneille, an Addison, a Pope, a Voltaire inspire?" The free-market economist in him came out at the end of his argument when he maintained that sumptuary laws were essentially ineffective to achieve his objective of sobriety. The social good that he wanted could come only by creating the proper economic conditions. Usually a conservative, Pinto emphasized that he proposed "no agrarian laws, no new division of property, no violent methods." He held up as a model the example of England, where all the classes worked seriously in a relatively free economy.[18] The economic outlook of this essay was conventional; there was as yet little foretaste of the radical views he would propound in his book.

Pinto was very clearly trying to join the contemporary enlightened world of letters. Wherever possible he made known his reactions to what was being said by important writers. His encounter with Diderot, for example, left traces in Diderot's writings that give the inescapable impression that Diderot regarded Pinto as a libertine.[19] On the other hand, the one essay that Pinto addressed directly to Diderot, a few pages on card-playing, hardly reflects the libertine spirit. Pinto took a characteristically moderate view

[18] *Ibid.*, pp. 333–42. It is indicated there that those pages represent the original text of Amsterdam, 1762. I have not seen such a separate edition of the French. The separately published English text (*An Essay on Luxury* [London, 1766]) is an expanded version.

[19] In two places in his writings, Diderot makes reference to certain "erotic tendencies" of this Jew Pinto, whom he has known in Paris and La Haye. The first is an anonymous remark in *Le neveu de Rameau,* which was written in 1762 (*Oeuvres,* V, 479–80). The second is in his *Voyage de Hollande* of 1774 (*ibid.,* XVII, 405), where he names Pinto and makes an uncomplimentary remark, but there Diderot made someone else the "hero" of the story of a not-paid-for assignation. As Theodor Reinach said, these remarks are consonant with the possibility that Pinto was something of a bon vivant, but the exact facts are obscure ("Les Juifs," *REJ,* VIII, 143–44).

of the fad for playing cards which had swept Europe. He admitted
that there were certain bad results from card-playing. Men and
women were thrown together more often and there were, therefore,
more sexual liaisons. Other passions, especially avarice, did come to
the surface. On the other hand, Pinto argued, card-playing was a
harmless way of having these passions express themselves; it thus
served a useful purpose in helping to avoid larger ills. Pinto paid his
respects at the end of the essay to Diderot's idea that the human
passions are the source of all sublime achievements and Diderot's
corollary that directing human energy into card-playing was against
the best interests of culture. Pinto, nonetheless, maintained that
cards were a civilizing influence.[20]

His most important work was the *Traité de la circulation et du
crédit*.[21] He first sketched out this work, according to his own
account, during his stay in Paris in 1761. When he published the
final version he was not in the least bit diffident; he spoke in the
tone of a man who was certain that he knew better than even the
greatest figures of the century. He had outgrown his own earliest,
conventional ideas to propose an utterly new approach to economics.
Pinto was very nearly right on both counts.[22]

The essence of the issue between Pinto and all the other economists of the age was the question of the economic function of the
public debt. A corollary was the issue with which he had already
dealt in his essay on stock speculation, the utility of the stock

[20] *Traité*, pp. 345–52: *Lettre de l'auteur a Mr. D. sur le jeu des cartes*.
This essay was printed originally as a pamphlet in London in 1768, and it
appeared there in the same year in English: *On Card Playing. In a Letter
from Monsieur de Pinto to Monsieur Diderot. With a translation from the
original, and observations by the translator*. The only copy of this English
translation known to me, that owned by the British Museum, was destroyed
by fire during the bombing of London in World War II.
[21] Pinto's *Traité* was published in Amsterdam in 1771. An English translation was published with notes in London in 1774 under the title *An Essay
on Circulation and Credit*. See also the end of Chapter IV.
[22] The greatest admirer of Pinto in modern times was Werner Sombart.
In his *Die Juden* (p. 113) Sombart maintains that, in the *Traité*, Pinto had
already said everything that the nineteenth century was to discover about
public credit and the stock market. In Sombart's view, Adam Smith represented the end of the eighteenth century and Pinto was the beginning of the
modern age in economics. In his *Das Wirtschaftsleben* (p. 191) Sombart maintained that Pinto was the first economist to understand that the growth of
credit depended on the increase of precious metals in Europe.

market, of those who speculated in it, and of the *rentiers* who derived their income from interest. Berkeley, Bolingbroke, and Montesquieu had maintained that *rentiers* were useless, since they lived
off the labors of others. Mirabeau, the elder, had argued the early
physiocratic case that the only source of wealth was the land and
the only tax that should exist was a single head tax on income from
land. David Hume had attacked the practice of borrowing by the
state as incontrovertibly ruinous.[23] All of these figures and their
views Pinto mentioned by name in order to define his very sharp
disagreement with them.[24] Nonetheless, his treatise elicited little
response. Adam Smith was indeed the only major economist to
react at all to Pinto's views and he censured an author, whom he
did not name, for holding the "insane view" that credit was a social
good and that the stock market was good for the economy.[25]

Pinto began his treatise by defending the national debt as an
economic good against all its critics. He very consciously was the
first to maintain that funding had been the cause of the enrichment
of England. The payment of regular interest by the state meant
that the actual capital debt was never repaid. The result was—this
is the first new note in Pinto—that the national debt was a device
for creating, artificially, new capital. The money realized by state
loans was spent largely in the country; it thus increased the real
wealth of England by putting it to use, while maintaining it as capital in loan bonds. State borrowing was therefore a way of reusing
the same money. "The enormous sum which the national debt represents never existed at any one time. The magic of credit and circulation has produced this mass of wealth successively with the
same money." [26] Pinto had no doubt that the tax burden represented
by interest payments was a very small price to pay for the creation
of new capital. Indeed, interest payments themselves were a form
of increasing wealth, because those who received them spent the
money and thus supported many people who sold them goods and

[23] The most pointed attack is on Hume, who was a personal friend. For
Hume's denunciation of public credit, see "Of Public Credit" in his *Essays*,
pp. 355–72.
[24] Pinto, *Traité*, pp. 13–35. See Chapter IV for Pinto's relation to the
physiocrats.
[25] Sombart, *Die Juden*, p. 113.          [26] Pinto, *Traité*, p. 47.

services. The difference between England and France, which should by its natural resources be the prime economic power in Europe, was to be found in their economic systems. France was laggard because it had the most primitive system of circulation. It had not funded its national debt in the way that England had, and it therefore had not realized the benefit of "having the right hand give to the left." [27]

Pinto saw in circulation and in increased commercial activity the engine of social change. He understood that the growth of commerce since the discovery of America had made the making of a fortune easier, and it had therefore been the cause of establishing "a rough kind of liberty and equality." [28] Pinto denied Hume's thesis that the public credit is bad for the poor because they were taxed heavily to pay for it, by asserting that the only way to help the poor was to increase total commercial activity. Anything that increased circulation, even some of the activity of the hated tax farmers of France, was to the good. Against the bullionist economists he argued that the amassing of specie, without an adequate credit system, did not enrich a country. He cited Spain and Portugal in evidence; they had derived much gold from the mines in America but had not used it properly to erect a system of credit. In economic matters "we are still children; our children will perhaps become men." [29]

What is national wealth? In very conscious answer to all the contemporary economists, and especially to the physiocrats, Pinto argued that every form of capital and income was to be considered part of national wealth. He regarded not only land, mines, and fisheries as capital, but also all forms of credit. Such paper is true and indestructible wealth, and it is not even diminished, like goods, by consumption. Every source of income, including even the money that is spent by tourists within a country, was to be regarded as part of the national wealth.[30] He argued that the increase of population, the great good of eighteenth-century economics, depended not merely on land but on total production of all kinds. The purpose of statecraft was twofold: to encourage all of the various economic

[27] *Ibid.*, p. 90.    [28] *Ibid.*, p. 57.    [29] *Ibid.*, p. 150.
[30] *Ibid.*, pp. 153–57.

pursuits to realize their maximum and to conciliate their various disagreements.

As an economist Pinto was far ahead of his time. There was in his thought more than a shadowy anticipation of the Keynesian economics of the last generation [31] and of the very contemporary economics based on the gross national product. Philosophically Pinto was an "enlightened" intellectual of his day in his belief in the idea of progress. He defined this most clearly in the opening pages of the one book that he wrote on a philosophical theme, his *Précis des arguments contre les matérialistes*. Materialism was the most radical thinking at that moment among the leaders of the Enlightenment. Figures such as d'Holbach were scandalizing more moderate men, including even Voltaire, with their utter denial of the existence of God. Pinto's book was in direct answer to d'Holbach's bold statement of his atheism.[32] Pinto joined the debate by agreeing with the generally accepted premises of all advanced thinkers of the eighteenth century that mankind was indeed improving. Reason and its corollary, education, were more prevalent. Pinto defined one quarrel with the spirit of the age: its atheism, which is ever more ferocious, seductive, and widespread. It is not even necessary to argue whether, on philosophical grounds, atheism is the truth. Even if it is, the mass of men require the belief in God to hold vice in check. Pinto acknowledged his intellectual debts to others and made no pretense of originality in this book. He quoted liberally from Rousseau, Newton, Galileo, Pascal, Francis Bacon, Bayle, Fontenelle, and Voltaire.[33] His climactic argument was quoted from the *Phédon* of Moses Mendelssohn, the book in which that thinker had attempted to prove the immortality of the soul. Pinto took over

[31] Pinto advanced his most "Keynesian" argument in direct opposition to the physiocrat Mirabeau. Pinto maintained that a state is not a family and that it should not run its finances on the principle of a family head, that is, don't owe money. In a state, Pinto argued, such a notion is "vicious." "What may ruin an individual will not, always, ruin a state." What a state spends remains within a country, increasing circulation and economic activity (*ibid.*, pp. 209–10).

[32] Pinto's *Précis* appeared in La Haye in 1774. D'Holbach's statement of the case for materialism, his *Système de la nature*, had appeared anonymously four years before in Paris; the book had caused a great scandal and a furious debate.

[33] Pinto, *Traité*, pp. 22–77, in which he gave a summary of the views of the major contemporaries, or near contemporaries, on religion.

from Mendelssohn his "new proof" of the immortality of the soul
—if no substance is ever destroyed, neither can the soul be.

Pinto asserted that his philosophical argument did not depend
on the belief in revealed religion. He gave a broad hint that he
wanted to avoid this whole question in order not to become impaled
on the issue of the relative merits of the Christian and Jewish claims
to being the bearers of the true revelation. Instead he asserted the
notion of Rousseau, among others, that "there is a constant and
universal revelation which every man can consult, by using his
reason in good faith and by looking into the depths of his heart." [34]
Illogically, despite the Deistic arguments Pinto used in the bulk of
the book, he maintained, without even attempting to prove it, that
prayer can indeed change God's mind, just as advocacy can change
the mind of a human prince. Pinto was aware that this notion was
not of one piece either with his philosophical argument or with
his stance as an enlightened thinker, for he added immediately that
prayer helps man, by reminding him of the virtues that can help
sustain him: "Here is the reason for the prayers of enlightened
men." [35] Pinto's attempt to defend religion led him to associate
Spinoza with those thinkers who were the source of the contagion
of irreligion.[36] In this, as we shall soon see, he was followed by
another enlightened French Jew, David Gradis. Pinto ended the
volume with the sigh: "Happy is the age, happy are the men to
whom it will not be necessary to prove that there is a God and that
they have a soul." [37]

In economics Pinto went his own way; in religion he was a moderate; in politics he appeared as a conservative at the beginning
of the American Revolution. He was very busy in the year 1776
pamphleteering against that rebellion. He debated with both a
doctor from Kingston, Jamaica, S. Baretto, and an anonymous
author, both of whom argued against him in favor of the revolutionaries. Pinto extolled legitimacy, as opposed to the efforts of the
Americans, which were leading to "the overthrow of order and true
liberty; . . . it is the temper of Oliver Cromwell." Pinto acknowl-

[34] *Ibid.*, pp. 112–13.          [35] *Ibid.*, pp. 114–15.
[36] Pinto did not regard Spinoza as dangerous, because his work was known
only to a few (*ibid.*, p. 12).
[37] *Ibid.*, p. 138.

edged that he was pro-English; he added that he followed both Montesquieu and Voltaire in these views. It should be noted that Pinto's favorable reference to Voltaire in this connection was being written at a moment when Guénée's book against Voltaire's views on the Jews, in which Pinto was heavily involved, was going into its fourth edition in Paris. Pinto believed that it was to the interest of all the European powers to obstruct the independence of America. The English colonies, once they were sovereign, would inevitably dominate the colonial possessions of all the European powers in central and southern America; they would take away the bullion produced by their mines. Indeed, the real, ultimate interests of the five great colonial powers, Portugal, Spain, England, France, and Holland, was to band together in a confederacy in order to guarantee the peace and order of the world. Such a confederacy, he argued, should together pacify North Africa and secure the freedom of Greece.[38]

The defense of legitimate authority is the recurring theme of all Pinto's writing on the American Revolution. In his view, Britain was not fighting to stamp out this rebellion in order to enforce a tax on tea, but rather to defend the basic principles of political order. The legitimate right of sovereignty must be maintained by force, if necessary, or else the result would be creeping anarchy throughout the world.[39] This theme of legitimate power and of the various European countries orchestrated in a larger system of peace

[38] Pinto's first two letters on the American Revolution appeared separately in French in 1776; see Szajkowski, *Franco-Judaica*, Nos. 1583–85. The two letters were published together in translation into English that very year in London under the title *Letters on the American Troubles*.

[39] Pinto developed this point in the third pamphlet that he wrote in 1776. This one was in answer to an anonymous debater who had jointed the argument between him and Baretto. This concluding pamphlet is entitled *Réponse de Pinto*. It should be noted that Pinto's arguments against the revolutionaries in America were based on different premises than those of the contemporary Tories either in England or America. These were arguing for legitimacy on the premise that governments had been instituted by God and kings were His necessary agents (see Davidson, *Propaganda and the American Revolution*, p. 279). Pinto was not debarred by his Jewishness from believing this even of gentile kings, but he chose to argue against the American Revolution in the name of history, order, the protection of individual liberties, and the political interest of all the powers of Europe. These were almost precisely the terms in which Edmund Burke would argue against the French Revolution after 1790.

and order was not a new idea, then, in Pinto's mind. As early as 1762, when he began his debate with Voltaire about the Jews, Pinto had ended his original pamphlet by arguing that religious differences have no economic importance. He had hinted to Voltaire that all of the great men of Europe had been working on reconciling the various national and religious interests and not on exacerbating them. Pinto had added that the real differences among men are not based on their religions, but on their economic interests. He gave as proof that Rome and Carthage had fought not over religion but over their clashing economic desires. Pinto had ended that pamphlet by saying that he had "the confused germ of a system of conciliation" in his mind but that he needed time to contemplate it further. His notions, he acknowledged there, derived from the dream of the Abbé de St. Pierre.[40]

Pinto had indeed returned later in the 1760s to the contemplation of the question of international peace and harmony within society. In 1771, when he published the *Traité,* he used the occasion to put all of his earlier essays on subjects other than the Jewish question into collected form. One of them, his *Lettre sur la jalousie du commerce,* was devoted to considering the relationship of sound economic principles to the true objects of statecraft. Pinto laid down as a fundamental principle that the object of the state is not to dominate other states but to achieve social harmony and peace. This purpose requires healthy international commerce, for if the bordering states are in misery and cannot pay for the goods that are exported to them, one's own country would inevitably be depressed. The good of each state, therefore, requires the good of all. In this opinion Pinto was at one with the newest tendencies of mercantilist thought at that time.

[40] Pinto, *Apologie,* pp. 46–47. Charles Irenée Castel de St. Pierre published *Projet pour rendre la paix perpetuelle en Europe* in 1713, based on an earlier short essay the year before. These ideas appeared in several later editions and in several forms. St. Pierre believed in the political status quo—that an international order should guarantee each sovereign in the territories he possessed, and that he should be restrained from seeking more. The armed forces of Europe as a whole should be used to put down insurrections, for stability was to the interest of all the powers. In economic thought, St. Pierre denied the notion then current among mercantilists that there was a fixed amount of trade, and that a country could increase its own only by taking it from others. (See Hemleben, *Plans for World Peace,* pp. 56–72.) In all these opinions, Pinto followed him.

Pinto challenged the more autarchic forms of mercantilism further by arguing that a branch of commerce that is useless to one state may be the lifeblood of another. Even in areas in which an individual nation has major commercial interests it is to its advantage to share with others, because no one can hope to dominate any one field completely. The true key to the flourishing of European society is to raise consumption, and the function of the colonies is therefore to serve an ever-growing market.

Pinto was aware that his thinking owed something to his devotion to the Dutch state. He believed it was the major trading nation of the day, and it required international peace, for its economic health, more than any other. He was arguing that the rest of Europe was evermore in the Dutch situation, that every national economy in Europe was becoming less self-sufficient and more interwoven.[41] Pinto now regarded long wars as unthinkable, on economic grounds, because they were too expensive. He proposed that the money that was being spent on making wars should be used to encourage agricultural production. Sighing that "unfortunately peace is ordinarily only an interval in which open hostilities cease, only to recommence with greater violence," Pinto concluded that a concert of the great commercial and colonial powers would represent "the happiness of the human race and the glory of the age." [42] Five years later, in response to the American Revolution, Pinto was again to return to his dream of the legitimate, existing political order of Europe as the cornerstone of international peace.

Pinto was not the only Jew of rank to appear in French letters in the 1770s. The most famous Jewish writer of the day, Moses Mendelssohn, knew of Pinto's work in defense of the Jews against Voltaire. Mendelssohn was not put off by any of the expressions of Pinto's pride in being a Sephardi: he asserted that if the Jews had a few additional such redoubtable controversialists on their side, their estate would be raised throughout the world.[43] Mendelssohn's own work had its echoes in French. The controversy with Johann Kaspar

---

[41] Though Pinto did not say so, this essay was in answer to David Hume's "Of the Jealousy of Trade" (*Traité*, pp. 334–38). Their points of view were identical, except that Pinto was much more pro-Dutch and he defended Holland against a slur by Hume.

[42] *Traité*, pp. 227–88.

[43] Quoted in Wijler, *Isaac de Pinto*, p. 56.

Lavater, into which the Frankfurt lawyer J. B. Kölbele had jumped, was summarized in a French volume that appeared in 1771 at the very height of that affair. Lavater, a Swiss pastor, had asked Mendelssohn to be baptized. The French compiler was a partisan of the most extreme Christian view, that Mendelssohn should indeed seize the opportunity and convert immediately, "if he is not too tainted with the arrogant contemporary philosophy!" It is revealing that it was Mendelssohn's philosophical enlightenment rather than his Jewish faith that was regarded as the bar to his accepting Christianity. Despite its hostility, this book had the merit of introducing Mendelssohn's view on Judaism to the French reading public. This compilation contained Mendelssohn's first anwer to Lavater's initial challenge to him to accept Christianity, as well as his reply to Lavater's second letter and to Kölbele's first intervention in the dispute.[44]

In 1772 Mendelssohn's most famous philosophical work, his *Phédon*, appeared in French translation in Berlin. A completely different translation appeared in the same year in Paris. In the preface to this version the translator printed extracts from Mendelssohn's first answer to Lavater, and he went on to praise him as superior to Plato in his learning and as equal to him in style. Despite these eulogies, Mendelssohn was attacked in this preface for being a Jew, but it is probable that the translator was saying this for effect because the volume was published legally, with the approval of the French censors.[45] As we shall see below, this philosophical work by Mendelssohn had one other connection to France, in addition to its use by Pinto. It was translated into Hebrew by an "enlightened" young man from Metz, Isaiah Berr Bing; this version was published in Berlin in 1786.

All of the figures discussed so far were, in one sense or another, not really French Jews. Mendelssohn, of course, was a Jew of Berlin. Péreire had been born in Portugal and came to France as a young adult. Pinto was perhaps born in Bordeaux and he did live briefly

[44] This book appeared anonymously: *Lettres juives du célèbre Mendels-Sohn.*
[45] There were many editions of Mendelssohn's *Phédon* in French. The first, representing a translation by Burja, was published in Berlin in 1772. A different translation by Junker "of the Academy of belles-lettres in Göttingen," was published in Paris and Bayeux in 1772.

in Paris, but for most of his life he was identified with Holland. The first native-born Portuguese Jew to write on general topics in French was Louis Francia de Beaufleury, a scion of the very prominent Francia family of Bordeaux. Francia made his appearance in French in 1783 with a short volume in which he suggested new means of dealing with the growing problems of begging and poverty.[46] Francia himself seems to have been the first professing Jew admitted to practice as a lawyer in France. He described himself on the title page of the book as a lawyer at the bar of the *parlement* of Bordeaux, and this description is confirmed in the official approval to the censor. He was even a member of the Academy of Rome, but he did not belong, clearly because he was a Jew, to the one in Bordeaux, his home town. This exclusion was the source of an incident that clouded the whole question of the originality of his first work.

The issue of mendicity in France had been raised before the learned world by the Academy of Chalons-sur-Marne in 1777, when it responded to the growing problem by offering the question as the topic for an essay contest. It received over a hundred entries and, even though none of them was judged good enough for the prize, so large a number of writers was evidence of an enormous public interest. Mendicity had indeed been growing in France, and many towns, although Bordeaux was not among them, had reacted by forbidding begging. The problem had outgrown the traditional ways of dealing with it, through the alms of the religious parishes. Francia therefore had written a proposal for dealing with the question and had read it to a few friends at the end of 1782. His proposals attracted the attention of the Bordeaux Academy. A commission was appointed, which reported favorably, but one of its members opposed Francia's reading his work at an open session of the entire body because Francia was not a member. This individual, de Ladebat, soon read an essay of his own on the subject, which Francia maintained was plagiarized from him. He therefore published his own work both as a contribution to the public good and in order to "protect" his authorship.

The essence of Francia's suggestion was that an end be made of the haphazard distribution of alms by individual parishes, both be-

[46] M. L. F. D. B. [Louis Francia de Beaufleury], *Projets.*

cause it was an ever-growing expense and because it was encouraging begging as a profession. The hordes of beggars, with no prospect of a fixed occupation, were a dangerous element, and some of them had in recent memory made riots against noblemen and tax farmers. What needed to be done was to put the poor to work, preferably by sending them back to their native places. In each community there should be a central bureau, such as the one that had been recently opened in the city of Amiens, to deal with its specific situation. In that city of 40,000 there were 5,000 beggars. Francia proposed that every community should be divided into geographic sections and that each area be visited regularly so that an accurate central register of all the poor could be kept. Help should be dispersed directly to them by delivery to their individual homes so that there could be a continuing check on their situation and on their need. There should be a fixed schedule, based on the cost of living, as a guide to the size of support given to each family. His further suggestions were that, even though Bordeaux was a center for the import-export trade, it should establish some manufacturing, especially in weaving, to create jobs. There should also be a pawnshop set up to grant small loans to the poor at no interest, with the basic capital for this project to be provided by donations.

Francia did not mention directly at any point that he was a Jew, and there was no hint that his suggestions had anything to do with the pattern already existing in the Jewish community from which he came. Among the Sephardim in Bordeaux there had been, for at least a century, a central register of all the poor, with constant inspection of their estate by the communal authorities. Wherever possible the community did try to find jobs, and the level of support was adjusted to the total budget of each family. Free loan funds existed there, as everywhere else in the Jewish world of that day, as a matter of course. It is likely that these traditional Jewish practices were in Francia's mind when he made his suggestions to the wider civic community.

Francia showed another kind of interest in the public welfare, in several suggestions that he made for fire and health insurance on the widest possible basis. In this connection it is not far fetched to see a biographical motif. Members of his family had been involved very prominently in marine insurance in the middle years of the eighteenth century, and two of them had been condemned to death in a notorious scandal that involved fraud, by faking the sinking of a ship.[47] In his writing about insurance in the 1780s there was, of course, no overt reference to the earlier squabbles and tribulations of his family.

In a supplement added to his book about poverty, Francia reproduced the text of a *mémoire* that he had read at a meeting called in Bordeaux's city hall in 1782, in which he proposed that fire insurance be created either by the citizens themselves or through commercial companies.[48] In either case, the financing should be through the issuance of stock and the rates should be based on the classification of buildings according to their size and their susceptibility to fire. Francia returned to this theme of insurance in a pamphlet he published in 1785 as an appendix to his volume on the poor and fire insurance.[49] Here he took issue with an earlier scheme for hospital insurance. This plan had been announced in 1754; it was based on the notion that the insuring company should run hospitals of its own to provide for those insurees who fell ill. Francia suggested a medical insurance that would provide direct payments to insurees. He added a proposal for a lottery to dispose of the annual surplus that he envisaged would accrue to the company. In this same pamphlet Francia also returned to the question of poverty, with a rather silly essay against employing men as domestic servants. He maintained that they were ruined by such service since they lost the habit of work and became beggars. He therefore proposed that men under thirty be forbidden to leave the countryside to come to town as servants.

None of Francia's writing made any difference in either the realm of action or of thought. His essays were quite typical of hundreds of such performances by "enlightened" provincial intellectuals. Neither did the writings of David Gradis, his contemporary in Bor-

[47] Szajkowski, *Franco-Judaica,* Nos. 1118–21; Cirot, *Recherches,* pp. 57–58; see also Chapter V.
[48] Francia, *Projets,* pp. 83–96.
[49] *Supplément au projets.* This was a pamphlet of forty-eight pages.

deaux, make any significant impression. Gradis was much more important both in commerce and in the inner affairs of the Bordeaux
Jewish community. He was the head of his family's famous sea-
trading firm during the last years of the *ancien régime* and thereafter until his death in 1810. His avocation was writing works of
philosophical theology. Gradis' volumes were privately printed and
they had little circulation or impact. These books are today great
bibliographical rarities, yet they are important for what they reveal
about the outlook of the author and of the Jewish oligarchy of Bordeaux that he led. None of Gradis' work was published until the
middle of the Revolutionary era, but what he wrote properly belongs in an account of Jewish intellectual activity in France before
1789, and not only because it is obvious, a priori, that his intellectual
outlook had been formed by then. There is, as we shall soon see,
other evidence of what he and his circle were thinking before 1789.
Gradis was the first Jew in France to attempt to face the question of
defining his faith in the light of a considerable reading of modern
thinkers.

Gradis' philosophic position was that reason is against the notion
that creation could have been ex nihilo.[50] He regarded this as inconceivable intellectually for, "from nothingness to being, there is an
infinite distance, which no power could ever have bridged." Gradis
argued Hebrew philology to maintain that the traditional translation of the first verse of the Bible is a mistranslation. It does not
mean "to create something from nothing," but rather it means "to
make." Gradis boldly attacked the Pharisees, the doctors of Jewish
law, who had handed on a "false notion" of the creation and this

[50] Gradis' first philosophical book was published anonymously, "par un négociant dont le nom et le commerce sont tres anciens à Bordeaux." It appeared
in the Revolutionary year 6 (1797) under the title *Courte dissertation sur
l'origine du monde, au réfutation du système de la création.* Gradis' Jewish education derived from his studies with David Athias, the rabbi in Bordeaux in
his time, and with Mordecai Tama, who was head teacher of the Jewish school
of the Sephardim. He was really from the Papal States and served also as the
rabbi of the Avignonnais in Bordeaux (see Chapter VII). Tama's appointment
to the school in 1783 was recorded in the Bordeaux *Registre,* Nos. 516, 517;
he evidently came then from Paris, where Azulai had met him earlier (*Maagal
Tov,* p. 115). Before the Revolution, Gradis is reputed to have published some
brochures on political economy (the favorite topic of his contemporary, Isaac
de Pinto), but no copies of these essays are known to exist. See the bibliographical article on David Gradis in Carmoly, *La France israélite,* pp. 145–57.

mistranslation of the Bible to the Christians and the Moslems. The rabbis had been guilty for at least a thousand years of spreading false religion, and it was Gradis' purpose to rescue the Bible from the Talmudists. It is important to note that this philosophical position of Gradis was consonant with the actual practice of Jewish education in the Bordeaux community of his day; Azulai had seen with horror that the curriculum did not contain any rabbinic sources.[51] In 1806 Gradis repeated his fundamental opposition to the Talmud, which Azulai had heard three decades before, at a meeting of the Bordeaux Jewish community: "The Jews of Bordeaux and Bayonne are quite far from wanting to make the Mishnah and the Talmud a fundamental premise of their religious discipline, as the other Jews do; they exclude from their faith anything that does not conform to good sense and to the literal meaning of the Bible. These alone are the bases from which they derive all the religious dogmas that they can accept." [52]

In his battle against the doctrine of the creation ex nihilo Gradis, in a sequel to his first work, defended his views against Bayle, Basnage, and others. (It is revealing that he mentioned no writer later than Voltaire.) He did not even hesitate to invoke some unnamed cabalists in support of his views, even though he was contemptuous of them in other connections. Nonetheless, Gradis was also involved in defending his rational religion against atheism, and even in defending Judaism against apostasy. Like Pinto before him he disliked Spinoza, whom he called "an atheist guilty of treason to his religion." [53] In his very last book, however, an embattled Gradis was having to defend religion against the materialists. "The true use

51 "In the evening I was invited to the school, to hear the examinations which take place when children pass from one class to another. In the school they teach only the Bible, and they even exclude the commentaries of Rashi, because he quotes the Midrash and the rabbinic commentaries. Maimonides is also excluded from this curriculum. Woe to the eyes which have seen such things! May there be an end to such sins!" (Azulai, *Maagal Tov*, p. 114; see Chapter VII).

52 Szajkowski, "Quarrels," *Horeb*, XIV–XV, 257.

53 D. G. [David Gradis], *Discussions*. The remark about Spinoza is on p. 36. This volume and the earlier one were published by Gradis two years later, with considerable additions, under the title *Essai de philosophie rationelle sur l'origine des choses et sur leur éternité future*. The additional argument is against the Deistic notion of God as watchmaker and in favor of a God who enters into personal relationships with men (*ibid.*, p. 275).

of philosophy is to bring us to God and to show us, in the very evidence of nature, the necessity of the first cause." Without the theistic faith, "man will make his gods of his stomach, of his senses, in a word, of himself." [54]

The Westernization among French Jews during the second half of the eighteenth century left its traces not only in the books that a few wrote but also in those that some owned. Louis Francia's father owned a considerable library, as did such people as Abraham Rodrigues Péreyre of Bordeaux and Israel Valabrègue in Paris.[55] This intellectual Westernization was but one expression of a continuing process, the earliest traces of which are to be found in the changing life styles of some Jews. The hold of ancient Jewish custom was weakening after 1750 in small but significant circles of all the separate parts of French Jewry, but the largest impact was felt first among the Portuguese.

On his first trip to Bordeaux, in 1755, the famous traveler Azulai did not want to eat in the house of Benjamin Gradis, who was then the head of the family, but he did not suggest that there was any real doubt that Benjamin Gradis was a religiously conforming Jew of at least the average sort.[56] At about that time there were several cases in the minutes of the Bordeaux Jewish community of public infractions of religious law. It was recorded in 1748 that Joseph Rodriguez Péreira and his son Raphael Dacosta were each fined 100 livres for mocking the dogmas of Judaism and breaking the laws of the Sabbath and the holidays. Three years later a certain Lesons was fined 12 livres and ordered not to shave for a week for having placed a lock on his door during Passover.[57] Such incidents were not recorded in the later years of the century, but not because the Jews of Bordeaux had become more pious. When Azulai was in Bordeaux for the second time in the winter of 1777–78 he reported, "The *parnassim* and the leaders of the Sephardim came to visit me. To begin with, I received them coldly, and afterward the conversation lasted a long time, the subject being philosophical speculation tend-

[54] Gradis' last philosophical volume was no longer either anonymous or signed only with his initials. His name appears on the title page of *Discussions philosophiques sur l'athéisme.*
[55] Szajkowski, "Secular Private Libraries," *Kirjath Sefer,* XXXV, 495–598; idem, "La vita intellettuale," *La Rassegna Mensile di Israel,* XXVII, 122–29, 179–91.
[56] Azulai, *Maagal Tov,* p. 36.        [57] *Registre,* Nos. 166, 186.

ing towards heresy." Azulai reported on Abraham Gradis, then the head of the family firm and the uncle of David Gradis, that he was "respected in the royal court of France, a man of great wealth, who was worth several millions. . . . He is one of the greatest of the heretics who do not believe in the oral law and who eat forbidden foods in public." Azulai visited Gradis at his home, where he could not help being impressed by a garden in which there were many flowers and trees native to America, where the Gradis firm had major economic interests. Azulai had trouble getting money from the wealthy in Bordeaux, and he reported in anger that the man who gave him the most difficulty, the incumbent head of the community, Solomon Lopes, was known not to obey the laws of *Niddah* in his relationship with his wife (the prescribed separation during and immediately after menstruation).[58]

In the winter of 1777–78 Azulai revisited not only Bordeaux but also Paris. He was even more horrified by what he found in the capital than by what he had found in southeastern France. The acting rabbi, then, of the Avignon Jews in Paris, Mordecai Tama, whom Azulai did regard as a scholar, drank wine in gentile taverns. There was no doubt that most of the communal leaders in Paris were living outside Jewish law, and several admitted to keeping gentile mistresses.[59]

Azulai's account of Paris is confirmed by evidence from the police archives of that city. There are accounts there of young Jews having commerce with Christian girls and living ostentatiously enough to ape the nobility. After 1752 there was a group of about twenty young Sephardim in Paris, the first generation born there, who carried swords and behaved like the wildest of young nobles. In 1761 one of the young Avignonnais, Moise Astruc (who was later to threaten to convert to Catholicism), fought a duel with Buhot, a police inspector. There was no comparable group of wild bucks among the smaller group of Jews in Paris who came from eastern France, but there were instances among them too of such escapades as keeping actresses of the Royal Theatre.[60] Paris was the Jewish

[58] Azulai, *Maagal Tov*, pp. 115–16.

[59] *Ibid.*, pp. 119–24.

[60] L. Kahn, *Les Juifs de Paris au dix-huitième siècle*, pp. 53–58; *idem, Les Juifs de Paris sous Louis XV (1721–1760)*, p. 16. Elie Worms of Sarrelouis was hiding in Paris in order to live with an actress who was his mistress.

"frontier" before 1789 because the very nature of the situation in the capital, where Jews were living on sufferance in the eighteenth century, reduced religious and communal restraints upon the conduct of individuals.

It would be false to give the impression that the traditional Jewish way of life and the inherited rabbinic learning were evaporating rapidly in Paris and among the Sephardim of southern France. Liefman Calmer's personal library contained all of the basic classics of rabbinic literature.[61] David Gradis, on the evidence of his own writings, had a good education in medieval Jewish literature as well as in the Bible. It is true that the rabbis of Bordeaux were of no distinction, evidently because the lay oligarchy insisted on dominating all the affairs of the Jewish community. In the early years of the Revolution the lay leadership of the community reported to the authorities of Bordeaux on the estate of Jewish life. They did not hesitate to characterize their own rabbi contemptuously as "merely a casuist" of no importance.[62] Azulai did not think very much more of the rabbi of Bordeaux in 1755, Jacob Athias. The lay leaders of the community were then in controversy with their rabbi over the qualifications of a ritual slaughterer (shohet). Azulai had considerable personal sympathy with the rabbi, but he overruled him nonetheless. It is clear from the context of the discussion both in Azulai's travel diary and in the minutes of the Jewish community that Azulai felt that Athias was a man of little learning.[63]

On that trip and on his earlier journey, Azulai was in Bayonne and he gives us a much more positive impression of its Jewish life. The kinds of questions he had to answer in Bayonne, about the minutiae of ritual, clearly reflected a life of learning and tradition.[64] Until poverty overtook Bayonne in the second half of the century, it had been the seat of rabbis more distinguished than those in Bordeaux. Raphael Meldola was there in the middle of the century, and his son David Meldola remained in touch with the community.

[61] Loeb, "Un baron Juif français," AIF, XLVI, 197–98.

[62] Archive de la Gironde, V, 13.

[63] Azulai, Maagal Tov, p. 36; Azulai's decision in this case, in his own hand, is in the Registre, No. 240.

[64] Azulai, pp. 36–37, 110–13. In Bayonne, on his second trip, Azulai was asked such questions as whether it was proper for people to cry out aloud in the synagogue during the repetition by the cantor of the Eighteen Benedic-

In David Meldola's book of responsa, which appeared in 1753, there were a number of questions from Bayonne and even a learned responsum by a local layman from that city. One of the entries in the volume is evidence of the continued existence there of a voluntary society of pietists who had taken upon themselves the rule of fasting on the day before the new moon.[65] Certain processes of intellectual and linguistic acculturation must have been going on there, too, because immediately after the beginning of the Revolutionary era there was a Jewish Jacobin society in Bayonne, which for a while governed the Jewish quarter on the other side of the bridge, St. Esprit. This group was, however, significantly less antireligious than the usual run of Jacobins, including those in control in Bayonne itself.[66]

---

tions. On the other hand there were leaders in the Jewish community of Bayonne in 1777 who asked Azulai theological questions which showed, that like their peers in Bordeaux, they too had been influenced by the *philosophes* (pp. 111, 117).

[65] Raphael Meldola was rabbi in Bayonne in 1737, the year in which his son David arranged for the publication in Amsterdam of his responsa in four volumes, entitled *Mayyim Rabbim*. None of the material in this work reflected the situation in Bayonne, for the responsa represent the conditions in his native land, Italy. David Meldola's own work, *Divrei David*, does have a number of questions from Bayonne. In No. 8 Daniel Péreire of Bayonne is found questioning a contradiction between two passages in the Talmud on the laws of ritual purity. Rabbi Abraham Jeshurun Cardozo discussed with Meldola the local custom of a group who fast the day before a new moon. Isaac Hezekiah Lopes de Fonseca asked Meldola a relatively simple question about liturgical procedure (No. 55). A more troubling issue was the local ordinance passed in 1700, during the rabbinate of Isaac DaCosta, and confirmed by the rabbis of Amsterdam, that anyone who married in private without parental agreement is not validly married. This occupied four entries in the book, Nos. 73–76. A rich layman, Moses de Robles, defended this ordinance, in excellent Hebrew, on the ground both that French law forbade anyone under twenty-five to marry without parental consent, and such marriage was, therefore, equivalent to rebellion against the state, and that the community had a right to annul a marriage in order to protect the morality of its young. Meldola was not at all sure of this conclusion, and it is evident from the discussion that such ordinances were desired by the *parnassim*, without too great concern about the fine points of talmudic law. The issue was the same in Bordeaux, where the communal leaders often exercised the power to nullify marriages contracted without their permission (*Registre*, Nos. 248, 481, and 503). A direct reflection of Raphael Meldola's rabbinate in Bayonne is to be found in a pamphlet that he published in Amsterdam in 1734, *Parshat ha-Ibbur*. The subject was the devising of the necessary legalisms to permit Jews to carry things on the Sabbath in the streets of their neighborhood in St. Esprit without infringing talmudic law.

[66] E. Ginsburger, *Le comité*, p. x.

## The Traditional Jewish Culture of Eastern France

The level of Jewish religious devotion and conduct, even among those who were beginning to follow Western practices before 1789, was highest in eastern France. The sermons of Jonathan Eibeschütz provide good evidence of this. Preachers have always exaggerated the evils against which they were inveighing; we can therefore be sure that the situation was no worse than he described. Much of what he preached in Metz in the 1740s has been printed. Eibeschütz repeatedly attacked those who shaved. The social intercourse between the sexes was too free. Fashionable clothes were being adopted, especially by the women. Gentile wine was being drunk, and there was a certain carelessness in some of the technicalities of Sabbath observance, especially in the opening of the mail, which religious law forbade on the Sabbath. The children of the rich were neglecting the study of the Torah and people were no longer marrying their daughters to scholars. The imitation of gentile ways was extending to such lengths that some Jews were no longer wearing ritual fringes, except inconspicuously as an undergarment. This catalogue of sins—and these were the worst that Eibeschütz could muster—is a far cry from the contemporary behavior among the wilder youths of Paris or the heretical communal leaders of Bordeaux.[67]

[67] These various remarks by Eibeschütz are repeated over and over again in his sermons, which were collected in the *Sefer Yaarot Devash;* that book is cited here according to the edition of Karlsruhe, 1779–82. See especially pp. 3, col. 2; 6, col. 4; 7, col. 4; 8, col. 4; 9, col. 1; 21, cols. 3 and 4; 22, col. 4; 34, col. 4. Many dozens of additional citations could be given in which he repeated these themes in sermon after sermon. Eibeschütz was also concerned about those who were playing cards, or who were beginning to shave their beards, or who were wearing wigs. Perhaps his most interesting remark is against "people who sin in their souls by beginning to be 'enlightened.' " This plague had broken out among Jews, because some were saying that God wanted the service of the heart and ethical conduct and not the observance of the commandments of Jewish law (p. 10, col. 3). This was the very first echo of "enlightened" thinking in Hebrew letters in eastern France, but it cannot have represented any serious movement, since Jewish observance was still very strong in that region in the next generation. Eibeschütz also deplored, in a sermon preached in 1744, the interest of Jews in current political affairs and in the wars between nations. All of this, he maintained, is irrelevant to Jews, who should waste no time in observing military maneuvers or in rejoicing over

The situation had not changed to any marked degree forty years later. The interim chief rabbi of Metz, after the death of the famous Asser Lion (R. Aryeh Loew), was Oury Cahen. In 1792, fearful that all of his learned writing would be forgotten because of the disturbed age in which he was living, Cahen printed a selection of his novellae and sermons. The persistent themes of Cahen's calls to repentance were the same as those of his great predecessor. People were drinking wine of non-Jewish provenance. They were going to theaters and cabarets, thus creating far too loose social intercourse among the sexes. Cahen did not suspect that there was real sin but he added that sinful desires were aroused in such situations. He knew that the wealthier Jews, and especially the women, were attempting to imitate the fashions of the rich gentiles. The ancient traditions of charity were not being adequately observed.[68] His list of sins did not include such things as breaking the Sabbath and non-observance of the sex laws of Judaism, all of which were already prevalent among the Portuguese.

The older ways of life were of course much more strongly rooted in eastern France, and they continued with little change into the Revolutionary era. Among the many contemporary accounts of the temper of Jewish life in that region at the end of the *ancien régime* and during the beginning of the age of the Revolution, two are perhaps the most interesting. One is an anonymous memoir by a Jewish peddler from Lorraine, which appeared in 1841, supposedly on the occasion of his hundredth birthday. This account tells of his receiving a conventional education in Hebrew, the Bible, and the Talmud up to the age of thirteen, after which the author, as was usual among the poor, went peddling in the country with his father. In those days "we all wore the same [specifically Jewish] clothes, and the beard appeared to all of us to be a commandment." The author tells

---

military victories (p. 29, col. 1). That card-playing was indeed a problem for the pietists of Metz and the region is evident from a decision in 1777 in the *Pinkas*, 102a. People were freely transgressing a by then ancient prohibition against playing cards anywhere within five hours' travel of Metz. Repeated fining had not helped to lessen the evil. Those who bet, and played cards or billiards, were now punished severely by being forbidden any honors in the synagogue for three years; they were permanently prohibited the right to take oaths or be witnesses.

[68] Cahen, *Halakhah Berurah*, p. 14.

us that at the time of writing the "enlightened" Jews were no longer
observing the Sabbath, but this was unheard of in the days of his
youth.[69]

There is another account, by a more interesting figure from a
higher point on the social scale, which describes the situation immediately after 1800. Its author was Paul Drach, who was born in
1791 into a rabbinic family in Strasbourg. Drach received a classic
Jewish education. By the age of twelve he was admitted to the
primary section of the school of Talmud at Ettendorf, and he advanced by quick degrees to the higher schools in Bischheim and
Westhoffen. These *yeshivot*, which are here recorded as existing in
the early 1800s, were evidently the successors of those that had been
established many years before to cultivate higher Jewish learning
in Alsace. The curriculum even during the Revolutionary era was
still entirely the study of the Talmud. Drach himself studied Greek
and Latin privately, and his father began to be alarmed by the possibility of his turning away from the faith, but Drach persisted.[70]
Drach eventually went to Paris as the son-in-law of Emannuel
Deutsch, a deputy chief rabbi of France, and he himself was the
head of a Jewish school there. He eventually converted to the Catholic faith, along with a number of other figures from eastern France.
Several were to have important careers in the church.

To the very end of the *ancien régime* the rabbinate of the region,
and especially of the city of Metz, was quite distinguished. Metz
itself was served in the eighteenth century by such luminaries as
Joshua Falk (1734–41), Jonathan Eibeschütz (1741–50), and Asser
Lion (1766–85). To be sure, none of these figures was from the
locality, but we cannot deduce from this that there was lack of
rabbinic learning among the scholars of the town. There was an
ancient rule in the communal constitution of Metz that, in order to
avoid controversy, any rabbi called to its leadership must have no
relatives resident in the city.[71] This rule was not observed among

[69] Ben Lévi, "Mémoires," *AIF*, II, 686–91; III, 459–61.
[70] Drach, *De l'harmonie*, I, 34–44.
[71] There have been several histories, in whole or in part, of the rabbinate
of Metz. The best was by A. Cahen, "Le rabbinat de Metz," *REJ*, VII, 103–15,
204–26; VIII, 255–74; XII, 283–97; XIII, 105–26. The earlier studies were
by Tsarfati [Terquem], "Rabbins de Metz," *AIF*, I, 25–31, and the criticism
of this piece by Carmoly, "Bemerkungen," *Israelitische Annalen*, II, 61–62,

the Alsatian communities, where the rabbinic office was more closely identified with political and economic affairs. The various rabbis in the region were official appointees of such local potentates as the Bishop of Strasbourg or the directory of the nobility of Lower Alsace, rather than electees of the Jewish community.[72] Communal figures of great wealth who were possessed of some learning often managed to get themselves appointed to the rabbinic office, clearly in order to exercise control over the destiny of the entire Jewish community. To recall two incidents that have already been mentioned: In the earlier years of the century the very wealthy and well-connected Samuel Lévy was, for awhile, the chief rabbi of Lower Alsace, which post he abandoned when he went to Lorraine, to his financial disaster, as the unofficial finance minister of the Duke of Lorraine.[73] In the 1780s in the city of Bischheim, the home of Cerf Berr, there was a running battle over the leadership of the Jewish community between his family and the other wealthy families of the community, the Lehmanns. Each clan had its own rabbi, Cerf Berr's being his brother-in-law, the future first chief rabbi of France, David Sinzheim.[74]

Although Alsace was less of a center of Jewish learning than Metz, despite its far larger Jewish population, it had a certain amount of intellectual activity. There were several schools of higher learning in the Talmud in the province. In 1777 the leaders of Alsatian Jewry met for a general review of the Jewish situation in all of its aspects,

---

80–81, 96, 185–86. For the practice in Metz to call rabbis from outside the community see A. Cahen, VIII, 271.

[72] In 1681 the king confirmed Aaron Worms, of Metz, as the chief rabbi of Alsace. This office was soon divided into two, one rabbi of Upper Alsace and the other for Lower Alsace. The bishop of Strasbourg, the count of Hanau, and the directorate of the nobility of Lower Alsace all fought to maintain the right to appoint their own rabbi. See, in general, Merlin, *Repertoire universel*, VI, 247–48; see also Chapter VII.

[73] M. Ginsburger, "Samuel Lévi," *REJ*, LXV, 274–300. Lévy's father and his step-mother, Glückel, tried to dissuade him from his venture in Lorraine; see *Zichronot Glückel*, pp. 134–36. For comparative material from the careers of other contemporary Alsatian rabbis, see *idem*, "Samuel Sanvil Weil," *REJ*, XCVI, 54–75, 179–98.

[74] *Idem*, "Les familles Lehmann et Cerf Berr," *REJ*, LIX, 106–30. This quarrel was settled by judgment of Benjamin Hemerdinger, the rabbi of the Jewish communities in the territories of the nobility of Lower Alsace. The judgment was unfavorable to Cerf Berr, but he accepted it. See also *idem, Histoire*, pp. 18–31 and Chapter V, fn. 138.

including the need to reorganize the structure of their communal government. Among the many things that were decreed, two decisions are of interest at this point. Individual Jews were forbidden to avoid the authority of the official rabbis of the province on religious questions, in favor of those scholars whose personal authority they seemed to be accepting. The leadership also established one higher academy of Jewish learning for all of Alsace in place of the various individual houses of study that were in existence then. They were, in particular, abolishing the long-existing schools at Mutzig and Ettendorf in favor of the new creation. This central *yeshivah* was to be supported from the proceeds of any fines that were levied by the syndics, from taxes on dowries, and from free will offerings. In order to make sure that the knowledge of the Torah should not disappear, it was even decided that half of the tuition for the primary education of children of the poor would be paid from communal funds.[75]

This concern for Jewish education had been reflected in Metz in a communal ordinance a century earlier, when it was decreed that the community would pay a set scale of tuition for those who required such help.[76] This remained a constant concern throughout the eighteenth century. It was quite usual there for the wealthy to create pious foundations for the support of teachers and poor students. To recall another incident that has already been described in part, in 1761 Moshe Belin gave 25,000 livres to the Metz community as a capital fund, the interest on which was to be used for the higher education of twenty-four poor children from Metz, and three who would be admitted from the academies of Alsace, Ettendorf, and Mutzig. This foundation, it should be pointed out, and several others that were created in Metz had the clear additional purpose of providing an income and freedom from communal taxation for scholarly relatives of the rich founders, who were appointed to the teach-

[75] The JTS Library possesses a pamphlet of eight pages in Hebrew and Yiddish representing the communal regulations that were decreed in 1777 and printed for distribution: "Extract from the minutes of the province, of the meeting of the representatives of the communities on Iyyar 21, 5537." See Chapter VII.

[76] A. Cahen, "Enseignement," *REJ*, II, 303–305.

ing, quasi-rabbinic offices.[77] That which Metz had ruled out in
relation to the office of chief rabbi, the acquiring of the post through
family influence, thus became the normal way in which all the lower
offices were filled. The posts of teachers of Talmud and rabbis of
the individual synagogues were, essentially, purchased and given as
benefices by the wealthy donors of large sums to pious purposes.

How high was the level of indigenous Jewish learning? The
elected chief rabbis of Metz and some of those who were called to
Alsace from outside France were of the very highest contemporary
standing. The indigenous figures were not of the same stature, but
it cannot really be maintained that there was a decline in the course
of the century. Even during the last decades of the *ancien régime*,
as it fought against an ever greater burden of taxes and debt, Metz
continued to maintain a *yeshivah*, where its chief rabbi could teach.
The commitment to support students from other places was made
not only, as was to be expected, in the rabbinic contract that it gave
the famous Asser Lion, thus clearly continuing a well-established
custom; it also appeared as late as 1787 in the contract that it offered
Herschel Levin, the rabbi of Berlin, to occupy this post.[78]

The state of classical Jewish studies in eastern France by indigenous scholars is shown both by the few books that they published and by the large number of unpublished manuscripts that still
exist in the various archives. After the death of Asser Lion there was

[77] *Pinkas,* 39a–b, and Chapter V. Belin used the creation of this foundation
to get his son-in-law, Itzig Pousweiler, appointed as rabbi of one of the synagogues in Metz. His salary came from the trust, but the community had to
grant him freedom from taxation. It finally agreed to do so, even though
Pousweiler was independently wealthy. The initial sub-appointments on this
trust, as teachers, went to Akiba Treni and Oury Phoebus Cohen, both of
whom were authors of learned works printed in Metz. Another example is
the case of David Terquem (*ibid.*, 50b–51a). He gave the community 12,000
livres, with the understanding that it would support two scholars from the
interest, but he asked that his own assessed capital worth be reduced by
this amount. The question was compromised by giving him a reduction of
6,000 livres.

[78] *Ibid.*, 65b: Clause 22 of the rabbinic contract of Asser Lion read, in
part, as follows: "The community obligates itself to support (as usual) twenty
students, for instruction by the chief rabbi, and five more besides." This
clause was repeated and even strengthened in 1787 (*ibid.*, 141a), when twenty-
five students were again authorized, plus the provision that more could be
added at the pleasure of the community.

an interregnum, and no chief rabbi of Metz was appointed until
the days of Napoleon. The three men who jointly acted as the rabbis
of the Jewish community were all local scholars. Two of them published, after 1789, quite respectable collections of novellae and
learned sermons, and one of the two, Aaron Worms (the great
grandson of Worms, the chief rabbi of Alsace in the seventeenth
century), became chief rabbi of Metz before his death in 1836.[79]
Among the many unpublished collections of learned writings there
are quite competent novellae by an otherwise unknown scholar from
Bischheim, Raphael Cohen, which were finished in 1785, and comparable productions by several rabbis from various parts of Alsace.[80]
In 1821 the library of Jacob Mayer, the rabbi of Strasbourg, was
catalogued. The manuscript list of his books reflects wide learning
in all branches of classical Jewish scholarship.[81]

Eastern France was the very edge of the world of eighteenth-
century Ashkenazi Jewish learning, and students from far away did
not come readily to its academies. Nonetheless, there was an indigenous audience and even a commercial market for higher talmudic Jewish learning. Otherwise the fact that several Jewish
presses were created in the last several decades of the *ancien régime*
is incomprehensible. Despite the difficulties these endeavors en-
countered, they were begun on the presumption that the community needed their productions.

[79] The three who served were Oury Phoebus Cohen, Mayer Charleville, and
Joseph Gouguenheim, with Aaron Worms as a deputy for instruction (A. Cahen, "Enseignement," *REJ*, II, 106, 120).

[80] The Schlamme collection in Mulhouse contains a collection (MS No. 1)
of "Novellae and sermons by Raphael Cohen of Bischheim," dated 1785. The
University Library in Strasbourg contains several comparable collections by
Alsatian rabbis (MS Nos. 57, 58). There is considerable material in manuscript of the rabbis of Metz, with Eibeschütz being particularly well represented. It appears that his disciples during his years in Metz copied out his
lectures on Talmud and his sermons. Strasbourg MSS 12, 13, and 79 contain
novellae and sermons by Eibeschütz and his immediate successor, Samuel
Hillman. Among the MSS of the *Ecole rabbinique* in Paris, Nos. 64 and 82
contain novellae by Eibeschütz and Hillman; Eibeschütz is also represented
in Nos. 72 and 73. Mayer Charleville was the author of all the novellae in
No. 148 (194 pp. in MS) and some of those in No. 68. Rabbi Wolf of Pousweiler appears as an author both in Strasbourg MS 57 and in the *Ecole rabbinique* MS 82.

[81] Strasbourg MS 99: a catalogue written by Jacob Weill in 1821 of the
books of Jacob Meyer, chief rabbi in Strasbourg. For Meyer's biography, see
M. Ginsburger, "Jacob Jeqil Meyer," *AIF*, XCIV, 154–55.

## Jewish Printing in France

Jewish printing did not begin in France until the latter half of the eighteenth century,[82] when two presses appeared almost simultaneously, one in Metz and the other in Avignon. The press in Avignon began in 1765, a year later than the one in Metz. It was founded by two partners, Isaac Naquet and Mordecai Cremieu (Carmi), who was later to become rabbi of Carpentras and a figure of some importance in France during the period of the Revolution and the Napoleonic Empire.

The first venture of the Avignon press was a prayer book, containing special prayers (*piyyutim*) for the Sabbath and the order of service for a number of other occasions, according to the rite of the four ancient Jewish communities in the Comtat Venaissin. This volume was paid for and its text was corrected by two young partners who underwrote this venture, Isaiah Vidal and Mordecai Venture. They were also the translators into Provençal of two of the *piyyutim*, for the circumcision ritual, that appeared in this volume. The next, and evidently the last, publication of this press appeared two years later in 1767. It was a prayer book of the local rite.[83]

[82] The first example of Hebrew printing in French preceded the two pioneer Jewish presses by more than two centuries. Robert Étienne (Stephanus), the second in the line of the famous family of printers, produced two editions of the Hebrew Bible in Paris, 1539–44 and 1544–46, as well as several volumes of lesser importance. See Darlow and Moule, *Historical Catalogue*, p. 706; Renouard, *Annales*, pp. 54, 65; Friedberg, *Bet Eked*, p. 1073, but the date for the last volume of the first edition that Friedberg gives, 1620, is in error. Renouard, p. 47, identified the very first Hebrew printing of any kind in France with an alphabet and Ten Commandments that Robert Etienne produced in 1539 as a rehearsal for the composition of the Bible. There was also some Hebrew printing in Strasbourg in the years 1544–49. Even more certainly than in Paris, there was no Jewish participation of any kind in this endeavor. The press in Strasbourg was created to serve the needs of students at the university. The senior professor of Hebrew at the time was Paul Fagius, who had worked earlier with the famous Jewish scholar Elijah Levita in the conduct of a Hebrew press in Isny. Most of the productions of the Strasbourg press seemed to have consisted of books that had been printed earlier in Isny. All that is known to remain of this press is a copy of the *Targum*, the Aramaic translation of the Bible, with a Latin translation by its side. No trace of this press is to be found in the later history of Hebrew printing in France. See Rostenberg, "The Printing of Hebrew Textbooks in Strasbourg, 1544–1549," *Journal of Jewish Bibliography*, II, 47–50, 92.

[83] Friedberg, *Toldot ha-Defus ha-Ivri*, p. 91.

By far the more important was the press that began in Metz. Between 1764 and 1789, with an interruption of four years (1772–75), it produced forty-seven titles. These represented not only prayer books and the like for popular consumption but also solid works of advanced talmudic learning. This press was founded by Moses Mai.[84] He was a member of a family that had resided in Metz since the beginning of the eighteenth century and he was himself one of the community's *parnassim*. In his early years as publisher Mai had to print his books on the press of Joseph Antoine, a local printer, because Mai had not obtained royal permission for his own press. In his first year of publishing Mai produced three titles, each of them characteristic of a genre that he was to cultivate in his later efforts. The most important from the point of view of rabbinic scholarship was the first edition ever printed of that part of the *Assefat Zekenim*, the collection of commentaries culled from the earliest authorities by R. Bezalel Ashkenazi, which related to the tractate *Bezah* of the Talmud. That Yiddish was still very much alive as the everyday language of Alsatian Jewry is proved by Mai's other two publications of that year, a prayer book with Yiddish translation, "in the language spoken by the Jews of this Province and their mother tongue," and the first Yiddish translation of Daniel Defoe's *Robinson Crusoe*.[85] In the next year Mai produced four liturgical texts, all with Yiddish translations except for a Passover Haggadah, and the novellae of R. Simon ben Adret on the Talmudic tractate *Ketubot*. The year after, 1766, was marked by three more liturgical publications and by the appearance of a volume in a new genre, a short summary of Hebrew grammar by a local scholar, Jacob Joseph Sofer, with Yiddish translation.

Perhaps the most significant aspect of the publication program of Moses Mai's press was his work in publishing local scholars. When the press was founded the famous Asser Lion, the author of the classic work of talmudic literature entitled *Shaagat Aryeh*, was rabbi in Metz, and Mai had begun his press with the rabbi's support and approbation. In 1781, four years before his death, the last original work by that great figure to be printed in his own community in his lifetime appeared. The work was entitled *Turei Even;* it was Asser Lion's last work, a brief commentary on several minor tractates of the Talmud. Mai printed other original productions by local scholars. In 1767 there appeared a commentary on the Talmudic tractate *Zebahim;* the book was called *Mayyan Ganim* and its author was Akiba Treni of Metz. Two years later Mai published another original work by an Alsatian rabbi, Issachar Ber ben Judah Lima of Ribeauville; it was a commentary on the *Tosefta,* a parallel text to the first layer of talmudic literature, in this case limited to the elucidation of the part of this text that referred to the talmudic tractate *Bezah.*

This press also paid attention to the works of scholars who had been rabbis in Metz earlier in the century. In 1785 a volume of novellae entitled *Kiryat Hannah* appeared. Its author was Gershon Coblentz, who had been a deputy to the rabbi of Metz early in the eighteenth century. In 1789 the third volume of the novellae of Jacob Reischer, who had been the rabbi of Metz from 1719 until his death in 1733, came off the press.[86] Between 1789 and 1792, when the serious career of the press came to an end, there also appeared three volumes of the *Meorei Or,* a critical commentary that was eventually to reach seven volumes, on most of the tractates of the Talmud and a considerable part of the first volume of the *Shulhan Arukh,* by Aaron Worms. Worms was a favorite disciple of Asser Lion; in the interregnum that succeeded the death of that great figure Worms served as his successor in the post of head of the rabbinical college in Metz. Worms was a personage of some consequence in the religious affairs of his community and of all eastern France throughout the period of the Revolution, and thereafter until his death in 1836. The concluding volume of his *Meorei Or* was published in 1825. It represented the end of serious talmudic publishing in Metz.

[86] The first two parts were published in Reischer's lifetime, the first in Halle, 1709, and the second in Offenbach, 1719.

The most important effort of the press of Moses Mai was his attempt to publish a small-scale, student edition of the Talmud.[87] Mai's announced purpose was to print the whole of the Talmud, not in its usual order, but to bring out individual volumes in the order in which they were being studied in the *yeshivot* of Alsace, and especially in the school in Metz. The tractates *Shabbat* and *Bezah* appeared in 1768, *Berachot* and *Niddah* in 1770, and, after a fateful interruption of which we will speak in a moment, the last volume in this series, *Rosh Hashanah,* appeared in 1777. The contents of the original publications by local scholars that Mai was publishing in the same period prove that he was actually serving the need that he had in mind. There was an obvious relationship between the appearance of the tractate *Bezah* in 1768 and the publication in the next year of a commentary to that volume, by Issachar Ber of Ribeauville; the tractate *Rosh Hashanah* was followed four years later by Asser Lion's novellae on that volume, which probably represent the lectures he gave in the Metz *yeshivah* when that part of the Talmud was the object of study.

Nonetheless this project brought disaster to Moses Mai. There was not enough of a market in Metz and Alsace alone for these talmudic productions and Mai therefore attempted to sell them elsewhere. This involved him in controversy with the Proops brothers in Amsterdam, the publishers of large folio editions of the Talmud. Mai explained that his format was different and he volunteered not to sell in Holland, but this did not satisfy his opponents. By 1771 Mai was bankrupt and had to leave Metz. His type was divided between his son Nathan (who later joined Mai in founding a press in Hamburg), and his son-in-law Godechaux Spire Lévy, who reopened the press in June, 1775, after he finally obtained royal permission, which Mai himself could never get, to print in his own name. An interesting sidelight on Mai's bankruptcy is provided by a decision taken in the Rabbinic Court in Metz in the late summer of 1772. The community itself had lent Mai 5,000 livres from its own funds, at the rate of 7 per cent, to help him continue his press. It had a lien on a thousand volumes that he had produced, half of which were Bibles

---

[87] See his broadsheet announcement reprinted in Friedberg, *Toldot ha-Defus ha-Ivri,* p. 88.

and the other half, prayer books. After investigation it was discovered that all of these books together, even if they were in perfect
condition, were not worth more than 2,500 livres. The Rabbinic
Court issued an order permitting the communal authorities of Metz
to take the books and to attempt to satisfy at least part of their lien
by selling them.[88] Mai himself did not return to Metz until 1789, the
year his son-in-law died, when he came back to rejoin his grandchildren for the last three years of his life. It should be noted here
that all of the serious original publications by this press appeared in
the two periods that Moses Mai was at the head of it and that its
productions in the hiatus between were, with two exceptions, either
reprints or prayer books.

### "Enlightened" Literature

Spire did, however, publish the first examples of "enlightened"
literature in Hebrew to appear in Metz. Moses Ensheim had returned to Metz in 1785, after four years as a tutor to the family of
Moses Mendelssohn, to attempt to make a living as a teacher of
mathematics.[89] Ensheim belonged to the literary circle that founded
the famous journal of reviving modern Hebrew literature, *Ha-
Meassef*. In 1787 Spire published a slim volume of riddles by Ensheim, which made card-playing their target. In the next year a
poem by Ensheim appeared. We know also that David Hamburger
published an occasional poem, written for the inauguration of a

[88] YIVO MS, I, 40a–b.
[89] For Ensheim's biography see Graetz, *Geschichte der Juden*, XI, 135–36.
He was born in Metz ca. 1760 and died in Bayonne in 1839. Ensheim was an
accomplished mathematician, but as a Jew he was refused a teaching post at
the newly founded *Ecole centrale*, for which he applied on his return home to
Metz from Berlin. Ensheim aided Abbé Grégoire in preparing his famous
*Essai sur la regénération des Juifs* and in his later pleading for the Emancipation. Ensheim did not, however, appear in the first three volumes of *Ha-
Meassef*. The fourth volume (1789, pp. 69–72) contained, anonymously, the
text of his *Three Riddles*. In the next year Ensheim appeared as the author of
an ode to the *Assemblée Nationale*, after the fall of the Bastille and the declaration of the rights of man. A characteristic stanza reads as follows:

House of Jacob! You are sated with woe,
You have fallen terribly, through no fault,
May your heart be strong in hope
Your salvation is approaching and your day of deliverance. (pp. 33–37)

Torah scroll in Metz in 1787, and that this work, which was based on Maimonides' thirteen articles of the faith, was reprinted in the next year.[90]

The most important echo, however, of the Berlin Enlightenment in pre-Revolutionary Alsace was a volume that appeared not in Metz but in Berlin in 1786. It was the first Hebrew translation of Mendelssohn's *Phédon*, his defense of the doctrine of the immortality of the soul. Isaiah Berr Bing, one of the young enlightened literati of Metz, was the translator.[91] The task was completed during Mendelssohn's lifetime and found favor in his eyes, according to a flattering introduction to the volume which was supplied by Naftali Herz Weisel, the most important figure of the Berlin Enlightenment after Mendelssohn. Weisel praised Bing as truly "enlightened," as one of his spiritual children, and he concluded the introduction with a sonnet in Bing's honor. Bing's Hebrew was indeed worthy of Weisel's praise, for it is an excellent example of the contemporary style of the "Berlin circle."

The circle of Mendelssohn was not, however, the only source of a modern kind of influence in Franco-Jewish literature of the generation that preceded the Revolution. Some "enlightenment" came from indigenous sources, by the rather easy shift from Judeo-Provençal to French on the part of scholars of Hebrew from the Papal States. Mordecai Venture was the author of a prayer recited in Paris on March 5, 1768, by the Jews of Avignon and Bordeaux at a special service of supplication for the recovery of the Queen of France from an illness.[92] Bernard de Valabrègue, the interpreter for Hebrew and

---

[90] This work is listed in *Ha-Safrut ha-Yaffah be-Ivrit* (Jerusalem, 1927). According to Zeitlin, *Bibliotheca hebraica*, it was entitled *Shemesh* in the reprint of 1788. I could not find the work or any biographical information about the author.

[91] Bing was born in Metz in 1759 and died in 1805. He was very close to Grégoire. See Tcherikower, "Jewish Efforts towards Emancipation" in *The Jews in France*, II, 18–19. Tcherikower is, however, in error in terming him the very first Alsatian Jew to be a writer in French. Quite apart from the fact that his French was not good, he was almost certainly preceded by his rival Berr Isaac Berr. In Weisel's account the manuscript of the translation was shown to Mendelssohn by a friend of Bing's resident in Berlin during the author's last days. The intermediary was probably Moses Ensheim.

[92] I have not seen it, but a copy was offered for sale in 1954 by M. Sanders, a London bookseller: *Prière Prononcée le 5 Mars 1768 par les Juifs Avignonais de Bordeaux demeurant à Paris, à l'occasion de la maladie de sa Majesté LA*

Oriental languages at the Royal Library, was the author of some poems based on Psalms 20 and 71, which were recited in Paris on June 11, 1775.[93] The occasion was a special service by the Jews of Avignon and Bordeaux residing there, convoked in honor of the coronation of Louis XVI. We have already mentioned the many efforts of Péreire in translating such services.

The first translation of the prayer book into French took place before the Revolution. It was composed by Venture, a considerable Hebrew scholar who was the author of a translation into Hebrew of the Targum Jonathan, the ancient Aramaic translation of the Book of Esther, in addition to the works already mentioned.[94] His pioneer translation of the prayer book (he followed the custom of the Spanish-Portuguese Jews and not his own native rite) appeared in Paris. The first volume, which appeared in 1772, contained the daily and Sabbath prayers, as well as certain ancillary material. Volume two (1773) contained the service for the High Holidays and volume three (1774) contained the orders of prayer for the major festivals. After an interlude of nine years the fourth volume appeared in 1783, presenting his translation of the special prayers for the fast days.[95]

Venture wrote a preface to his work, which gave some interesting information on the audience he expected for his translation. His reasons for undertaking it were threefold: there were some Jews who did not know Hebrew well enough to understand the prayers and some in that day already knew no Hebrew at all; he wanted the women to understand; and he was eager that non-Jews have "a correct idea of why we pray to God." Venture said some sensible things about the difficulties of translating a language and text so foreign to

---

*REINE de France, pour demander à Dieu le rétablissement de sa santé.* Composé par M. Ventura (Paris, 1768). See Szajkowski, *Franco-Judaica*, No. 1680.

[93] Valabrègue became "interprète du Roi" at the royal library in Paris in 1754. Azulai (*Maagal Tov*, p. 129) met him there in 1778 and disliked him intensely, calling him a braggart and ignoramus. For the prayers he translated, see Szajkowski, *Franco-Judaica*, No. 1681.

[94] *Patshegen Ketav* (Amsterdam, 1770).

[95] The title page of this fourth volume for the first time identified Venture as "sécretaire-interprète" at the royal library in Paris. Azulai, *Maagal Tov*, did not speak of such an association by Venture in 1778, when he met him, in a context where it would have been mentioned, if Venture had already achieved this position.

the genius of French. His most deeply felt remarks were towards the end of the preface. He had done his work not to replace the Hebrew of the service with French, but in order to lead all his brethren to study the sacred tongue; he had labored for those who knew nothing and he had, therefore, carefully added elementary notes on all the necessary rituals. Venture was himself an orthodox Jew, but the fact that his translation was needed reflects a "modern" situation as early as 1772.

All of these beginnings of stirrings towards modernity in the last couple of decades before 1789 were not, except among the Sephardim, very deep. As we have seen from the sermons of Eibeschütz, and there is corroborating evidence in a number of regulations to be found among the decisions of the Metz community, the beginnings of acculturation to modern styles of life were being felt in the circles of the rich. There was as yet no serious intellectual acculturation. A few representative figures of the younger generation in eastern France were acquiring, privately, a knowledge of French. These people all looked to Berlin, to the circle of Moses Mendelssohn. The leading "enlightened" intellectuals in eastern France in the 1780s were Isaiah Berr Bing, Berr Isaac Berr, and Moses Ensheim. It is significant that all three were punctiliously observant in religion, in the manner of Mendelssohn and Weisel.

So too were all the major communal leaders of eastern France, who also were involved in the circle of Mendelssohn. Cerf Berr himself was a personal friend of Weisel. Weisel wrote two odes in 1785, which appeared in the issue of Ha-Meassef (the periodical of the "Berlin circle") for the next year, in praise of Louis XVI and of Cerf Berr personally for the abolition of the body tax on Jews in eastern France. In the superscription of the lines praising Cerf Berr, Weisel characterized him as "God-fearing and zealous for the divine commandments." [96] There was further evidence in Ha-Meassef that this was true, for there was an apology to Cerf Berr in the preface to the 1788 volume of the journal, where Cerf Berr appeared as defender of the orthodox beliefs. He had written a letter taking angry exception to an article appearing in 1786 that had implied a Deistic view of morality and a denial of the faith in reward

[96] Ha-Meassef, 1786, pp. 33–34, 48–49.

and punishment.[97] Cerf Berr was quite evidently important to this circle as a main supporter, and he was not alone. In various lists of subscribers Abraham Berr of Metz appeared as underwriting five subscriptions and other figures from the region, such as Lipman Landau of Nancy, were also mentioned.[98] The wealthy leaders of the Jews of eastern France are second only to those of Berlin itself as supporters of the beginnings of the Berlin Jewish Enlightenment, but they were clearly among the most conservative element in religion who were partisans of the movement. The break with tradition was to come in eastern France in the next generation, under the impact of the Revolution and not before.

### The Battle for Jewish Rights

Both elements in France, the Sephardim and the Ashkenazim, were involved in the agitation for Jewish rights that came to a head in the last fifteen years of the *ancien régime*. As was said earlier, in political connections their interests were different, however. The Sephardim had undergone a century of acculturation; at least their leaders had entered the world of French manners and even of French culture. They already had most of the rights to which they aspired, and their activities after 1776 were primarily defensive, to ensure nothing would happen to bring them trouble. For the Ashkenazim the battle for their rights was vital, and their activities on their own behalf were the cutting edge of their entry into modernity.

The literary battle for Jewish rights was really the prime contemporary intellectual effort of French Jews in the last three decades of the *ancien régime*. The participation of Jews in French intellectual culture in general, despite such figures as Pinto and

[97] *Ibid.*, 1788, preface.
[98] *Ibid.*, 1786, pp. 64, 211. This is to be compared with a total initial list of about 200 subscribers (*ibid.*, 1785, p. 16). Rich Jews from eastern France also furnished important help to various of the publication projects of this circle. Moses Halphen of Strasbourg was one of a dozen or so subscribers to the publication of the Five Scrolls in Hebrew and German by Joel Brüll and Aaron Halle (*ibid.*, 1788, p. 240). Lipman London and Seligman Papenheim of Nancy were listed in support of Isaac Eichel's project, to publish Maimonides' *Guide to the Perplexed* with two medieval philosophical commentaries (*ibid.*, p. 264).

Péreire, was not large. It was more a harbinger of the future than a
present achievement. The Westernized Jewish intellectuals before
1789 could not really personally avoid the Jewish question in favor
of an involvement in general cultural issues. Francia did indeed
attempt this, but it is revealing that his attempt was made after
1776. In that year the Sephardim had achieved their heart's desire
by being granted the right to live and trade all over France on an
equal plane with all Frenchmen, and they thus felt that for themselves they had no further battles to fight. There were two periods
in the fight for Jewish rights: the years between the appearance of
Pinto in 1762 until 1776, when all the writing was done by Sephardim and Avignonnais, and the years to 1789, when the Sephardim
were completely silent in public and the battle was taken over by
leaders and writers from Metz, Nancy, and Alsace. To be sure, each
group played a role in the thinking and the arguments of the other.
These roles were not always, as we shall soon see, those that have
been conventionally ascribed to them.

It has been said time without number that Pinto's sole purpose
was to defend the rights of the Sephardim and that he had no concern for other Jews. Credence is lent to this notion by the fact that
the occasion of Pinto's *Apologie des Juifs* was an internal squabble
in Bordeaux and Paris between the Sephardim and the Jews from
Avignon, against whom Pinto was bringing his influence to bear.
The opening pages of the *Apologie* do contain such remarks as "a
Portuguese Jew from Bordeaux and a German Jew from Metz appear to be two entirely different beings." [99] There is, however, much
more to the relationship of Pinto to other Jews than such words
quoted alone imply.

In the first place, Pinto was himself aware, as he asserted in a
letter to Péreire that was published in one edition of his pamphlet,
that the good of the Portuguese might have to be bought with the
woe of the Germans and the Avignonnais, "but unfortunately one is

[99] There were two early editions of the *Apologie,* both of them anonymous.
One was in Amsterdam 1762 and the second, undated, in Paris. The Amsterdam edition is entitled *Apologie pour la nation juive:* it has as its subtitle
the title of the Paris edition, *Réflexions critiques sur la premier chapitre du
VII<sup>e</sup> tome des oeuvres de monsieur de Voltaire au sujet des Juifs.* The citations
here are from the Paris edition, p. 16.
Pinto was attacking, directly, the article "Juifs," which had appeared in
an edition of Voltaire's historical writings, published in Geneva in 1756. (The

often reduced to empiricism, in politics as in medicine." [100] Pinto regarded it as his duty and Péreire's to defend the rights of the Portuguese while doing their best to make peace with the others by helping them as much as possible. The essence of Pinto's argument on behalf of the Portuguese tried to do just that. He did, indeed, make the point that has always been quoted against him by his critics, that only the Portuguese were descended from the tribe of Judah and that they had always lived apart from all the other children of Jacob, marrying only among themselves and maintaining separate synagogues. This was "history," however, and Pinto did not seriously expect that anyone would be impressed by the argument. Both Voltaire and his other contemporaries brushed aside this part of what Pinto said. The point which Pinto was making in that passage was that today, in 1762, the Portuguese were to be distinguished from all other Jews: "They do not wear beards and are not different from other men in their clothing; the rich among them are devoted to learning, elegance, and manners to the same degree as the other peoples of Europe, from whom they differ only in religion." The Portuguese are honest businessmen, almost never usurers, and they have been of great use to the economies of the countries that have admitted them. They have the vices that go with such virtues—a taste for luxury, prodigality, laziness, and "womanizing"—the vices of "great spirits."

Pinto admitted that other Jews, mostly German and Polish ones, were depressed in manners and culture, but there were among them, especially in Amsterdam and London, where they had lived in some freedom, men "who are the most upright people in

---

piece was part of the work that was later titled *Essai sur les moeurs; Oeuvres complètes,* ed. Moland, XI, 110–45.) If his immediate purpose had been to answer Voltaire, why did Pinto wait six years? Voltaire's work provided more than the pretext, however. The statesmen and men of affairs whom Pinto was trying to influence on behalf of the Sephardim, such as the Duke of Richelieu, who was then the military governor of Guienne (the province that included Bordeaux), were all reading Voltaire. Indeed, Voltaire and Richelieu were well known to be life-long friends (Cole, *The First Gentleman of the Bedchamber, passim*). What Voltaire was saying as historian, precisely because of its tone of critical realism, appeared to be the least ideologically questionable and, therefore, the most influential aspect of his writings. See Chapter IV regarding the parallel controversy between Hénault and Péreire; see Chapter IX for an extended discussion of Voltaire.

[100] *Ibid.,* pp. 9, 19–23, 26–29, 43–44.

the world and who do business with the utmost honesty." Indeed, these Jews should be admired for the great advantages they have renounced in order to remain faithful to their religion. What was wrong with them had been caused by persecution: "Is it astonishing that, deprived of all the advantages of society, . . . condemned and humiliated on all sides, often persecuted and always insulted and degraded," that these Polish and German Jews are what they are?

At the very end of his pamphlet Pinto quite clearly responded to another element in the encounter of an early Jewish intellectual with the thought of the Enlightenment. He was aware that the new, secularizing intellectual world might be hospitable to the individual Jew who totally abandoned that identity in the name of being a *philosophe*. Clearly Pinto himself was a candidate for such a step, but he answered that there were enlightened men among the Jews who would not "because of the delicacy of their emotions" trade away their religion. They respected the Divinity enough to worship his decrees in private, to be Deists in their inner hearts. They were not the less worthy of praise for having the firmness to remain, because of "greatness of soul, in a religion which is proscribed and held in contempt."

At the very beginning of the propaganda by Jews for their equality in the world, Pinto thus stated three themes: There was a segment of the Jewish community that was worthy of equality because it was already living the highest culture and manners of the majority. The depressed mass of the Ashkenazim were what they were, not by their nature, or even by their faith, but because of persecution and exclusion; more favorable conditions would change them. The attachment of Westernized Jews to their Jewish identity was to religion, but that religion was no longer the orthodox faith, for such men philosophized like other contemporary intellectuals. They persisted in remaining Jews because it was dishonorable to abandon a persecuted community. Mendelssohn quite correctly hailed this pamphlet because much that was going to be said in the next thirty years, mostly by disciples of his or people under his influence, was already outlined within it.

The immediate contemporary reviews of Pinto took exception to his distinction between the Portuguese Jews and all the others. A writer in *The Monthly Review* argued against Pinto that the Polish and German Jews, "so far as they are Jews, are probably no worse than their brethren." [101] Somewhat less bluntly, the same point was made in answer to Pinto in the *Bibliothèque des sciences et des beaux arts*.[102] Both reviewers were nonetheless aware that the real argument for any higher consideration for the Portuguese was that they had been richer and better educated, that is, more Westernized. In the most important answer to Pinto, the letter that Voltaire wrote him, all that Pinto had said about the distinction between Portuguese Jews and the rest was ignored entirely. The issue for Voltaire was Judaism. Voltaire was willing, grudgingly, to allow Pinto to remain a Jew, evidently in awareness of Pinto's illogical attachment to his persecuted tribe, provided Pinto would be a *philosophe*.[103] In Pinto's own response to the critical reviews he insisted that he had not been partial to the Portuguese, but that he had tried to defend all Jews. Pinto insisted again that the faults of the majority of the Ashkenazim were created by their persecutors.[104] Two years later, after Pinto had published his response to his critics, an anonymous pamphlet in London counter-attacked him. On internal evidence the author was either a Jew or someone very pro-Jewish indeed. He criticized Pinto for not defending all Jews equally and for not veiling the faults of the Ashkenazim. The central assertion of this anonymous pamphleteer was that the cultural differences between the Portuguese and other Jews were lessening, which could only mean that a segment of the Ashkenazim was beginning to arrive at comparable wealth and Western culture.[105] This reply to Pinto accepted his premise that inner Westernization was a precondition for the attainment of equality by the Jews.

The next stage in the discussion of the Jewish question in France by Jews revolved directly around economic questions. The decree of 1767 broadening the right of admission to the guilds had evoked, as we have seen, an immediate battle in Paris.[106] The Jewish question became more prominent in France in the 1770s for a variety

[101] *The Monthly Review*, XXVIII (1763), 570.
[102] *Bibliothèque des sciences et des beaux arts*, XVIII (1762), 509–12.
[103] *Correspondence*, XLIX, 131–32.   [104] *Réponses.*   [105] *Réflexions.*
[106] See Chapter IV for the discussions by Péreire, Valabrègue, and Lacretelle.

of reasons. When the Portuguese finally succeeded in 1776 in obtaining their last major favorable decree during the *ancien régime*,
it was clear in the text of that decree itself that the main motive for
this broad recognition of their rights was no longer precedent
reaching back to 1550. It was, rather, an awareness that the Portuguese Jews as a whole were sufficiently French to be worthy of
these privileges. The decree itself gave as its reason the fact that
these Jews had given service to commerce "without there ever
having resulted any inconvenience to our other subjects from their
particular usages." [107] On the other hand, in 1777 the battle over
the false receipts began to rage in Alsace, and the issue that was
immediately raised there was precisely that of the commercial honor
and usefulness to the country of the Jews of eastern France. The
kindest things that royal officials could find to say were that the
Jewish moneylenders were no less miserable than their debtors.
Here the question was radically different from what it had been
in the earlier phase. It was not the moving of the royal government
to recognize the usefulness and the cultural estate of Portuguese
Jews by giving them rights, but rather asking the government to
use its power in such fashion as to change the Ashkenazi Jews.

It was at this moment, in the year 1776–77, that the very height
of the literary debate was reached in French letters. In 1776 the
Abbé Antoine Guénée's book, which contained as its basic kernel
Pinto's pamphlet of 1762, went into its third edition in Paris and in
the next year Voltaire answered him at length.[108] By that point, however, the immediate issues raised there were already beside the point.
The Portuguese avoided getting involved in Guénée's fight with
Voltaire. Pinto himself remained silent. All this made sense because
the policy of the Sephardim henceforth was to try to protect what
they had. They would take an interest in some progress for their
brethren in eastern France providing that nothing happened which
would include them to their disadvantage with these others. The

---

[107] Léon, *Histoire des Juifs de Bayonne*, p. 152.

[108] Voltaire's *Un Chrétien contre six Juifs* appeared in 1777 in Geneva (the
title page read "La Haye"). Guenée (1717–1803) was then the teacher of
the children of Louis XVI's brother, the Count of Artois. He had already published some volumes in defense of Christianity and his object in his *Lettres de
quelques Juifs* was to continue that effort. Guenée took no further part in the
debate about the Jews.

Jews who appeared after 1776 to argue the case for their rights were all therefore from eastern France.

Almost all of the figures within the Jewish community who participated in this argument were in the immediate orbit of Moses Mendelssohn. It was to Mendelssohn that Cerf Berr, the unquestioned leader of the Ashkenazim in France, turned for literary help in defense of the Jews of eastern France. Mendelssohn persuaded Christian Wilhelm Dohm, an official in the Prussian court, to write a volume in defense of the Jews. This book was conceived as an answer to the contemporary attack by the leader of Alsatian anti-Semitism, Hell. Dohm's essential argument was the one that had already been advanced by Pinto and Valabrègue, that the way to solve the Jewish problems was to change the conditions under which they lived.

The German original of Dohm's book (*Über die bürgerliche Verbesserung der Juden*) was being prepared in 1781, the very year during which the emperor of Austria, Joseph II, was known to be working on a new decree governing the life of the Jews in his empire. When this *Tolerenzpatent* finally appeared at the beginning of 1782 a summary of it was included in the French edition of Dohm's book, which appeared that year, with the additional comment that this decree was conceived in the spirit of Dohm's thinking. Mendelssohn's own reaction to the decree of Joseph II was equally positive, although he himself shortly had second thoughts. He soon saw a conversionist tendency. In his book *Jerusalem* he said, with proud anger, that if equal rights for Jews had to be purchased at the cost of their religion, Jews must forgo such a bargain.[109] At first blush, however, this "enlightened" act was hailed in France as an example to its new young monarch, Louis XVI. Naftali Herz Weisel, the most important figure in Mendelssohn's circle, reacted immediately to the decree of Joseph II by publishing his famous short book in Hebrew, *Divrei Shalom ve-Emet*. This volume was translated forthwith into French by the very first Jew in eastern France to appear in French letters, Berr Isaac Berr.

[109] Katz, "To Whom Was Mendelssohn Responding in his *Jerusalem*," *Zion*, XXIX, 112–32. On the debate between Mendelssohn and Dohm regarding the organized Jewish community, see the beginning of the next chapter.

He had been born in 1744, the youngest of the children of Isaac Berr, a rich banker, who was one of the three leaders of the Jewish community of Lorraine, a post which the son was in due course to occupy himself. Berr Isaac Berr had received a first-class talmudic education under Jacob Perle, the chief rabbi of Lorraine, but he also was taught French by private tutors.[110] As a literary man Berr Isaac Berr had made his debut in French, as did most of the other figures whom we have been discussing, by translating a patriotic religious service.[111] His publication of Weisel's work in French had a much more direct, contemporary purpose. The argument of this work turned in two directions. Facing the governments of Europe, Weisel had repeated with great eloquence the argument that the present estate of the Jews, and especially their lack of secular knowledge, had been created by persecution. Jews had only one crime, "that of being born of Jewish parents and of having followed their ancient faith." The Jews must indeed change their ways and add to their traditional religious studies the knowledge of science and European languages; the Jews must become "enlightened." This enlightenment would, however, be of no use if Jews remain excluded from all normal economic pursuits, including the professions. Weisel therefore hailed the work of Joseph II, for he saw it as the first step towards both objectives: reeducating the Jew and bringing him into society.

Both in Weisel's own time and later, the impact of this work led to many misunderstandings. The decree of Joseph II was far less pro-Jewish, and in many senses far more harmful, than Weisel understood. He has been much blamed for this enthusiasm. Moreover, the first half of the book made the case at such length for the modernization of Jewish education that the argument of the second

[110] For Berr Isaac Berr's biography see Carmoly, *La France israélite*, pp. 54–62. Berr's French translation of Weisel appeared under the title *Instruction salutaire adressée aux communautés juives qui habitent paisiblement les villes de la domination du Grand Empéreur Joseph II* (Berlin, 1782). This pamphlet was reprinted in Paris in 1790, during the battle before the *Assemblée Nationale* for the rights of Jews in eastern France. That edition was prefaced by an exchange of letters between Berr and the Abbé Maury, in which the latter remained unconvinced that the Jews could cease to be an *imperium in imperio*.

[111] Szajkowski, *Franco-Judaica*, Nos. 1651, 1660. These were two special services ordered by the syndics of Lorraine to pray for the health of Louis XV during his last illness, and then to mourn his death in 1774.

half—that it was up to the powers to make room for the new Jew
—tended to be obscured. The rabbis of central Europe attacked
Weisel immediately, and bitterly, as a heretic.[112] It is instructive
that no such comment was forthcoming from eastern France, not
even from such a pillar of the traditional faith as the aged chief
rabbi of Metz, Asser Lion. In the context of the immediate situation
in eastern France, Weisel's position, as translated by Berr, made
sense. The lay leaders of the depressed Jewry of the region were
then thinking very much along his lines. They imagined cultural
Westernization by the Jews as part of a "social compact" between
the Jews and the state. The Jews would do their share to regenerate
themselves if the state would only do its part by increasing their
economic opportunities. By 1782, in the twenty years since Pinto
had said it first, this argument had been the ever more crystallized
thesis of all pro-Jewish discussion of the problem of the Ashkenazim,
including their own writings about themselves. It must be added
that this discussion was proceeding in an age which imagined that
the solution of all social problems was to be found not in any
automatic processes but in direct governmental regulation and intervention.

[112] On the controversy occasioned by Weisel's views, the most convenient
summaries are in Waxman, A History of Jewish Literature, III, 114–20, and
Klausner, Modern Hebrew Literature, I, 120–34.

## ◄§ VII §►

## *The Jewish Community*

In the years immediately before the Revolution, the question of the organized Jewish community was at the very heart of the debate about the future of the Jews, producing overt conflict between most of the Jews and most of their friends among the gentiles. The leaders of both the Sephardim and the Ashkenazim continued to argue in the 1780s that the power of the organized Jewish community should be maintained and even strengthened. On the other hand, moderate gentile opinion was largely opposed to continuing any Jewish legal separatism. Even while such figures as Dohm and Mirabeau spoke for maintaining some Jewish autonomy, they envisaged this as a transitory phenomenon; the organized Jewish community would wither away and die as the Jews entered fully into the economic and social life of the majority.[1] Towards the end of his life, in the 1780s, the acknowledged intellectual leader of the "enlightened" Jews in Europe, Moses Mendelssohn, was openly

[1] In making his proposals for the future Dohm did advance the suggestions that Jews should continue to have their autonomous communal structure, and that they should retain the power of excommunication. The right to live and be judged by their own laws was part of giving them "full employment of the rights which belong to them as men" (*Réforme politique,* pp. 163–66). Nonetheless, this must be read in the light of two other elements in his book. One was the fact that he had been commissioned by Cerf Berr to answer Hell; the appendix to Dohm's volume contained the *mémoire* of the Alsatian Jews, which strongly pleaded for increased powers of inner control for the rabbis and the *parnassim.* Dohm himself argued, in his own name, that legal equality for the Jews would soon bring a modification in the Sabbath law so that they could serve in the army; indeed, he continued, the separatist rigor of Jewish law, in general, would change the moment that the Jews could regard society as their own (pp. 190–92). It is implicit (though Dohm did not make it explicit) that Jewish legal autonomy would soon disappear, by the choice of the Jews. Mirabeau managed in the same short book to praise Mendelssohn for his be-

and forthrightly opposed to maintaining any Jewish communal separatism. Having defined Judaism as a religion, he argued that it had no right to ask for more than free assent from its believers. Nevertheless, Cerf Berr and his circle, despite their very close relationship to Mendelssohn, were entirely opposed to him on this point.[2]

The Sephardim in France were as adamantly committed to maintaining the jurisdiction of the Jewish community as were the Ashkenazim. In 1773 the oligarchs in Bordeaux again proceeded to strengthen their authority over stray Jews who were trying to move into the city.[3] Four years later their agent in Paris, Péreire, was very pleased to accede to a request from the police of that city (a request he had undoubtedly engineered) that he be the official registrar of all arriving Jews who claimed to be Sephardim and that he decide whether they had valid reason to remain in the city. In a parallel action the police asked the agent of the Jews of Metz, Hadamar, to perform a comparable function among the Ashkenazim.[4] As we have already seen in several connections, in the 1770s

---

lief in the absolute separation of church and state and to agree with Dohm that the internal authority of the rabbis over the Jews should be upheld by the state (*Sur Moses Mendelssohn*, pp. 24–25, 88–89). The total drift of Mirabeau's argument is to presume that equality would ultimately obviate the need for any special policing of the Jews by their own authorities and that it would wean them from their separatism. See also Chapter X.

[2] Mendelssohn's mature views on Judaism and the prospects for equality for the Jews were in his *Jerusalem*, which appeared in 1783. He argued directly against Dohm's proposal that Jews retain the right of excommunication: "Neither the state nor the church has the right to compel belief" (*Gesammelte Schriften*, III, 319). Mendelssohn first answered Dohm almost immediately at length in the introduction to the German edition in 1782 of Menasseh ben Israel's *Vindiciae Judaeorum* (*ibid.*, pp. 193–202; and Rotenstreich, introduction to the Hebrew translation of *Jerusalem*, in *Small Writings on Judaism*).

[3] The syndics decreed on December 26, 1773, that those who lodged any new Jewish arrival had to inform the community within twenty-four hours; the beadle had to keep his own independent check and he was equally responsible for informing the syndics (*Registre*, No. 417). This internal decision was given the force of law in 1787 when the municipal authorities of Bordeaux decreed that the Sephardim could and should police all Jewish strangers, both for the interests of the police and to further the need the Sephardim themselves felt "to spare themselves the embarrassments which came from popular prejudices, which associated them with whatever difficulties others of their religion had with the law." This decree is listed in Szajkowski, *Franco-Judaica*, No. 280; see, in general, Cirot, *Recherches*, pp. 70–72.

[4] The official letter to Péreire from Lenoir, the head of the police in Paris,

and 1780s both of the major segments of French Jewry were ever more involved in attempting to control the increase in the population of the poor and to remake into "useful" people those who remained in France. The Jewish community was itself bidding for the role of becoming the direct agent for "improving" the mass of Jews, and Jewish leadership was everywhere asking for more authority in order to be equal to these tasks.

Despite the apparent increase in the powers of the organized Jewish community in the years immediately before the Revolution, it would be wrong to deduce that Jewish internal organizations were becoming stronger. The contrary is true. Late in the eighteenth century the corporate Jewish bodies all over Europe were in ever greater financial trouble. Communal taxes were becoming harder and harder to collect, especially in those areas where smaller towns were subservient to larger cities or to regional structures.[5] This larger process was very much at work in eastern France. The *parnassim* in Metz kept trying, without great success, to force the Jews in the surrounding countryside, the *pays messin*, to pay a substantial portion of a communal budget. The Jewish provincial organization in Alsace was having trouble with many of its constituent communities.

And there were other internal battles. Powerful figures or groups fought each other, often over clashing economic interests, and the

was dated November 15, 1777. A printed copy of the document is in the archives of the Israel Historical Society in Jerusalem; see also Detcheverry, *Histoire des Israélites de Bordeaux*, pp. 108–109. Hadamar was first appointed in 1761 for three years at the derisory salary of 60 livres a year, for very part-time services (Metz *Pinkas*, 40b). This post was given to Moshe Bischa in the winter of 1785; he was appointed for a term of six years at the salary of 600 livres per year (*Pinkas*, 131a). Hadamar had moved back to Metz in April, 1784; a local businessman sued him later that year and specified that he had recently returned to Metz (Szajkowski, *Franco-Judaica*, No. 698). For Hadamar's services to the French authorities in Paris see Hildenfinger, *Documents*, pp. 190–94, 196–98. After Péreire's death in 1780 he was succeeded by David Silveyra (*ibid.*, p. 256). On December 7, 1777, the syndics of Bordeaux met to honor Péreire for obtaining the *lettres patentes* of 1776 and for his appointment by Lenoir, the lieutenant-general of the police, to be in control of Sephardi arrivals. The Sephardim were quite upset that all kinds of Jews were settling in Paris and pretending to be Sephardim. This new control would keep other Jews from using rights that belonged only to the Portuguese and it would save the Portuguese embarrassments caused by their being identified with the bad conduct of such people (*Registre*, No. 455).

[5] Baron, *The Jewish Community*, II, 351–63.

controlling elite of bankers, army purveyors, and shipowners was more and more hated by the masses. These fights were taking place in public, often as legal actions in various civil courts. In Bordeaux the Sephardim had largely succeeded in their attack on the Jews from Avignon, but the hidden cost of the victory appeared in the form of a debate in French opinion, far from complimentary, about the Jews as a whole and about the authority of the Jewish community. In Metz, despite all the efforts of the community, some of its richest figures did not hesitate to step outside the internal Jewish law courts in the hope of getting satisfaction in the civil courts.

This fraying of communal authority was, however, not the most significant factor in the definition of the question of Jewish autonomy on the eve of the Revolution. There was another basic element in the situation, a premise unique to France. It was little noticed in its own time and no attention has been paid to it thereafter, precisely because it was not overt. From their very roots in the sixteenth century, a crucial difference had arisen between the communal structures of the Sephardim and the Ashkenazim. The Portuguese communities had arrived in southwestern France as marranos, whereas the Ashkenazim had begun in Alsace and Lorraine as avowed Jews. In most respects the Jewish communities that arose in both places were comparable in their structures and in their powers, but the differences were crucial. As the Sephardim ceased being marranos towards the end of the seventeenth century and organized Jewish communities in the open, they never acquired, or even attempted to acquire, civil jurisdiction over cases involving Jews. They continued their pattern of recourse to French courts, and they were ever more conscious of the fact that this made them more like the Christian subjects of the crown.[6] This was totally unlike

[6] In 1753 the intendant de Tourny proposed that all the Jews in Bordeaux, including the Sephardim, be evaluated for their usefulness to the state and that those who were not of any value be expelled, regardless of the legal precedents. The syndics responded to this threat with a petition to Paris in which they argued for the rights of the Portuguese Jews in France. The climactic point was that the Dutch and other merchant communities in Bordeaux were subject to the law of France and to no jurisprudence that was particular to themselves; therefore, they could not be expelled on simple suspicion, without due legal process. The Portuguese Jews had the right to claim the same safeguards "because they participate in the same justice and they ought there-

the situation in eastern France, where the Jewish community fought hard to the very end for civil jurisdiction over Jews. Long before the Revolution the Sephardi community existed for religious and charitable functions but, unlike the Ashkenazi community, it did not have its own law courts. Here in embryo was a rough distinction between "church and state," between the private business of the Jews and their participation in the larger society. In the immediate debate that led to the Emancipation, the existence of this model had large consequences. The Sephardi and the Ashkenazi communities both discharged religious and charitable functions; these were universally acknowledged as proper. Almost as universally, legal separatism, which did not exist among the more acculturated Sephardim, was condemned as obnoxious.

It would be an exaggeration to maintain that the major causes for the dissolution of the organized Jewish community by the Revolution came from within Jewish experience. Among the Sephardim themselves even purely religious compulsion, which the community had always exercised from the day it became avowedly Jewish, was eroding in the last decades before the Revolution. As we have seen, Azulai found Deists and breakers of the ritual law among the Sephardi leaders in France during his second trip to that country in the winter of 1777–78. These changes were taking place because contemporary thinking about religion was making itself felt among Jews. It was an increasing certainty among all the modernists of all the faiths that even with regard to internal dogmas and practices compulsion was wrong. The largest cause of all for the abolition of the organized Jewish community was, of course, the over-riding principle in the name of which the Revolution was made: the abolition of all special status and special exception. However, the Sephardi community that had evolved towards the end of the eighteenth century was of considerable significance. It was very much in the minds of those who thought about Jews. The two forces that the emancipators of the Jews wanted to use in order to

fore to be judged by all of the same laws, including those which guarantee the safety of individuals; they are subject to the local judge wherever they live, and their status ought to be the same as that of other subjects of His Majesty" (*Registre,* No. 219).

improve the Jews of eastern France were broader rights legislated by the state and an inner loosening of the tight Jewish ghetto. The Sephardim provided an example of both, before the Revolution.

The differences between Sephardi and Ashkenazi communal patterns in France did not derive from immemorial roots in the separate traditions of these two Jewries. Before the expulsion from Spain the Sephardim had exercised such broad autonomous judicial powers, both civil and criminal, that in some places they could even impose the death penalty.[7] The communities that the exiles created after 1492 did not all regard it as a benefit that their civil cases were tried in general courts. In Venice, for example, they fought a losing battle against the city over the imposition of its civil jurisdiction upon them.[8] In London, on the other hand, the situation paralleled that in Bordeaux. The first *ascamot* (communal regulations), which were adopted in 1664, prescribed that Jews must first attempt to arbitrate their business disputes before the authorities of the Sephardi community; if that failed they were free to go to the general courts of law.[9] It is instructive that in London as in Bordeaux the Jews had been admitted through a back door, without formal recognition.

There were, thus, two types of Jewish community in France in the eighteenth century. Their differences figure in the events that led to the Emancipation, and they were ended by the acts of 1790 and 1791. The Revolution put an end to the structure of Jewish self-government; yet, in all respects in which both these communities were similar before the Revolution, the patterns of their inner cohesion largely persisted thereafter. Both the similarities and the differences require more detailed discussion.

[7] Baron, *The Jewish Community*, II, 71–75, 241.
[8] Roth, *The History of the Jews of Italy*, pp. 368–69. The situation in Italy was not uniform. In the Papal States Jewish legal autonomy was suppressed, except for strictly religious matters around 1700; Jewish civil jurisdiction persisted in Leghorn, Modena, and Mantua.
[9] Hyamson, *The Sephardim of England*, p. 29.

## Cemeteries, Abattoirs, Synagogues, and Schools

Every Jewish community throughout history almost invariably has begun its corporate existence by acquiring a cemetery. The Sephardim, having arrived as marranos, were inevitably first buried with the rites of the Church in the cemeteries of the various parishes to which they formally belonged. Indeed, the cutting edge of their coming out into the open as Jews was their acquisition of cemeteries of their own. The pattern was the same in all their places of settlement. They first acquired a separate burial ground, which was given to them in their quality as "Portuguese merchants." Towards the end of the seventeenth century and in the early years of the eighteenth this separate piece of ground or some other land that was acquired by an organized communal body became an avowed Jewish cemetery.

The first and most rapid example of the entire process took place not in the major communities of Bayonne and Bordeaux but in the village of Peyrehorade. The noble House of Orèthe sold the Portuguese a cemetery of their own in 1628. It is not at all clear whether they were permitted at this early date to dispense with the services of the Catholic clergy, but it cannot be doubted that they were burying their dead as Jews fifty years later; a tombstone of the year 1678 bore the Jewish date 5438. In the nearby town of Bidache, on the territory of the Duke of Gramont, there was a Jewish cemetery as early as 1669; here a Jewish date appeared on a tombstone in 1677.[10]

The two major Jewish communities, in Bayonne and Bordeaux, acquired their first separate cemeteries later than in Peyrehorade. In 1654 one of the parishes of St. Esprit, the suburb of Bayonne where Jews were permitted, assigned a separate piece of ground for the burial of the Portuguese. In the year 1671 this piece was formally ceded to the Portuguese community. In those days it is likely that Jewish dead were still being buried without overt Jewish ceremonies, but it is possible that at least there were already no

---

[10] E. Ginsburger, "Les Juifs de Peyrehorade," *REJ*, CIII, 36; Léon, *Histoire des Juifs de Bayonne*, pp. 196–97. Inscriptions in the Hebrew language did not appear until 1712 in Bidache and 1720 in Peyrehorade.

Catholic ones either. That Jewish funeral practices came into the open in Bayonne soon thereafter is quite certain. In 1689 the ground of the existing Jewish cemetery was taken over by the crown, which intended to build fortifications there. The year before the Jews had bought their own cemetery and by 1693 an inscription in Hebrew appeared on a tombstone. After that such inscriptions occurred as a matter of course.[11]

The situation in Bordeaux was more complicated. In the sixteenth and seventeenth centuries the Portuguese were buried as Christians in the cemeteries of the Catholic parishes in which they lived. Towards the end of the seventeenth century they began to be buried not by the parishes but in the cemeteries of four convents. The quality of the deceased as Jews was now being avowed; the convents were much more cooperative than the parishes in allowing Jews to be buried without Christian ceremonies. The first truly separate Jewish cemetery was not acquired until 1710. The very first entry in the minute book of the *Sedaca* recorded a decision to lend the monastery of the Cordeliers 600 livres in order to have a separate piece of ground for the burial of the Portuguese. The *Sedaca* also agreed to enclose this new cemetery with a wall. At this point there existed a society to perform the Jewish burial rites (*hebera kaddisha*), and as the head of such an organization Alexander Mezes figured in the establishment of this cemetery. Indeed, he personally lent the community the money necessary for the acquisition of the ground.[12] In Bordeaux the *hebera kaddisha* was not in control of the cemetery. The right to be buried there was used, from the beginning, as an effective incentive to pay communal taxes. In 1745 the rule was made explicit that no one could be buried in the cemetery without permission of the head of the *Sedaca*.[13]

Towards the end of 1736 the whole matter of Jewish funerals in Bordeaux was completely freed of all memory of the community's marrano past. A royal decree directed that after January 1, 1737, Jewish funerals should be registered with the civil authorities in Bordeaux and formal permission should be granted by them. The

---

[11] Léon, *Histoire des Juifs de Bayonne*, pp. 199–211.
[12] *Registre*, No. 1.  [13] *Registre*, Nos. 45, 124.

Church, therefore, had nothing further to do with the situation, **not** even as a complacent bystander. Later that year, in September, the *Sedaca* itself appointed someone, at a salary of 100 livres a year, to keep a register of births and deaths; such records were kept throughout the eighteenth century until the era of the Revolution. The very last instance of the *Sedaca's* involvement in the question of a cemetery was in 1764, when the community bought an additional piece of ground at a price upwards of 11,000 livres. In order to finance the cost the *Sedaca* borrowed funds that had accumulated for the support of its educational facilities. It needs to be added that, despite the bad feeling between the Sephardim in Bordeaux and all the other Jews who had settled in the community, and especially those from Avignon, the *Sedaca* never made any difficulty whatsoever over burying other Jews in its cemetery.[14] It is to be presumed, since these others were not taxpayers in the *Sedaca*, that those who could afford it paid the Portuguese for this service.

In eastern France the acquisition of Jewish cemeteries was a more straightforward process. In the course of time a network of regional cemeteries was acquired. Some of these, such as the cemeteries in Rosenweiler and Ettendorf, existed as early as the sixteenth century. There was a Jewish cemetery in Haguenau far back into the Middle Ages, but the earliest tombstone in the presently existing cemetery dates from 1654. The cemetery at Selestat is known to have been established in 1622. The one at Jungholz, which was serving thirty-five Jewish settlements in Upper Alsace towards the end of the eighteenth century, was established in 1655. At that time there were no Jews actually living in Jungholz, but a group representing Jews in nearby towns bought a cemetery from the noble family of Schauenburg. This ground was enlarged several times through further purchases during the eighteenth century. The cemetery was administered by a regional organization, which derived its funds not from contributions by the various communities, but by directly taxing individuals; the local representatives to the administrative body seem to have acted as collectors. The administrators were under the authority of the provincial Jewish organization; in 1787 they asked permission from Cerf Berr, in his capacity as syndic of

[14] Cirot, *Recherches*, pp. 139–42; *Registre*, No. 326.

all the Jews in Alsace, to tax the people who used this cemetery in order to raise 1,000 livres with which to pay the cost of erecting a fence.[15]

The most important Jewish community in eastern France was, of course, in Metz. The formal admission of the first Jews to Metz in 1567 must have required immediate arrangements for Jewish burials, but all traces of the earliest cemetery have been both lost and forgotten. The first record appeared in 1619, when the Jews were allowed to establish a cemetery at the edge of the neighborhood in which they lived, at the Porte Chambière. There were two difficulties with this piece of ground: it was on the bank of the river Moselle and thus subject to flooding, and some of the royal fortifications of the city were nearby. In 1690 the Jewish community of Metz, having grown, had to purchase additional ground for a new cemetery. Concurrently, it made the substantial contribution of 20,000 livres to the royal project of building fortifications for the city. This payment was made to defray the cost of building the new battlements in such fashion that the old Jewish cemetery would not be disturbed. The community also contributed a large sum, variously given as 35,000 or 50,000 francs, to the building of an embankment, so that the river would not flood this sacred ground. There were several further attempts in the eighteenth century to take away the Jewish cemetary and use the ground for military purposes, but the community always succeeded in fighting off the threat.[16]

Every Jewish community must be supplied with kosher meat. There is no record of how this was managed in the course of the seventeenth century by the Portuguese, or whether they even dared engage in kosher slaughtering. As early as 1711 an abattoir existed in Bordeaux, as a facility owned by the Jewish community. It was leased out in that year to a private enterprise for 465 livres a year, and by 1752 the cost of this lease had risen to 3,400 livres.[17] A bakery for the production of matzot also existed in Bordeaux throughout the eighteenth century and it was equally a monopoly

[15] M. Ginsburger, *Israelitische Friedhof*, pp. 11–31; Scheid, *Juifs d'Alsace*, pp. 269–319; Joseph Bloch, "Le cimetière," *REJ*, CXI, 141–59.

[16] Netter, "Les anciens cimetières," *REJ*, LI, 280–302; LII, 98–113; M. Ginsburger, "Les anciens cimetières," *REJ*, LII, 272–83.

[17] *Registre*, Nos. 4, 195.

of the *Sedaca;* in 1762 its lease brought 600 livres. Access to the ritual bath was also controlled by the syndics. The poor were permitted there without the payment of a fee, but the keeper of the bath was specifically forbidden to permit anyone to have access to it without permission of the syndics.[18] The price of both matzot and kosher meat depended on whether the consumer was a taxpayer and therefore of some financial substance, or a receiver of charity. In Bordeaux a tax of 5 per cent was levied on kosher meat in the middle of the eighteenth century, for the support of Jewish education.[19] There is no record in Bordeaux of any trouble with the gentile guilds over the existence of the Jewish abattoir; even in Bayonne, where the local guilds consistently fought with the Jews, the matter of Jewish enterprise in the supply of their own meat was never a cause for battle.

In this area, too, the situation was somewhat different in eastern France. In the various territories of Alsace the right to have an abattoir was controlled by the local powers, either noblemen or cities, and the Jews had problems with gentile butchers who had leased that right. The major stumbling block was the fact that Jews did not eat the hindquarters, and thus sold them to gentiles. Furthermore, since many more animals generally had to be slaughtered than the ultimate number that were pronounced kosher, the Jewish abattoir always had meat to sell to the general grade. The resolution of these quarrels tended to take several forms. First, the Jews had to offer for sale to the gentile butchers the meat they did not use; only if they refused could Jews sell it directly to non-Jews. The number of animals that Jews were permitted to kill was often fixed and regulated; if the Jews needed more they had to obtain such animals from the gentile butchers. In some places Jews rented directly from noblemen the right to have their own abattoirs.[20] Indeed, in the Alsatian Jewish *mémoire* of 1717 in which they asked for a general charter of economic and communal liberty, one of the

[18] *Registre,* Nos. 83, 193.

[19] The constitution of the school organized by the syndics at the end of 1760 specified that the manager of the facility for kosher meat had to remit every three months the proceeds of a tax of 5 per cent on the meat to the treasurer of this *Thalmud Thora* ( *Registre,* No. 280).

[20] Hoffman, *L'Alsace,* IV, 343–44.

requests was for the right to keep a butcher shop wherever there were more than six families in one place, on the understanding that they would sell their meat at a price substantially higher than the price prevailing in the general trade.[21] In Metz, Jews undoubtedly had the right to provide their own meat supply from the very beginning of their settlement. The first formal document dates from 1636, when the Jews were permitted to slaughter animals for their own food with the understanding that they would pay imposts levied on this activity equal to those paid by all other butchers. At that point the number of animals they were permitted to kill was fixed but this restriction was lifted in 1674. In the eighteenth century the Jewish abattoir in Metz was being used by a number of Jewish butchers who were private entrepreneurs under the supervision of the community.[22]

In eastern France to an even greater degree than among the Portuguese, the tax on kosher meat was a basic form of continuing taxation to help support the Jewish communal budget. Indeed, anti-Semites were arguing as late as 1780 that the permission for Jews to sell unused hindquarters in the general trade represented an indirect form of taxing Christians to support the organized Jewish community.[23]

Cemeteries and the supply of kosher meat are by their very nature public functions. Such services could be arranged only through some form of permission by government and it generally required community organization to arrange for them. A synagogue is a

[21] Pour les Juifs établis en Alsace, p. 3.

[22] Clément, La condition des Juifs, pp. 160–61. Among the permanent officials of the Metz Jewish community there was a beadle who was charged with keeping account of the number of animals that were slaughtered and declared kosher in the abattoir (obviously so that taxes on meat levied by the communal organization would be paid in full). In 1761 a committee of butchers was appointed to control the quality of the meat; seven years later they were replaced by a board of five inspectors who were charged with overseeing every aspect of the abattoir, including the prices the butchers charged. Regular elections for this board were held every three years thereafter (Pinkas, 4a, 37a, 69a).

[23] In Bollwiller the Jews had to pay the seigneur a tax of 16 sols, 8 deniers per ox, and 13 sols, 4 deniers per cow. The Jewish community collected instead 40 sols per animal from the lessee of the kosher abattoir and used its profits to help support the communal budget. The local bailli Jacquot (who disliked Jews) argued in a complaint to the intendant that ultimately all of this was paid by Christians (Hoffman, L'Alsace, IV, 345).

different matter, for it is possible for Jews to conduct a formal religious service wherever ten adult males can be gathered together to make up a quorum. As occasional or even as continuing bodies such congregations can exist in private homes. For that matter, much more formal, communal congregations could be housed in buildings or parts of buildings, with tacit permission of the authorities, without any public sign of their function. This was the situation in Bordeaux and Bayonne. Though the practice of Judaism was overt in Bordeaux by 1707, there was no open synagogue. A visitor eight years later attested to the fact that the existence of regular Jewish worship was well known but there was no public place of worship.[24] Throughout the eighteenth century a number of synagogues existed in various private houses. The Gradis family even maintained one of its own. The Jews from Avignon had their own place of worship, and Ephraim, the hero of the battle over the supervision of kosher wine, kept a synagogue in his house for the Ashkenazi Jews. The community itself maintained a synagogue, that of the *Hebera*,[25] and it was very likely in existence before 1710. In Bordeaux the *Hebera* performed most of the religious functions throughout the eighteenth century. Unlike in Bayonne, however, where the *Hebera* grew into becoming the overarching communal organization, in Bordeaux it remained subject to the control of the syndics of the *Sedaca*.

The existence of synagogues was both equally well known and equally semi-clandestine in Bayonne. In 1710 the clergy of a collegiate church in St. Esprit complained that the Jews were chanting too loudly in their synagogue, which was very near the church. The governor of Bayonne forbade this practice but gave the Jews permission to assemble for prayer in another house some distance away.[26] Azulai attested to the fact that he worshiped and preached during his first stay in Bayonne in 1756 in a dozen synagogues.[27] All of them were conventicles maintained on the premises of in-

[24] Léon, *Histoire des Juifs de Bayonne*, p. 46; Detcheverry, *Histoire des Israélites de Bordeaux*, p. 112.

[25] Cirot, *Recherches*, p. 178. The list of synagogues that he gave was based on all those mentioned in the registers of the ritual-circumcisers in the eighteenth century.

[26] Anchel, *Les Juifs de France*, p. 140.

[27] Azulai, *Maagal Tov*, pp. 36–37.

dividual families; the most important was kept by the Brandon family on the third floor of a building of theirs. In 1750 the Bayonne community acquired a building in which it established housing for its rabbi as well as facilities for its school and matzot factory. A synagogue was established in this building, but the more centrally located Brandon synagogue seems to have remained throughout the eighteenth century and beyond as the major place of worship of the Jewish community. The city authorities of Bayonne in 1765 made a point of the fact that even at that late date none of the existing synagogues had any legal recognition; this was despite the fact, not mentioned in that brief, that the constitution of the Jewish community in Bayonne had been given royal approval a dozen years earlier.[28]

In Paris the situation was even more tenuous, for the obvious reason that the Jews had no right to live there at all. Nevertheless, after 1721 there were two Jewish hotels in the capital and prayer services were held in them, albeit with some secrecy. There were also even more private synagogues. The police persecuted these religious expressions. Once they even confiscated all the religious objects, including two Torah scrolls, that they found in the apartment of Jacob Worms, a Metz banker and army purveyor who spent much time in Paris. Nevertheless, both Jacob Worms and Samuel Lévy, when they were in the Bastille in the 1720s, managed to arrange, no doubt by paying the guards, to have kosher food brought to them; they were permitted to observe the Sabbath and say their daily prayers. Even some ritual slaughter for the provision of kosher meat managed to exist in Paris in the course of the eighteenth century.[29] It became public and overt in 1765 that there were synagogues in Paris. The Jews from Avignon and those from Bordeaux held their first patriotic services then and printed the texts.[30] As we shall soon see, this was the way in which the Sephardim in both Bayonne and Bordeaux "naturalized" their synagogues.

In eastern France the synagogues were not at all clandestine. In the various smaller communities of Alsace prayer services were held

[28] Léon, *Histoire des Juifs de Bayonne*, pp. 223–24, 91.

[29] L. Kahn, *Les Juifs de Paris au dix-huitième siècle*, pp. 41–45.

[30] The occasion was the illness of the dauphin; see Szajkowski, *Franco-Judaica*, No. 1679.

everywhere without any attempt to be discreet, though in most
places there were no separate synagogue buildings. Haguenau was
an exception; there was a separate synagogue building there in the
thirteenth century. When the city became French in 1648 permission for the building of a synagogue was soon obtained and that
edifice was dedicated in 1665; a public synagogue was maintained
there throughout the eighteenth century. The synagogues of Alsace
did not have a happy destiny, for they were frequently the objects
of vandalism by Jew-haters. The one in Haguenau was destroyed
by arson in 1676 but was rebuilt seven years later.[31] In Metz a communal synagogue existed by the middle years of the seventeenth
century. As we have seen, Louis XIV visited the building when he
was in Metz in 1656. In 1745 Eibeschütz preached a sermon at the
great event of the rebuilding of the communal synagogue.[32] The
community as a whole also owned a subsidiary synagogue, the
*Klaus,* which had been created by a pious foundation around 1700.
In the course of time, through establishment by gifts or because of
various communal pressures and quarrels, other synagogues arose.
There was constant battle between the leaders of the official community and the other synagogues and private conventicles. Offerings made at the main synagogue were a source of income to the
community, and the celebration of religious occasions elsewhere
diminished this revenue.[33] In Nancy the first Jewish families to be
admitted by the Duke of Lorraine prayed in private homes, but in
1737 formal permission was given for the erection of a synagogue.
This building was enlarged in 1788.[34]

In the course of the eighteenth century both the Sephardim and
the Ashkenazim took great pains to recognize patriotic occasions.
In part, especially among the Sephardim, the motive was to bolster
their de facto right to have synagogues. By getting royal representatives graciously to accept these Jewish gestures (the order of service

[31] Scheid, *Juifs de Haguenau,* pp. 3, 78–80.
[32] Eibeschütz, *Sefer Yaarot Devash,* I, 41d.
[33] The sumptuary laws of 1769 contained the injunction that "no one could
pray in his own home, with a quorum of ten men, the fine being 3 livres for
each transgression" (*Pinkas,* 76b). Ten years later it was ruled that any individual who held such a service in his home had to pay 30 livres for each
occasion (*Pinkas,* 105b).
[34] D. Kahn, "Le ghetto de Nancy," *Revue juive de Lorraine,* VIII, 253–56.

was invariably printed and sent to the intendant or a comparable official) they established a desirable precedent. The earliest report of such a patriotic service is from 1706, when one was supposedly held in a synagogue in Bordeaux on the occasion of the birth of one of the royal princes. A printed copy of the order of prayer is not known to exist. Such occasions did, however, become quite usual in the middle of the century. Louis XV's trip to Metz in 1744 to be with his armies and his dangerous illness there gave rise to patriotic gestures both in Metz itself and in southeastern France. When the king arrived in Metz, the Jewish quarter was decorated in keeping with the adornments of the rest of the city. The synagogue itself was hung with tapestries and all the Torah silver was put on display. A delegation of the Jewish community participated in the reception for the king and one of their number even delivered an address in French.[35] During the king's illness there was a special service of intercession at the synagogue in Metz.[36] Comparable services took place in Bordeaux. The service in Bordeaux was, in fact, published in two editions, one in Spanish for local use and the other in French in Paris.[37] After this event there was not a single occasion in the life of the royal family that was not marked by such prayer services, especially among the Sephardim.[38] This tradition of patriotic services persisted into the era of Revolution and the time of Napoleon. The largest function of all these occasions both before 1789 and thereafter was to suggest that the Jews regarded themselves as an integral part of French society and the printing of these

[35] Begin, "Voyage," AIF, IV, 735–36.
[36] Szajkowski, Franco-Judaica, No. 1650.
[37] Ibid., Nos. 1664–66; these texts are in the JTS Library.
[38] The Registre in Bordeaux mentions a number of such patriotic occasions: an order on January 12, 1757, by the syndics for a day of prayer and fasting in reaction to Damiens' attempt to assassinate Louis XV (No. 251); intercession during the illness of the dauphin in 1765 (No. 341); prayers during the last illness of Louis XV in 1774 (No. 423); a special service, the birth of Louis XVI's son in 1781 (No. 495) and his second son in 1789 (No. 1784). On June 30, 1780, the princes of Conde and Bourbon visited the synagogue when they were in Bordeaux (No. 479) and in 1786 the syndics had a portrait of Louis XVI hung in their board room (No. 545). There were more special services in Bordeaux than were recorded in the communal minutes, and the Jews in Bayonne, Paris, Metz, and Alsace were as busy as those in Bordeaux in marking patriotic occasions. See Szajkowski, Franco-Judaica, Nos. 1648–82, for a bibliography of such services; many of these texts are in the JTS Library.

services was part of the campaign of the Jews to be recognized as such.

Everywhere, among both the Sephardim and the Ashkenazim, the community as a whole accepted the obligation of providing for the education of the children of the poor. The continuing concern of the Ashkenazim for both elementary and higher Jewish education has already been mentioned in other connections. Some further details about the involvements of the communal organizations should be added here. When compulsory education was decreed in Metz in 1689, all children below the age of fourteen were required to go to school for the full day and those between fourteen and eighteen had to attend at least one hour of class each day. Parents who disobeyed the rule were threatened with expulsion from the city.[39] In 1751 the community created a central elementary school. This institution had two major divisions; the Bible was taught in the elementary class and advanced Talmud and the commentaries, as well as the legal codes, were taught in the higher class. This central school was financed by the interest on funds that had been left in various wills, as well as by special additional taxation.[40] In Alsace, because of the scattered nature of the Jewish population, no such central elementary school was possible. The provincial communal body continued to subsidize the tuition of the children of the poor in private schools to the end of the *ancien régime*.[41]

It seems clear that the organized communities in Bayonne and Bordeaux accepted responsibility for Jewish education at a very early date. The minute book of the Jews in Bordeaux, which was begun in 1710, has no mention of the founding of a school. The earliest entry concerning Jewish education was in 1731, when the incumbent teacher at the school maintained by the community was fired for unspecified reasons. The text of that entry, and of the further minutes in which the rabbi Jacob Haim Athias was appointed head of the school, implied that this institution had long been in existence. This school, and its successors, also served those who

[39] A. Cahen, "Enseignement," *REJ*, II, 303–305.  [40] *Pinkas*, 6b.
[41] *Extract from the minutes of the provincial organisation of the meeting on Iyyar 21, 5537* (in Yiddish and Hebrew), clause 24 (copy in the JTS Library); on Jewish education in general, among both the Sephardim and Ashkenazim, see also Chapter VI.

could pay tuition.[42] In Bayonne there existed as early as 1709 an organization called the *Santa Yesiba;* this was probably a brother-hood concerned with Jewish education, though it is possible, in the Sephardi usage of such terms, that this group existed for charitable rather than educational purposes.[43]

The Jewish school in Bordeaux seems to have disappeared in the middle years of the century, for it was refounded in 1760. Its ad-ministration consisted of a committee that was appointed by the leaders of the *Sedaca* and was responsible to that body. The course of study was Hebrew language and grammar, the Bible translated into Spanish, and the prayer book. The health of the children was checked, especially against communicable diseases, by the doctors of the community. The poor families who were on the list of those supported by the *Sedaca* were ordered to send their children to this school or be penalized by denial of any further support. This set of rules was twice amended, in the years 1761 and 1767, but there apparently was continuing difficulty in maintaining the institution. In 1772 a number of individuals petitioned that it be reconstituted and that a tax of 5 per cent be put on the kosher meat in order to provide its budget; the *Sedaca* approved the request.[44] In 1774 what amounted to a new constitution for a reorganized school was passed. The most interesting element in these new rules had to do with curriculum. It was ordered that the students be taught "Hebrew grammar as perfectly as possible and that they be instructed in our best commentators: that is to say, those who were themselves the best grammarians and were therefore most attached to the literal sense of the Bible, which is the sole means of discovering the true commandments which God has enjoined upon us." For the first time French and arithmetic were introduced as part of the regular curriculum.[45] On the evidence of this curriculum, with its clear bias against the Talmud, it is no wonder at all that Azulai was outraged when he visited this school three years later.

There was never a *yeshivah* in Bordeaux. There may have been, at least during the first half of the eighteenth century, some higher

[42] *Registre,* Nos. 58, 62.
[43] Léon, *Histoire des Juifs de Bayonne,* pp. 364–65.
[44] *Registre,* Nos. 273, 280 (the statutes of 1761), 400.
[45] *Registre,* No. 422.

Jewish learning in Bayonne, but even there such an effort took the form, at most, of a study circle of local residents who had some education in the Talmud. Unlike those in Amsterdam, the Sephardim of France did not regard it as their immediate responsibility to establish and support a center for higher Jewish education. On the other hand, even during periods of economic stress the Ashkenazim never wavered in accepting responsibility for attempting to remain an international center of Jewish learning. To be sure, the academies in Metz and in Alsace were not as distinguished as those in Bohemia and Poland, but to the very end of the eighteenth century they were serious and respected.

The Sephardi and Ashkenazi conceptions of the content of Jewish education were radically different long before the Revolution. Quite apart from the Deistic flavor of the Sephardi curriculum, the social assumptions that underlay it presumed an entry by choice of all Jews into the culture of the general society. In communal terms they were, however, in agreement: both Sephardim and Ashkenazim regarded education as an unquestionable responsibility of the organized community.

## Religious Controls and Controversies

Both the Sephardim and Ashkenazim were vitally concerned with policing Jewish religious conduct. We have already noted that in 1755 Azulai was called upon in Bordeaux to decide an issue involving one of the ritual slaughterers in the congregation; he reluctantly decided against the views of the incumbent rabbi, Jacob Haim Athias.[46] The question of supervision of the making of kosher wine was, as we have seen, a cause of friction, both within Bordeaux and with other communities that would not accept local Sephardi supervision as adequate. A major and most troublesome religious problem, both in Bordeaux and Bayonne, was the issue of Jewish marriages. In Jewish religious law a marriage is valid if it is contracted in the proper form in the presence of two witnesses. No permission is required from any authority, but the organized communities of the

[46] Azulai, *Maagal Tov,* p. 36; Azulai's decision was written into the *Registre* in Hebrew in his own hand (No. 240).

Sephardim could not countenance such laxness. If such were permitted, young people would be marrying without the consent of their parents and nothing could be done about it. As we have noted earlier, the Sephardi communal authorities repeatedly forbade the practice and such marriages were even annulled on a number of occasions. The last such act to be recorded took place in Bordeaux in 1783. The tribunal convoked for that purpose is of especial interest. Despite all the old tensions and battles of the Sephardim with the other Jews in Bordeaux, this court of religious law consisted of the Sephardi rabbi, David Athias; Mordecai Tama, the rabbi of the Avignonnais in Bordeaux (who was then also acting as a teacher in the Sephardi school); Ephraim Philip, evidently the rabbi of the Ashkenazim in the city; and an invited visitor, Isaac Nahon, the rabbi of Tetuan in Morocco.[47]

Another peculiarity in the situation regarding marriages was the question of divorce. During the *ancien régime* only Jews had the right of divorce in France. The community organization, with the help of the rabbi, was the authority that decided such cases. There seem to have been very few divorces in the course of the eighteenth century. The most famous involved the Bordeaux-born banker Samuel Peixotto and his wife, Sara Mendes Dacosta. These two had been married in London in 1765 and had then moved to Bordeaux. In 1770 Peixotto went to Paris, leaving his wife behind. He sued for divorce in Paris, on the grounds that in Jewish law a husband had an absolute right to divorce his wife. The case dragged on, and during Azulai's second visit to Paris Peixotto attempted to enlist him on his side. Azulai refused. When he came to Bordeaux later in the journey, the wife (who had evidently come to Bordeaux to fight the case) gave him a handsome contribution for the academy in Hebron. In a brief on her behalf in the year 1779 Azulai was quoted, as an authority on Jewish law, in support of her refusal to be divorced. In the summer of that year this case was referred by the civil courts in Paris to the Sephardi community in Bordeaux to pass judgment on the question in accordance with Jewish usage. They dragged their feet, no doubt, because both protagonists had powerful family connections in Bordeaux. The

[47] *Registre*, No. 514.

whole matter soon became academic when Peixotto went to
Spain in 1781 and converted, with great pomp, to the Catholic
faith (the king himself was one of the godfathers).[48]

The Ashkenazi communities were equally concerned about the
control of marriages and divorces. It was repeatedly ruled in eastern
France that no wedding could take place without permission, but
no case of the voiding of such a marriage on the simple ground that
it was contrary to communal regulations is known among the
Ashkenazim. Both in Metz and in Alsace this control by the community had more than religious significance. In Bordeaux and
Bayonne taxes on dowries were unimportant as revenue, but among
the Ashkenazim it was a source of income that was significant to
the communal budget. On the average, the Sephardim charged 3
livres per 1,000 as the cost of permission to be married; the Ashkenazi rates were, minimally, 1 per cent of the total worth of the
wedding settlement on both bride and groom, and the rate was
from 4 to 8 per cent if either the bride or the groom were from
outside the community.[49] In both Bordeaux and Bayonne there
had never been a fixed maximum, even in theory, of the number
of Jewish families allowed to live in a community. In eastern France
permission to be married could be granted only in the light of the
on-going conflicts over the size of the Jewish communities.

The most important differences between the Sephardim and
the Ashkenazim in the realm of religion were not in details. Their
stances were essentially dissimilar. Among the Sephardim personal
religiosity was becoming ever more tepid. The community remained
formalistically orthodox, but laxness in faith and practice was ever

[48] An inexact account of this affair was given by Malvezin, *Histoire des
Juifs à Bordeaux*, p. 230. The most recent account, with emphasis on Azulai's
participation, is in Benayahu, *Rabbi H. Y. D. Azulai* (in Hebrew), pp. 50–51.
See also Azulai's own remarks in *Maagal Tov*, pp. 121, 164, and the *Plaidoyer
pour la demoiselle Sara-Mendes d'Acosta*. One of the crucial issues in this case
was whether the Jews did indeed have the legal right to divorce in France;
this had never been tested or doubted before.

[49] The amount in Bordeaux was fixed at 2 livres per 1,000 of dowry in 1711,
3 livres per 1,000 in 1736, and at the discretion of the syndics in 1766
(*Registre*, Nos. 3, 74, 349, 350; Cirot, *Recherches*, pp. 75–76). In Metz the
rates remained stable throughout the eighteenth century; 4 per cent was
charged on the dowry of a bride and 8 per cent on the worth of the groom, if
they came from outside Metz (*Pinkas*, 37a, and Clément, *La condition des
Juifs*, p. 116).

more in vogue at the very top of the social pyramid and was descending to the mass. The controlling elements among the Ashkenazim, on the other hand, remained seriously orthodox until the Revolution and beyond. The Jews of eastern France had indeed been divided by a major religious quarrel that arose in the middle of the century. It was much more traumatic and serious than any of the quite unimportant incidents over which there were arguments among the Sephardim, but by its very nature this storm could just as well have broken out a century earlier. Indeed, it was the last act in western and central Europe of a drama that had begun with the appearance of the false messiah, Shabbetai Zvi, in the Near East in the middle years of the seventeenth century. This controversy began in 1751 with the accusation by Jacob Emden that Jonathan Eibeschütz was secretly an adherent of the sect of believers in Shabbetai Zvi. Eibeschütz had just gone to Altona from Metz, and the war between the two took place on the stage of the whole of European Jewry. It is true that the dominant elements in the Metz leadership and in Alsace succeeded in suppressing Eibeschütz's supporters, but the contemporary documents indicate that this quarrel was much more divisive among the Ashkenazim in France than has appeared on the surface.

Eibeschütz had been rabbi in Metz until 1750 and the crucial charges against him were based on five amulets he had issued to various individuals in the Metz community. The texts of these amulets were copied in Metz, and they were transmitted to Altona in copies that had been certified, at separate times, by the scribes of the Jewish community and by a royal notary. In the interpretation of his enemies these amulets, when decoded, proved that Eibeschütz was invoking the power of Shabbetai Zvi to help the people to whom he had given them. He, of course, denied these explanations as false and vicious. Eibeschütz's immediate successor in Metz, Samuel Hillman, was one of the most bitter, active, and unrelenting of his opponents. Nehemiah Reischer, who held office both as a deputy to the rabbi in Metz and as the rabbi in Lorraine, had been a friend, student, and supporter of Eibeschütz; he had been instrumental in getting Eibeschütz his original appointment as rabbi in Metz, but by 1751 Reischer was bitterly hostile. He wrote to Jacob Emden, the arch-opponent of his former friend, with unrestrained venom, rising to the wild crescendo that Eibeschütz had connived in allowing his own daughter to prostitute herself for money. In one of Hillman's letters he mentioned, as evidence of Eibeschütz's propensity for dangerously heterodox cabalists, that he had treated Moses Hayyim Luzzatto, the Italian-Jewish poet, cabalist, and messianic dreamer, with great respect when that excommunicated figure had come through Metz. In the spring of 1751 followers and former students of Eibeschütz proclaimed in the city of Lublin, Poland, that Reischer and Moses May, the leading lay opponents of Eibeschütz, were excommunicated. This action was forthwith declared to be null and void by formal proclamation in both the synagogues of Metz.[50]

In the course of the controversy Eibeschütz was often accused of having no friends left in Metz, because no one there rose in his defense. This argument was used by his enemies to establish presumptive proof of his guilt. This is exaggerated. The Jews of Metz were bitterly divided over Eibeschütz and an enormous battle was being waged there. Mordecai Gumprich, one of the two Jewish scribes in Metz who had certified the transcriptions of the amulets, wrote to Eibeschütz later in 1751 that he had done this under duress. It is instructive that Gumprich did not claim in this letter that the text had been falsified. He did maintain that he continued to study Eibeschütz's teachings in secret. There were intimations in Gumprich's letter that a conventicle of Eibeschütz's disciples continued to exist in Metz. Some of these were men of high station. Gumprich mentioned that Wolfe Treni (who belonged to a family that was consistently represented throughout the century among the *parnassim*) was an adherent.[51] Writing in 1751 from Cracow, Jacob Joshua Falk, Eibeschütz's immediate predecessor as rabbi in Metz, reminded the *parnassim* that he had warned against Eibeschütz's original appointment. He begged them now

[50] The text of the amulets and of the certification by the trustees of Metz, a number of letters by Hillman and Reischer, and the text of the proclamation in the two synagogues of Metz on Sivvan 11, 5511, are all to be found in the anonymous short volume *Sefat Emet ve-Lashon Zehurit,* which was published in 1752 by one of Emden's followers.

[51] Gumprich's letter was printed by Eibeschütz in his volume of self-defense, *Luchat Edut,* 15b–16a.

to unite and to follow their present rabbi.[52] It is thus clear that Falk was attempting to strengthen Hillman's hand amidst division among the leaders. In 1752 Samuel Halberstatt, the rabbi in Haguenau, wrote to Eibeschütz that he could not publicly declare himself in opposition to "men of the fist and the strong arm. I am actually a wanderer in a strange land; how can I fight the leaders, for if they are aroused, they will expel me." Halberstatt had come to Alsace from his native Prague in 1745, after the expulsion of the Jews from that city by the Empress Maria-Theresa, and he had been helped by his teacher and friend, Eibeschütz.[53]

On the evidence of these various letters, the leaders of Metz, who had once unanimously wanted Eibeschütz as their rabbi, had become bitterly divided over him during his stay in Metz. They were now in their majority his violent opponents. Nevertheless, even though there was an appearance of unity in Metz in opposition to the former rabbi, this unity was far from complete. It is always dangerous to argue from silence of documents, yet it cannot be entirely accidental that in the last minute book during the *ancien régime* of the Jewish community in Metz, the *Pinkas*, which was begun in 1749, the pages that might possibly have had reference to actions taken during this controversy are ripped out. The community seems to have wanted to forget this painful episode as quickly as possible. Nevertheless, it would be unreasonable to presume there were no echoes of this titanic battle in Metz during the second half of the century. If human nature is any guide, these enmities must have smoldered for many years. What effect these shocks may have had on the fabric of religious faith and practice we cannot determine on the basis of available evidence. It is at least a reasonable presumption that the quarrel was sufficiently destructive, in several ways, to make it easier for French ways and ideas to penetrate the ghetto.

Whatever may have been the deepest effects of the quarrel over Eibeschütz, on the surface inner Jewish religious life in eastern France went on in the old grooves until the period of the Revolution. There were, indeed, numerous cases of bastardy in the second

[52] *Sefat Emet*, the letter of Jacob Joshua Falk (the book is unpaged).
[53] *Luchat Edut*, 45a; on Halberstatt, see Scheid, *Juifs de Haguenau*, p. 82.

half of the century in Metz (there were some also in Bordeaux), but it would be wrong to deduce from this that moral conduct had, indeed, become markedly looser. In the very heydey of orthodoxy in Metz in the last years of the seventeenth century, during the rabbinate of Gershon Ashkenazi, he was already paying considerable attention to such breaches. Social intercourse between the sexes was becoming a bit freer. Eibeschütz in his sermons in the 1740s was much occupied with this question. The Alsatian communal regulations of 1777 included a prohibition of the practice of having boys and girls promenade together on Sabbath and holidays. They were advised to spend their time, instead, in the company of a scholar, listening to his instructions.[54] Even the social intercourse of engaged couples was regulated in 1776. The craze for playing cards and billiards and for betting, which were well-known vices in all of European society at that time, were specifically prohibited in 1777 by a communal regulation. Even those who were being held in the Jewish jail in Metz were forbidden to play cards to pass the time.[55]

An elaborate code of personal conduct was published in Metz in 1769. Sumptuary laws of this nature had been enacted for many centuries everywhere in the Jewish world. A number of such codes were being written at that time by the Jewish communities of the Papal States. In Metz itself such a code had existed in 1690, and it too was based on earlier sources.[56] The Metz regulations of 1769 thus stood in a line of established tradition.[57] The opening clauses of this last and most elaborate attempt to regulate personal be-

[54] Gershon Ashkenazi wrote three responsa about illicit pregnancies (*Hiddushei ha-Gershuni*, Nos. 1, 28, 93); for Eibeschütz's concern with this question, see *Sefer Yaarot Devash*, I, 18d; for Alsace, see *Extract from the minutes*, clause 23.

[55] See *Pinkas*, 41a, 50b, 52b, 93b for various cases of bastardy and for the proclamations of penalties and excommunications; for the prohibitions against free social intercourse and cards and billiards, see *Pinkas*, 101a, 102a, and Chapter VI.

[56] Cahen, *Règlements somptuaires, passim*. Sumptuary laws from 1690, 1691, 1694, and 1697 were printed in this short book, in French translation.

[57] For medieval sumptuary laws in Italy and Castile in the fifteenth century, see Finkelstein, *Jewish Self-Government*, pp. 292–93, 373; in general, see Baron, *The Jewish Community*, II, 301–307. The Ashkenazim in Amsterdam promulgated three sets of sumptuary laws, in 1709, 1717, and 1722, which were quite similar to those in Metz (*Takkanot li-Seudah*, in the JTS Library); see also the communal constitution, in Yiddish and Hebrew, in Amsterdam in 1737 (*Takkanot ha-Kehillah*, in the JTS Library).

havior were devoted to the question of sobriety in dress. Even the wives of the rich, those who possessed fortunes of more than 15,000 crowns, were forbidden to come to synagogue or promenade in public places in outer garments of muslin, linen, or silk, but they could wear such clothes within the Jewish quarter. Servant girls who were not natives of Metz could not wear silk even on Sabbath or the holidays. The amount that could be spent on the entertainment of guests at such events as weddings and circumcisions was severely limited. At an engagement, regardless of the station of the families involved, only four plain cakes and four sugar cakes could be served. At a wedding where the dowry was less than 6,000 livres, only three musicians could be employed. However, where the dowry was over 10,000 livres, the principals could entertain their guests as expensively as they might wish.

This code contained more than sumptuary rules. Conduct in the synagogue, and especially talking in the synagogue, was regulated, and all private prayer conventicles were forbidden. When gentile dignitaries came to visit, no one but the *parnas* or someone designated by him was allowed to talk to such a personage. No one could remain in Paris for Passover or the high holidays without express permission of the community. "Steerers" to bring trade in off the streets were forbidden to drift over in front of the stores of competitors. Any meat brought to Metz from outside could not be sold in the city, even if local taxes were paid on such an import. In this code all forms of gambling were forbidden, bringing a fine of 39 livres for each transgression. but in 1769 an exception was still made for those in jail.[58] It is, no doubt, too fanciful to imagine that this exception was canceled eight years later because some Jews were finding their way to jail in order to gamble with impunity.

Among the Sephardim in France only one attempt in Bayonne was made in the course of the eighteenth century to publish sumptuary regulations. Such codes did exist in Spain before the expulsion. The Jews from Avignon in Bordeaux, who came from a community in which such rules were being enacted repeatedly in the eighteenth century,[59] never attempted to follow the pattern of their

[58] This code, in 125 clauses, is in the *Pinkas*, 76a–84a.
[59] For sumptuary laws from the Papal States, see Roth, "Sumptuary Laws," *JQR*, XVIII, 357–83; Dianous, "Les communautés juives," *Ecole nationale des chartes, positions des thèses*, 1938, pp. 31–36; see also in the next volume

home community. In arguing for the Sephardim of France in the 1760s Isaac de Pinto maintained that they shared with the top elements of contemporary Christian society in a love of display and high living. These were the "vices of great souls." [60] The high bourgeois who led the Sephardi communities did, indeed, live well on a very public scale. As we have seen in the discussion of the economy of Bordeaux, the whole of its merchant group, and not only the Jews, were foreigners. To live publicly in the life style of the high bourgeoisie was very much less of a problem for Jews in Bordeaux than in eastern France. The rich Ashkenazim were, however, straining against both inner Jewish tradition and the virulent and visible angers of the gentile society surrounding them. Samuel Lévy at the beginning of the century lived on a princely scale in Nancy and Cerf Berr ran a large house in Strasbourg in the 1780s.[61] They both fought hard, and not very successfully, to achieve public acceptance of this way of life, for in eastern France visible Jewish wealth was an enraging sight. Sumptuary laws were being enacted among the Ashkenazim throughout the eighteenth century for two reasons: both the older religious pieties and the older anti-Jewish hatreds were still strong.

## Taxation

The crucial function of all the organized Jewish communities in France involved taxation. The central bodies were responsible for covering the internal budget of the Jewish community. They also collected the royal and local taxes, for these were imposed on the Jews in lump sums. For both these purposes the community assessed individuals according to its judgment of their abilities to

---

(1939) of the same series, Dianous, "Les Juifs d'Avignon," pp. 53–59. The one attempt at enacting sumptuary regulations among the Sephardim was made by Raphael Meldola during his rabbinate in Bayonne (Léon, *Histoire des Juifs de Bayonne*, p. 378).

[60] Pinto admitted with evident pride, in his response to Voltaire, that the vices of the Portuguese were luxury, prodigality, chasing women, and not working (*Réflexions critiques*, p. 23).

[61] Lévy's high style was described by M. Ginsburger, "Samuel Lévi," *REJ*, LXX, 294; Lévy had many servants in Nancy and gave expensive balls. For the angers that were evoked by Cerf Berr's large homes in Bischheim and Strasbourg, see Hoffman, *L'Alsace*, IV, 359.

pay. Central Jewish bodies succeeded everywhere in enlisting the aid of civil powers in collecting even those taxes that were levied to cover the internal Jewish budget. There were differences among the communities: for example, the Jews of Metz had a far greater tax burden than those of Bordeaux. Nevertheless, in all essential respects Sephardi and Ashkenazi communal authorities behaved everywhere in the same way.

In Bordeaux, the original role of the *Sedaca* was to support the poor. In the early years levies for this purpose were enforced by internal sanctions, through denying access to the religious services of the community.[62] In 1730 the intendant, de Boucher, acceded to a request from the leaders of the *Sedaca:* recalcitrant Jews who refused to pay the assessments of the syndics would be pursued by the civil police.[63] This tax, called the *annuel,* varied in the course of the second half of the eighteenth century from the figure of 2,000 livres in 1744 to a high of 9,754 livres in 1780.[64] There were also assessments for extraordinary purposes. In 1766 the Jews in Bordeaux were paying an annual tax of 3,000 livres in order to be released from the obligation of taking part in civic guard duty on Sabbath and Jewish holidays.[65] Both in Bordeaux and Bayonne local and royal officials received regular gifts. Occasionally there was the need to bribe somebody; [66] a number of times in the course of the

[62] In 1711 those who refused to pay were denied access to the abattoir and the ritual bath; their newborn sons would not be circumcised and their dead would not be buried until the family had squared the account in full (*Registre,* No. 5). In 1726 only half of a total of 3,000 livres was collected (*Registre,* No. 36) and two years later the threats that were first made in 1711 were repeated by the syndics (*Registre,* No. 41).

[63] The text of this decree is in the JTS Library; see also Cirot, *Recherches,* p. 51.

[64] Here are some of the amounts given in the *Registre:* 2,000 livres in 1744 (No. 107); 2,400 livres in 1746 (No. 133); 3,425 livres in 1767 (No. 362); 5,475 livres in 1769 (No. 380); 2,796 livres in 1775 (No. 425); 7,700 livres in 1777 (No. 451); and 9,754 livres in 1780 (No. 480). After 1767 a surcharge of one-fifth was generally added to the *annuel* to pay for the special expenses involved in the Passover holiday.

[65] *Registre,* No. 352. In that deliberation of June 7, 1766, there is record of an unsuccessful intervention with the intendant, de Boutin, to reduce the amount of this payment from 3,000 to 2,400 livres.

[66] The budgetary annex to the *Règlement* of the Jews of Bayonne, approved by the king in 1753, listed sixteen such charges. Out of a total communal budget that year of 7,881 livres as much as 3,190 represented such special

eighteenth century the Jews in Bordeaux were either asked for or offered special donations. They made large patriotic gifts for outfitting warships at least twice during the wars of the second half of the century.[67]

We do not know how the royal taxes were collected from the Sephardim in the seventeenth century while they were still marranos, or in the early years of the eighteenth, as the *Sedaca* was becoming the official representative of the Jewish community as a whole. It is probable that they were being treated as a merchant guild and that, therefore, there was some separate body that divided the taxes among the individual Portuguese Jews. This function was acquired by the *Sedaca* at least as early as 1738. In that year the basic royal tax, the *capitation*, was mentioned for the first time in the minutes of the community. The intendant fixed the sum at 3,100 livres and the syndic of the *Sedaca*, aided by a committee, assessed their shares upon all the individual taxpayers. By 1772 the total amount of the *capitation* was 7,230 livres. In 1789 it was 9,400 livres.[68] The other basic royal tax was the *vingtième* that was collected in all of France as a percentage of the volume of business activity. How this impost was collected from the Jews in Bordeaux is not entirely clear. They seem to have paid a sum that was levied upon them as a community; at least some of the Portu-

---

payments (Léon, *Histoire des Juifs de Bayonne,* p. 149). In 1754 Jacob Rodrigues Péreire induced the Jews of Bordeaux to lend 6,000 livres to an unnamed lady "qui par luy et par ses aliances peut être utile à la nation" (*Registre,* No. 228). In 1762 this sum was not yet repaid, and the debt was then assigned to M. Douin, the principal secretary of the Count of Saint Florentin, the minister of the royal household, for his help in securing permission for them to not mount patrol on Sabbaths and festivals (*Registre,* No. 306). In 1777 Péreire was paid 3,000 livres as reimbursement for "certain sums" he had given to a M. de L.B. (*Registre,* No. 455). The reason for this bribe is not indicated, but it could hardly have been unrelated to the granting of *lettres patentes* of June, 1776.

[67] The most important of these attempts to raise their taxes failed. In 1749 the administrators of the *hôpital de St. André* tried to get 10,000 livres per year from the Jewish community. They argued that the old arrangement of 1693, by which the Jews were freed from supporting the *hôpital,* involved only small numbers and little wealth, whereas the present community was far larger and controlled half the commerce of Bordeaux (Cirot, *Recherches,* pp. 31, 44–45). For the donations to the buying of warships, see Chapter V, fn. 43.

[68] *Registre,* No. 78; Cirot, *Recherches,* pp. 40–41; Szajkowski, *Autonomy and Jewish Communal Debts,* p. 25.

guese figured together with other individual bourgeois of the city on individual tax rolls.[69]

The situation in Bayonne was essentially the same. In 1753 the Jewish community was given official approval of its communal constitution. That document included a precise internal budget. The cost of maintaining the poor was roughly 2,500 livres a year, which was substantially the same as in Bordeaux. Almost all the rest of a budget of 7,800 livres went to pay gratifications to various officials of both the royal and the local government and to satisfy the share of the Jews of the royal tax on meat, wine, and oil. This constitution could obviously set no limit on the amount of taxes that the civic authorities or the king might in the future impose on the community, but it had long been taken for granted that the Jewish communal authorities had the responsibility of paying these taxes in a lump sum. All the taxes that the *Hebera* in Bayonne assessed had behind them the force of the civil powers, and they could use the police to confiscate the goods of those who refused to pay.[70]

The tax situation in Metz was basically the same. The royal taxes were levied on the Jews in a lump sum and the communal organization raised the required amounts through its own schedule of internal taxation. As in Bordeaux, the Jews were thus being treated for tax purposes as a kind of merchant guild. In Metz, too, the basic royal tax was the *capitation*. During the eighteenth century, until 1766, the city authorities made the Jews pay one-fifth of the total amount for which Metz as a whole was responsible. In that year the Jews succeeded in convincing the intendant that their share should be reduced to one-sixth of the total. They paid a comparably large proportion of the *vingtième*. This tax rose from an average of 2,100 livres at the beginning of the century to 7,700 livres immediately before the Revolution. There was a variety of other, less important, minor taxes, such as payments in lieu of the obligations that Christians had for housing soldiers or working on the roads.

The most important special feature of the situation in Metz was the Brancas tax. The Jews had given large cash gifts in 1710 to the

[69] Cirot, *Recherches*, pp. 40–41. Until 1753 the syndic was responsible for collecting the royal taxes. In 1753 he relinquished this task and it was given to an official appointed for this specific task (*Registre*, No. 211).

[70] Léon, *Histoire des Juifs de Bayonne*, p. 150.

Duke of Brancas, the son-in-law of the president of the Metz *parlement,* and to the Countess of Fontaine, the daughter of the royal lieutenant in Metz. These gifts ceased when the president and the lieutenant died. During the period of the regency of the Duke of Orleans, the beneficiaries succeeded in obtaining an order that each Jewish family in Metz pay an annual tax of 40 livres to the duke and the countess (who was then the mistress of the regent). This original arrangement in 1715 was revised three years later. A new edict permitted the existence of 480 Jewish families in Metz, and the new tax ("for the right to dwell" in Metz) was changed into an annual charge of 20,000 livres, to be paid by the community as a whole. The Jews battled against this imposition, both in the years when it was being decreed and in 1735 and 1750 when there were further renewals. They did not succeed in securing its abolition until the Brancas tax was declared illegal by the National Assembly in 1790. Altogether it had cost the Jews of Metz almost two million livres.[71]

The Metz Jewish community also had to support its own elaborate internal structure of rabbis, synagogues, education, and, especially, social services for the poor. As in Bordeaux, it frequently had to find the money with which to purchase special favors or influence.[72] A problem peculiar to Metz was the relationship of its authority to the growing number of Jews in the surrounding countryside, the *pays messin,* whom the communal authorities in Metz were trying to make pay a share of at least the Brancas tax.[73] By the 1780s the corporate budget of the Metz Jewish community had approached a figure of 150,000 livres annually; this represented the enormous sum of more than 350 livres per family. The *parnassim* attempted to raise these amounts by an elaborate schedule of taxation. Basically, each individual was taxed according to

[71] Clément, *La condition des Juifs,* pp. 102–19.

[72] In February, 1786, Moise Weill, who was then the agent of the Jews of Metz in Paris, gave the Marshal de Broglie 1,000 livres, which he "accepted very graciously." This was evidently an annual gratification. In 1789 Weill gave presents of geese to a number of ministers, but he was still two short for Necker, the minister of finance (Szajkowski, *Autonomy,* pp. 160–61).

[73] There were continuing frictions. In 1776 a conference was called of the representatives of all the villages and it was decided that tax assessments would henceforth be made directly by the Metz communal body and not by local officials (JTS, MS 01922).

his income. There were also consumer taxes on meat and wine. The right to live in the city was sold for a minimum of 600 livres and whoever emigrated from Metz had to pay a tax of 8 per cent of his total worth.[74] Income did not keep up with mounting expenses, and the Jewish community was constrained to borrow ever larger amounts of money.[75] The Metz Jewish authorities made frequent use of the civil police to enforce their tax assessments.[76]

The situation in Alsace was the most complicated of all. The king himself levied a tax on the Jews for the *droit de protection* and the various local noblemen imposed a charge, the *droit d'habitation*, on each Jewish family living in their territories. Both of these taxes were paid directly by the individual families. The amounts did not vary according to income. As in Metz and in Bordeaux, all the other royal taxes imposed on the Jews were collected from the community as a whole. In Alsace, too, these included the *capitation* and the *vingtième*, as well as payments by the Jews in lieu of their working on the roads.[77] There were also various minor taxes and

[74] There were frequent problems with taxes on every level of Metz Jewish society. After the death of the army purveyor, Moses Belin, two of his sons-in-law, Seligmann Wittersheim and Wolf Urshil (Beer) negotiated in 1761 for reductions in their taxes (*Pinkas*, 36a, 37a). Moses Spire got a reduction of 1,750 livres in 1770 (*Pinkas*, 85a). Hendele, the daughter of Meir Treni and the sister of Wolfe Treni, reluctantly paid 6,400 livres as the 8 per cent tax on her assets when she moved to France in 1770 with her husband, Isaac Reis (*Pinkas*, 86a).

[75] The Jews in Metz paid one-sixth of the *capitation* collected in the city in 1757–66 (55,248 livres as against 221,777 livres from the non-privileged bourgeois) and 9,648 livres of a total of 57,736 livres of city taxes in 1789. In the years immediately before the Revolution expenses outstripped income by 40,000 livres a year (Szajkowski, *Autonomy and Jewish Communal Debts*, pp. 29–30).

[76] There were many attempts to increase tax income. In 1761 the mode of collection was changed; the poorest taxpayers would now pay every two weeks and the middle group once a month (*Pinkas*, 37b–38a). This new arrangement evidently did not work, for a once-a-month collection from everybody was ordered in 1777 (*Pinkas*, 105a). In 1781 Jews living in the city were forbidden to buy meat from the abattoirs in the *pays messin*, for "the income from the local abattoir is necessary for the payment of taxes" (*Pinkas*, 120b). It was recorded in the minutes for 1752 that the *parnassim* had the right to sue in the French courts those who did not pay taxes (*Pinkas*, 9b). Eibeschütz made reference to this practice in a sermon in 1747 (*Sefer Yaarot Devash*, I, 98a). In 1782 the situation had worsened; the community got consent from the intendant that it could enlist the police power to confiscate and sell the goods of those who did not pay taxes (*Pinkas*, 123a).

[77] Scheid, *Juifs d'Alsace*, p. 133; Hoffman, *L'Alsace*, IV, 375–85.

"gratifications." The province-wide Jewish organization was also responsible for those internal expenses involving the Jews of Alsace as a whole. The two major items in this budget were the financing of higher Jewish education and the paying of the costs for legal and political actions in defense of Jewish rights and in the various attempts to broaden them. For all of these purposes the necessary taxes were collected on a sliding scale; the assessments were made by the financial officers of the provincial organization on the basis of their estimate of the wealth of the individual taxpayers.

In Alsace, as everywhere else among the Jews in France, there were two persistent problems: the concealing of assets from the tax assessors and recurring suspicions of favoritism on their part. On occasion the leaders of the Jewish community in the province were accused of trying to make all the Jews pay for political actions that their enemies said they had really undertaken on their personal behalf in order to achieve results that would accrue to their immediate economic benefit. At least once the syndics were even accused of lining their own pockets with money they were raising by special taxation to pay the pretended costs of protecting the Jews against non-existent dangers. In 1729 an action was brought against three bankers, the brothers Meyer, Mathis, and Baruch Weyl (the first two were the syndics of the Jews in Alsace). They had imposed a special levy of 15,000 livres to recover a loan they had supposedly made to the communal organization. The accuser, Paul Lévy, alleged that all this was done for the bankers' personal profit; they were pretending political influence they did not possess and blowing up a false fear that the Jews were in danger of being expelled from Alsace.[78]

In the second half of the eighteenth century, the taxes paid to the king by the Jewish community organization in Alsace consistently amounted to between 20,000 and 25,000 livres. Charles Hoffman, the author of the most comprehensive history of the province in the eighteenth century (and who had a pronounced bias against the Jews), went to great lengths to prove that the Jews of Alsace were better off than the Christian majority, citing as his

[78] Hoffman, *L'Alsace*, IV, 392. In this affair the intendant rejected the accusation.

major evidence that the Jews paid relatively less in royal taxation. It is true that the amount seems small, even astonishingly so, especially if we recall that the *capitation* and the *vingtième* cost the 3,500 Jews in the region of Metz about as much as it cost the 20,000 in Alsace. It is, nevertheless, inconceivable that the Jews in Alsace were the beneficiaries of any real favoritism. The royal taxes were only part of the burden that was borne by the nearly 200 small Jewish settlements, for each of these communities had to pay very substantial taxes to local powers. The initial cost of the right to live in a place, or the repeated costs of permission for one's children to get married and remain in the community, were well-nigh ruinous. Internal Jewish budgets in each individual town, and especially the cost of supporting their own poor, were high. For example, there were fewer than 70 families in Haguenau in the middle of the eighteenth century. The normal local tax bill was of the order of 800 livres a year, but all the other costs were staggering. Quite apart from the poor, this small community supported eight Jewish communal functionaries and their families.[79] The most important consideration is that, as we have seen earlier, the radical increase in Jewish population in Alsace throughout the eighteenth century was not among the rich or even the middle class. Even those who had a few livres with which to buy the right of residence often became poor in the process. The province-wide tax bill to the royal government remained stable as the population rose because these imposts continued to be paid from the wealth of a few. The very stability of the royal taxes despite rising Jewish population, in an age when the French treasury was ever hungrier, is the most conclusive proof of the marked misery of Alsatian Jews before the Revolution.

### Defender of the Jews

All the Jewish communities in France lived in considerable and continuing fear. This was true even in Bordeaux as late as the middle of the eighteenth century, even though the Sephardim had

[79] Regarding the cost of being admitted to Haguenau or having married children stay there, see Chapter V; for a list of communal functionaries and of the poor in 1784, see Scheid, *Juifs de Haguenau*, Appendix, pp. xxxix–xlii.

royal assent to live openly as Jews and despite the fact that their importance in the vital sea trade was growing rapidly. The very first communal constitution to be recorded in the minutes of the *Sedaca*, in the year 1736, contained a solemn declaration: "In order to safeguard our existence it is against our interests that any matter that concerns us should come to the knowledge of the gentiles. To ensure that no information should pass to them, we hereby decree that any individual who will inform the gentiles of any matter of consequence which can harm the *Sedaca* will be excommunicated and fined in accordance with the full rigor of the law." [80] The safe-guarding of Jewish existence and Jewish rights required discipline and obedience under the most favorable circumstances. Despite many revolts, communal leaders generally succeeded in imposing their authority because they discharged this most sensitive and crucial function. By common consent it was their responsibility to defend not only the rights of the community as a whole, but also individual Jews. Indeed, every relationship of the Jews with the outside world almost invariably became a matter for formal or behind-the-scenes communal action.

It was only during the very last years of the *ancien régime,* when the winds of the Revolution itself were beginning to blow, that all the Jewish communities, both Ashkenazi and Sephardi, were some-what involved together in discussing the future of Jewish rights in France with the royal government.[81] This was not the dominant pattern even during the Revolution, for the Sephardim and the Ashkenazim for the most part continued to act separately. To be

[80] *Registre,* No. 74, clause 2.

[81] Especially in the light of the frequent references to the tensions over com-munal taxation between the community of Metz and the Jews in the *pays mes-sin,* it is significant that in 1785 the *parnassim* of Metz made all the villages share in an action that the *kehillah* was bringing before the *parlement:* the local authorities were raising taxes on two of the village Jewish communities, in St. Jean and in Barchingen, and the *parnassim* were defending them (*Pinkas,* 131a). See Chapter X for the actions of the late 1780s. Only one occasion is known of an attempt at political involvement by the Ashkenazim of the Sephar-dim. Eibeschütz wrote to Bordeaux from Metz to enlist help for the interna-tional political action by Jews to defend those whom Maria-Theresa was ex-pelling from Prague in 1744–45 (Graetz, "Einige handschriftliche Briefe," *MGWJ,* XVI, 426–30). For this dawning effort of international Jewish diplo-macy, see, in general, Mevorah, "Jewish Diplomatic Activities," *Zion,* XXVIII, 125–69.

sure, their objectives were different, but it was also true that each of the major communities, and every one of its components, had long been accustomed to dealing directly and independently with a bewildering variety of civil powers. Nevertheless, there was a fundamental similarity in structure; in discharging these defensive political functions the Sephardi and the Ashkenazi communities behaved in exactly the same ways. Throughout the era of the *ancien régime* both elements kept lobbying in Paris at the royal court; both largely succeeded in cultivating good relations with royal intendants in the provinces in which they lived and both did not hesitate to do battle against largely unfriendly local jurisdictions. Everywhere the leaders of Jewish communities were, as we shall soon see, the representatives of the richest families. Their personal importance and political connections were crucial to the defense of the Jews as a whole. In large part, despite the many battles over tax assessments, the Jewish masses accepted the authority of these oligarchs because they paid the major share of the bill for the organized Jewish community. The ultimate source of their power was, however, their influence with government. Whether it was in their dealings with the king or the Duke of Lorraine or some obscure *seigneur* in Alsace, the Jews who really commanded interest were the rich, who brought ready and visible financial advantage. Poor Jews existed by the good graces of the rich. The Jewish masses had no choice but to accept the situation, for the alternative was to have no real protection at all.

The need for the Jews to secure new *lettres patentes* at the beginning of each reign has already been mentioned in various connections. Such actions required the use of influence in Paris and the payment of large sums to the royal treasury. These monies had to be raised by special imposts. Generally the sums were so large that they could not be realized by immediate taxation. All the communities had to resort at various times to large-scale borrowing. In Bordeaux the Jews borrowed 30,000 livres in 1776, probably to pay the cost of achieving the *lettres patentes* that year, which granted them the largest rights they ever attained before the Revolution. There was then, for the first time, no direct large payment to the crown, but the "hidden cost" was evidently large. In 1775 the provincial organization of the Jews of Alsace borrowed 24,000 livres. By 1778, when the battle over the "false receipts" had begun, Cerf Berr, as syndic, was authorized to borrow another 50,000 livres; 100,000 livres was indeed borrowed in 1784. The mounting debts of the Jewish community in Metz were caused not merely by the cost of the taxes that it had to pay but also by the expensive battles it fought. It tried repeatedly to get rid of the Brancas tax; throughout the eighteenth century it was always fighting to protect its economic rights against recurring attacks by the *parlement* of Metz.[82]

Despite their increasing activities in attempting to limit the Jewish population, both the Sephardim and the Ashkenazim did try to protect their own. In 1744 the Jews of Bordeaux responded to pressure against the growing numbers of the poor by offering a list of Ashkenazim to the intendant for expulsion; they argued for the right of all Portuguese Jews to remain.[83] In Alsace in 1746 the syndics managed to convince the military governor of the province that only the foreign-born poor be expelled but not those born in Alsace.[84] One of the minor brushes of the community in Metz with the *parlement* took place in 1763, when the civic authorities ordered a general inspection of the Jewish quarter to look for criminals, which meant no doubt those who were making a living illegally. The community organization succeeded in obtaining permission to conduct this inspection itself, quite obviously in order to protect at least some Jews from expulsion.[85] A battle of a different order took place in Bordeaux in 1751. Six of the leading Jews of the commu-

---

[82] Szajkowski, *Autonomy and Jewish Communal Debts*, pp. 29–30, 102, 131–32. In Bordeaux part of the cost of the *lettres patentes* of 1776 was financed by using the endowment of the *Thalmud Thora* (a sum of 6,690 livres), which had been invested with four of the richest Jews in the community (*Registre*, No. 444, the deliberation of August 28, 1776).

[83] *Registre*, No. 110: "It seems useful to send out of Bordeaux a number of Ashkenazi and Italian Jews, who come here and are thus making the situation more difficult for our own Portuguese poor." See also Chapter V.

[84] The complaint that the Jews in eastern France were protecting too many of the poor kept recurring. In 1789 the *bailli* of Dorlisheim complained that the number of the wandering poor kept increasing in Alsace because all the rabbis were protecting them (Scheid, *Juifs d'Alsace*, p. 220; Hoffman, *L'Alsace*, IV, 347).

[85] *Pinkas*, 49b.

nity by then already owned land and an attempt was made to make
them pay taxes. These individuals argued that, in the light of the
*lettres patentes* of 1723, their status was that of bourgeois of a free
city, like all the other bourgeois of Bordeaux, and that all Jews were
therefore exempt. Even though this matter involved only a handful
of the wealthiest individuals, the *Sedaca* as a whole paid the cost
of this defense.[86] No doubt some of the individual Jewish taxpayers
were less than happy over their involvement in this action, even
though it helped establish a broader definition of the rights of the
Sephardim. There is direct evidence that the actions by the organized communities in Bayonne and in Bordeaux to achieve royal
recognition of their respective communal constitutions in 1753 and
1760 were also not pleasing to certain elements in the communities.
As we shall soon see, there were bitter battles over the taxing power
that these documents were confirming to the syndics. Nevertheless,
the recognition of these constitutions was an important political
achievement.. The leadership was obviously more popular in 1731,
when it avoided a threat to Bordeaux to tax its Jews 40 livres per
family, an amount patterned after the Brancas tax in Metz. In
1749 the *Sedaca* was equally successful in avoiding a threat by the
administrator of the St. André poorhouse to make the Jews pay
10,000 livres per year towards its upkeep.[87]

Such attempts to make the Jews pay more money to local powers
were endemic in Bayonne. When the Jews had arrived at St. Esprit
they had found it prudent to give the curate of the parish in which
they lived an annual pension of 400 livres. By the middle of the
eighteenth century the local clergy wanted a large increase consonant with the growth of Jewish population. The Jews responded
by refusing to pay anything at all, maintaining that their original
act had been a free-will offering. The syndics of the Jews of Bayonne
took this case on appeal from the local judges to Paris and won
their suit.[88] This battle, even though there were several recurrences,

[86] The cost of this action was raised by levying a special tax, one-third of
the *annuel* (*Registre*, Nos. 190, 191). The battle was won before the *Cour des
Aides* (Cirot, *Recherches*, pp. 39–40).

[87] Cirot, *Recherches*, p. 31.

[88] Léon, *Histoire des Juifs de Bayonne*, pp. 53–56.

was a minor affair. The major concern of the Jewish community was its continuing battle with the local authorities over Jewish economic rights.

A particularly sensitive issue was the matter of conversion to Christianity. There were a number of cases among the Sephardim in the course of the eighteenth century, and almost all of the leading families were directly involved. The whole issue became particularly painful in Bordeaux in the 1720s, when three daughters of Alexander Mezes (he had been the head of the *hebera kaddisha* in 1710) were converted. In this and in other cases around the same time, some of the converts were children who had been baptized, or taken to baptism, by Christian maids. Mezes never succeeded in regaining his daughters, but the Jewish community as a whole did secure a royal decree in 1728 that forbade the Church to accept any converts who were under the age of twelve.[89] This decree was later cited at least once in a comparable situation by the Ashkenazim in eastern France.[90]

Among the Ashkenazim, even more than among the Sephardim, most of the relations of the organized communities with the gentiles revolved around economic issues. In one of his sermons during the summer of 1745, Jonathan Eibeschütz made the point that the community he was addressing stood high in virtue of defending any Jew who was in trouble with the authorities. It was an ancient rule in Metz that the *parnas* in office had, as one of his prime responsibilities, the duty to immediately exert his influence on the civil authorities whenever he was informed that any individual Jew was in their hands for any reason.[91] The situation was essentially the same in Alsace. In December 1754 Hirtzel Lévy was executed in Colmar for a robbery he did not commit. His family fought for twenty years, unsuccessfully, to have his memory cleared. Even though the legal briefs in the case were signed by his survivors, the participation of the Alsatian Jewish community in these actions was

[89] The saddest part of the Mezes affair was that, when hope was gone for the return of these three children, their mother wanted to convert in order to enter the monastery in which they were being kept, but she was refused (Malvezin, *Histoire des Juifs à Bordeaux*, pp. 158–68).

[90] Szajkowski, *Franco-Judaica*, No. 1439; a comparable decree for Alsace was issued in 1784 (*ibid.*, No. 1448).

[91] Eibeschütz, *Sefer Yaarot Devash*, I, 67a; *Pinkas*, 134a.

very thinly veiled. An intervention of a different order took place in 1766, when the authorities in Alsace decreed that Jews could employ Christians to do those chores which, because of religious scruples, Jews could not do for themselves on Sabbaths and holidays.[92]

The most important defensive activities of the Alsatian provincial organization were, of course, in the area of Jewish rights as a whole. This had continued throughout the eighteenth century, in many confrontations. The climactic occasion was the affair of "false receipts." Hell, the central anti-Jewish figure in this affair, complained bitterly about the provincial organization and argued for its abolition.[93] He was not alone. A colleague of his, another local judge in Alsace, a certain Jacquot, wrote to the intendant in 1780 that the Jews of Alsace have a leader "who is like their king, because they regularly pay him large tribute which only God knows how he uses." [94] Jacquot was, of course, attacking Cerf Berr, and he knew full well to what purpose that leader was using the funds of the provincial organization. Within the Jewish community itself not even his enemies ever charged Cerf Berr with motives of personal gain.

The Alsatian enemies of the Jewish communal bodies were not moved by a humane regard for the masses of the Jews, who were supposedly groaning under the oppressive yoke of their leaders. The purpose of men like Hell and Jacquot was to try to destroy the community structures in order to remove the prime protector of the Jews. As we have said earlier, the organized Jewish communities were also under attack before the Revolution from other quarters. The mainstream of pro-Jewish, "enlightened" opinion wanted to abolish them because, especially in eastern France, the organized communities represented the coercive power of the Jewish tradition and religion. These "enlighteners" had no doubt that the Jewish individual had to be liberated from this negative environment. An-

[92] Szajkowski, *Franco-Judaica*, Nos. 1332–35, 109.

[93] "Regarded and treated in every society as plague-bearers, in this province [of Alsace] the Jews are a corporation; they meet, deliberate, and elect their leaders; they have their own judges even for purely civil matters, a privilege of which the Protestants of this province, even though they are Christians and good citizens, cannot boast. This is a nation within a nation; in the midst of a great state, here is a powerful small state which knows how to protect its subjects" (*Observations sur l'affaire des Juifs d'Alsace*, p. 100).

[94] Hoffman, *L'Alsace*, IV, 393.

other theme was coming to the foreground after the middle of the eighteenth century. The organs of the Jewish community had ever more made at least some of the poor expendable, and angers were mounting. Some of this ire was, as we shall see, being heard by responsible Frenchmen who were not anti-Semites. By the 1780s it was clear on all sides that the powers and functions of the Jewish communities and the whole legal status of the Jews would have to undergo radical revision. The authority of oligarchs and rabbis was in serious question, but how had the structure of their rule evolved?

### Communal Organization and Internal Quarrels

The beginnings of Jewish communal organization in southwestern France are obscure. In 1629, more than half a century before the first traces of an avowed Jewish community appeared in Bordeaux, there was mention in one document of a syndic of "new Christians." [95] This is an isolated bit of evidence, but it is probable that the Portuguese had some form of community organization even in their marrano phase. In the middle of the seventeenth century, when Colbert was encouraging foreigners to come to Bordeaux, the Dutch, the Irish, and the Germans were each organized there as *nations.* The "Portuguese merchants" were no doubt being dealt with comparably.[96] The existing minute book of the *Sedaca* began in 1710, but one of its first entries is evidence that this body was heir to an older tradition. An early entry in the minutes spoke of the need to keep records, since "our old minute books are lost." [97] This remark may have referred only to the records of the preceding two decades, after the avowedly Jewish community had been organized in the 1690s; it is conceivable however that the reference was to preceding forms of communal organization.

In Bayonne or, to be more exact, in St. Esprit, the suburb in which

[95] Szajkowski, "Relations Among Sephardim, Ashkenazim and Avignonese," *YIVO Annual,* X, 189.

[96] Cirot, "Recherches," *Bulletin hispanique,* X, 364 (this article is not identical with the book by the same name); in the eighteenth century the Portuguese were inscribed on the general list of *corps et métiers* as a particular corps (see Chapter V, fn. 18).

[97] *Registre,* No. 3; references to specific pages in such older minute books were made in 1722 and 1723 (Nos. 27 and 29).

the Jews dwelt, the semi-marranos were organized as a community by the middle of the seventeenth century. Apart from the evidence of their joint activities in purchasing a cemetery, there is record of one Jewish community ordinance that was issued in 1666.[98] The basic Jewish organization in St. Esprit was the *Hebera*. Its functions were parallel to those of the *Sedaca* in Bordeaux, and it was run in a similar manner by an oligarchy. The continuing cause of internal battles was taxation. Aggrieved individuals did not hesitate to sue the leadership of the *Hebera* in various jurisdictions. In 1749 a royal order was issued to make sure that such complaints would not clutter up all the courts. It was directed that henceforth those who objected to actions by the *Hebera* could appeal only to the royal intendant.[99] As a result of these internal quarrels, and of the problems raised by the continuing immigration of poorer elements, the *Hebera* proposed its constitution, an elaborate document in forty-four articles, for approval by the intendant. He granted formal sanction in January, 1753. The Jewish community was recognized as a legal corporation and its actions were given official force. The three syndics and the other ten members of the ruling body were to continue, as before, to be elected annually by their predecessors—and not by anything approaching universal suffrage. The leaders were thus a self-perpetuating group. These thirteen officials were in sole and complete charge of making up the tax roll and of enforcing collections. Since "vagabond German and Italian" Jews kept arriving, their stay was limited to three days. The dominant oligarchy was thus given a free hand to run the affairs of the Jewish community.

We do not know when, exactly, the *Hebera* in Bayonne was transformed into the basic and sovereign organization of the community and when the decision was taken to allow a handful of the

[98] The *Réglements* of 1753 mentioned an *ancien registre* of the community that contained a regulation against unauthorized weddings dated 1703. The next article referred to a regulation passed in 1666, but it was not clear from the text that this act reflected an already fully organized community (Léon, *Histoire des Juifs de Bayonne*, pp. 141–49, for the full text of this constitution). We do know that this rule was reenacted in 1700 by Isaac Da Costa, when he was rabbi in Bayonne (see Chapter VI, fn. 65).

[99] That the members of the ruling group would elect their successors was established by a royal decree of March 29, 1741. The decree regarding taxes was issued on June 28, 1749 (MS copies of both acts are in the JTS Library).

wealthiest families to rule. The dates of the comparable actions in Bordeaux are documented. Until 1714 the officers of the *Sedaca* were chosen to deal with the poor. The next year the rhetoric of the minutes changed, to indicate that the syndic and his deputies were now being elected to take charge of all matters of concern of the community. The control by the oligarchs was instituted in 1716. At a meeting held on April 7 of that year a decision of May 25, 1711, was annulled. The earlier arrangement had been that all contributors to the *Sedaca* would have the right to vote in its elections. It was now decreed that "in order to avoid unpleasantness, when the time comes to elect a *gabbai* and his deputies, no one can participate at the election meeting, or in deciding any question that involves our poor, except those who have already held the office of *gabbai*." [100]

The controlling families in Bordeaux fought two essential internal battles in the middle years of the eighteenth century: against the Avignonnais Jews and against Portuguese dissidents. They won against both, largely because of the activity in Paris of Jacob Rodrigues Péreire.[101] In 1754 the *Sedaca* accepted his advice to "lend" 6,000 livres to an unnamed lady, "who by herself and by her connections might be useful to the nation." [102] Two years later the relationship between Péreire and the *Sedaca* was regularized by his acceptance of a life pension of 400 livres to represent it in Paris.[103] Despite his great reputation and connections, Péreire could not persuade the royal court against extending commercial rights to the Avignonnais, especially since the six leading families who were petitioning the king were supported by the *parlement* of Bordeaux, but he did succeed in keeping control of the organized Jewish community in the hands of the Portuguese. When the Avignonnais were given commercial rights in 1759, the act ignored their request to organize their own community.[104]

In 1760 the leaders of Bordeaux followed the example of Bayonne. They strengthened their power by getting royal approval for a com-

[100] *Registre*, Nos. 10, 11.

[101] The only biography of Péreire (La Rochelle, *Péreire*), though primarily concerned with his work for deaf-mutes, has considerable information about his Jewish activities; see pp. 119–25, 273–74, 277–79, 385–98, 444–60.

[102] *Registre*, No. 228.          [103] *Ibid.*, No. 248a.

[104] Malvezin, *Histoire des Juifs à Bordeaux*, p. 211.

munal constitution. Their *règlement* was much briefer than that of
Bayonne. Its author was Péreire, who signed it along with thirteen
*anciens* from Bordeaux. The motivations for its enactment were
given in the preamble: "There was dissension in the Jewish community and there had been much squabbling, especially over taxation,
for a number of years." The crucial provisions of this act were therefore twofold: The police power of Bordeaux was made available as
constraint against those who refused to pay their share of the
*annuel* for the poor, and strong action was taken against "vagabonds
and men without means of support." After a vote by a majority of
three-quarters of the *nation*, the undesirables were to be expelled.[105]

This clause was directly related to the fight with the Avignonnais.
A list of 152 such "undesirables" was compiled and given to the
Duke of Richelieu, the military governor of Guienne. Most of the
people on the list were Avignonnais; only the six families who had
the right to live in Bordeaux under their recent *lettres patentes* were
spared. Richelieu issued the decree of expulsion in September, 1761,
and before long almost all of those named in the order actually did
leave Bordeaux. The quarrel was not yet ended, however, for the
Avignonnais were still petitioning for their own autonomous community. Péreire enlisted the aid of Isaac de Pinto, who was a friend
of Richelieu's. Since the requests of the six Avignonnais families
were still pending, Pinto wrote to Richelieu in 1762, emphasizing
the superiority of the Sephardim over all other Jews. The final result
of all this lobbying was a decree issued in May 1763, which was
perhaps even written by Péreire for the royal officials in Paris. The
Avignonnais were given the right to elect their own syndic and to
prepare their own tax roll, but they were denied all other expressions of autonomy. The crucial matter of control of the Jewish population, the decision on whether to exclude new arrivals, remained, in
law, in Sephardi hands.[106]

For lack of evidence we cannot be sure about Bayonne, but there
can be no doubt that the arguments about taxation in Bordeaux
had no basis in class. These were not fights between the oligarchy

[105] The complete text of this communal constitution is in the *Registre*, No.
279; there is a pamphlet copy of this act in the JTS Library.
[106] Malvezin, *Histoire des Juifs à Bordeaux*, pp. 212–16. The involvement of
Pinto in this affair had important consequences; see Chapters VI and VIII.

and those it oppressed; it was, rather, a series of squabbles among
the leading families. The very first recalcitrant mentioned in the
*Registre*, in 1711, was Jacques Lopes, who had refused to pay an
assessment of almost 88 livres, in a special tax roll that was 600
livres for the entire *nation*.[107] Despite repeated threats of excommunication and the use, after 1730, of civil constraint as well, important individuals continued to refuse to pay taxes. There was a
long battle between 1733 and 1742 with a branch of the Mendes
family. The recalcitrants finally had to pay 670 livres, which was
close to the top rate in those years.[108] The last major quarrel took
place in the 1760s. The dissidents were led by two brokers, Moses
and Joseph Azevedo. They produced a table of the twenty living
former syndics of the *Sedaca* to prove that these represented,
through family relationships, a small group of nine families. The
other party was not much more democratic however. They numbered less than a third of the current tax roll of 171, but they paid
one-third of the taxes, and there were some very wealthy men
among them. After a two-year battle the quarrel was ended by royal
decree in 1766.[109] All else was left untouched (that is, the proce-
dures for assessing internal Jewish taxes), but there was a change
in the mode of making up the tax roll for the royal imposts. For this
purpose two *non-anciens* were added to the taxing committee of
seven *anciens*. This change really did nothing to diminish the power
of the former syndics, for it was they, and not the general body, who
chose the *non-anciens*. This was the last major internal quarrel before 1789; its result was to leave the dominant rich families in secure control.[110]

[107] *Registre*, No. 3.                    [108] *Registre*, No. 107.
[109] The story of this quarrel is told in all the histories of the Jews in Bordeaux. The most recent discussions are in Szajkowski, "Relations Among
Sephardim, Ashkenazim and Avignonese," *YIVO Annual*, X, 186; and "Internal
Conflicts," *HUCA*, XXXI, 167–80. This second study is almost entirely devoted to the Bordeaux tax fight in the 1760's; its appendix reproduces the
minutes of the meeting of the fifty-two dissidents on June 24, 1764, from a
notarial file in the archives of the departement of Gironde.
[110] It is true that from time to time after 1766 one of the dissidents appeared
as a *non-ancien* among the tax assessors. A list of these appointees from 1766
to 1786 appears in the *Registre*, No. 448; it is headed, for 1766, by the Mendes
who fought the *Sedaca* from 1733 to 1742; in 1785 one of the two *non-anciens*
was a son of Moses Azevedo.

An oligarchy was equally in control in Metz. The names of the *parnassim* between 1753 and 1789 were recorded in the *Pinkas* (minute book) of the community. During the whole of this period the office was monopolized by perhaps a dozen families. For example, the banker Hertz Halphen of Nancy, who maintained his right of residence and active participation in the Jewish community in Metz, was first elected as *parnas* in 1756 and he was still in office in 1789. Meier Treni was in office from 1753 until his death some time after 1762; his son Wolfe Treni was elected *parnas* in 1765 and remained in office until 1780 (it should be remembered that Wolfe Treni was cited in 1751 as a secret adherent of Eibeschütz during the controversy over the amulets he had written in Metz). In 1753 Zalman Cohen was elected *parnas*. He died in office and was replaced in the next election in 1756 by his son Sender, who remained a *parnas* through consecutive reelections until after 1774. Sender Cohen soon died, but by 1783 his son Hertz was elected *parnas* and he was still in office in 1789.[111] Once a man had been elected for the first time, it is clear that it was presumed that he would remain in office, through reelection, until he died. The fact that he had been in office made it likely that his principal heir would be elected in his turn.

Even though the mode of election was technically rather democratic, there were large property qualifications for the office of *parnas*. This meant of course that the electorate had to choose its leaders from among a handful of rich families. The earliest fragment of a communal constitution dates from 1699. At that moment all of the Jewish taxpayers of Metz were electing a group of forty people who in turn elected eleven people who in turn chose a communal administration which served for three years. In 1699 the administration consisted of five *parnassim* and a committee of seven to assess communal taxation; after 1702 the number was reduced to four *parnassim* and five tax assessors. There was also a committee of

111 The first election of Meir Treni and Zalman Cohen was recorded in the list of *parnassim* in the *Pinkas*, 11a; three years later, when Halphen and Sender Cohen were first elected, the army purveyor Moshe Belin also first came into office, remaining a *parnas* until his death after the elections of 1762 (20b); Wolfe Treni's first election was recorded in the minutes of 1765 (60b); Hertz Cohen was first on the list of *parnassim* in the election notice on 125a.

seven charged with protecting those Jews in town who had not yet acquired royal permission to live in Metz.[112]

This form of election was abandoned sometime before the middle of the eighteenth century, as is proved by the regulations prescribed for the choosing of *parnassim* in 1752 (the first to appear in the *Pinkas*). All of the essential features of the Metz constitution were present in this document, for the later revisions of the rules, as they were made every three years on the eve of the new elections, repeated its essential provisions. The electoral college for choosing *parnassim* consisted of ninety-nine people, thirty-three from each of three orders in which the community was divided, according to wealth. The top group consisted in 1752 of those whose total financial assets amounted to 10,000 crowns or more; the middle group was worth at least 4,000 crowns and the poorest had more than 600 crowns. The property qualifications varied somewhat through the years but the principle of a division into three orders was never changed. Out of this larger body of ninety-nine, twenty-one electors, seven from each order, were chosen by lot. On election day they were locked into the executive chamber of the community until the election was over and the *parnassim* had taken the oath. In 1752 there were nine *parnassim* (the number varied slightly through the years); [113] no two who were related even to the degree of being married to second cousins could serve at the same time. To be eligible for the office of *parnas* one needed to have the legal right to live in Metz, even though it was permissible to be living elsewhere at the moment; to have been married a minimum of thirty-two years; to be worth at least 5,000 crowns; and to have once served as administrator of the charity for the poor (these qualifications were adjusted in detail but never in essence through the years).[114]

---

[112] Kaufmann, "Extraits," *REJ*, XIX, 115–30.

[113] The number of *parnassim* was reduced to eight in 1762 (*Pinkas*, 43b); it was lowered to seven in 1768 (70b) but became nine again in 1771 (89a). The lowest number was six in 1783 (125a). The number was set prior to each election, but it always reflected the presumption that all the living *parnassim* would be reelected.

[114] In 1762 the property qualifications for *parnas* were set at a capital of 10,000 crowns, if a candidate had the semi-rabbinic degree of *haber*, and 20,000 crowns if he did not. Three years later the property requirement was made the same, 20,000 crowns, in all cases (57a), but in 1768 this amount was halved (70a). The property test was halved again to 5,000 crowns in

A quorum for the transaction of business was a minimum of seven of the nine *parnassim*. If fewer than seven *parnassim* were in town at the same time, the number was brought up to nine by co-opting by lot from among the thirty-three electors of the wealthiest group. Upon his election a *parnas* had to pay all back taxes that he owed. Without the consent of a general meeting of all the electors, the *parnassim* were forbidden to give away more than 60 livres to any individual. They were enjoined to litigate any dispute between the community and an individual before a Jewish court of law, but they could take disputes over taxes to gentile courts. Each of the *parnassim* served in turn for a month (in some later arrangements this became two months) as the executive officer of the community.[115]

In Alsace Jewish communal organizations existed on two levels. In most of the individual communities the *parnas* was elected by universal suffrage of all the taxpayers; in some he was appointed by the *seigneur* on whose territory the Jews were living. Everywhere the prime function of the *parnas* was to carry out the orders of the local noblemen. Wherever the *parnas* was chosen by internal election, he had to be confirmed in office by the overarching Jewish

1771 (88a), but the amount then began to climb again: it was ruled in 1772 that anyone elected for the first time had to possess 20,000 crowns (125a); in 1786 a *haber* needed 12,000 crowns and others had to possess 15,000 crowns; in 1789 the respective amounts rose to 15,000 crowns and 20,000 crowns (142b).

115 The *parnassim* of Metz controlled an elaborate structure of government. There was a *gabbai* for charity as well as one in charge of education, a committee of seven tax collectors, and another committee of nine inspectors who were especially charged with collecting the Brancas tax (*Pinkas*, 5b, describing the structure in 1751). There was also, of course a *hebera kaddisha*, for the burial of the dead, which acquired early the function of supervising the studies in the communal schools (4b), as well as many other fraternities for study or charitable endeavor. There were a large number of paid officers; a beadle, a synagogue-crier, a night watchman (he also checked on the sick in the Jewish hospital), two or three doctors, four cantors, and two scribes, not to speak of the chief rabbi and his deputies (*Pinkas*, 4a, 4b, 13a, 23a, 33a). The *gabbai* for charitable concerns was a kind of tax farmer. He was responsible for furnishing in cash the amounts that were pledged by individuals to charity. This *gabbai* was to recover the money by collecting the pledges, but there was always trouble. In 1772 a professional collector was hired, at a fee of 5 per cent of whatever he brought in (91b). The *gabbai* evidently continued not to have enough funds, for in 1776 a committee investigated the hospital and was upset that he had not provided adequate food, heat, and bedding. The *gabbai* was ordered to mend his ways and give the sick "tea, sugar, preserves, and like foods" which they required (101b).

provincial organization and, if that was necessary, by the intendant
or some other royal authority. The *parnas* could be deposed by his
constituents if he were using his office to express personal grudges.

The provincial organization was headed by two *parnassim*, who
were called either *préposés* or *syndics* in French. There was also a
general treasurer, who was represented in each community by a
collector of taxes and assessments. The *parnassim* and other officers
were chosen at a triennial election held in the spring of the year. It
is likely, though not absolutely certain, that the electors were the
*parnassim* of the individual communities. One of the functions of
the triennial meeting of this province-wide Jewish assembly was to
set policy on a variety of matters. The session of 1777 occupied itself mostly with taxation, but the delegates also enacted some
sumptuary rules and they even reaffirmed an older rule dividing the
direct care of the indigent sick equitably among all the Jewish communities of the province.[116] At the next meeting, in 1780 at Cerf
Berr's home in Bischheim, to defend the Jews against the economic
and political attacks in the affair of the "false receipts," it was decided to press for the abolition of the body tax in Strasbourg and
to get a new charter of rights for the Jews in Alsace. Money was
appropriated to initiate not only political action but also to encourage pro-Jewish propaganda.[117] It was no accident that Dohm's book
in defense of the Jews appeared with the support of Cerf Berr the
very next year, in 1781, containing as an appendix the *mémoire* on
behalf of the Alsatian Jews, which had been drafted at the gathering
in Bischheim. We do not have a minute book of the Alsatian Jewish
provincial organization, and it cannot therefore be proved that there
were any formal property qualifications for the office of syndic.
Nevertheless, it is clear that this office was invariably held by the
richest Jews in the province, who, like the Weill brothers early in
the century or Cerf Berr at the end of it, possessed important political connections.

[116] The Alsatian Jewish provincial organization is described in detail in Hoffman, *L'Alsace*, IV, 331-33; see also *Extract from the minutes of 1777*, clause
2. The directory of the nobility of Lower Alsace appointed not only a rabbi
but also two *parnassim* for the Jews in their territories; see M. Ginsburger "Elie
Schwab," *REJ*, XLIV, 262–63.
[117] Scheid, *Juifs d'Alsace*, p. 245.

There were even more quarrels within the Ashkenazi oligarchies (there were many more Jews in eastern France) than among the Sephardim. In Metz, for example, formal Jewish communal structure began quite peacefully in the year 1595, when the Jewish population in the city was only 120. An act of organization was translated into French and deposited with the royal governor of the city, who signified his assent by accepting the document. At that moment the Jews were ruled by six *parnassim*, one of whom was a rabbi. It did not take long for a major fight to begin. In 1627 Moses Cohen of Prague was elected as rabbi by the group in power. Some dissidents refused to accept this choice and they even imported into town a rabbi of their own. Revealingly, the rebels accused the leaders of knowing how to stay in power through their knowledge of the French language and their ready access to governmental authorities. That there was some substance to this charge was proved by the outcome of the quarrel. The military governor of Metz, the Duke of LaVallette, sided with the men in power and even expelled some of their opponents, including their rabbi.[118]

At the very end of the *ancien régime* such quarrels, which had been going on throughout the years in Metz, were still vitriolic. In 1782 a pained decision was reported in the *Pinkas*. The communal authorities revoked the right of Jacob Coblenz to live in Metz. He was a ringleader of a group of malcontents who had already been fined ineffectively. The entry in the minute book is illuminating: "The rebels are increasing lately and they are unlawfully raising their raucous voices against the *parnassim* of our community . . . thus hoping to weaken their authority. It is their intention to subvert the dispensing of justice by the *parnassim* so that everyone can henceforth do what he wants and what pleases him." Three years later there was the most flagrant abuse of all. One of the incumbent *parnassim*, Wolfe Cohen, instituted suit in civil court against his own colleagues and against the interim rabbis of the community. According to the regulations for the election of *parnassim* in 1789 he was debarred for life from ever holding any office in Metz because of his recourse to the secular courts.[119]

[118] A. Cahen, "Le rabbinat de Metz," *REJ*, VII, 205–14.
[119] *Pinkas*, 123a, 142b.

The internal battles in Alsace were equally bitter and common danger did not bring unity. Some of the many quarrels among the lay leaders have already been mentioned: in 1715 to 1717 the syndics and Isaiah Brunswick were fighting over who was to represent the Jews before the king against an attempt by the Alsatian cities to restrict Jewish commerce. A decade later the syndics were accused of being self-serving and venal and in 1781 Cerf Berr and the Lehmann family split the community of Bischheim. It is understandable why in the regulations enacted by the assembly of 1777 it was again ruled that all the Jews in Alsace had to obey the general syndic of the province and that, in case of disobedience, he could fine a rebel up to 150 livres.

Perhaps the greatest cause of controversy within Alsatian Jewry was its rabbinate. The first rabbi for all of Alsace was Aaron Worms of Metz, who was named to that office by Louis XIV in 1681. This over-all authority did not last, for when he died in 1697 the Jews of Lower Alsace got permission to have their own rabbi. In 1700 Samuel Lévy managed through family connections to get himself elected rabbi jointly in the towns of Ribeauvillé and Bergheim and to be recognized as successor to Worms as rabbi of all of Upper Alsace. When Lévy left to become the "court Jew" of Leopold of Lorraine, his successor, Samuel Sanvil Weil, tried to claim jurisdiction over all of Alsace. There had, however, been a rabbinate in Haguenau since the middle of the seventeenth century with either authority or pretensions to authority over the Jews of Lower Alsace. In 1721 Elie Schwab, of the same wealthy Metz family that had produced Samuel Lévy, became rabbi in Haguenau through family influence. He got formal recognition that year from Louis XV as rabbi of all of Lower Alsace, by alleging that he had been chosen by the Jews of the region. The directorate of the nobility of Lower Alsace opposed this royal action on the ground that they had not given their consent and that the Jews had themselves previously elected Samuel Weil. In actual fact Schwab had been elected by the Jews in Haguenau to the post in that town only. In 1734 he was battling with Samuel Maennel Seligman, the rabbi of Bouxwiller, for authority over the Jews in two small towns, Oberbronn and

Niederbronn. Schwab was not above writing to the *Conseil Souverain* of Lower Alsace that his opponent was "an ass by his very nature." His enemies replied in kind by attacking Schwab's character. This quarrel was finally settled in 1738. A royal decree confirmed the following authorities in their rights to name rabbis in their territories: the Bishop of Strasbourg, the Count of Hanau-Lichtenberg, and the directory of the nobility of Lower Alsace.[120]

In the last decades before 1789 what had evolved from all these quarrels, in which Jewish factions, various local authorities, and the royal power were all involved, was roughly the following: There were a number of more or less officially recognized rabbis in a variety of Alsatian towns. There were four rabbis in Lower Alsace and one in Upper Alsace who had full legal recognition and civil as well as religious authority over the Jews in their regions. The question of the civil authority of the rabbis had been the major issue in all the battles over that office—and it is this civil authority of the rabbinate, and of the Jewish communities in eastern France in general, which was the crucial difference between the Ashkenazi and Sephardi communities as a whole.

### Nation in Exile or Merchant Guild?

From the very beginning of organized Jewish life in Metz the *parnassim* had absolute power over the inner life of the Jews. The act of organization on July 12, 1595, had specified that they were to "govern, judge, and forbid" all the Jews in Metz. Very early in the seventeenth century the royal power fully accepted the assumption on which the Jews had organized themselves in Metz, that they were to conduct their internal affairs in the manner that was usual in the nearby communities of Germany and in the central European Jewish world as a whole. The leaders of the Jewish community maintained consistently that this included their right to jurisdiction even in civil cases that involved Jews. On this issue there was a

[120] On the authority and powers of the rabbinate of Alsace in general, see Hoffman, *L'Alsace*, IV, 334–44. For some of the battles among the rabbis, see M. Ginsburger, *Les Juifs à Ribeauvillé* (a pamphlet); "Mutzig," *Souvenir et Science*, IV, Nos. 5, 10; "Elie Schwab," *REJ*, XLIV, 104–21, 260–82.

continuing battle throughout the whole of the *ancien règime*, with dissidents in the Jewish community itself and especially with the *parlement* of Metz.

In 1624 the Duke of LaVallette confirmed the Jews in their power to judge religious and civil cases involving only themselves, "as has been customary since they were established in the city." One of the early acts of the newly organized *parlement* of Metz was to agree in 1634 to the proposition that the Jews had the right to inner self-government "in religion and in their inner concerns." This last phrase was vague and it left the *parlement* room for the next century and a half to oppose repeatedly the power of the Jews to exercise independent civil jurisdiction. This question generally came up again when a dissident individual within the Jewish community, dissatisfied with some decision of the *parnassim* in a matter in which he was involved, tried to overturn the civil jurisdiction of the Jewish community and go to law. There were such incidents in 1694 and again in 1706 and 1709.[121]

At the beginning of the new reign of Louis XV the regent issued *lettres patentes* in 1718 that confused rather than clarified the situation of Jewish civil jurisdiction. This decree of 1718 dealt with the whole gamut of Jewish concerns in Metz, among them communal autonomy. It permitted the Jews to keep for themselves, for cases involving only Jews, the right to be tried by their rabbi; the lay heads of the Jewish community could "make all their internal rules, including those regarding religion, customs, ceremonies, and taxes." [122] This formula was interpreted in due course by the Metz *parlement* to mean that the rabbinic tribunal had the status merely of an arbitrator, and that Jews were to be judged in civil affairs not by local civil courts, but according to their own law. A French translation of the code of Jewish civil law, the *Choshen Mishpat*, was now necessary. Such a volume was deposited with the *parlement* in 1743. This text was found to be too prolix, because of "the great amount of the nonsense of their rabbis, in which the Talmud and their other books abound." Lançon, one of the lawyers practicing before the *parlement*, undertook to make a usable extract from the "formless

[121] A. Cahen, "Le rabbinat de Metz," *REJ*, VII, 111, 206, 215, 257–59.
[122] The text of this decree is in Clément, *La condition des Juifs*, pp. 278–85.

chaos." [123] For almost half a century thereafter a French court was thus regularly in the business of judging Jews by interpreting a talmudic law book.

From the very beginning of its organized history the Jewish community had exercised the right of supervising the execution of wills and the appointing of guardians for minors. Who was to do this was invariably specified in the contracts between the Jews of Metz and the rabbis they elected. Both in 1708 when Abraham Broda was called to Metz and in 1766 when Asser Lion was appointed it was specified in their contracts that the rabbi could act alone in appointing temporary guardians for minors; after three months he could make a permanent appointment, but only with the approval of the parnassim.[124] Asser Lion evidently ignored this provision and consulted only his rabbinic deputies in such matters, for the parnassim decreed in 1779 that he must desist from this practice and share the power of appointment with them.[125] The control of wills was a major issue, for considerable economic patronage was involved. It was the largest single element in the business of the rabbinic court in Metz.

Testamentary decisions in rabbinic law were those that were most likely to be challenged in the French courts. In particular, the dower rights of the widow were very much less in talmudic than in French law and it was therefore to her advantage to try to overturn rabbinic jurisdiction.[126] The most important such case occurred in 1759. The widow of Bernard Spire Lévy refused to accept a Jewish decision that was unfavorable to her. When the Metz Jewish community attempted to enforce the decree of its tribunal by excommunicating her, she went to parlement to appeal both the decision

[123] Lançon, Recueil des lois, introduction; the on-going battle of the Jews with the parlement of Metz is described in detail in Clément, La condition des Juifs, pp. 48–89.
[124] The text of the rabbinic contract of Abraham Broda is printed in Braude, The Broda Family (in Hebrew), pp. 12–18; the very similar contract of Asser Lion was recorded in Pinkas, 64a–66a.
[125] Pinkas, 107b.
[126] In talmudic law a widow receives the amount specified in the marriage contract and the capital worth of her dowry. In the customary law of Metz a widow, including step-mothers, shared equally with the children in all household goods and debts owed the deceased (see Jager, Transmission héréditaire, p. 54).

and the excommunication. On January 30, 1759, the Jewish authorities in Metz were utterly forbidden to make any future attempt to preserve their civil jurisdiction over Jews. The *parlement* went further, to rule that the community could not use excommunication to enforce rabbinic decisions even when the rabbis sat as arbitrators and, in the most sweeping action ever, the Jews of Metz were prohibited from enforcing their discipline on internal matters such as squabbles within the synagogue. In 1765 the Jewish community petitioned *parlement* against this act. In the Jewish brief precedents were quoted from the royal decrees in their favor, but the *parnassim* knew that these arguments would not impress the *parlement*. They therefore advanced other considerations. They insisted, in the first place, that religion is an indivisible thing which must control every facet of conduct, including civil conduct. If the rabbis could not enforce their decrees through excommunication, their authority would become nil. Most feelingly, the *parnassim* added that since the decree by the *parlement* the Jewish leaders of Metz had had "sad experience; since this decree they have been witness to a decline of standards of conduct, for there was an increase in gambling, in luxury, in attendance upon shows and in loose habits in other areas; they had tried, ineffectually, to bring some remedy, but they had found that only rebelliousness and contempt were meeting their chastisements." [127]

The Jews of Metz could get no satisfaction from the *parlement*, but they did succeed some years later in getting a new decree in their favor from the king. At the beginning of the new reign of Louis XVI *lettres patentes* were issued, on February 3, 1777, in which it was specified that the rabbi and the lay heads of the Jewish community should be maintained "in their jurisdiction over all those matters which concern the cases of Jews against Jews, in the civil realm, only; it is forbidden to any Jew to refuse to accept this jurisdiction in such cases." When the *parlement* of Metz registered this decree it refused to accept its meaning at face value. The *parlement* added the reservation that the rabbinic court had jurisdiction only if Jews chose to arbitrate their differences before it but that no Jew

[127] A *nosseigneurs de parlement, supplient humblement les syndics de la communauté des Juifs de cette ville* (a copy of this brief is in the JTS Library).

could be compelled to go to Jewish justice. The *parnassim* of Metz fought against this interpretation but not everyone in the community conformed (and, as we have seen above, not even all the *parnassim* obeyed the rules). It was recorded in the minutes in 1781 that some people were ignoring the *lettres patentes* of 1777 and going to the general courts. The Jewish community announced that it would sue to stop them and that it would make them pay the cost of such actions.[128]

One of the points of issue in this battle over civil jurisdiction was economic; who was going to collect the fees that pertained to the right of judgment? This was very much in the foreground in Alsace. The right to dispense justice in courts of lowest resort belonged to the innumerable petty noblemen of the province. It had long been held that they could not act personally and directly as judges in their immediate fiefs. They had to appoint magistrates, who were called *baillis,* but the *seigneurs* shared in the proceeds from court costs and from the fines that were levied by their officers of justice.[129] The *baillis,* who were mostly venal, had a personal stake not only in the fees but also in the graft that they could collect. In 1681 when Louis XIV had confirmed Aaron Worms as rabbi for all of Alsace, the decree had specified that "he should exercise functions comparable to those of the rabbi in our city of Metz." Even though the *Conseil Souverain* of Alsace tried to maintain in 1719 that rabbinic jurisdiction in Alsace did not include the right to execute wills and appoint guardians, this decision was reversed in the next year. Throughout the eighteenth century the authority of the Jews over civil cases that involved only themselves was even stronger than in Metz itself.

The noblemen in Alsace were not particularly unhappy in this separate Jewish legal structure, for they lost nothing by it. In general, one-half of the fines levied by the various Jewish tribunals were paid over to the *seigneuries* in which such a tribunal sat. One of the issues, therefore, in the innumerable battles among rabbis in the province, who were always fighting to extend their jurisdictions, was the financial interest of the appointing power. *Seigneurs* were interested in having Jewish cases tried on their territories and not

[128] *Pinkas,* 120b.   [129] Livet, *L'intendance d'Alsace,* pp. 225–26.

taken elsewhere, as they sometimes were, to Metz or even to Frankfurt. As early as 1698 the directorate of the nobility of Lower Alsace had established a rabbi and two syndics on their territory, avowedly in order to keep their Jews from having recourse to justice elsewhere; this action was reaffirmed in 1722.[130] There were troubles in Alsace, too, over Jews who defied the community and had recourse to the general courts. The regulations published in 1777 by the triennial Jewish assembly reiterated the continuing prohibition against such breaches of discipline.[131]

It is not at all accidental that the most vehement opposition to Jewish civil jurisdiction did not come in Alsace from the *Conseil Souverain* but from the *baillis*. In Metz the *parlement* was a court of first resort and it was therefore in direct collision with the exercise of Jewish justice. The *Conseil Souverain* of Alsace, sitting at Colmar, was a court of appeal, to which cases came from the rabbinic courts quite as normally as from the lower courts manned by the *baillis*. These local feudal magistrates were, however, in conflict with the judicial organs of Jewish autonomy. Hell, who led the attack on the Jews and on their self-government after 1777, was the *bailli* of Landser. He spoke for many, probably for most, of his peers. Aside from churchmen, these lowest judicial officers were the most important literate anti-Semites in Alsace on the eve of the Revolution.

There was none of this in Bordeaux and Bayonne. To be sure, not many cases of business conflicts involving only Jews were ever litigated before the civil courts in southwestern France. The Sephardim evidently settled such arguments among themselves, no doubt by arbitration before the syndics, as the Bordeaux regulation of 1738 required. Inheritance cases did get into the civil courts with fair frequency, because the syndics never tried to impose Jewish testamentary law.[132] It is absolutely clear that the rabbis of the Sephardim had no civil jurisdiction; they did not even participate in arbitrations. In the communal constitution of Bayonne in 1760

---

[130] Hoffman, *L'Alsace*, IV, 334–39.        [131] *Extract from the minutes*, clause 8.

[132] There were many more cases about estates among the Sephardim than in the rest of French Jewry; see Szajkowski, *Franco-Judaica*, Nos. 1009–10059, where all but ten of these legal briefs and documents, which referred to testamentary matters, were of Sephardi provenance.

it was specified that "the rabbi will take no part whatsoever in the affairs of the *nation;* he will confine himself only to those matters which directly involve his ministry." This decision was perhaps a reaction in Bayonne to the one attempt to institute a rabbinate of far broader powers. During his regime Raphael Meldola had tried to make the community conform to stricter religious norms; he fought to exercise the kind of rabbinic power that was customary in his home community of Leghorn.[133] In Bordeaux in the eighteenth century the role of the rabbi was inferior even to that in Bayonne. When Jacob Haim Athias was appointed to office in 1738, it was specified that "he should take charge of all the spiritual functions of the *nation.*" This meant that he was in charge of purely ritual functions. Even in that area he was pulled up short by the lay leaders in the next year, when without permission of the syndics he forbade a ritual-slaughterer to practice his trade. Athias was suspended from office in 1752 in the midst of a quarrel with the syndics; he was reappointed only on the promise that he would not "fall back into his evil ways." His son and successor, David Athias, was a synagogue functionary and the chief teacher in the religious school. An undated document from the eighteenth century is particularly sad. The intendant himself was inquiring of the Jews why their syndics had "so little respect and deference for their rabbi." [134]

Among the Ashkenazim the *parnassim* did indeed do battle with the rabbis over their respective roles and powers, but this was a battle among equals over questions of substance, involving the civil law of an autonomous "nation in exile." Throughout the *ancien régime* the rabbis of Metz were men of the highest distinction. Without exception, they were authorities in rabbinic law to whom questions were sent from the whole of central and eastern Europe.

[133] Léon, *Historie des Juifs de Bayonne,* p. 147 (clause 23 of the *Règlement* of 1753) and p. 387 (Raphael Meldola in Bayonne).

[134] *Registre,* Nos. 85, 205, 275: Cirot, *Recherches,* pp. 81–82. The syndics of the Sephardim of Bordeaux were of the same opinion about their rabbi after the Revolution. In a report to the prefect of the police (undated, but from the 1790's) the syndics wrote that there was one rabbi in Bordeaux who was "simply a casuist" with no authority. They added that rabbis could "never figure in any political deliberations or in any meetings that regulated the internal behavior" of the Sephardim (*Archive de la Gironde,* V, 13).

Indeed, a comparison of their large output of responsa with the little such writing among the Sephardim is revealing. There were only two collections of responsa that bore some relationship to Bayonne. These were the volumes of the two Meldolas; these books contained almost no decisions on issues of civil law. The few such questions that occurred in the last section of Raphael Meldola's *Mayyim Rabbim* were all of Italian provenance. On the other hand, one-third of the responsa by Jacob Reischer and Gershon Ashkenazi were devoted to issues of civil law. The rabbis in Alsace were not uniformly as distinguished, but their role was the same as that of the rabbi in Metz.[135] Even in Alsace there were some exceptional scholars. Samuel Lévy had received a first-class talmudic education and his stepmother Glückel deplored the fact that he did not devote himself to what she regarded as his obvious career, that of becoming a light of learning and a rabbinic leader for the entire Ashkenazi world. Samuel Halberstatt had come to Alsace from the post of deputy rabbi in the greatest Ashkenazi center of that day, the Jewish community in Prague.

The whole structure of the Sephardi community was founded on a different presumption; they were not organized as a people but rather as a merchant guild, which employed various functionaries to serve them, rabbis among them. This merchant guild did, indeed, try to keep its poor and its quarrels out of the public eye, but this was a matter of circumspection. Before the law it was to the interest of these merchants to try to achieve, as they ultimately almost did in the decree of 1776, the status and the stance of the rest of the French bourgeoisie. The emancipation of the Sephardim was, therefore, a quite different and far easier matter than the emancipation of the Ashkenazim. When the Ashkenazim were finally given equality in 1791, the immediate expectation of the emancipators was that the Jews of eastern France would reorganize the whole of their lives, both as a community and as individuals, in the Sephardi mode.

The battles of the Jews for enlargement of their rights and the beginnings of their acculturation were important as "preparations"

135 All the questions of business in parts two and four of Meldola's *Mayyim Rabbim* were from Italy; for the contrasting situation in Metz see Gershon Ashkenazi, *Hiddushei ha-Gershuni*, and Jacob Reischer, *Shevut Yaakov*, part 3.

for their emancipation. To gain their cause it was, however, not enough for the Jews to insinuate themselves into any possible new economic openings and push, maneuver, and plead for increased rights. They had to convince French opinion and the makers of French policy. We must turn now to the complicated discussions of the "Jewish question" in France as a whole in the eighteenth century.

## ❧ VIII ❧

## *Churchmen and the Jews*

The eighteenth century was the "age of the Enlightenment," of Voltaire and the *philosophes*—but it was also the age of statesmen, economists, and abbés. Some of these were "enlightened," others were influenced to some degree by the new thinking, and still others opposed or ignored it. This age was intoxicated with words, especially with those in print. One sometimes gets the impression that every literate person had a printing press next door to his study. Everything, including the Jews, was being debated b᷄ everybody.

Voltaire was the dominant figure, and all his life he could not let go of the question of Jews and Judaism. Discussions by historians of the Jewish question in his age have therefore tended to become considerations of the relationship between the Enlightenment and the Jews. It has been assumed as self-evident that the emancipation of the Jews by the Revolution was a direct result of the new 'hinking of the *philosophes*. As we have already hinted, this construction is much too simplistic. We shall soon see that the *philosophes* were themselves divided and subdivided on the Jewish question, in very complicated ways; there was no straight line from their corporate outlook to the granting of equality for the Jews. But the *philosophes* were not the only group in France in the eighteenth century that was discussing the Jews. The church and the state had both begun seriously to rethink the Jewish question in the days of Colbert. In the eighteenth century each of these discussions moved in a separate and paradoxical direction.

It must be remembered that before the Revolution began no

responsible statesman or economist believed in immediate emancipation. The great majority were meliorists, who wanted to broaden the economic rights and opportunities of the Jews with a view to bringing them into society. A hyper-modern minority, the physiocrats, tended to doubt that even a meliorist approach was possible. In the Church, the situation was just the reverse. The overwhelming majority of the clergy, even some of the most literate among them, continued to hold to medievalist, anti-Jewish opinions into the Revolutionary era. This is proved beyond any doubt by their *cahiers* of 1789.[1] Nonetheless, a significant quasi-secret, quasi-sectarian minority, composed of some of the best clerical intellectuals, had moved towards the view that the Jews should be treated with kindness—and the root of the newer outlook of some of these abbés was in theological considerations. How did these changes occur?

The debate that had been reopened among clerical intellectuals by Spinoza's *Theological-Political Tractate* continued in even more complicated ways in the eighteenth century. In this debate there were religious writers who simply repeated, to the very end of the century, the medieval view that the Jews were damned and that their suffering had to persist as punishment for their rejection of Christ. A typical spokesman for this view was the Abbé Perrin des Chavanettes. He was a follower of Bossuet, whom he quoted frequently as the ultimate authority. In 1769, when Chavanettes published a theological history of the Jews from the creation to the destruction of the Temple of Jerusalem, the Jewish question was very much a current intellectual issue. The debate between Pinto and Voltaire had been underway since 1762, and the first entry of the liberal abbé Antoine Guénée, who intervened in this argument, had taken place in 1765. Chavanettes' interpretation of Jewish history was not influenced at all by these discussions. He did not slant his version of biblical Jewish history to defend ancient Judaism against Voltaire. His concluding remarks about the Jews after the

---

[1] The positions taken in the *cahiers* on the Jewish question have been summarized in Liber, "La convocation," *REJ*, LXIII, 184–210. The exceptions to the rule that the *cahiers* were overwhelmingly anti-Jewish are to be found in an occasional position by a group of the nobility or the third estate and never in a *cahier* by one of the clerical assemblies. See, also, the discussion of this point in Chapter X.

beginning of their exile were an unalloyed restatement of the dominant medieval view:

The Jews have been made to wander for more than seventeen centuries all over the world. This exile represents the final seal on all the prophecies which foretold that they would be punished for their deicide. Despite all their attempts, they have not been able to succeed to this day in creating a nation, a state, and an established government of their own. The Jews are the objects of hatred and general indignation, which pursue them unceasingly and propel them from one country to another. What a frightening picture of both inflexible justice and unbelievable blindness.[2]

A comparable attitude was taken, at least most of the time, by a more important and more complicated figure, the Abbé Charles Louis Richard. Unlike Chavanettes, Richard was very much involved in the "actions and passions" of his time. When the Parisian Jewish banker Liefman Calmer bought the barony of Picquigny in 1774 and attempted to appoint priests to two benefices on that land, Richard immediately joined the battle of the pamphlets. He wrote that the Church, as the bride of Christ, must reject "ministers at its altars whom a descendant of the killers of Christ is presuming to appoint to them." Jews had no rights to make such appointments because they were "avowed enemies of the Christian religion and of the Catholic Church." Richard reached the climax of his invective in declaring that

a Jew is a born and sworn enemy of all Christians. It is a principle of his faith to regard them as blasphemers and idolaters who should be put to death, and whom he should harm as much as he can without endangering himself. The Christians in turn regard Jews as the God-killing executioners of Jesus Christ, the man-God, whom Christians adore and accept as their Messiah, their supreme head, their immortal Savior.

In the light of his outrage at this incident involving Calmer, Richard had to answer the question as to why the king had granted this Jew letters of naturalization. He tried to "absolve" Louis XVI by suggesting something that Richard obviously did not believe himself, that the king had been tricked and had not known that Calmer was a Jew. Without expanding on the implications of the distinction, Richard concluded the essay by asserting that the naturalization of a Jew could mean merely that "only useful rights" have been con-

[2] Chavanettes, *Discours*, pp. 147–48.

ferred on him; a Jew could have no rights that were incompatible with his status as "a Jew, foreigner, and enemy." [3]

This attitude of Richard's was not limited to Jews. He was concurrently engaged in pamphleteering against the growing movement to give freedom to the Protestants in France. The legalization of Protestant marriages was being debated at that time as a direct outgrowth of Turgot's attempt to get civil rights for Protestants at the beginning of Louis XVI's reign. Richard took the uncompromising position that there could be no rights for error. He obdurately insisted that legalizing Protestant marriages would do injury to the general good of the state in both the spiritual and temporal realms. The function of the state was to serve the true Catholic faith. [4]

In arguing these medievalist views Richard even descended to anonymous pamphleteering of a most scurrilous kind. He wrote a letter purported to be by the "rabbi of the synagogue of the Jews of Metz" to Mordecai Venture, whom Richard called "the rabbi of the synagogue of Paris." This title was reasonably accurate, for Venture was then the most considerable scholar among the Jews of Paris. He was serving as specialist in Hebrew at the royal library and he did fulfill rabbinic functions, unofficially, for the Jews of Paris. In this letter the "rabbi of Metz" announced to his colleague in Paris that he was calling a Sanhedrin to "instruct" Calmer not to appoint any priest to a benefice unless that priest is circumcised. If Calmer did not obey he would be expelled from the synagogue. Perhaps the strangest aspect of this pamphlet was the use which Richard made of Voltaire. As we shall soon see, Richard's major work was done in the defense of the faith against Voltaire's criticism. Richard nonetheless invoked Voltaire to help make an anti-Jewish point. The last lines of this "letter from Metz" is an exhortation of Calmer to follow the example of that good Christian, Voltaire, who had suggested that the Abbé Guénée, as the defender of the Jews, should be circumcised—all the more reason, Richard added, in his pose as a rabbi of Metz, why the holder of a benefice

[3] Richard, *Recueil,* especially pp. 84–85, 92, 96, 105. For the rest of the literature on this battle see Szajkowski, *Franco-Judaica,* Nos. 1199–1259.

[4] Richard, *Les Protestants;* for this debate, see Chapter IV.

conferred by a Jew should be required to enter the covenant of Abraham.

Richard continued in this vein in a "letter of a Parisian Jew to a Jew in Germany." The Parisian was ecstatic over the dignity that was accruing to all Jewry through Liefman Calmer. The "writer" asked that it be announced to all the Jews of Germany "that the time of their deliverance is near and they will soon, in their turn, rule over the Christians all over the world." Calmer would build the Jews beautiful synagogues after destroying all the churches.[5] In the debate against Calmer Richard thus took the low roads of traditional anti-Semitism in his anonymous pamphlets and the high roads of theological anti-Judaism in his signed essays.

There was, on the other hand, a kinder tradition even among orthodox Catholic theologians. This school of thought descended from Fleury. Here, too, Voltaire played a considerable role in helping it crystallize, but it was not so much the Voltaire who despised the Jews in the present, but rather the one who mounted a life-long, unrelenting attack on the Old Testament. As we have seen, Fleury had idealized the Old Testament. His work was to be remembered for a good century later even by some men of the Enlightenment. D'Alembert, for example, was most impressed by Fleury; he saw in Fleury's depiction of human life of Old Testament times and the days of the early Church the highest adumbration of the natural life: "In reading Fleury one imagines, at least for a moment, that one is Israelite and Christian." [6] The most important intellectual figure of the century, Voltaire, was not impressed however.

Fleury's outlook was followed by Dom Augustin Calmet, the leading orthodox Catholic scholar among Voltaire's contemporaries. As is well known, Voltaire spent much of his energy mocking this abbé. Calmet was a most prolific writer who maintained throughout his work an attitude of fairness to Jews, not only of the biblical era but even of the medieval and contemporary ages. The entries about Jewish matters in his *Dictionnaire historique, critique,*

---

[5] Both these "Letters" appeared in 1777 in an anonymous pamphlet of ten pages. They were headed, respectively, *Lettre du rabbin de la synagogue des Juifs de Metz au sieur Liefman Calmer, propriétaire de la baronie de Picquigny* and *Lettre d'un Juif de Paris à un Juif d'Allemagne.*

[6] D'Alembert, *Oeuvres*, X, 20–21.

*chronologique, géographique et littéral de la Bible* were unfailingly fair, although his information was sometimes inaccurate. His main source was Léon de Modena, whose work he knew in Richard Simon's French translation. For example, Calmet's article on Passover repeated no blood libels, not even to refute them. The account of the Sanhedrin implicitly absolved the Jews for at least part of the guilt for the death of Jesus, because Calmet emphasized that the Sanhedrin no longer had the right to decree capital punishment at that time.[7] In his *Histoire de l'Ancien et du Nouveau Testament et des Juifs pour servir d'introduction à l'histoire ecclésiastique de M. l'Abbé Fleury,* the story of the biblical history is told with approval as the preamble to the larger revelation that followed in Jesus. Calmet was, however, fair and courageous enough, when he blamed the Jews for the death of Jesus, to add that they had biblical reason since they held that he was not the son of God. "In effect the law of Moses condemns blasphemers to death." [8] In the whole of Calmet's work there is a recurring note: he had a preference for "enlightened" Jews, such as he imagined Maimonides or his favorite authority, Leon de Modena, to have been.

Calmet's work was continued by Richard, who was the chief editor and author of an ecclesiastical dictionary.[9] All the entries that had direct reference to Jews and Judaism were largely under the influence of the earlier work of Calmet, but there were crucial differences. The most important was the article on the Talmud, which did not follow Calmet's objective account. It was a long and vicious attack: "In its history and chronology the Talmud contains not only pitiful dreams, ridiculous fables, and obvious falsehoods, but it also blasphemes against the religion of Jesus Christ." Richard proceeded to give a list of the "errors" of the Talmud, no less than thirty-eight in number, in which he mostly ridiculed the folklore of the Talmud by taking it literally.[10]

On the other hand, especially when he was confronting Voltaire,

---

[7] Calmet's *Dictionnaire* first appeared in Paris in 1722 in two volumes; see II, 147, 327–28.

[8] Calmet's *Histoire* was published in Paris in 1719 in two volumes; the edition being quoted here is a "new and corrected" one, Paris, 1737, III, 653.

[9] See Moulaert, *R. P. Richard,* p. 8. The actual title of Richard's massive *Dictionnaire,* in answer to Voltaire, was *Bibliothèque sacrée.*

[10] *Richard,* V, 200–201.

Richard followed Calmet in unfailingly approving of those Jews who seemed to him to be in some measure beyond the Talmud and its superstitions. On Menasseh Ben Israel, of seventeenth-century Amsterdam, he wrote: "He was of the Pharisaic sect but an honest man of good character. He had all the civic virtues which one could wish. He possessed quick understanding, sound judgment, and a light but sharp wit." Richard took a comparable attitude to Maimonides: "This doctor was one of the finest scholars among the Jews, and he was perhaps the one most removed from their superstitions." Richard added that Maimonides, in his work on Jewish law, had the virtue of excluding "the majority of the tales and impertinences which abound in the Talmud." [11] The implication is thus very clear that for a Jew to be minimally acceptable in the world he must abandon the law of the Talmud. Another stroke was thus added to a theory about Jews, emanating from orthodox Christian theological circles, which attributed what was wrong with them to the Talmud and suggested that if they would return to the Bible and its simple virtues they would approach again the level of high civilization and morality. Jewish "enlighteners" in the next generation and the one after were to make much of such notions.

Richard's massive work was contemporary with the earliest stages of Voltaire's *Philosophical Dictionary*. The first five volumes of Richard appeared in 1762 and the first edition of Voltaire's work, representing his broad onslaught on every aspect of the Bible, was published in 1764. The industry of writers in those days is almost unbelievable; the enormous supplementary volume to Richard's work was in print, in well over six hundred folio pages, in 1765. It was written as a counter-attack on Voltaire. Richard announced that it was his task to combat the denigration of religion by the *philosophes*, for "the *philosophes* confuse all ideas; their frightful ideas overturn and destroy every religious principle, there is no God or king, or faith or law." Under the pressure of Voltaire Richard turned, in the supplementary volume, into a much stronger defender of ancient Judaism. In the article on religion in this new

[11] *Ibid.*, VI, 413–14.

book he argued that the laws of Moses are indeed imperfect if they are compared to the laws of the New Testament but that they were the highest dispensation prior to the appearance of Jesus. Richard rejected all of the arguments of the "unbelievers and Deists" against the truth and divinity of the Pentateuch. The conclusion of a long and detailed argument was that the New Dispensation had abrogated the judicial and ceremonial law of the Old, but the philosophical doctrines about God, the moral precepts, and the love of God and of neighbor were all clearly to be found in the doctrine of the ancient Jews, and that they were still in force.[12] The first response to the appearance of Voltaire's *Philosophical Dictionary* was thus to make again the same inevitable connection that had been made when Spinoza's work had appeared: the defense of the Jewish Bible was a necessity for the defense of Christianity. This connection was now appearing in the work of an abbé who was and remained a considerable anti-Semite.

Nonetheless even Richard was not an anti-Semite all the time. Anger at Voltaire and some carry-over from Richard's praise of the Jews of the Old Testament united, in one of his works, to produce at least a mild defense of the Jews of his own day. At the very time that Richard was attacking both the Protestants and Liefman Calmer, he also mounted a large-scale personal attack on Voltaire. This work was a fanciful depiction of the journey of the soul of Voltaire among the famous shades of the past, both believers and non-believers, including Machiavelli, Spinoza, and Marcus Aurelius, among others. All of these were put on the stage by Richard to say how wrong they were in not being good Christians and to argue with Voltaire. In the last chapter the protagonists were Voltaire and the Jew Trypho, who had been the Jewish figure in the church father Justin Martyr's *Dialogue* between a Christian and a Jew. In addition to attacking Voltaire for his writings against the Bible, Trypho charged Voltaire with his lack of compassion for the Jews and with aggravating their misery. Richard did not emphasize this particular theme, for here too his purpose was to defend Christianity, even through the mouth of Trypho. Nonetheless at the very

[12] *Ibid.*, VI, introduction and 428–29.

end Richard had Voltaire confess "my bad faith, my calumnies, and all the other errors into which I had fallen when I spoke of the Jews." [13]

Protestants as well as Catholics were constrained to defend the Bible against Voltaire in those years. The work of Fleury was by then a century old; it had gone through many editions and it was in use among Protestants, too. In 1771 a group of anonymous Protestant writers answered Voltaire by publishing their own commentaries on and additions to Fleury. The essence of Voltaire's persistent attack on the Bible was that the religion of the Old Testament was most unreasonable. The Protestants answered that, quite on the contrary, ancient Judaism represented the very religion of reason: "This people is the only one that exhibits a law conforming to all the ideals of justice, truth, and holiness, which are engraved in our hearts; in a word, a law that is a faithful expression of the law reason constantly sets before our eyes." It was a little unclear in the context of this passage whether the anonymous author, who was arguing here against Voltaire's *Philosophie de l'histoire*, meant his praise only for the ancient Jews or whether at least some of it was intended for the Jews of his day. At the end of the essay the author maintained the conventional pro-Jewish argument that the Jews were no worse than other people of the day, and that many of the faults attributed to them must be blamed on the persecutions that they had suffered: "This nation which is so interesting to Christians should not be despised by a *philosophe*." [14]

A century of theologically orthodox Christian discussion after Fleury produced, in its own way, a new theory about the Jew. The total movement of the discussion in all its nuances was towards a notion that was never completely articulated, but which was ever more the inherent premise: the Jew should be brought closer to society as a whole, on the condition that he free himself from the Talmud; or conversely, by freeing himself of the Talmud the Jew would as a matter of course come closer to society. These ideas seem on the surface not to differ from the medieval Christian view

[13] The book was published in 1775 anonymously: *Voltaire parmi les ombres;* see pp. 305–23. There was a second edition in 1778, which took note that Voltaire had now really gone to the next world.
[14] *Essais historiques,* preface.

that the Talmud ought to be burned, as it repeatedly was in the Middle Ages, because its doctrines were inherently pernicious and because it was the major force barring the Jews from accepting baptism. Nonetheless, the atmosphere within which these ideas were repeated, at least among the contemporary elements of orthodox believers, was essentially different. The burning of books was ever less a respectable occupation in the 1770s; so was forced conversion. This newest Christian approach suggested that the Jew should be freed of the Talmud by being treated with some respect and kindness. Even Richard, the most anti-Semitic of the orthodox writers, sometimes took this tack, for he put into the mouth of Trypho an expression of outrage at the personal disrespect with which Voltaire had treated Jews.[15] Once the Jew returned to his biblical roots, having been persuaded by the arguments of reason to leave the Talmud, these abbés imagined that he would be closer to the situation in Judaism itself out of which Christianity arose. There would then be hope that the Jew would be open to seeing that which he did not see the first time he was in that situation, when Jesus appeared, and that he would now accept the light of the new dispensation.

The identification of biblical Jewish life with the life of nature and reason, and the projecting of this life as the one proper to Jews in the present, was a new, powerful, and important idea. In the hands of Fleury, Calmet, and Richard this kind of Jew was identified with the most "Western" figures of post-biblical Jewish history, especially Maimonides, whom they praised, because they imagined that this figure, who had in reality been a supreme master of the Talmud, was its enemy. These ideas were taken over in a body by the Hebrew "enlighteners," the disciples of Mendelssohn, who began the task of the intellectual modernization of Jewish life in the years immediately before the French Revolution.

It has been something of an historic puzzle as to why these Jewish "enlighteners" chose, out of all the possible layers of Hebrew style that were available to them, to write in biblical Hebrew.[16] They preferred the Bible to the Talmud and they glorified Maimo-

15 Richard, *Voltaire parmi les ombres*, p. 308.
16 Klausner, *Modern Hebrew Literature*, I, 163–64.

nides as rationalist philosopher and man of science at the expense
of Maimonides the Talmudist. The answer to the question is that
perhaps at that moment in the history of European letters and
culture this was really the only model of Westernization available
to them. "Enlightened" Jews could not then easily become *philosophes* and thus enter the world of culture; at the very least, those
who wished to remain Jewish could not accept such an invitation.
The only model, therefore, for the Westernization of Jews in a
way acceptable to some serious body of opinion, while they yet
remained Jews, was the image created by orthodox abbés of Jews
for whom the Talmud was no longer the essence of their religion
and culture. No Jew who wished to remain one could accept this
vision in its overt, orthodox, conversionist form—but this was not
the only version that was appearing at the time, even among abbés.
There was a Jansenist view that was, from the Jewish standpoint,
more liberal.

## Jansenists and Millenarians

Fleury and his disciples, and the commentators on his work, were
largely descended from Bossuet. There was much more radical
thinking about the Jews among an offshoot of Jansenism founded
by a younger contemporary, the Abbé Jacques Joseph Duguet. A
direct line of almost a century of millenarian speculation about the
Jewish question leads from Duguet to Grégoire, the churchman
who was central to the struggle for the emancipation of the Jews
at the beginning of the Revolution.

Pascal himself had not differed from the prevalent orthodox view
of the religious destiny of the Jews: they were damned to dispersion
because of their rejection of Jesus and they would be restored to the
Holy Land as part of the "end of days," when their conversion
would be part of the miracles that would end man's sinful history.[17]
Jansen had been equally orthodox on this question. In the debates
in the eighteenth century between Jansen's millenarian-minded disciples and their more orthodox opponents, he was invariably quoted
against some of his own followers.[18] The main target was Duguet.

[17] *Pensées*, No. 640. See also chapter III.
[18] Rondet, *Le rappel des Juifs*, pp. 254–55.

That prolific abbé had been the author of innumerable works of biblical exegesis, in which he had attempted to harmonize the teachings of the Old Testament and the New through the use of allegorical interpretation. In his hands the Old Testament had become one vast book of allusions, which were hidden beneath the seeming plain sense of the text. A main point of his exegesis was to insist that those passages in the Old Testament that Christian theology had conventionally understood as foretelling the future glory of the Church really applied to the Jewish people. Duguet insisted that Israel meant not the new Israel, the community of Christian believers, but the old Israel, the physical seed of Abraham. The heart of a truly redeemed Christianity therefore had to be the Jews.[19]

Duguet was thus preoccupied with the question of converting the Jews. For two reasons he could not postpone that event. His biblical exegesis pointed to the conclusion that the conversion of the Jews was, on theological grounds, a necessary and separate preamble to Christian eschatology and not, as in the orthodox recension, one of the several miracles that would take place concurrently at the end of time. More immediately, he was reacting together with all the intellectual leaders of French Christianity at the end of the seventeenth century, including Fénelon and Bossuet, to the religious upheavals since the days of Calvin and to the beginnings of agnosticism among the upper classes. There was much despair for the future of Christianity and, indeed, of Christendom, particularly in the circles of Port-Royal. Duguet was certain that the only possible divine answer to the cataclysms that had shaken Christianity was the "second coming." His apocalyptic speculations pointed to the year 2000, but this event would be preceded by centuries of preparation.[20] The central task of Christianity was thus to approach the Jews. They became for Duguet not a repentant

[19] The only full-length biography of Duguet is Chatélat, *Etude sur du Guet.* In this study no attention is paid the millenarian side of Duguet. This aspect, and Duguet's followers, are treated at some length in Lémann, *L'entrée des Israélites,* pp. 263–84, but one must guard against Lémann's anti-Jansenist, orthodox Catholic bias.

[20] The apocalyptic views of Duguet were handed down by oral tradition among the Jansenists; they had not been written out by him. See Gruenebaum-Ballin, "Grégoire convertisseur?," *REJ,* CXXI, 390. Did Duguet owe anything to the theology of Peyrère? It is an open possibility.

prodigal son, finally returning to the bosom of the Church, but rather something much more grandiose, the indispensable tool for the Church's restoration and regeneration.

This millenarian preoccupation, with its highlighting of the Jew, was henceforth a central theme of Jansenism in France in the eighteenth century. The *convulsionnaires* of the 1720s and 1730s, as they frothed at the mouth and prophesied the imminent divine judgment, announced as part of their vision the imminent return of the Jews.[21] Duguet himself was still alive and writing in those years (he died in 1733), and his point of view was maintained in the next generation by a number of disciples. The argument came to a head in the last two decades before the Revolution in a series of bitter exchanges between two scholarly churchmen, Laurent Etienne Rondet and François Malot.

Rondet was the editor of an edition of the Bible with commentaries, which had appeared in Avignon. Though not a priest, he was a considerable scholar and an orthodox Christian. In his biblical commentary Rondet had upheld the orthodox position that the conversion of the Jews would be part of the Apocalypse and that it had best be left to that miraculous event. In 1776 Malot published anonymously in Avignon itself a pamphlet attacking this view. Malot maintained that the work of converting the Jews was a basic activity of the Church, coextensive with its entire career, and that it was not to be left for a short apocalyptic moment. Indeed, the end of the world itself would not take place in three miraculous years, which was the plain sense of the Book of Revelations. Following Duguet, Malot maintained that there would be a long interval and evolution from the conversion of the Jews to the "last day." He did not hesitate to take issue with ancient Christian writers who had believed that the Apocalypse would happen very quickly, for in Malot's opinion his own generation was far closer to the end of history than were the Church fathers and was therefore far better able to judge how the end would occur. Malot's most interesting remark, for our present purposes, was made out of his awareness that the conversion of the Jews was no easy task because men did not easily abandon their ingrained beliefs or even their

[21] Lémann, *L'entrée des Israélites*, pp. 272–73.

prejudices. He added that the task of converting the Jews was made all the harder because "the persecutors strike fear [among the Jews] and impede the progress of the Gospel by their cruelties and their tricks." [22]

Rondet answered Malot in the next year in a substantial book, *Dissertation sur le rappel des Juifs*. It is clear from the preface to this volume that there was great personal anger between the two, and the controversy had already spilled over, in the fall of 1776, into several periodicals. Rondet repeated his view, and he buttressed his position not only with elaborate biblical exegesis but also by invoking the authority of Bossuet, Calmet, and the ancients against Duguet, the only major figure, and a modern one at that, whom Malot could cite. Apart from denying both Malot's arguments and the credentials of his authorities Rondet concluded this elaborate counter-attack by arguing that men had no right to engage in speculation about the date when the "end of days" would come.[23]

The battle continued directly between the two in two more volumes. Malot expanded his original pamphlet into a book of more than three hundred pages, which contained some interesting additions to his earlier views. He reaffirmed the belief that his own generation had more authority in interpreting what was meant in the eleventh chapter of the Book of Revelation than did the ancients. They had had no knowledge of the size of the earth, since America

[22] The initial pamphlet by Malot was published anonymously: *L'époque du rappel*. The remark about persecution is on p. 20; see also pp. 15, 35–36, 66–69.

[23] Rondet, *Le rappel des Juifs*, preface. In the fall of 1776 this controversy between Rondet and Malot spilled over into the periodical press. the *Journal ecclésiastique*, the *Nouvelles ecclésiastiques*, and even the *Mercure de France* (*ibid.*, p. xxix). It is especially necessary to emphasize that this controversy between Rondet and Malot was well known in its day because their books and pamphlets were forgotten and are today great rarities. Rondet had first entered the battle with the millenarians on the issue of the Jews fifteen years earlier. The Abbé Jules Deschamps, the follower and successor of Duguet, had published a work, *Rappel futur des Juifs*, in 1760 and Rondet answered it the next year with a short work, *Israel vengé*. Rondet denied the millenarian view in this, his very first essay on the subject, by maintaining that the conversion of the Jews was not a pre-condition to the end of days. I have not seen either work and, indeed, no copy of the volume by Deschamps is known to exist in any of the major libraries. This interchange between Deschamps and Rondet is briefly mentioned by Lémann, *L'entrée des Israélites dans la société française*, p. 274; these two works are listed in Szajkowski, *Franco-Judaica*, Nos. 1536, 1538.

had not been discovered in their day and their awareness of the geography of Asia had been spotty. The ancients could, therefore, imagine the conversion of the world in three and a half years, but eighteenth-century man knew better. The ultimate future of the Jews, once they were converted, was not a return to the physical Jerusalem; it would be their entry into the general society of a redeemed Christendom. Malot deduced from his own interpretation of Revelation that the conversion of the Jews would take place in the year 1849.[24]

Rondet's response was much more temperate than his contribution to the earlier discussion. We learn from him that there had been much apocalyptic calculation about the date of the conversion of the Jews, not so much by Duguet as by some of his disciples. An anonymous clandestine *Lettre*, which had appeared in 1739, had even been bold enough to predict the year 1748. These speculations had been based on attempts to interpret the ninth chapter of Daniel. Rondet's view was that it was indeed probable that the conversion of the Jews would take place in the next century, but only in the time of the Antichrist, and as an immediate preamble to the Apocalypse.[25] Malot continued the argument in at least two more fairly lengthy pamphlets. In 1782 he defended himself further against Rondet by continuing to insist that 1849 was the true date when the Jews would be converted and that such apocalyptic speculation was permissible.[26] In the next year Malot answered two separate attacks on him by the editor of the *Feuilles hebdomadaires*, and the matter at issue again was the right to speculate on apocalyptic matters.[27]

This millenarian debate had thereby mushroomed from an internal debate among theological scholars, in books and pamphlets, to a continuing argument in the church journals and even in periodicals of general circulation—and this was happening at the very

[24] Malot's book was published anonymously under the same title as his pamphlet. It was marked "second edition," and it appeared in Paris, with the approval of the censors, in 1779. See pp. xxi–xxii for his "modernist" stance and p. 210 for his date for the Apocalypse.

[25] Rondet, *Supplément*, pp. 493, 501, 561.

[26] Malot, *Suite et défense*, pp. 186–88. Malot reported here that Duguet had calculated the year 2000 as the date of the "second coming" (p. 201).

[27] Rondet, *Seconde lettre*, p. 13.

height of discussion of the Jewish question. In their arguments about the true date of the "second coming" the millenarians were talking only to themselves, but they were adding some new notes to the on-going discussion about Jews. For theological reasons of their own they were emphasizing that Jews were not incidental to the millennium, or part of some broader turning of all humanity; the Jews were crucial. Not even the most pro-Jewish of the *philosophes* had gone so far as to make the treatment of the Jews the touchstone of his future secular millennium; as we shall soon see, some could even imagine creating the new world without doing anything at all for the Jews. The latter-day Jansenists were unique in emphasizing that the need to approach Jews in love in the secular realm was central to the future of all humanity. Since the "second coming" was imagined as a process, Duguet's disciples were willing to begin with unconditional kindness towards the Jews. The abandonment of the Talmud or, ultimately, conversion could be left to time.

There were theologians who were even more liberal than that. The anonymous author of an answer to Richard was, perhaps, not a vicar, as he announced himself to be, but there were some such vicars to be found in the 1770s. He argued that "intolerance is in every sense a child of darkness"; the New Testament and every precedent of the early church opposed the persecution of other faiths. Fleury was invoked as having maintained that in the present, enlightened age one had to be tolerant even of heretics; the murder of the Jews by the Inquisition was quoted by the writer as a vile example of intolerance. The economic argument was also made that Protestants were bankers, manufacturers, and businessmen and that France could not afford to lose such people by emigration.[28] In this work, however, these ideas were not applied directly to the Jews, and there was even a hint that the author of this pamphlet did not regard the Jews of Alsace as one of the natural and valid communities of that province.

Another writer, de Boissi, did say precisely the same things in relation to Jews, directly. He wrote a supplement to the history of

[28] Anonymous, *L'intolérance éclairée*, place of publication not specified, 1777, pp. 6, 11–12, 30, 139, 189. This work too belonged to the debate about the rights of Protestants that marked the beginning of the reign of Louis XVI.

the Jews by Basnage. De Boissi ignored completely whatever there
had remained in Basnage himself of the Christian theologian, who
believed in the superiority of Christianity, and he praised Basnage
for being free of such an idea. In de Boissi's opinion, whatever was
wrong with the Jews had been created by persecution: "One is
horrified by these cruelties which degrade humanity; one must
listen to the voice which commands that we should not persecute
or kill people because they did not accept the truths which we believe." [29] This is, of course, the rhetoric of the Enlightenment. It is
a far different stance from the one taken towards Basnage's work by
an orthodox Catholic writer, Jean Liron, at the beginning of the
century. He had criticized Basnage bitterly for blaming several
early French saints and bishops, especially Saint Ambrose, for persecuting Jews. Liron had sneered at Basnage as a Protestant; he
added that "a Jew of Amsterdam, had he undertaken to write the
history of his people, would have spoken of Saint Ambrose more
justly." By the end of the century there were at least some abbés
who would not defend medieval persecutors of Jews.[30]

Both the Jansenist impulse and that of the *philosophes* were
present in the most important liberal abbé of this time, Henri
Grégoire, who wrote the prize-winning essay in the Metz essay
contest and who later led the battle in the Revolutionary *Assemblée
Nationale* for the emancipation of the Jews. Grégoire had received
his earliest Christian education at the hands of followers of
Duguet.[31] He was certainly aware of the storm that had been
aroused over the conversion of the Jews by the famous interchange
in which the Swiss pastor, Lavater, had asked Mendelssohn to convert to Christianity. Grégoire had met Lavater a few years after that
debate, when the young curé was traveling abroad.[32] In 1788
Grégoire responded to a letter by a Protestant minister in Strasbourg, Ehrmann, by agreeing that the Catholic Church continued
to hope for the conversion of the Jews. He added, "I have preached

[29] De Boissi, *Dissertations critiques;* the quotations in the text are from the
preface, I, pp. ix–xi.
[30] A. M. J. M. D. [Liron], *Le temps de l'établissement,* p. 73.
[31] Gruenebaum-Ballin, "Grégoire convertisseur?," *REJ,* CXXI, 389.
[32] *Mémoires de Grégoire,* I, 17.

on this question in the church of Lunéville in the last year or two and I hope to publish a complete work on this question."[33] In 1810, when Grégoire finally succeeded in publishing his account of all the contemporary religions, a work in two volumes entitled *Histoire des sectes religieuses*, he asserted that "the Catholic Church maintains its sweet hope that the Jews will enter its bosom." He advised that Christians should give up the crime of persecuting the Jews, as a means of moving towards the day when all men would be united in the same faith.[34] Grégoire remained a Jansenist to the end of his days; he was even the head of a circle of millenarians in the Paris of Napoleon.[35] For our present purpose the most important remarks that he made were those that occurred before the Revolution, in the very book in which he pleaded the cause of the Jews. Much of his argument repeated Dohm and Mirabeau, that the evils of the Jews were created by persecutions and that they would be cured by equality, but Grégoire's climactic point was that "the granting of religious liberty to the Jews would be a great step forward in reforming and, I even dare say, in converting them, for truth is most persuasive when it is gentle."[36]

Grégoire was helped in his work for the Metz essay contest by a life-long friend who was a moderate Jewish "enlightener" and a follower of Mendelssohn, Isaiah Berr Bing. This has been somewhat of a puzzle, since Bing was an orthodox Jew and certainly not a candidate for conversion. In the light of the alternatives available to him, in his concern for the acceptance of the Jew in the general society, Bing's action is less puzzling. Grégoire's mildest version of millenarian conversion hopes was almost the most accepting position that Bing could find, especially as it was made milder still by the more secular side of Grégoire's outlook.

Nonetheless, some crucial ambiguities remained. Bing published his views on the Jewish question in 1788. He recognized that eco-

[33] M. Ginsburger, "Zwei unveröffentliche Brief," *Festschrift zu Simon Dubnows siebzigsten Geburtstag*, p. 206.
[34] Grégoire, *Sectes religieuses*, II, 401–402.
[35] Gruenebaum-Ballin, "Gregoire convertisseur?," *REJ*, CXXI, 394–96.
[36] The secular, conventionally "enlightened" side of Grégoire's views on the Jews was summarized in his *La régénération*, pp. 151–54. The remark about converting occurs on p. 123.

nomic and cultural changes in the Jews were necessary, but he avoided prescribing any program beyond an undefined equality. It was clear from his total approach that to prescribe would involve him in criticism of the existing Jewish community, for which he was not prepared. What indeed was the new Jew to be? "More productive" and "enlightened"—but what did this mean? [37]

Christians were able to prescribe with greater freedom, but their prescriptions were not much clearer. A century of economic and religious discussion had come to a climax in two radical churchmen, Mably [38] and Grégoire. On the human level Grégoire knew many Jews on a friendly basis, and Mably seems to have known none. By temperament Mably was far more a lover of humanity in the abstract, whereas Grégoire had a much more concrete involvement in people. Mably was certainly much less inclined to see any good in the Jews. Nonetheless, there was a fundamental convergence between the two on the Jewish question, and they spoke for many who disagreed with them on matters of detail and even of essence. By the 1780s advanced thinkers had largely settled the question that the Jews belonged within European society, and the earlier, medieval premise that they ought to be excluded was, at very least, no longer self-evident. Among both the theologians and the economists this new premise had not been derived primarily from the explication of enlightened abstractions about the rights of man. Its immediate roots were in millenarian theology and in *raison d'état*.

But, having accepted, and even having helped create, the new premise that the Jews ought to be admitted into society, theologians and economists had agreed without any doubt that they were accepting not of the concretely existing one, but of some new Jew that they would remake, or who would remake himself, in the image of what they thought he ought to be. There was a price on the Jew's ticket of admission into society.

What would happen after the Jew paid this price? Would society admit him, accepting the fact that at least this new Jew had a right to be a lasting phenomenon? This question could be answered only

[37] See the discussion of Bing in Chapter X.
[38] For Mably and late eighteenth-century economic thinking about Jews see the end of Chapter IV.

on the basis of some vision of contemporary society as a whole. In the years before 1789 such a broader outlook could no longer come from the realm of theology or even from economics. That theory came from Montesquieu, and it was defined in opposition to Voltaire.

## ⋖§ IX §⋗

## *The Men of the Enlightenment*

The men of the Enlightenment divided into pro-Jewish and anti-Jewish figures largely on the basis of theoretical differences. Nonetheless, although they sometimes couched their comments in the rhetoric of high principle, these remarks were very often related to current events. Indeed, the closer some of the *philosophes,* and especially Voltaire, came to contemporary issues the more obviously anti-Jewish they became in contexts where their abstract principles could have permitted them to argue the other side.

Three major events brought the Jews to public notice in the course of the eighteenth century. The first was the recurrence of persecution of the marranos in Portugal after 1721. In the forty years that followed 139 people were burned, so that the middle of the century represented a period of notorious ferocity. The climax was the great auto-da-fé in Lisbon in 1737, in which 12 marranos were burned at the stake. These persecutions in Portugal caused a renewed wave of refugees, including some who found their way to France. This was the age in which the *philosophes* were mounting their strongest attack on the obscurantism of the Church. It required no great love of Jews for anti-clerical thinkers to oppose the Portuguese Inquisition, for these persecutions could be invoked as crucial contemporary evidence of the true nature of the Church. Discussion of these events, however, inevitably led to argument about what was proper and just in relation to Jews.

Marranos themselves had played a part in causing western Europe in general, and in France in particular, to look with increasing horror on the Inquisition. The whole of a quite rich literature of the marrano diaspora, as it spread to France, Holland, England, and throughout the Mediterranean basin, was suffused with the memory of auto-da-fés in Spain and Portugal. In France itself some of the marranos who came to Bordeaux were, as we have seen, of intellectual importance. That Montaigne had no love for the Inquisition is well known. There was, in the seventeenth century in Rouen, a small but intellectually important marrano center. This group was led in the 1620s by Moses Pinto Delgado, who was a distinguished poet in Portuguese. Antonio Enriquez Gomez was in Rouen in the 1640s, after having spent some time in Bordeaux, on his flight from Madrid. He published a pamphlet in Spanish against the Inquisition in Rouen in 1647. More such writings will, no doubt, yet be discovered, but there was even more propaganda against the Inquisition by word of mouth, as refugees told their tales of horror to every sympathetic person.[1]

Two situations in France itself, involving Jews of that country, were of some public importance in the middle of the eighteenth century. There was the long battle in Bordeaux between the dominant and older Sephardi Jewish community and a newer, smaller group led by several families from Avignon. The argument spilled over not only into antechambers of political figures but also into the writings of literary men. It ultimately involved the entire question of the situation of the Jews and of what was to be done with the several kinds of Jewish communities that were present in France.

Isaac de Pinto has been alluded to several times, but some matters mentioned in earlier connections need to be recalled here briefly. Whether he was born in Bordeaux or not, he had close relationships not only with the Sephardim of the city, but especially with the military governor of the province of Guienne, the highly intelligent libertine, the Duke of Richelieu. In 1762, towards the end of the quarrel between the Sephardim and the Avignonnais in Bordeaux, Jacob Rodrigues Péreire asked Pinto to write to Richelieu in support of the Sephardi position in the quarrel. Pinto's letter, dated May 20,

<hr />

[1] Roth, *A History of the Marranos*, pp. 322–38, 343–48. Regarding the marrano center in Rouen, see *idem*, "Les marranes à Rouen," *REJ*, LXXVIII, 113–55. The work by Gomez against the Inquisition, entitled *Politica Angelica*, has been republished with notes and a biographical sketch by Revah, "Un pamphlet contre l'Inquisition d'Antonio Enrique Gomez," *REJ*, CXXI, 81–168.

1762, made the point that the Portuguese Jews were descended from a different tribe from all other Jews; being superior to all the rest, they deserved more consideration. In the immediate sense this intervention was not a great success, for the Avignonnais got most of the rights they requested, despite Pinto's intervention. This quarrel did, however, act as the spur for Pinto's major work in defense of the Sephardim, his *Apologie des Juifs*. It was cast in the form of a reply to an attack by Voltaire six years earlier in his article on Jews in the seventh volume of the 1757 edition of his works.[2] Pinto had not answered Voltaire then because he had just read that book. In the preface to his work Pinto told that Péreire had asked him to write the *Apologie* as a further piece of propaganda in the continuing campaign of the Sephardim. They were working to protect the rights they had accumulated through two centuries and to broaden them further. This "response" to Voltaire was thus, in part, a device to lend importance to Pinto's defense of the Sephardim by linking it with the greatest literary name of the day. In larger part, it represented a correct estimate that Voltaire was the most serious adversary of the Jews in that day. At any rate, Pinto's slim pages led directly to the expansion of this attack in the next few years by the Christian theologian, the Abbé Antoine Guénée, and to the further rebuttals by Voltaire, both in the letter with which he responded to Pinto in 1762 and in the book *Un Chrétien contre six Juifs*, in 1777, in which he answered the arguments of Guénée. The local argument between the Sephardim and the Avignonnais was thus an immediate impulse for the most famous of all the discussions of the Jewish question in the last decades of the *ancien régime*.

The misery, growing size, and economic conditions of the Alsatian Jewish community, and of the rest of Jewry in eastern France, increasingly became public issues after the middle of the eighteenth century. Despite all restrictions imposed both by the central government and by local powers, poor Jews who were fleeing from con-

2 The text of Pinto's letter to Richelieu was reprinted in Malvezin, *Histoire des Juifs à Bordeaux*, pp. 213–14; see also the only full-length study of Pinto, by Wijler, *Isaac de Pinto*, p. 43. For the famous exchange of letters between Pinto and Voltaire, see the texts in the critical edition of Voltaire's correspondence, *Correspondence*, XLIX, 98, 131–32. Regarding Pinto see also chapter VI.

tinuing troubles in Poland and central Europe had kept drifting to western Europe. The local Jewish communities, which were ever more burdened by their presence, tried fitfully to stop the flow, but without success. The peasants of Alsace were heavily in debt to Jews, most of whom were themselves as badly off as their debtors. All of this came to a head in the "affair of the false receipts," which was the center of attention in eastern France in the last two decades before the Revolution.[3] Two cases involving Jewish bankers and army purveyors occasioned public battles. The Alsatian army purveyor, Cerf Berr, fought in the 1770s and the 1780s with the city of Strasbourg, which attempted to defend itself against the royal decree under which he claimed the right to live in that city. Many briefs and counter-briefs were broadcast in order to influence public opinion. The newspapers took note, and not only in France. Cerf Berr was a Jew whose "usefulness" the king himself had hailed. The rights that properly pertained to such a Jew became another focus of the literary debate about the Jewish question.[4] An even more interesting affair involved Liefman Calmer, the Jewish banker and army purveyor resident in Paris who had bought the barony of Picquigny in 1774. The acquisition of this land automatically conferred upon him the feudal rights that went with it and the right to appoint priests to a benefice that depended on the barony. As we have seen, this second situation occasioned an important controversy, both in pamphlets and in a lawsuit, over whether a Jew could appoint Christian clergy.[5]

The movement towards freedom for the Jews outside of France in several places in the course of the eighteenth century also made a difference to enlightened discussion. Amsterdam was near at hand and many of the leaders of the Enlightenment, such as Diderot, had personal experience of its Jewish community.[6] Voltaire knew,

[3] See Chapter V.

[4] Much of the material on the battles of Cerf Berr before the Revolution is to be found in the first volume of a privately printed work about the family as a whole. It was written, in four volumes, by one of Cerf Berr's descendants (Levylier, La famille Cerf Berr).

[5] See Chapters V and VIII.

[6] There are two echoes, both uncomplimentary, of Diderot's visit to Holland. The first is in anecdotal form in his Le neveu de Rameau, written in 1762 where he told a discreditable tale about a lascivious Jew of Utrecht (Oeuvres

though not happily, Jewish bankers in both London and Berlin. The nearly successful effort to achieve legal equality for the Jews in England in 1753 was noted throughout the world of civilized discussion in Europe. There was also an increasing awareness of the comparatively small number of Jews in the English colonies in America, who were living in great freedom without harm to society.[7] The participation of these Jews in the American Revolution, and the complete equality that was theirs without question even before the promulgation of the Constitution of the United States in 1789, were well known in Europe.

At the other end of the European horizon was the Turkish empire. The false messiah, Shabbetai Zvi, had appeared there without hindrance after 1648, to the astonishment of many Christian travelers and other commentators. There was considerable interest, in France in particular, in the appearance of the false messiah. Among the fairly numerous contemporary accounts in Western languages of the career of Shabbetai Zvi, at least four were in French. There is no evidence that the appearance of this messianic movement among the Jews gave any impulse to French millenarian thinking about the Jewish question. Shabbetai Zvi does not seem to have been a source for Duguet and his school. What this incident did do was to emphasize to European minds that such a picturesque occurrence could happen outside Christian Europe, in an environment where several religions were somehow or other coexisting. Viewed through certain kinds of glasses from Paris, the situation of the Jews in Turkey seemed to be no worse than that of the Christians, since

---

*complètes*, V, 479–80). The second was a straightforward traveler's account in his *Voyage de Hollande,* written in 1744. Here he referred to Pinto ambiguously as someone he knew in both Paris and The Hague (*ibid.,* XVIII, 405). In a longer passage in the same essay Diderot told of his impressions of the Jews of Amsterdam. He gave the Jews credit for being more moral than the rest, but he disliked the noisy atmosphere in their synagogues. He noted that they were free to engage in all kinds of commerce and in medicine, but that they could not become artisans. Diderot emphasized that the Jews of Amsterdam had the right to acquire land and that they enjoyed the protection accorded to citizens, though they were excluded from public office. However, several Jews had been made barons as reward for their services to the Dutch state (*ibid.,* pp. 431–33.

[7] In his important defense of the Jews, *Réforme politique,* Dohm both evoked the American example, that the American revolutionaries were battling together for freedom (pp. 32–33, 119), and the Act of Naturalization in England in 1753 (p. 98).

both were minorities in a Moslem society. Jean-Baptiste de Boyer, the Marquis d'Argens, could imagine a Jew in Constantinople speaking freely to Christians about their religion and their history.[8]

## Montesquieu and d'Argens

The Christian Inquisition in Portugal and the comparative religious freedom in non-Christian Turkey were the immediate impulses for the first important discussions in the eighteenth century of the Jewish question. Montesquieu reacted in *L'esprit des lois* to the burning at the stake of an eighteen-year-old girl with a most eloquent denunciation of the Inquisition. He cast it in the form of an argument written by a Jew:

You complain, he said to the Inquisitors, that the emperor of Japan is having all the Christians in his domain burnt on a slow fire; but he could answer you: "We treat you, who do not believe as we do, as you treat those who do not believe as you do." . . . But it must be stated that you are far more cruel than this emperor. . . . We follow a religion which you yourselves know was once beloved by God. . . . You think that he no longer loves it; and because you think this you torture with steel and fire those who cling to this pardonable error of believing that God still loves that which He once loved. . . . If you do not want to be Christians, at least be human: treat us as you would if you had neither a religion to guide or a revelation to enlighten you and had to act only on the basis of the weak intimations of justice with which nature endows us. . . . We must warn you of one thing: in future ages if someone will dare say that in the century in which we live the peoples of Europe were civilized, you will be cited as the evidence that they were barbarous; and your image will be such that it will dishonor your age and make your contemporaries the object of hatred.[9]

[8] In his tempestuous career, which included experience in Germany for a decade, through the period of Voltaire's disgrace in Berlin, d'Argens spent time earlier in Constantinople, where he became friendly with a Jewish scholar named Fonseca, who reappears as Aaron Monceca in the *Lettres juives* (see Bush, *The Marquis d'Argens*, p. 6). In 1763 it was d'Argens who pressured Frederick the Great into giving Moses Mendelssohn the status of a "protected Jew" in Berlin (Kayserling, *Moses Mendelssohn*, pp. 123–26).

For contemporary European reactions to the appearance of Shabbetai Zvi, see the literature listed in Scholem, *Shabbetai Zvi*, pp. 833–37; Scholem maintains that Shabbetai Zvi had no effect on Christian millenarianism at the time (*ibid.*, p. 82) but Scholem makes no reference to French Catholic millenarianism. Traces of such influence may yet be found there.

[9] Montesquieu, *Oeuvres complètes*, II, 746–49. This passage is from *L'esprit des lois*, which was first published in 1748.

Montesquieu was aware that all the religious had a tendency to persecute and that an oppressed sect could turn around, immediately as it came to power, and oppress other faiths. The state must oblige the various religions to leave each other in peace. This toleration did not mean that the state opposed all of the sects. On the contrary, he argued in *L'esprit des lois,* "We are here men of politics and not theologians; even for theologians there is a difference between tolerating a religion and approving it." Some of the sects were culturally and spiritually inferior, but men cannot be changed even by good laws, for that would be too tyrannical. Freedom and exposure to other better customs would move men to change themselves.[10] In this general view Montesquieu was reasserting the outlook of French skepticism, of Charron and Bodin; he was also reaching back to the view of the *politiques* at the end of the sixteenth century, who had tried to compose the quarrel between Catholics and Huguenots in France by suggesting a distinction between the state and religion. In the *Lettres persanes* Montesquieu had introduced a broader perspective, that of Islam. The discussion of religion thus became more than an affair in Europe between Judaism and Christianity. For Montesquieu, tolerance had become a universal necessity in the eighteenth century because in the world as a whole there was a bewildering variety of custom and opinion.

From this perspective Montesquieu responded in his *L'esprit des lois* to the on-going argument about the respective merits of the ancient Jews and Greeks. The theologians and the doctrinaire enlighteners had been arrayed on that battle-line with great bitterness since Spinoza. Montesquieu argued that there was merit in both of these ancient cultures. The laws of Moses and the different laws of Solon had each been created, wisely, in the context of a specific time and place. Solon's claim to the Athenians that he had given them the very best laws meant in reality that he had given them the very best laws under which they were capable of living. "When divine wisdom said to the Jewish people, 'I have given you good precepts,' this means only that they have a relative value. This consideration answers all the criticisms which one can level against the law of Moses."[11]

[10] *Ibid.,* pp. 564–65.     [11] *Ibid.,* p. 571.

Montesquieu's earliest and most famous statement on the Jews was in the *Lettres persanes*. Writing in 1721 he termed Judaism the "ancient trunk," which produced the two branches, Christianity and Islam. The Jews were just as obstinate as the Christians in believing in their possession of the truth. The situation was getting better for Jews, for the spirit of intolerance was beginning to evaporate in Europe. Nevertheless, Montesquieu did not like the Jews uncritically. Usbek wrote to Ibber in the *Lettres persanes* that there were, of course, Jews in France, precisely as there were Jews in Persia, and both these Jewish communities were alike. "Know that wherever there is money there are Jews." [12] A more revealing opinion still is to be found in his unpublished papers, which were not printed until the nineteenth century. He excepted the Bible from his strictures because it was divinely inspired and, apart from the purely historical works, the author put nothing of his own into it. However, the works of the rabbis represented the spirit of slaves. The rabbis, indeed, did not really understand their own sacred, biblical texts. "Ignorance, which is the mother of traditions . . . had created new notions." These rabbinic works fashioned the continuing low taste and character of the Jews, for their rabbis had not "one among them of even a minor order of genius." [13]

This was Montesquieu at his most Christian, but this private opinion was unknown in the eighteenth century. His public utterances were the ones that influenced history, and he was understood from them to favor tolerance of the Jews. Those who were to quote him in the debates about the Jews would sometimes make no distinction between complete cultural laisser faire, that is, the policy of letting the Jews be themselves, and the more pervasive idea that freedom was the sole means of improving the character of the Jews. On this point, Montesquieu himself had been equally contradictory.

It is, perhaps, not too farfetched to suppose that Montesquieu's awareness of the Bordeaux Jewish community had something to do with the liberalism of his public views in relation to Jews. He was in office in the *parlement* of Bordeaux in the years 1716–26,

[12] *Ibid.*, I, 218–19.
[13] Weill, "Un texte de Montesquieu sur le Judaisme," *REJ*, XLIX, 150–53.

the decade when the Jews of Bordeaux were coming out into the open. It was in 1723 that this *parlement* registered the decree of the king giving Portuguese Jews the right to openly practice their religion in France. The persecutions in Portugal were occurring during those years, and marranos were escaping to Bordeaux with great frequency. Although little direct contact between Montesquieu and the Jews has yet been proved, it is inconceivable that there should not have been some.[14] What is more, as we have seen, the kind of Jews who were present in Bordeaux at that point in the century were still quite traditional in their religion and outlook, but they had already undergone a moderate amount of acculturation in France. A close reading of all of Montesquieu's published remarks on the Jews gives the impression that this is the image he had in mind when he spoke of tolerance for them.

Montesquieu's defense of religious liberty in general owed something to his conception of human cultures as determined by climate and environment. Montesquieu himself used the notion of the negative influence of the environment to be rather contemptuous of Jews, in private, but he believed firmly that change was possible. D'Holbach was to use the same idea differently; he argued that the Jews were a creation of a climate and environment that made them totally and hopelessly foreign to Europe. This was, of course, a long step towards the notion about race that was to be held by Gobineau in the next century. In the eighteenth century, however, Montesquieu's concept of many cultures, which derived their difference from varying origins in nature, was understood as a liberating, egalitarian idea. It is incontrovertible that later in the century Montesquieu was consistently quoted by all those who were on the side of the Jews, either in the past or in the present.

Montesquieu's stance "outside" of the European culture was also used by a contemporary, the Marquis d'Argens, an enlightened writer who was famous in his own time and widely read, although he is now almost completely forgotten.[15] D'Argens published his

[14] Francia de Beaufleury (*Histoire de l'établissement*, p. 43) asserted that Joseph Cordozo, a doctor who was a convert, was a friend of Montesquieu.
[15] On d'Argens see Bush, *The Marquis d'Argens*. Mornet attests to the great reputation and influence that d'Argens had in his own time (*Les origines intellectuelles*, p. 34; see also Lion, "Rousseau et d'Argens," *Revue d'histoire lit-*

criticisms of the contemporary scene in three works, which were really one, all written in the same tone. They were entitled *Lettres juives, Lettres cabbalistiques,* and *Lettres chinoises.* On the one hand, d'Argens used the Jews as Montesquieu had used the Persians, to provide a stance from which European superstitions and religion could be criticized. In this use the Jew was no living figure. The only relation he bore to Jewish reality was that it was presumed that he was particularly capable of criticizing Christianity because of the intimate relationship of early Christian history with Judaism. Otherwise, the Jew was an abstraction, a symbol of enlightenment. Precisely because he was such an abstraction the Jew of d'Argens was depicted as a radical critic of his own tradition, who nowhere defends it in its inherited form. In the second letter his "Jew" Aaron Monceca, having just arrived in France, wrote "back home" to Constantinople criticizing Christianity for its changeability.[16] The attack continued in the next letter, where d'Argens contrasted the rabbis, who supposedly teach only reason, with Christians, who are full of superstitions. This argument built to the conceit of Monceca that "I have discovered in Paris Jews without number, who are Jews without believing that they are, and even without knowing it."[17] The argument was that all advanced people in Europe were Christians only externally; they really believed in Judaism, that is, in the reasonable doctrines of d'Argens. Indeed, the advanced spirits of Paris were really marranos, like the Jewish ones in Spain. Judaism was the highest religion, in this argument, not because of its age, or because it gave birth to the biblical faiths, or because it was true revelation, but because it conformed more to reason than either Islam or Christianity.[18]

On the other hand, d'Argens managed to suggest that, whatever Judaism in his abstracted version might be, the existing Jews had much wrong with them, and that it was their fault. He managed to assert obliquely, in the "testimony of a Mohammedan," that for a

*teraire de la France,* XXXIII, 418. In its own time the *Lettres juives* were read by absolutely everybody in the literary world of Paris. The most recent study of the Jewish question in d'Argens is by Brav, "Jews and Judaism," *Studies in Bibliography and Booklore,* IV, 133–41. See above, fn. 8.

[16] *Lettres juives,* I, 12      [17] *Ibid.,* pp. 25–26.      [18] *Ibid.,* p. 105.

time Jews sacrificed children on their altars in France. The denial
of this "report," which appears in the text in the words of the
"transmitting Rabbi," was less convincing than the fact that d'Argens mentioned such a canard at all. In *Mémoires du Comte Vaxere,
ou le faux-rabbin*, a pot-boiling novel d'Argens wrote about the
time of the publication of his *Lettres juives*, he "dedicates" the
book to Isaac Meio, "Jew of Metz, usurer and rabbi." [19] In the
"dedicatory letter" d'Argens did indeed say that Meio was more
generous than was the norm among usurers. Nonetheless, even
though his avowed purpose was to show that there could be good
Jews, the good were by definition those who had entered polished
and reasonable Christian society, as the heroine of the novel finally
did. The end of the prefatory letter best reflected the ambiguity of
d'Argens' view of the Jews:

I declare that I have not really quite made up my mind about you, because my aim was not to prove in this book that there can be well-
mannered and obliging usurers, but rather to show that in all religions
there are people of much merit; it is this which has prevented me from
choosing you as one of my heroes. If ever I decide to write a story
about illustrious usurers I give you my word that you will have a distinguished place in it. [20]

In the preface to the third volume of his letters, which he addressed
to the rabbis of Amsterdam, d'Argens argued, tongue in cheek, that
there were perhaps ten Jesuits in the world who were humble, ten
Italian prelates who were learned, etc., and that, therefore, it was at
least conceivable that there were ten Jews who were enlightened
and were not usurers. He concluded this "defense" of of the Jews
as follows: "If your nation is in general less virtuous than several
others, it nonetheless has, like the others, some fine people and
great men." [21]

D'Argens' penchant for enlightened Jews was not entirely an
abstraction. He distinguished between the miserable and ignorant
Jews, whom one saw in Metz, Avignon, and certain other French
cities, and those other Jews whom one found in some number in
Holland and Venice, "whose decisions on matters of the mind

[19] *Mémoires du Comte de Vaxere* was published in Amsterdam in 1737.
[20] *Ibid.*, p. 105
[21] *Lettres juives* (ed. of 1738), III, unpaged introduction.

are often of much greater value than those of the best of the academicians." [22] There was in this compliment more than a hint of the idea that such enlightened people were on the way into advanced European society, and that a change of religion would not stand in their way, very much. In the course of the correspondence, d'Argens' "enlightened" Jewish spokesman did convert to "reasonable" Christianity. "The Talmud of the rabbis is a hundred times more ridiculous than that of the Koran." The Karaites, the Jewish sect who rejected the Talmud, were the most reasonable. Nothing was higher than the Jewish religion in its Karaite form, or for that matter, in its ancient Essene version; nothing was more detestable than the same religion as practiced by the majority of Jews, who follow the Talmud, in the tradition of the Pharisees.[23]

D'Argens faced the question of the reason for anti-Semitism, rejecting the notion that it was due to difference in religion. He insisted that its real source was in the bad conduct of Jews. D'Argens argued that the Jews were hated for their avarice and bad faith, so that those among them who were honest were punished for the sins of the guilty. The rabbis should therefore devote themselves to writing books of morality, rather than the nonsense which most of them were producing. Unfortunately, so d'Argens maintained, the rabbis teach the Jews to be more avaricious. He rejected the defensive argument, which was used by pro-Jewish writers throughout the century, that the avarice of the Jews is pardonable because they are persecuted. The force of this essay on anti-Semitism was to blame the existing Jewish tradition and Jewish way of life for what was wrong with the Jews, and not their circumstances of exclusion and persecution. The way to end the Jewish problem was for the Jew himself to become "enlightened," to detach himself from his tradition.[24]

D'Argens was of course aware of the suffering of the Jews under the Inquisition, and he consistently opposed that most shocking example of intolerance. With contempt he wrote of the Inquisition, "The day that they condemn a Jew to the flames is for them a day

---

[22] *Ibid.*                            [23] *Ibid.*, pp. 85, 87.
[24] *Ibid.*, pp. 47–53. Here, as throughout his work, d'Argens was bitterly critical of the Talmud.

of pleasure and triumph." [25] Montesquieu had been moved by such thoughts to defend the Jews and religious liberty in general. D'Argens in effect "explained" that the stubbornly unenlightened Jews, who had remained attached to their tradition and their usuries, had brought much, if not all, of this on themselves. In the many decades of Voltaire's literary career, he was to affirm both these views.

### The Problem of Voltaire

Voltaire complained of the Inquisition all his life. He denounced the persecutions of the Jews many times as evidence of the unworthiness of the Church. In the *Sermon du Rabbin Akib,* he put in the mouth of the rabbi the same kind of argument that Montesquieu "quoted" from the eighteen-year-old marrano girl. Voltaire even went so far in that passage as to absolve the Jews of murdering Jesus, although he was not always so generous to the Jews on this point. Characteristically, however, Voltaire did not content himself in the *Sermon* simply with saying such things as: "Let the fanatics, the superstitious, the persecutors, become men. . . . What was the Jews' crime? None other than that of being born." [26] This is the kind of thing he was saying early in his career, in 1723, in the *Henriade:*

> In Madrid, in Lisbon it [fanaticism] lights its fires,
> These solemn pyres, where unhappy Jews
> Are sent ceremoniously by priests
> For not having abandoned the faith of their ancestors.[27]

Even there, in the *Henriade,* Voltaire soon found occasion in talking of the hatred of Henry III, who was about to be assassinated, to remark again of the misery of the Jew, but also to balance that remark with a swipe at their "ancient mass of superstitions." A generation later Voltaire, again at his most liberal, in the

[25] D'Argens added that the cruelties of the Inquisition happened only in Portugal and Spain, and not in France, where at worst the Jews were exiled (*Lettres juives,* I, 27).
[26] *Oeuvres complètes,* XXIV, 281.          [27] *Ibid.,* VIII, 136.

climax of his argument in the *Sermon* could not forget his contempt for Jews:

Your enemies today add to your criminal account that you stole from the Egyptians . . . that you have been infamous usurers, that you too have burnt people at the stake, and that you have even been guilty of cannibalism. . . . I admit that we too have been a barbarous, superstitious, ignorant, and stupid people; but would it be just to proceed to burn the pope and all the monsignori of Rome at the stake, because the first Romans kidnapped the Sabines and despoiled the Samnites?

On the surface this was generous, for Voltaire was suggesting that the ancient Jews had been no worse than the ancestors of the Europeans as a whole; nonetheless there was a barb in his flat presumption, which he was to continue repeating all his life, that the ancient Jews had indeed been guilty of the worst kind of abominations. Voltaire then moved on to one of his most eloquent passages on tolerance: Let Christians, he exclaimed, "stop persecuting and exterminating the Jews, who as men are their brothers and who as Jews are their fathers. Let each man serve God in the religion in which he is born. . . . Let each man serve his king and his country, without ever using obedience to God as the excuse for disobeying the law." [28] Here Voltaire appeared at his most similar to Montesquieu, but this was not the dominant note in his writings about Jews.

Diderot went to the other extreme. He managed to attack the Inquisition and the Church all his life without mentioning the persecution of the Jews at its hands. There was only one such passage in defense of the Jews, and not a very warm one, in all his writings. It occurred in the *Encyclopédie*, in the article on the Crusades:

A third horde, consisting of more than 200,000 people, half of whom were women and the rest priests, peasants, and school children, followed in the footsteps of Peter and Dodescal; but the fury of this last horde fell particularly on the Jews. They massacred them whenever they could find them; these brutish and impious people believed that they could properly avenge the death of Jesus by slitting the throats of the little children of those who had crucified him.[29]

[28] *Ibid.*, XXIV, 284.  [29] *Encyclopédie*, XIV, 245.

On the other hand, Diderot's articles in the *Encyclopédie* on Jews and Judaism said not a word in moral defense of the persecuted Jew, or in sympathy with him.[30]

The attack on the divinity of the Bible was the consistent theme of Diderot's work, even in the earlier period of his life when he was still a Deist. This theme was already present in his *Pensées philosophiques,* which was first published in 1746. Reason stands against all inherited religious traditions.[31] In his *La moisade,* which was written around 1768, Diderot criticized the Old Testament very sarcastically, attacking it in the manner of Voltaire with all of Voltaire's usual arguments, including the factually erroneous one that 23,000 people (the Bible gives the number as 3,000, but the error is constantly repeated by Voltaire as well and by d'Holbach) were killed for worshiping the golden calf. "And you, angry and brutish people, vile and vulgar men, slaves worthy of the yoke which you bear . . . go, take back your books and remove yourselves from me." Diderot was for religion and against superstition; "the philosopher must prepare minds so that the theologian may more easily enlighten and convince them."[32]

Like d'Argens, Diderot was hostile to the Pharisees and admired the Essenes.[33] In one version of his views on the question of Jews Diderot had the same preference for "enlightened" Jews that d'Argens displayed. He gave an account of a visit to the Jewish quarter of Amsterdam and to its synagogues. He disliked what he saw at the synagogue because of its noise and lack of decorum. He found a difference between various kinds of contemporary Jews: "The shaven Jews are rich and are regarded as honest men; one has to be careful with the bearded ones, who are not particularly scrupulous. There are some very educated people among the Jews."[34]

It therefore cannot be argued that even the hatred for the Inquisition, which was universal among the *philosophes,* and their awareness that marranos were its target led them invariably to

[30] See the only larger study of Diderot and the Jewish question, Sänger, *Juden und Altes Testament,* p. 30.
[31] Diderot, *Oeuvres complètes,* I, 145, 154, 155, 163; see also Wilson, *Diderot, the Testing Years, 1713–1759,* pp. 236–37.
[32] *Diderot,* IV, 118–27.    [33] *Encyclopédie,* XV, 342–45.    [34] See fn. 6.

pro-Jewish conclusions. Their contact with enlightened Jews, or with Jewish misery, did not produce the same results among all. On the contrary, the men of the Enlightenment tended to divide on the basis of their underlying relationship to the whole of the Jewish question. The central figure was, of course, Voltaire.

The relationship between Voltaire and the Jews has been much interpreted and argued. Voltaire did have two direct, unfortunate dealings with Jews at various points of his life. The first was with the Jewish banker Acosta in London in 1726; the second occasion was his famous battle with the court Jew Hirschel in Berlin in 1750–51. The substance of the earlier incident is that Voltaire came to London with a letter of credit on DaCosta, but DaCosta soon went bankrupt, causing Voltaire to lose almost all of 20,000 francs. The later story involved a shady investment that Voltaire made in Berlin with Hirschel, a lawsuit, and the ultimate breaking of relations between Voltaire and Frederick the Great.[35]

Heinrich Graetz, the greatest Jewish historian of the nineteenth century, gave two reasons for Voltaire's views on Jews: he was opposed to Christianity, which derived from the Bible; and every Jew, including all the figures of the Bible, reminded him of his two Jewish enemies.[36] In a more recent study by Herbert Solow, the view was advanced that Voltaire's attack on Jews and Judaism was rooted not in these specific encounters but in other factors. He was a hedonist, whose anti-Jansenism shaded over into anti-Judaism. The attack on Judaism, to which his attack on the Jews of the present was incidental, was but a larger part of his life-long battle with Christianity and the Bible.[37] Two contemporary studies of this question are in substantial agreement with Solow, although each has emphasized a different part of Solow's thesis. Peter Gay has maintanied that Voltaire "struck at the Jews to strike

[35] There is one letter in English by Voltaire to Nicolas Claude Thieriot on October 26, 1726, in which he tells the story of his unfortunate dealing with the Jewish banker: "At my coming to London I found the damned Jew was broke. I was without a penny, sick to death of a violent ague, a stranger, alone, helpless, in the midst of a city wherein I was known to nobody." (*Correspondence*, II, 36). There are a number of letters about the Hirschel affair (*ibid.*, XIX, 9, 24, 29, 33, 45, 53, 66). The writers include Voltaire, Frederick the Great, and his sister Wilhelmina, who was particularly mocking of Voltaire.
[36] Graetz, "Voltaire und die Juden," *MGWJ*, XVII, 161–74, 200–23.
[37] Solow, "Voltaire and Some Jews," *Menorah Journal*, XIII, 186–97.

at the Christians." The Jews could therefore enter Voltaire's new heaven, just like the Christians, by purging themselves of their despicable history.[38] Pierre Aubery has distinguished between Voltaire's views on the Bible and his views about the Jews of his own time. Aubery has argued that all of Voltaire's charges against Jews were meant for the ancient Jews and that the only attack he repeated on those of the present was his dislike for their absurd attachment to their tradition.[39] The cure was clear: let them abandon their particularism and become "enlightened."

All of these explanations of Voltaire's attitude to the Jews can be denied, with adequate citations from Voltaire himself. In his counter-attack on Guénée, Voltaire denied Guénée's aspersion that his anger at Jews was based on his experiences with individuals who had done him harm by asserting, "I have forgotten about much larger bankruptcies by good Christians without complaining. I am not angry with any Portuguese Jew; I respect them all." [40] Voltaire's famous letter in answer to Pinto in 1762 has often been invoked as the crucial proof of his view that enlightened Jews, which in his time meant essentially Jews of Spanish-Portuguese extraction, were, or could be, acceptable to him. Did he not conclude his apology to Pinto by saying to the Jew, be what you please, even a Jew, "but be a *philosophe*." This "proof" is questionable. In the first place, Voltaire never completed his apology by making any correction of the slightest consequence in his future writings about Jews. More important, eleven years later, in 1773, Voltaire, who was always at his frankest in his letters, wrote about Jews of Spanish-Portuguese extraction in the English colonies. It is clear from the context that the man to whom he was writing, Jean Baptiste Nicolas de Lisle de Sales, had said something approving about these people (more will be said about this later). Voltaire replied as follows: "I know that there are some Jews in the English colonies. These marranos go wherever there is money to be made. . . . But that these circumcised Jews who sell old clothes

[38] Gay, *The Party of Humanity*, pp. 97–108; see also his earlier statement in *Voltaire's Politics*, pp. 351–54.
[39] Aubery, "Voltaire et les Juifs," *Studies on Voltaire and the Eighteenth Century*, XXIV, 67–79.
[40] *Un Chrétien contre six Juifs*, in *Oeuvres*, XXIX, 558.

to the savages claim that they are of the tribe of Naphtali or Issachar is not of the slightest importance. They are, nonetheless, the greatest scoundrels who have ever sullied the face of the globe." [41]

It is clear from Voltaire's obsession with the financial honor of the Jews in the Bible and throughout history that he was angry, at least much of the time, because of the memory of his dealings with the Jews. He did, indeed, attack the Bible to get at Christianity, but no one can read his attacks without the mounting conviction, based on hundreds of his references to Judaism and the Jews, that most of the time he regarded them as radically different. Almost every discussion of the question, up to the most recent ones by Aubery and Gay, has offered the explanation that there was something in Voltaire's stance which was a carry-over, even in the mind of this ex-Christian, from the endemic anti-Semitism of the Christian tradition within which he was nurtured. The force of this explanation is that it has enabled those who offer it to view Voltaire as ultimately tolerant. What there was of Jew-hatred in the Enlightenment, even though it is to be found among some of its chief spokesmen, was therefore a passing phenomenon. Voltaire, Diderot, and d'Holbach can be imagined as having been engaged in freeing themselves, in their own lives, of Christianity and its last negative effect on them, anti-Semitism, as part of their battle to breed all such notions out of European culture as a whole. In this interpretation, Jewish exclusiveness and stiff-neckedness were but one of the many illiberal traditions that men must conquer and reject in the name of freedom.

This may perhaps have been the nature of Voltaire's inmost feelings. Some case can be made for such an interpretation, for Voltaire was an unsystematic thinker. He wrote an enormous library in the course of his long life, and he contradicted himself on many matters. It is possible, therefore, to interpret the overwhelming weight of the remarks disdainful of the Jews as representing his past and the relatively few pro-Jewish remarks can be seen as the dawning of his true, lasting convictions. Nonetheless, this interpretation cannot be valid. In the first place, what was

[41] *Correspondence,* LXXXVI, 166.

in Voltaire's inmost heart, and why it was there, cannot be determined even by the most delicate of psychological analyses. It is an inherently insoluble question. There are, however, two questions that can be answered: What did Voltaire's contemporaries understand him to say? What was his legacy to the next age?

In his own time Voltaire's work encouraged anti-Semitism; it was a major obstacle to the freedom of the Jews. For the next century he provided the fundamentals of the rhetoric of secular anti-Semitism. These two considerations create a large presumption that Voltaire himself was an anti-Semite, but this question is really not very important. His role in history was that of the crucial architect of the ambivalences that surrounded the Emancipation. His work made a fundamental contribution to its debacle.

## Voltaire and His Contemporaries

Overwhelming evidence shows that both Jews and gentiles, whether "enlightened" or not, unanimously regarded Voltaire as the enemy not only of biblical Judaism but of the struggling Jews of his own day. Everyone understood him to mean more than that the Jew was the most difficult of all peoples to enlighten and regenerate. He, Diderot, and d'Holbach were understood to be teaching that the Jew was hopelessly and irretrievably alien.

In the last years of his life Voltaire was living in Ferney, on the edge of Alsace, where bitter battles where being waged between the Jews and their enemies. A man as attuned as Voltaire was to every immediate event must have been aware of what was going on at his very doorstep. There were no direct echoes of these encounters anywhere in his writings or his letters, however; his comments towards the very end of his life were, as we shall see, all the testier about the usuries and the bad character of the Jews.

In the 1760s and 1770s Jews in France were fighting for the right to abandon usury and to enter the guilds. They were attempting to take the first step in becoming new men, of precisely the kind that Voltaire supposedly wanted. The Jews were sufficiently in tune with the newer currents of thinking to welcome every friendly voice that could be enlisted in support of such a policy. This was the period in which Voltaire fought the battle for the rehabilitation of the memory of Jean Calas, the Protestant who had been victim of a judicial murder in Toulouse in 1762. Whatever scores an abbé like Guénée may have had to settle with Voltaire on account of religion, the Jews themselves would certainly have turned to Voltaire in arguments about economic rights, social restratification, and political freedom if they had felt there would be any entrée. Had he not, indeed, said to Pinto in 1762, "Be a philosopher"? Several Jews of Alsace, who were familiar with the world of books, found the obscure young lawyer Lacretelle to defend them with "enlightened" arguments in the battle for their right to enter productive occupations, that is, to take the first step towards becoming "philosophers," but they did not seek Voltaire. Nor can it be said that the Jews of Alsace hesitated to go to him because there were aspects of Jewish existence they knew Voltaire did not like. Dohm, Mirabeau, and Grégoire, whom Jewish leaders did enlist and perhaps even paid to write on their behalf in the 1780s, were also not uncritical admirers of the Jews. For that matter, neither was Lacretelle.

This argument from silence would not be convincing if it could not be proved that all the anti-Jewish pamphleteers in the last two decades before the Revolution, and especially in Alsace, invariably based their arguments not primarily on inherited Christian prejudices but on the post-Christian anti-Semitism that was defined for them by Voltaire. They usually invoked his authority directly. By the same token, all the pro-Jewish writers never quoted Voltaire except as the enemy. They almost always based themselves on Montesquieu and counter-attacked Voltaire. This is all the more striking because these defenders of the Jews agreed in suggesting that the object of their pleading was not the Jew of the day but the one to be remade in the image of enlightened philosophy, the one that Voltaire supposedly would find acceptable.

In the year of Voltaire's death, 1777, the famous affair of "false receipts" began in Alsace. The organizer of the ring that made these forged documents, which were given to the peasants by the hundreds to enable them to claim that they had paid the debts they owed to Jews, was a local Alsatian judge, Hell. In 1779 he published a short book explaining his position, in which he offered a consistent account of his anti-Jewish views.[42] Though Hell never quoted Voltaire directly, it is clear from his book that he had read with great care the anti-Jewish pronouncements of the sage of Ferney.

Hell admitted, by implication, that the receipts were indeed forged but argued that this was a merited response of the Alsatian peasants to their despoilers.[43] He did make some use of Christian anti-Semitic clichés: "The blood of the righteous one whom they crucified has fallen upon them and upon their children." However, his main tack was to use all of the defamations of the Jews through history to prove that they were, indeed, guilty of bad conduct. Hell repeated the stock remarks of the enlightened writers: at least until the last century, the Jews had been guilty of the ritual murder of children.[44] He preferred the Karaites to the Jews who were attached to the Talmud,[45] but it was the latter who predominated in Europe, and he attacked the Talmud in precisely the same language that was to be found in the writings of the major figures of the Enlightenment. Like Voltaire, Hell enlisted the prophets in their attacks on the Jews to prove that their inherited character was bad.[46] The existence of an organized Jewish community, as a legally recognized corporate body, made the Jews all the more dangerous, both because they could press their economic claims and because they were a nation within a nation, and thus disloyal.[47] In the name of the people of Alsace he attacked the nobles for using their right to admit Jews and thus turn more despoilers loose on the peasants.[48] The forgeries of receipts were indeed, he admitted, a crime against God, but they were socially useful because the peasants were helped.[49] Hell concluded his argument with a double appeal to the judges who were to try the cases of the false receipts: the accused peasants were Christians and had a right to expect solidarity from the judges against the

---

[42] Hell, *Observations*.　　　　　[43] *Ibid.*, pp. 10–13.
[44] *Ibid.*, pp. 26. A comparable remark is to be found in d'Argens, quoted in the text of this chapter.
[45] *Ibid.*, pp. 33–34.　　　　　[46] *Ibid.*, p. 69.
[47] *Ibid.*, pp. 81–83; see also Chapter X.
[48] *Ibid.*, p. 87.　　　　　[49] *Ibid.*, pp. 107–110.

Jews.[50] In the second place, the peasants were the only class that really paid taxes since the rich paid almost nothing. The very least that the nobility could do for the peasant was to free him of the yoke of the Jews: "Therefore, gentlemen, pronounce your verdict and absolve us; it is in the interest of a thousand peasants who are about to be ruined; it is also to the interest of the state to which each citizen is dear." [51]

A few years later another writer, Foissac, used the anti-Jewish arguments of the Enlightenment quite overtly. His pamphlet *Le cri du citoyen contre les Juifs de Metz* was part of the battle against the Alsatian Jews that had been initiated by Hell. It is likely that "Foissac" was a pseudonym for Jean Baptiste Annibal Aubert-Dubayet, who was a captain of cavalry in Metz in the 1780s and later, for a short while, the Minister of War under the Directory.[52] The author of this pamphlet quoted Voltaire at the very beginning to the effect that Jews are perverse, ignorant, barbarous, and avaricious. He even pretended that he began by being grieved at the prevalent hatred of the Jews but that he had to conclude, after he got to know them, that they were deserving of this obloquy.[53] His major point was that every young officer was, upon arrival at his regiment, immediately surrounded by the Jews, who offered him loans with which to ruin himself.[54] The Jews were bad in ancient times and, as Voltaire knew, they remained so: "Monsieur de Voltaire, who knew the Jews very well, partly because of a difficult experience with them and partly because of close study of their history, stated, when speaking of them, that in all ages

[50] *Ibid.*, p. 123.

[51] *Ibid.*, pp. 123–36. On Hell's central role in the affair of the false receipts, see Chapter V.

[52] Both the identity of Foissac and the date of publication of his pamphlet are in some doubt. Szajkowski (*Franco-Judaica*, No. 1637) gives the date as 1786 and corrects the place of publication, which is given as Lausanne, as, in reality, Metz. The pamphlet was indeed published in 1786. It was suppressed by the *parlement* of Metz in a decree of July 8, 1786 (*ibid.*, No. 1638 and JTS Library). A response by the Jewish writer Berr Bing, *Lettre*, appeared in Metz in 1787. There is agreement in the secondary sources that the author was Aubert-Dubayet. The biographical articles about him in *La grande encyclopédie* and in the *Nouvelle biographie générale* both maintain that he was the author of this pamphlet, but both are in error in giving Paris as the place of publication and the date as 1788. On Bing and "Foissac" see also Chapter X.

[53] Dubayet, *Le cri du citoyen*, p. 2.      [54] *Ibid.*, pp. 10–12.

leprosy, fanaticism, and usury were their distinguishing characteristics." [55] The author of this pamphlet had a positive suggestion for the solution of the Jewish problem. It was that a wise
government should forbid them both their present occupations and
their residences in eastern France; it should direct them to the
vast, uncultivated lands of France. By working on the land the
Jews would become citizens of France and they would then be
worthy of that honor. [56]

The enemies of the Jews thus quoted Voltaire to prove that not
merely their religion but their essential and lasting character was
evil. It is more revealing still that the friends of the Jews in the last
twenty years before the Revolution were engaged in debating with
Voltaire, in the name of their version of a truly enlightened position,
at least as much as they were concerned with older, Christian
prejudices. A whole host of names, of a variety of outlooks, can be
added to the several abbés mentioned in the last chapter, all of
whom counter-attacked Voltaire in the name of Montesquieu.

Pinto had begun his *Apologie*, by quoting Montesquieu, to prove
that all men, including the Jews, are basically the same and that
the differences among them are made by climate. Guénée continued the theme. [57] He answered Voltaire as follows: "What kind
of philosophy is this which, dominated by hatred and dedicated
to the blindest prejudice, permits itself these outrageous attacks on
a people, the descendants of whom already have more than enough
about which to complain. Is this the philosophy of Montesquieu
and Locke?" [58]

Pinto's *Apologie*, first published in 1762, was reprinted in 1769
in Guénée's work, accompanied with footnotes by the abbé. The
whole of Pinto's work was based, as we have seen, on the idea
that those Jews who had entered Western society and adopted
Western manners were better than the rest, and that they were
thereby made worthy of equality. He argued for the Portuguese

[55] *Ibid.*, p. 19.
[56] *Ibid.*, p. 26; this last argument owed something to the physiocrats.
[57] On Guénée see Wright, "Le prêtre," *Bulletin catholique*, 17th year, no.
71, pp. 743–47. Guénée's *Lettres* was first published in 1769, and there were
numerous other editions, including translations into four languages.
[58] Guénée, *Lettres*, pp. 302–303.

that they "do not wear a beard and are in no way different in their clothing; their rich engage in scholarship, in elegant ways, and in ostentation to as great a degree as the other people of Europe from whom they differ only in religion." [59] Voltaire took no notice of this in his reply to Guénée and Pinto. It is even more revealing that some years later, in 1774, Pinto wrote a pamphlet against materialist philosophy, which was intended as a refutation of d'Holbach's *Système de la nature*.[60] Pinto's arguments were those of a man of the Enlightenment rather than those of a believing Jew. He did not once use the doctrine of Revelation or even quote the Bible. He accepted the notion that prayer changes nothing and was tolerant of atheists. It is simply inconceivable that Voltaire, who heard about everything, did not know that one of his old antagonists had written a book that was largely acceptable to him in its views. This was also the decade in which the image of Mendelssohn, the enlightened Jew of Berlin, was so famous in all of Europe. Voltaire ignored Mendelssohn completely. More immediately, he paid no attention whatsoever to the man he had once asked to be a philosopher, when Pinto was so evidently

[59] Guénée, *Lettres,* p. 46. In his original argument Pinto had been surprised that Voltaire, who had insisted that Judaism is the mother of Christianity and Islam, should have heaped such calumnies on the oldest faith. Guénée took issue with this in a footnote. He saw no contradiction between honoring ancient Judaism and yet rejecting its present form as having been superseded, by Christianity. It is wrong to attempt to convert people by fire and sword, but the Jews must be brought to the true faith by enlightened methods. "The fanaticism of some Christians does not represent the Christian religion. . . . Christianity is armed only with persuasion and with the good it brings with objectivity and with patience" (p. 11). Pinto had praised Jews for their fidelity, for they did not convert to improve their financial circumstances. Guénée added a footnote: "No one is inviting them to make business with their religion but rather to open their eyes to the light. One can have compassion for them and forgive them but one should not praise them" (p. 37). Pinto was pleased with Voltaire's defense of the Jews against the charge of Christ-killing, but Guénée did not find it so praiseworthy. He took issue with Pinto's assertion that Pontius Pilate had played the greatest role in the death of Jesus by remarking: "Can one really fool oneself about the facts or hide them?" On this point Guénée attacked the Jews quite violently. He held Voltaire, who had argued that the modern Jews could not be held responsible for any action by their ancestors, to be quite wrong (pp. 37–39).

[60] Pinto, *Précis.* Despite these heresies Pinto was, however, *parnas* of the Synagogue of Amsterdam and was buried in the Jewish cemetery of The Hague (Wijler, *Isaac de Pinto,* pp. 98–104). Regarding Pinto and Dohm, see also Chapter IV.

following that injunction—and this at the very time when Voltaire
was writing his invective against Guénée and Pinto!

On the heels of the publication of Hell's diatribe against the
Jews, Cerf Berr, the leader of Alsatian Jewry, with the aid of
Mendelssohn persuaded Christian Wilhelm Dohm, an enlightened
economist and government official of Berlin, to write a book in
defense of the Jews. Two editions were published in Germany, one
in German in 1781 under the title *Ueber die Buergerliche Verbesserung der Juden,* and the second in French in 1782 entitled
*De la réforme politique des Juifs.* Dohm's essential stance was to
denounce Hell's ideas as "unworthy of our century and of an enlightened people." [61] The basic principle of Dohm's economic theory
was that every state wants to increase its population.[62] Why not,
therefore, add to the population, painlessly, by reversing the policy
that was followed everywhere in Europe of hindering the increase
of the Jews. Dohm deplored the fact that no state had yet risen to
"the true and natural principles" of free trade.[63] In conventional
enlightened fashion, he argued that the faults of the Jews were
created by the conditions under which they were made to live
and earn a living.[64] Human character was not innate, but it was
created by climate, food, and the conditions of the environment.
In this Dohm of course followed Montesquieu. If the Jews were
given the opportunity and freedom, they would change and very
rapidly lose their bad habits. "The Jew is more of a man than he is
a Jew." [65] Dohm could have supported his case by quoting Voltaire (who had once said, "Be a philosopher," to Pinto) and it
would indeed have been impressive authority with which to demolish Hell. There is not a whisper anywhere in Dohm's book of a
presumption that Voltaire could be used in support of a program
to upgrade the Jews by changing their unfortunate circumstances.

That Voltaire was regarded as the enemy of the Jews of Alsace
is clear in an anonymous contemporary pamphlet that appeared
in 1781.[66] The author described himself as an Alsatian farmer.
The immediate impulse for this essay was no doubt the controversy involving Hell and the affair of the false receipts, although

---

[61] Dohm, *Reforme politique,* p. 78;     [62] *Ibid.,* p. 1.     [63] *Ibid.,* p. 14.
[64] *Ibid.,* p. 45.     [65] *Ibid.,* p. 35.
[66] *Sammlung von Aufsatzen,* ed. Schmoll, pp. 59–103.

the writer claimed that he was first impelled to think about the Jewish question by an essay contest about them that was held by the "newly created philanthropic society in Strasbourg," of which we have no other record.[67] This essayist argued on Christian grounds that it was a religious duty to love Jews. The author was, however, motivated by economic considerations and an "enlightened" outlook rather than by religion: "The purpose of the state is the power, wealth, and happiness of society, and not to make all men worship God in the same way. This would represent the greatest imperfection and unhappiness in the world; thank God that this idea will always remain a phantom."[68] The anonymous author defended the Jewish religion against all attacks, including those of Voltaire, on circumcision; he argued that, on the contrary, no aspect of this faith was detrimental to the state. The only ritual of the Jews that disturbed commerce was their observance of Sabbath, and he hoped that equality would ultimately create a change, even in that.[69] The author of this essay purported to be an Alsatian Protestant who saw some parallel between the situation of his community, which had been ennobled by persecution, and the Jews.[70] The essential thrust of his argument was that economic liberty is what men desire most and they would change all of the traditions of their past that stood in the way of its attainment. Why did our anonymous pamphleteer, who knew Voltaire's work well enough to argue with it, not quote him with approval in this connection? Obviously, he thought that Voltaire regarded the Jews as beyond regeneration.

As is well known, Mirabeau turned his attention to the Jewish question in the 1780s. The immediate impulse for his interest was a trip to Holland in 1784 and one to England in 1785. He was in Prussia in 1786 a few days after the death of Mendelssohn. Mirabeau was impressed by the enlightened minorities of the Jewish communities of the capitals of these three countries, and he was particularly taken with the image of Mendelssohn.[71] In the

[67] *Ibid.*, p. 60.           [68] *Ibid.*, p. 66.           [69] *Ibid.*, pp. 75–76.
[70] *Ibid.*, pp. 100–101.
[71] See Reiszner, "Mirabeaus Judenpolitik," *Morgen*, VIII, 122–30. There are remarks on the Jewish question in Mirabeau's four volumes which appeared in London in 1788, *Monarchie prussienne*, III, 453–64. Here he defended the

book that resulted from that trip, *Sur Moses Mendelssohn, sur la réforme politique des Juifs*,[72] he argued that the faults of the Jews were those of their circumstances. Mirabeau gave considerable weight to the proposition that the Jews themselves should be freed of the "dark phantoms of the Talmudists." [73] Judaism was, however, in Mirabeau's view not an immoral faith, and he defended this religion against both the older and the newer attacks. In the course of Mirabeau's argument he repeated Dohm's assertion that "the Jew is more of a man than he is a Jew." [74] Indeed, Mirabeau quoted quite freely from Dohm; [75] he attacked Hell;[76] and he invoked Turgot [77] and Rousseau [78] to support his pro-Jewish arguments. The nearest that he got to Voltaire was to refute what he termed a prevalent opinion that the Jews are bad by nature. He asserted that history proves that "the Jews, considering them as men and as citizens, were greatly corrupted only because they were denied their rights." [79] This, he insisted, should be realized by the enlightened minds who opposed this persecuted people and considered them bad by nature.

Two more cases in point are books written in defense of Judaism and the Jews by obscure writers in the 1780s. One was by M. Senger in 1785 entitled *L'esprit des lois mosaïques*. The very title was evocative of Montesquieu's famous *L'esprit des lois*. The theme of the book was to defend ancient Jewish jurisprudence in the name of cultural and legal diversity. "Even if all the peoples of Europe obeyed only one monarch, this prince would have to give them different sets of laws." [80] The intent of the author was to teach a positive appreciation of biblical Jewish law; although the enemies of the Bible were not mentioned by name, Senger was consciously answering the attacks by Voltaire and his followers and associates.

Another such defense was written at about the same time by Emile Claude Joseph Pierre Pastoret: *Moyse considéré comme*

---

Jews against the charge of usury, and he used the image of the Jews of Berlin, an already enlightened group, to prove that the Jews can indeed be remade by freedom.

[72] *Sur Moses Mendelssohn* appeared in London in 1787.      [73] *Ibid.*, p. 28.
[74] *Ibid.*, p. 66.      [75] *Ibid.*, p. 90.      [76] *Ibid.*, p. 63.      [77] *Ibid.*, p. 27.
[78] *Ibid.*, p. 36      [79] *Ibid.*, p. 57.
[80] Senger, *L'esprit des lois mosaïques*, pp. 8–9.

*legislateur et comme moraliste.* Pastoret had made his literary
debut in his native Marseilles as a disciple of Voltaire. The year
after the master's death Pastoret published an appreciative memo-
rial essay, *Eloge de Voltaire.* He remained a considerable admirer
of Voltaire and took the lead during the Revolution in having Voltaire included among the figures honored in the Pantheon that was
created in 1791. Nevertheless, Pastoret consciously dissociated
himself from Voltaire's views on comparative culture in general
and on the biblical Jews in particular. In a study of Zoroaster,
Confucius, and Mohammed Pastoret looked not for the foolishnesses
to mock in other traditions (as Voltaire had done in the *Essai sur
les moeurs*), but for those aspects of other cultures that he could
praise as approaching the great contemporary moral standard, "the
love of humanity." In the whole of this work Pastoret ignored
Voltaire completely and referred consistently to Montesquieu. In
the work on Judaism that Pastoret published two years later, the
attack on Voltaire was overt. He maintained, again, that all religions had been created by responding to climate and environment. Christianity was, indeed, superior to all other faiths, because
it alone had been universalized by the abolition of all practices
related to local culture and conditions. Judaism was, however, not
to be considered a vile tradition and its believers were not outside
culture. In effect, Pastoret's views reduced the distance between
the inherited culture of the Jews and the new world of moderate
eighteenth-century *philosophes.* It thus became more reasonable
to imagine that equality for Jews was both possible and useful. The
gulf between the Jews, even at their most "Jewish," and the new
world that ought to be born was not the vast chasm that Voltaire
had described.[81]

[81] See Pastoret, *Moyse considéré comme législateur et comme moraliste,* p.
10, 516–17. His work on the major oriental religions appeared in 1786: *Zorastre,
Confucius et Mohamet comparés comme sectaires, législateurs et moralistes.*
There was a second edition in 1788 (the one that I have seen), in the year
when Pastoret's work on Judaism was published. He was a moderate royalist
during the Revolution; he fled France in the Jacobin period and returned to
participate in the governments of the Thermidor and Napoleon. During the
Restoration he was made a peer of France, first as a count and then as a
marquis. In the twenty years from 1817 to 1837 Pastoret published his main
work in eleven volumes, a study of comparative law entitled *Histoire de la
législation.* For his biography, see *La grande encyclopédie,* XV, 77.

Senger did not figure at all on the battle for the emancipation of the Jews that took place between 1789 and 1791. Pastoret took no role of leadership on this issue, even though he was one of the minor actors in the drama of the Revolution. Mirabeau, until his death on April 2, 1791, was the towering figure in the Constituent Assembly. He was so well-known a proponent of emancipation of the Jews that he was charged with being in their pay. The majority that was eventually mustered to vote the decree conferring equality on the Jews consisted largely of men like these; they were acting on premises derived from Montesquieu.

These men were essentially secular thinkers. There was, also, an element of moderate religious opinion led by Grégoire among those who enacted the decree of emancipation. The men of religion did not agree with each other, and they did not necessarily all defend the Jews to the same degree, and yet in all their varieties they, too, quoted Montesquieu against Voltaire. Let us give three examples. A little-known Protestant professor, Jean Salchli, of Lausanne, was moved by the same essay that had occasioned Pinto's work to write a book in defense of ancient Judaism against Voltaire's attacks. At the very outset Salchli termed Voltaire a careless genius who did not know what he was talking about in his discussion of ancient Jewish civil and political law. Montesquieu was by far the greater political mind, being "the world's greatest expert on laws," and his authority in praise of Jewish law was to be preferred to Voltaire's attack. Salchli disagreed with Voltaire, point by point, about the Old Testament, but Salchli was himself an orthodox Christian in regarding the modern Jews as "this blind people." Nonetheless, like the Catholic Abbé Richard, Salchli could not help saying at the very end of his book that there were some things in Voltaire's writings about the Jews of his own century, "regardless of how despicable they might have become," that had gone much too far. Salchli defended them, albeit quite weakly, against Voltaire.[82]

Guénée, the most famous of those who debated Voltaire on the Jews, was somewhat more liberal in his theological outlook. His main purpose was, as a Christian, to defend the Jews of the Old

[82] Salchli, *Apologie de l'histoire du peuple juif suivant les auteurs sacrés,* pp. 3–7, 227–35.

Testament. Yet the very violence of Voltaire's attack made Guénée speak for even the Jews of his own time. As we shall soon see, Voltaire in his essay on tolerance that was occasioned by the death of Jean Calas had excepted the Jews from the principle of universal toleration, or had at very least strongly suggested that such might be done. Guénée, in his *Lettres,* the beginning of his original writings (as distinguished from his notes to Pinto's *Apologie,* which represented the first part of the book) was outraged that Voltaire could take such a view:

We have just read your *Traité de la tolérance.* . . . We have been greatly surprised to read that in a work which proclaims the ideas of kindness and humanity . . . we have again found you treating our people, our sacred books, and everything which is dear to us in a manner so contrary to the pose of equity and moderation that you adopt. Is it conceivable that so much contempt and hatred is present in the work of a philosopher of conciliation, who is a friend of the human race? [83]

Guénée's manner of writing was his pretense that he was himself a Portuguese Jew. These words were cast in the style of a Jew pleading for his own people, but there can be no doubt whatsoever that these were Guénée's own views as well.

The very last word among the clerics belongs to Grégoire, precisely because it was he who bore the brunt of the immediate battle in the years 1788–91 for the emancipation of the Jews. He was a curé in a parish under the ecclesiastical dominion of the Bishop of Nancy, de la Fare. The bishop was a vicious anti-Semite of the medieval kind, who spoke with great heat in the Revolutionary parliament against Grégoire's proposals for giving equality to the Jews. Grégoire retold this story in one of his books and he added, quite unnecessarily in the context in which the remark occurred, that Voltaire, "who had always shown himself to be the enemy of the Jews," had been as bad an anti-Semite as de la Fare.[84] In Grégoire's account the implication was very clear that in battling for the emancipation of the Jews he had had to fight for their freedom with the spirit of both the medievalist bishop and the leader of the *philosophes.*

As is well known, Grégoire made his public debut as a leader in the reconsideration of the Jewish question in 1787, when his work won first prize in the Metz Academy's essay contest on that subject. There were no overt references to Voltaire in this volume, although it is clear in the light of what has just been said that Grégoire had him in mind as he argued that Jews were not bad by nature and that freedom would regenerate them. This essay contest represented the climax of a century of discussion about the Jew. It was the hinge on which the debate made the last turn right before the Revolution. What was written about Voltaire by the other two prize winners, the Protestant Thiéry and the Jew Zalkind-Hourwitz, is therefore very revealing indeed.

Thiéry wrote that Voltaire had been unfair in attacking the religion and character of the Jews. They were not inhuman for sometimes hating their enemies and wanting vengeance. Thiéry was very angry, in general: "The enemy of the Jews whose blows have hurt most is M. de Voltaire, who has prostituted his genius in order to enjoy the strange pleasure of degrading and condemning the Jews." Thiéry quoted Montesquieu as the authority for giving all men, including Jews, freedom and equality.[85]

An equally revealing comment is to be found in the opening pages of the book by Zalkind-Hourwitz, the Polish-Jewish enlightener who figured in the Revolution as a Jacobin, he made very radical suggestions in 1789 for the means to be taken to reform the Jews. Hourwitz began by stating flatly, and as a matter of course, that what he needed to do was to defend the Jew not, as one would expect, against the attacks of continuing Christian prejudice or the hatred of the populace rooted in economic conflict, but against "the seductive eloquence of Voltaire and of all the other celebrated writers who are sworn enemies of all their fellow men who pray to the Supreme Being in Hebrew." In this book Hourwitz faced the issue of Jewish religion and, as a good enlightener, he agreed that Judaism as it existed, with its customs, was prejudicial to admitting the Jews to equality in society. He argued that the hold of Judaism on the Jews was exaggerated: "In a word, the devotion of German, Polish, and Portuguese Jews to their religion is of the same order as that of Spanish, German, and French Cath-

[85] Thiéry, *Dissertation*, pp. 49, 56.

olics to theirs." The force of Hourwitz's argument was that all of this can be easily changed by changing the conditions under which Jews live.[86]

This had been the position of Pinto in his *Apologie,* with which Voltaire had debated. Clearly Hourwitz did not deduce from that earlier debate that Voltaire would ultimately have been ready to open his arms to enlightened Jews—for was not Zalkind-Hourwitz most assuredly in his own mind a *philosophe?*

Voltaire's contemporaries, it is abundantly clear, did not doubt that he was an anti-Semite. Everyone was certain that he was, and everyone was just as certain that his distaste for Jews extended, for the most part, even to enlightened ones. They did not imagine that he disliked Jews because he was guilty of still retaining some Christian prejudices from his youth. On the contrary, they knew, as Mirabeau put it, that only a few of the men of the Enlightenment were pro-Jewish and that most had their own "enlightened" reasons for regarding Jews as no more within the pale of culture than the ancient Romans considered slaves to be when they talked of the rights of men in civilized society.

## Voltaire and Paganism

This analogy to the attitude of the Romans to their slaves is the key to the question not only of Voltaire's attitude to the Jews, but to that of other central figures of the Enlightenment such as Diderot and d'Holbach. At the very heart of the whole of Voltaire's outlook there was, as André Maurois has seen, a vision of universal history that was constructed in opposition to the orthodox one of Bossuet. Voltaire did not see the Jews and biblical history as central; he looked back to pagan, Greco-Roman antiquity as the golden age.[87] Then there had been true philosophy and culture. This would have been ruined by the advent of Christianity. In his own mind Voltaire was a Cicero *redivivus* who had come to recreate that world. The glory of the new age of enlightenment would be that Europe would be restored to its true foundations.

[86] Zalkind-Hourwitz, *Apologie des Juifs,* pp. 7, 82–83.
[87] See Maurois' preface to Voltaire, *Philosophical Dictionary,* p. xii.

In that ancient age, as Voltaire knew all too well, the Jews had been hated. Even then they had stood apart from the vision of a cosmopolitan world. Hannah Emmrich has observed, in the only larger study of Voltaire and the Jews ever written, that Voltaire regarded the Jewish character as a continuity from ancient times to the present. This lasting phenomenon had to be confronted again when the corner was being turned from the Bible towards a renewed Stoicism.[88] The obvious place in which to find the description of this confrontation was in the works of the Greco-Roman pagans who had last experienced it, in Voltaire's terms. The issue was more fundamental than the quarrel between Christians and Jews; it was the quarrel between the bearers of Western culture and those who had infected it with Oriental ideas.

The essence of Voltaire's view on the Jews, the key to the understanding of all the rest, is in one of his last serious writings on the subject. In 1771 he again adopted one of his favorite poses, that of a classic Roman, and wrote *Lettres de Memmius à Ciceron*. Voltaire put into the mouth of Memmius a description of Syria, in which the Jews were singled out as the very worst of men, hating all others and in turn hated by them: "The Persians and the Scythians are a thousand times more reasonable. . . ." He went on to praise Cicero for his anti-Semitic oration, *Pro Flacco*. The climax of this outburst read: "They are, all of them, born with raging fanaticism in their hearts, just as the Bretons and the Germans are born with blond hair. I would not be in the least bit surprised if these people would not some day become deadly to the human race." [89] Voltaire had thus, being an ex-Christian, abandoned entirely the religious attack on the Jews as Christ-killers or Christ-rejectors. He proposed a new principle on which to base his hatred of them, their innate character.

That the "racist" remark by Voltaire just cited is no accident can be proved further by something he wrote in the next year, in his *Il faut prendre une partie*. This piece was introduced as "the last word of Voltaire on metaphysics." It consisted largely of speeches by the adherents of various religions, and each one was, of course, designed to make that particular religion appear ridiculous. At the end, a "theist," Voltaire, reviewed each of the speeches. He said to

---

[88] Emmrich, *Das Judentum bei Voltaire*. She was also aware that much of Voltaire's attitude was rooted in Greek and Roman sources.

[89] *Oeuvres complètes*, XXVIII, 439–40.

the Jews, "You seem to me to be the maddest of the lot. The Kaffirs, the Hottentots, and the Negroes of Guinea are much more reasonable and more honest people than your ancestors, the Jews. You have surpassed all nations in impertinent fables, in bad conduct, and in barbarism. You deserve to be punished, for this is your destiny." [90]

Voltaire was, beyond any doubt, conscious of the fact that he was counterposing the Jews to the Greeks, to the disadvantage of the Jews. Perhaps his kindest essay on the Jewish spirit was his review in the *Gazette littéraire* of 1764 of M. R. Lowth's book, *Sacred Hebrew Poetry*. He approved of some of the poetic images of the prophets and he liked the pastoral quality of the Pentateuch, as literature. He even explained Hebrew imagery, in the manner of Montesquieu, as being rooted in the climate and manner of life of the ancient Hebrews. Nonetheless, he added that "one must state that this people had no idea of that which we call taste, delicacy, or proportion." [91] This notion was more explicit in one of Voltaire's very last utterances, *La Bible enfin expliquée*. In speaking of the Maccabees, Voltaire asserted that a new light was appearing for the human race in their time, and that light was coming from Athens alone. Men were becoming accustomed, little by little, to think more reasonably and to write with greater order and naturalness (the two evidently being identical in the mind of the neoclassicist). Even the Jews were being affected:

The Jews themselves had shied away from a bombastic, incomprehensible, and incoherent style . . . and one which resembles drunken dreams when it does not reflect the enthusiasm of divine inspiration. . . . The books of the Maccabees prove the point. We do not know who the authors were. It is enough to know that in general they were written in a style somewhat more human than that of all the earlier histories in the Bible and sometimes, if one may dare say it, closer to the eloquence of the Greeks and the Romans.[92]

[90] *Ibid.*, p. 549.  [91] *Ibid.*, XXV, 204.
[92] *Ibid.*, XXX, 273–74. That Jews continued to regard Voltaire's attacks on the Bible as attacks on themselves is evidenced in an interesting entry in the *Minutes* of the Mahamad of the Spanish-Portuguese Congregation of London, Vol. 106. Raphael Baruh was refused permission, on Hesvan 3, 5537 (the fall of 1776) to print a book entitled *Counter-explanation of La Bible enfin expliquée*. This decision was reversed five days later but I have not been able to find a work on the subject by Baruh. (I owe this reference to my friend, Dr. Richard Barnett, honorary archivist of the Congregation.)
It is equally likely that Baruh did not have contemporary political problems

Almost all the themes of Voltaire's attitude towards the Jews were on view in his discussion of them in his *Essai sur les moeurs,* which was written relatively early, in the 1750s. He was aware that it was the avarice of Spain that had led to their expulsion in 1492, but he insisted that the Jews had had a hand in bringing this on themselves, because they controlled all the money and commerce in the country. He knew that, in general, the Jews were milked dry in medieval Europe by being made to buy their rights dearly and that the accusations of ritual murder were a form of confiscation. He quoted Maimonides approvingly as one source of the idea that the Jews were the fathers of Christianity: "This people ought to interest us, because we ourselves are basically only uncircumcised Jews." Why, therefore, are the Jews hated? "It is the inevitable result of their laws; they either had to conquer everybody or be hated by the whole human race." This hatred began with the peculiarity of their religious laws, and it was strengthened by their animosity towards the uncircumcised Romans who conquered them. Voltaire ended this discussion by writing: "They kept all their customs, which are exactly the opposite of all proper social customs; they were therefore rightly treated as a people opposed to all others,

---

in mind at all. He may have projected this work solely to refute Voltaire's attacks on the Bible, in order to counter the negative influence of contemporary heresies on the faith of younger Jewish intellectuals. The last two roars of the dying lion were heard in 1776. Both Voltaire's answer to Guénée, *Un Chrétien contre six Juifs,* and his last great attack on the Bible as a whole, *La Bible enfin expliquée,* appeared in that year. We have seen in Chapter VI that the thought of the *philosophes* was then penetrating among the Sephardim; Azulai was arguing theology in the winter of 1777–78, in Paris, Bordeaux, and Bayonne. After the Sephardim in France had achieved their climactic rights in the *lettres-patentes* of 1776, Voltaire the anti-Jew with whom Pinto had debated seemed much less directly troubling to them than Voltaire the critic of the biblical faith.

This was all the more true outside of France, at least in the free environment of an English colony such as Jamaica. A volume was published there anonymously in 1788 under the title *Reason and Faith.* The author was the rabbi of its Jewish community, Joshua Hezekiah de Cordova. The purpose of this book was to defend true religion against "a Spinoza, a Collins, a Tindal, a Bolingbroke, a Hume, or a Voltaire." The audience to which this defense was addressed consisted of "ignorant youth deceived by believing themselves philosophers so soon as they become unbelievers" (p. 14). For the identification of the anonymous author and the discovery of the existence of a first edition of this work, published in Jamaica, see Korn, "The Haham de Cordova of Jamaica," *American Jewish Archives,* XVIII, 141–54; the edition in Philadelphia, 1791, has been known and is the one from which quotations here are taken; there was also a last edition published in Richmond, Virginia, in 1804.

whom they served, out of greed and hatred, out of fanaticism; they made usury into a sacred duty. And these are our fathers." [93]

The firmest proof of Voltaire's classicizing anti-Semitism is to be found in the specifics of the arguments that he adduced against Jews. Often he overtly quoted, and sometimes he even misquoted, classic sources. Even when he did not quote directly, his main charges, without exception, descended from that arsenal.

Over and over again Voltaire insisted that the Jews borrowed everything in their culture from others, that they were certainly not the teachers of the Greeks, that they were ignorant of the arts and sciences, and that their morality was inferior to that of the Greeks and the Romans. These themes are recurrent leit-motifs in his *Philosophical Dictionary*. In the article on Abraham he called the Jews "a small, new, ignorant, crude people," and he added that "a man must be either a great ignoramus or a great rascal to say that the Jews taught the Greeks." [94]

The Jews adopted all of their rites from the Egyptians. All of the sciences were unknown to them, for "their only science was that of brokerage and usury." [95] He praised Grotius by agreeing with his opinion that Alexander and Aristotle were superior to the Jews and reiterated that the Jews took all their customs from the powerful nations that surrounded them. The only thing that properly belongs to the Jews is "their stubbornness, their new superstitions, and their hallowed usury." [96] In his first answer to Guénée, in *La défense de mon oncle*, Voltaire even suggested that the Jewish religion was borrowed from the Greeks, by identifying Lot's wife with Eurydice and Samson with Hercules.[97] He went further along this line, stating this thesis not as a possibility but as a certainty in his *Dieu et les hommes:* the Jews were inveterate plagiarizers and there is not a single page of the Jewish books that was not stolen, mostly from Homer.[98] In his final answer to Guénée, *Un Chrétien contre six Juifs*, Voltaire admitted that there were probably some learned Jews in Alexandria, under Greek influence, but he denied the notion that the Jews themselves had any ancient learning. On the contrary, they were entirely eclipsed by the Greeks. "If we must talk

[93] *Oeuvres complètes*, XII, 159–63.  [94] *Philosophical Dictionary*, p. 62.
[95] *Ibid.*, p. 201.   [96] *Ibid.*, p. 499.
[97] *Oeuvres complètes*, XXVI, 428.  [98] *Ibid.*, XXVIII, 189–90.

of Jewry, we must state that they were a wretched Arabic tribe without art or science, hidden in a small, hilly, and ignorant land, as Flavius Josephus asserts in his reply to Apion." [99]

Josephus, of course, had said no such thing, but Apion indeed had. That writer of the first century, whose arguments are known to us entirely from Josephus' refutation, had charged the Jews with not producing any men of importance in the arts and sciences as compared with the Greeks.[100] Apion was repeating an earlier argument by Apollonios Molon, a writer of the first century B.C.[101] In the second century this notion was repeated by Celsus, the platonic philosopher.[102] The claim that had been made by Hellenistic Jews, notably by Philo, that the Jews were the teachers of the Greeks, was an affront to many of the Greek and Latin authors and they answered it by insisting that whatever the Jews knew they had acquired from others.[103]

Another charge that Voltaire repeated obsessively was that the Jews hate all other men. In his *Traité sur la tolérance à l'occasion de la mort de Jean Calas*, the very central statement of Voltaire's impassioned commitment to freedom, he added to his usual assertion that Hebrew is to Greek as the language of a peasant is to that of an academician, a concluding slur that God had repeatedly commanded the Jews to kill idolaters. Voltaire then left some shadow of a doubt as to whether that was still their law.[104] If it was, there would be no other course but to send them to the gallows. This might be the only instance in which intolerance would be a reasonable course.[105] The Jews were an intolerant people, whereas the Romans were tolerant, and the successors of the men of Rome were the enlightened men of today, "statesmen who are equally remote from superstition and fanaticism."[106] Writing to Jean François Herrault in 1768 Voltaire again contrasted the tolerance of the Romans, who permitted a synagogue in Rome, to the intolerance of the Jews.[107] At about this time, in *Bolingbroke,* Voltaire asserted

[99] *Ibid.*, XXIX, 504.      [100] T. Reinach, *Textes,* p. 134.      [101] *Ibid.*, p. 63.
[102] *Ibid.*, p. 166.      [103] *Ibid.*, p. x.
[104] *Oeuvres complètes*, XXV, 78.      [105] *Ibid.*, pp. 96–98.
[106] *Ibid.*, XXIX, 522–26. This passage is from his *Un Chrétien,* the reply to Guénée.
[107] *Correspondence*, LXVIII, 168–69.

that Jesus was born when there was still fanaticism, but some bits of decency had appeared among the Jews because of their long association with the Greeks and the Romans.[108] Voltaire repeated again and again that the supreme expression of a Jewish hatred of all men is that they, unlike all others, refuse to eat at the same table with other men.[109]

This charge against the Jews represented the most prominent and oft-repeated attack upon them in the classic sources. One of the earliest Greek writers about Jews, Hecateos of Abdere, had stated in the third century B.C. that Moses had ordained a way of life "contrary to humanity and to hospitality." [110] A century or so later, Posidonios of Apameos wrote that the Jews alone of all the peoples refused to have any social contact with others and considered all other men as their enemies. The charge was repeated by Apollonios Molon and of course by Apion, who asserted that the Jews "did not wish well to any foreigner, and especially not to the Greeks." The very accents of Voltaire himself are to be found in Philostratos, a Sophist of the first half of the third century: "This people had rebelled for a long time, not only against the Romans, but against all of humanity. People who have imagined an anti-social life, who do not participate with other men either at the table, or at libations, or at prayers, or at sacrifices, are more distant from us than the people of Susa or the Bactrians, or the most remote Indians." This theme continued among Roman writers, whom Voltaire certainly knew well. Juvenal had said that the Jew "was raised in the hatred of Roman laws." The Jew had been taught by Moses, in a secret book, not to point out the way to a traveler who did not practice the same ceremonies and not to lead someone who was not circumcised to water. Tacitus had said it all, in the way that Voltaire was to repeat all his life. This Roman historian had charged that the Jews had "an obstinate attachment to each other, an active concern, which contrasts with the implacable hatred which they harbor for the rest of mankind." [111]

The first Greeks to be aware of the Jews found in them a particu-

[108] *Oeuvres complètes*, XXVI, 220.
[109] *Ibid.*, XX, 525–26.    [110] T. Reinach, *Textes*, p. 17.
[111] *Ibid.*, pp. 56, 63–64, 133, 176, 293, 307.

larly burdensome enemy for, unlike all the rest of the peoples who came into the orbit of Greek influence, the Jews claimed that their religion and culture were superior. For Rome the most painful element in the encounter with the Jews was that Judaism, and soon Christianity, a Jewish sect, were making large missionary inroads in Rome itself and throughout the empire. The reaction was to speak against the destruction by the Oriental spirit, through the miasma of its presence, of the hold of the classic Roman virtues. This religion therefore had to be mocked, and the worst kinds of ceremonies and beliefs had to be attributed to it. Cicero called it a "barbara superstitio." Tacitus repeated a canard, already ancient in his own time, that the Jews worshiped the head of an ass. Plutarch of Cherone identified the cult of the Jewish God with that of Bacchus. And so it went in the writing of many other authors of the Greco-Roman period. Seneca brought the whole theme to a head: "The practices of this criminal people have prevailed so widely that they have been accepted throughout the world; the vanquished have become the lawgivers to the victors." [112]

The response of Roman philosophers and emperors of the first century was to try to free Rome of these pernicious superstitions. Suetonius recounts that Tiberius chased all Egyptian and Jewish cults, as well as all other foreign religions, from the city. Society had to defend itself against infection; this was the main thrust of Voltaire's position.

Voltaire was certainly uncomfortable, however, about his own feelings towards the Jews. This was clearest in his correspondence in the last two decades of his life. He defended tolerating the Jews, in a famous letter to d'Alembert in 1764, although he added that he was aware that the Jews had a history of persecuting others. Nonetheless, enlightened men must be tolerant, at any price.[113] It should be noted, however, that this letter was written at the very height of his interest in the Calas affair, when his rhetoric was at its most tolerant. The nucleus of Voltaire's view of the Jews, however, amounts to this: there is a cultural, philosophical, and ethnic tradition of Europe which descended, through the human stock of that continent, from the intellectual values that were

[112] *Ibid.*, pp. 238, 304–305, 263.    [113] *Correspondence,* LIV, 102–103.

taught by the Greeks. Those were in turn carried to all the reaches of the European world by the Romans. This is the normative culture of which Voltaire approved. The Jews are a different family, and their religion is rooted in their character. Christianity is the Jewish religion superimposed on people of a different world, both ethnically and culturally. It is somewhat better than Judaism because it has been affected by the nature of those who have adopted it and by their earlier, healthier tradition. It is possible to redeem Europe by reviving its attachment to its own fundamental nature and tradition. European men can be freed effectively of Christianity because Christianity is here a long-standing infection; it is not one of the foundations of the European spirit, deriving from its character. The case of the Jews is radically different. Being born a Jew and the obnoxiousness of the Jewish outlook are indissoluble; it is most unlikely that "enlightened" Jews can escape their innate character. The Jews are subversive of the European tradition by their very presence, for they are the radically other, the hopeless alien. Cure them of their religion and their inborn character remains.

These views of Voltaire represent more than unthinking rhetoric, for they were being stated in a context of debate within the Enlightenment. The counter-opinion being strongly held in the 1760s, and more especially in the 1770s, was that the Jews were not hopeless by nature. Let us examine one revealing exchange of views. If we do not have the exact text of de Lisle's letter to Voltaire in 1773, it seems a fair guess that their interchange had something to do with the contents of de Lisle's book *De la philosophie de la nature*. De Lisle had argued that "a Jew is a man before being a member of a sect, before being a usurer, even before he is a Jew; if we want him to stop trading deceitfully and believing in a ridiculous cult, let us behave like men towards him." [114] No, de Lisle insisted, basing himself on Montesquieu, the Jews are not monsters either in the physical or moral order. His account of all the persecutions that the Jews had suffered was based on the proposition that Juda-

[114] De Lisle de Sales, *Philosophie*, pp. 67–70. See also Meyer, "Attitude," *Studies on Voltaire*, XXVI, 1180, who maintains that this was the first work to argue for complete and unconditional equality for the Jews.

ism is a decent and humane religion and that the Jews had never ceased being men like all others.[115] It is true, that Voltaire had said these things himself on occasion, but when he found such things said by de Lisle he responded, as was quoted earlier, by saying that the Jews were hopeless and that they were the worst rascals that the world had ever seen.

### The "Coterie"

Voltaire's anti-Semitism must be seen not only in the context of those who argued against him but also as it was reflected in the work of those closest to him. He was not alone in adopting a classicizing stance from which to criticize the Jews. At the end of the 1760s, while Voltaire was writing very busily on all aspects of the subject, the work of an important scholarly figure who belonged to the Enlightenment, Jean Baptiste de Mirabaud, was published; it was a collection of the views of Greek and Roman writers on the Jews, entitled *Opinions des anciens sur les Juifs*. The date of publication is revealing; it was 1769, in the midst of a period of maximum use by Voltaire and, as we shall soon see, by d'Holbach of the "classical" perspective. Mirabaud provided the "proof texts." [116] He argued that the misery of the Jews was not a result of their rejection of Jesus, for the Jews were despised in antiquity, before Jesus appeared. The Jews were disliked in Roman times by writers such as Tacitus because they believed that their God was above all others, and they therefore, supposedly, hated the whole human race. Julian the Apostate proved this point by censoring the conduct of the Jews towards the Canaanites. Mirabaud quoted Horace and Juvenal as among the ancient writers who mocked the Jewish customs of fasting and circumcision. The Jews were despised in particular for their extraordinary credulity. The pagans, indeed,

[115] De Lisle, *Philosophie*, pp. 106–22.

[116] Mirabaud, *Opinions*; at the time this book appeared, Mirabaud had been dead nine years. It was evidently done by d'Holbach, or someone of that circle, from a manuscript that represented a more extended version of the book than its first edition in 1740. See Naville, *Paul Thiry d'Holbach*, pp. 153–54. That the circle of d'Holbach needed to revive this book in that very year is most revealing and instructive. For the two editions in 1740 of Mirabaud's original book, see Szajkowski, *Franco-Judaica*, Nos. 1527 and 1529.

spoke of miracles, but no one really believed in them; only the Jews were foolish enough to take miracles seriously. In the Diaspora the Jews had remained an identifiable community; they had not disappeared because they were attached to their superstitions. Clearly the only way to do anything with the Jews was to free them of their faith.[117] Granted, Mirabaud thus held the view that is commonly attributed to the whole of the Enlightenment: Judaism is the worst of the ancient superstitions because it is the source of both Christianity and Islam, but the progress of Enlightenment could free Jews of their religion and make them worthy people. This was the point of Mirabaud's argument in this book, which lumped Christianity with Judaism, as Jewish infections of the more reasonable earlier pagan culture.

On the basis of the same arguments Voltaire had gone further by affirming the unchanging character of the Jews, and so had d'Holbach. The main purpose of d'Holbach's labors was to destroy Christianity. In pursuit of that end he not only attacked the Old Testament but he even enlisted Jewish arguments against the Christian revelation. For example, he knew that Jews "counterpose to the interpretation of the Christians their own simple and literal explanations of the true sense of the Old Testament." [118] D'Holbach was particularly pointed in attacking the Talmud: "The Talmud and the writings of the rabbis are full of dreams, cabbalistic interpretations, old wives' tales, marvelous fables which the Jews have handed down from father to son and which are the reason why the works of the rabbis are rightly held in disrepute." He had no patience with modern Jews, whom he regarded, in this passage, as benighted, although no more so than any other believer.[119]

Nonetheless, there is a note in d'Holbach which is beyond a mere attack on Judaism in order to get at Christianity. Most of d'Holbach's work is translation from the English Deists, and he was therefore limited by his sources. L'esprit du Judaisme was probably his own original work and thus reflected his own basic position. He concluded that volume as follows:

[117] Mirabaud, pp. 1, 8, 10, 17, 20, 49–50.
[118] Examen, p. 95. This book is a translation of Collins, Discourse.
[119] Ibid., p. 141.

Europe! Happy land where for so long a time the arts, sciences, and philosophy have flourished; you whose wisdom and power seem destined to command the rest of the world! Do you never tire of the false dreams invented by impostors in order to deceive the brutish slaves of the Egyptians? Then, dare, oh Europe! Break the unbearable yoke of the prejudices by which you are afflicted. Leave to the stupid Hebrews, to the frenzied imbeciles, and to the cowardly and degraded Asiatics these superstitions which are as vile as they are mad; they were not meant for the inhabitants of your climate." [120]

D'Holbach was thus arguing that what was wicked in Christianity was not merely a Jewish invention, but that it was the attack of the Oriental spirit on European culture. This miasma had ruined the freedom and dignity of the European tradition, which should now free itself of its lasting Oriental plague. We even find in this volume an exception made for Jesus, of whom d'Holbach approved,[121] but he turned right around to say that the early Christians misconceived him and created a religion around him in the image of their Jewish prejudices. The "schismatic Jews, i.e., the Christians" have taken from the Greeks "most of the opinions out of which their spiritual mentors have, in age after age, constructed their religious systems." [122] Early Christianity succeeded because, unlike Judaism, it conceded to the European spirit. The Christian priestly class had increasingly inherited all the intolerance and superstition of their Jewish predecessors.[123]

Diderot had made no such distinction even in favor of Jesus. Though it has been argued that the slur on Jesus that occurred in his article in the *Encyclopédie* on Judaism—he called Jesus a "fanatical and obscure Jew"—was really not by Diderot, but that it represented a later gloss by the even more anti-religious Naigeon, this is of secondary importance.[124] Diderot's total approach was

---

[120] *L'Esprit du Judaisme*, pp. 200–201. This book is definitely not identical with Collins' *Discourse* of 1724. See above, fn. 118. I have compared these works. The entries in the Szajkowski and Tcherikower bibliographies and in the *Catalogue générale des livres imprimés* of the Bibliothèque Nationale, which assert that the two books are identical, are, therefore, to be corrected. For the attribution of this book to d'Holbach, see Naville, *Paul Thiry d'Holbach*, p. 415, and Mornet, "Bibliographie," *Revue d'histoire littéraire de la France*, 40th year, 259–81.

[121] *L'esprit du Judaisme*, p. xvi.      [122] *Ibid.*, pp. xix–xx.

[123] *Ibid.*, pp. 159–92.

[124] On Jacques André Naigeon (1738–1810), see the only full-length study,

to find something in the Jewish spirit, not merely in the dogmas of their religion (he treated Judaism as religion rather kindly), and to define that something as the enemy of humanity. In conventional enlightened argument, in exactly the manner of Voltaire and d'Holbach, Diderot liked all the Jewish sects except the Pharisees. Once he turned to the account of Jewish history after the destruction of the Temple, Diderot was no longer concerned with Pharisaic doctrine. His subject suddenly became the nature of the Jewish people. Of those who took refuge in Egypt after the Temple was destroyed, he wrote, "They brought with them their spirit of sedition and revolt and this caused a new massacre there." [125] In discussing the Talmud, Diderot had it both ways. He found that there was nothing good in it and that the Talmud regarded Christians as beasts, whom one can kill and rob. Diderot then denied that Jesus borrowed his materials or methods from the Talmudists, for the parables of the Talmud were very different from those used in the Gospels. He then turned around to assert that Jesus, "ce Juif obscur et fanatique," drew from the same basic source as the authors of the Talmud, but that his application of its parables was more spiritual.[126]

When Diderot reached his discussion of esoteric Jewish philosophy, the point at which we would expect to find him most sympathetic to Jews, he wrote as follows: among the Jews one will not find "any rightness of thought, any exactness in reasoning or precision of style, in a word, any of that which ought to characterize

---

Brummer, *Studien*. His first article for the *Encyclopédie* was on the subject of "Richesse," in 1765. Naigeon too, was a classicizer. In this essay he quoted heavily from Seneca and he argued, with many quotations from early Christian sources, that Christian morality was not an advance on paganism and at its best was a continuation of the Greek and Roman outlook (*Encyclopédie*, Lausanne ed., 1780, XXIX, 184–200). Naigeon also wrote the article *Unitaires* in the *Encyclopédie* (XXXVI, 107–29). This was the most radical statement by a member of the "coterie" of the notion that all religions are relative, that the only true religion is to obey the laws of the state, that the true shints are the good citizens, that the only impiety is to sin against the social contract, that religion is an institution of social control, and that the sovereign can change or even abolish any religion. Immediately after this statement of enlightened totalitarianism, Naigeon attacked the Bible from the point of view of historical criticism and ended with a slur on "the poverty and equivocations of the Hebrew language."

[125] Diderot, *Oeuvres complètes*, XV, 356.  [126] *Ibid.*, p. 365.

a healthy philosophy. One finds among them, on the contrary, only a confused melange of the principles of reason and revelation, a pretentious and often impenetrable obscurity, principles that lead to fanaticism, blind respect for the authority of the rabbis and for antiquity, in a word, all the faults that mark an ignorant and superstitious people." [127]

This diatribe is to be read in the light of his well-known opinion that Europe could be saved if the right philosophy could be substituted for superstition: "I have never attacked religion, which I respect; but I have attacked superstition, which hides behind the mask of religion and which disfigures it." [128] But Diderot's basic view was that the Jews could not be incorporated into other peoples: "This people should be kept separate from others." [129]

In Diderot's view, even as retouched somewhat by Naigeon, Christianity was superior to Judaism, but both religions were irretrievably damaged by the fundamental Jewish character of credulity, superstition, and fanaticism, which their founders gave to them. The over-all difference between Christians and Jews was that Christianity was a religious over-lay in Europe for people whose essential character was not Oriental, and who thus could be returned to their true nature if they were freed of religion. The task was much harder, if not impossible, for the Jew because his religion and his character were one.

The mainstream of the thinking of the Enlightenment, led by Voltaire, was absolutist. It imagined itself as a positive force for the making of a new world, and everyone had to be remade in order to be part of the new heaven. The particular disaster of the Jew was that the men of the Enlightenment were not entirely certain that he could enter the heaven even after he was remade. There was only one tradition of enlightened thinking that ran counter to all this intellectual absolutism, in the name of an appreciation of the Jew and Judaism as one of the many valid forms of culture and religion. That was the relativism of Montesquieu. Voltaire derived many of his arguments from the English Deists.

[127] *Ibid.*, p. 378.     [128] *Ibid.*, IV, 127. This quotation is from the *Moisade*.
[129] *Ibid.*, II, 97; this quotation is from Diderot's *Réponse à l'examen du prosélyte*, which was written in 1763.

Montesquieu admired the saving illogic of the English political system. Voltaire chose the diversity of human habits as the subject of his mockery; Montesquieu used this fact as the source of a life-long sermon on tolerance and respect for what exists.

With his finely attuned perception, sensitive to all the currents of the surrounding atmosphere, Voltaire could not help but pick up an occasional dire warning from the followers of Montesquieu. Predictably, his reaction was contemptuous and impatient: "I know well that it is said that the *philosophes* ask tolerance for themselves," he wrote to d'Alembert, "but it is foolish and stupid to say, 'when they arrive at power they will not tolerate any religion other than their own'; as if the *philosophes* could ever persecute anybody." Voltaire's dogged refusal to examine his own position is even more striking in the light of the remainder of his letter: "One will never be able to make fanatics flexible," he advised d'Alembert; "one must teach them to scorn and look with horror on the opinions for which they do battle." [130] And "fanatics" were, of course, those who held "unphilosophical" views.

The idea of freedom for all sorts of ideas was the major intellectual force for liberating the Jews at the end of the eighteenth century. The idea of remaking men to fit properly into the new society was the seed-bed of totalitarianism. The notion that the new society was to be a reevocation of classical antiquity was the prime source of post-Christian anti-Semitism in the nineteenth century. The vital link, the man who skipped over the Christian centuries and provided a new, international, secular anti-Jewish rhetoric in the name of European culture rather than religion, was Voltaire. The defeat of the emancipation of the Jews of Europe existed in embryo even before that process began.

[130] *Correspondence,* LIV, 102–103.

### ❧ X ❧

## *The Revolution*

In the last years of the *ancien régime* even reactionaries knew that France needed many reforms. Not even the most radical of the men who would soon be taking the oath of solidarity and resistance in the royal tennis court of Versailles knew that they were preparing a revolution. The reform of the Jews was on the list of the problems being discussed in the 1780s but, except in eastern France, this issue was nowhere a burning, immediate concern. After 1776 the Sephardi leaders of Bordeaux preferred to leave the question of the rights of their community undiscussed in the fear that any new general legislation could only lessen their status. These oligarchs had largely won their fight for a place in the economy and they were committed to keeping their poor invisible.

The painful issue that occupied public attention was the Ashkenazim. These Jews, as we have seen, were much more alien in culture and much poorer than the Sephardim; it needs to be reemphasized that they were also very much more hated by their neighbors. Their enemies kept agitating in the 1780s for an end to Jewish usury, but Alsatian anti-Semites were not willing to imagine any alternative place for the Jews in the economy. François Hell, the central figure in the affair of the "false receipts," kept proclaiming that "the assemblies of the Jews are a threat to public order," but he and the forces for which he spoke had no program for fitting these Jews into society after the destruction of their separatism. On the other hand, the Jews of eastern France themselves had reacted to the attack by lobbying and agitating for complete economic equality; nonetheless, they wanted to retain and even strengthen their cultural and legal apartness. Both these programs were impossible, and they were both to be brushed aside by the Revolution.

These counter-pressures were being exercised directly on the royal government in Paris, but the pamphleteers on both sides were speaking also to the generation that had arisen after 1750 and had been shaped by the Enlightenment. The mood in the highest councils of the government reflected several concerns. It was dominated by a pragmatic desire to bring an end to the turmoil in Alsace. In the last years before the Revolution there was a general tendency at the royal court towards bringing some order into the bewildering and conflicting mass of earlier precedents by which France had been governed for centuries. In relation to the Jews, the first actions of enlightened absolutism had been taken in 1782 in Austria by Joseph II, when he issued his Edict of Toleration, and this act became something of a paradigm for Louis XVI's government.[1] The new humanitarian thinking was an influence on the minds of at least some of his ministers. The mood of the intelligentsia was equally eclectic. At that moment the "new men" tended to believe that, with a few exceptions, the Jews were inferior people; many were convinced that this inferiority would last very long and some feared that the Jews were hopelessly debased. Nonetheless, in the 1780s the new thinkers, as a body, believed that it was the duty of decent people to do something for and about the Jews, for persecution was unworthy of enlightened people. No one suggested, at least not in public, that the Jews ought immediately be given equality. Their friends wanted to take larger steps towards reform than the royal government was ever willing to approve, but before 1789 both the government and the in-

[1] Joseph II issued a series of decrees about Jews in the fall of 1781, culminating in the *Toleranzpatent*, which was issued on January 2, 1782. The decrees abolished the body tax, opened some new economic pursuits to Jews (but with severe limitations), and gave some access to the universities. On the other hand, the restrictions on the residence of Jews where they had not previously been permitted were kept in force and Jewish numbers in Vienna remained strictly limited to those families who were individually tolerated. On these decrees, and especially on their relationship to the work of Dohm, see Graetz, *Geschichte der Juden*, XI, 74–76; for the contemporary reactions of Wessely, and the re-echo in France of his enthusiasm for the work of Joseph II, see the end of Chapter VI.

telligentsia were operating within the same framework in their separate considerations of the Jewish question.

In the wake of the agitation that had been occasioned by the beginnings of the affair of the "false receipts" there were evidently very serious deliberations in 1779 or 1780 by Cerf Berr and the rest of the leadership of Alsatian Jewry. They decided to make a new approach to the government and to ask for a fundamental reordering of the Jewish situation in their region. At that moment they had before them the opinion of Dohm, in the very book that Cerf Berr had commissioned in defense of the Jewish position, that Jewish legal autonomy should be limited to purely religious matters. Dohm had even found merit in an arrangement that would permit Jews, if they wished, to go to the general courts for judgment, though such decisions would be rendered by Christian judges according to Jewish law. Even though the leaders of the Jews of Alsace were very keenly aware that Jewish autonomy was under violent attack by their enemies, they consciously chose not to follow the moderate view of Dohm. The *mémoire* that Cerf Berr and his associates wrote no later than 1780 was allowed to stand as late as 1784 as the comprehensive summary of the Jewish position.[2]

The basic aims that were stated in the document were no different from those that the Jews of Alsace had announced as early as 1716. They asked for "a law which grants them both a free existence and the legal means of making a living." The essential theory on which they based their case was that the Jews represent a legal entity, a *corps* under the protection of the king. They were *sujets* who differed from all other subjects of the crown only to the degree to which any one order or group within the state differed from others in rights and privileges. The most insulting of all their disabilities was the *péage corporel*. Since the Jews had once been given the right to live in Alsace, under royal power to which they were obedient, they ought to share in the benefits of citizenship. Certainly, the Jews of Alsace should be freed from this tax, which might, at most, be continued for foreign Jews who came to France on business.

The authors of this *mémoire* suggested a program for the future

[2] See the beginning of Chapter VII and especially fns. 1 and 2.

consisting of three main provisions: complete freedom of commerce anywhere in Alsace, the strengthening of the power of the *parnassim* over the Jewish community, and the closing of the door to any new migration of foreign Jews into the province. The road away from usury was to give the Jews of Alsace commercial rights equivalent to those possessed by their brothers in Nancy, Metz, Bordeaux, and Bayonne. The broadening of their economic potential would enable them to bear their particularly heavy burden of taxes and to become useful to the state in such pursuits as providing horses for the cavalry and provisioning the armies. Cerf Berr was held up as the model whom the Jews of Alsace should aspire to emulate. The result of giving them freedom to live anywhere in the province and to engage in all kinds of business would be, they were sure, an improvement in the conduct of Alsatian Jewry and the disappearance of prejudice. Economic freedom would thus make them more useful and financially productive to the state and more acceptable to the gentile majority in Alsace.

To counter the objection that so liberal a regime would inevitably attract more Jews to the province, the leaders of Alsatian Jewry asked for the severest royal restrictions on new arrivals. The inner autonomy of the Jewish community was also, it was maintained, of great benefit to the state. By strengthening the power of the rabbis and making them the sole judges of first resort in disputes between Jews, rebellious spirits would cease troubling the various law courts. The police powers of the *préposés* (*parnassim*) should be increased, so that they could control unruly Jews.[3]

[3] The text of this mémoire was printed as an appendix in both the German and French editions of Dohm's work. It was written and most probably submitted to the *Conseil d'Etat* no later than 1780, for in the German edition (p. 80) Dohm referred to it as having reached him the year before. The wording of the section on the *péage* is the ultimate source of the crucial phrases in the decree of January, 1784 (Compare Dohm, French edition, pp. 228–31). That Cerf Berr was known to be the architect of this act is proved by the entry in the Metz *Pinkas,* p. 128a, where he is given a lifetime honorary post of syndic of the Metz Jewish community as reward for this achievement. The almost always reliable Robert Anchel erred in relation to this *mémoire* by Cerf Berr. He found a copy of it, undated and without signature, at the *Archives Nationales* (F 12 854 B) and presumed that this document was later than the decree of January, 1784. He therefore wondered why this document ignored the abolition of *péage*. A comparison of the archival text with Dohm's proves that they are identical. Hence there is no mystery. (See Anchel, *Les Juifs de France,*

The response of the royal government to these requests, and to the continuing problems in Alsace, came in 1784, in two decrees which were the *ancien régime's* last major enactments concerning the Jews. In January, 1784, Louis XVI forbade the *péage* in perpetuity and irrevocably in every jurisdiction subject to his sovereignty, "regardless of whether they belong to cities and communities, ecclesiastic or lay lords or anyone else, of whatever quality." A body tax, the decree stated, puts the Jews in the same class with animals and "it is repugnant to the feelings we have for all our subjects to allow a tax on any one of them to remain which seems to degrade mankind." [4] There was more than a hint in this decree that things would not go smoothly, for in the text the *Conseil d'Etat* recognized that by abolishing the *péage* it was hurting the revenues of various jurisdictions; the door was left open for future discussion of indemnities. The foreboding of the *Conseil* was realized immediately. There was resistance by the independent city of Oberbergheim and, much more important, by Strasbourg.[5]

Those who resisted this decree were more angered by its rhetoric than by their loss of revenue from the *péage*. If humane and "enlightened" considerations were becoming the basis of royal policy, there was reason to fear that there would soon be a really large increase in the rights of the Jews in Alsace. Such fears could only grow with careful reading of the new decree, for it contained two motifs of considerable economic and juridic importance. On the economic side the language of the act announced that the abolition

pp. 217–19.) Betting de Lancastel, *Considérations sur l'état des Juifs dans la société chrétienne*, pp. 55–56, quoted from the text of this *mémoire* and gave the date of its submission to the *Conseil d'Etat* as 1779.

[4] *Edit du Roi portant l'exemption des Droits de péage corporel sur les Juifs du mois de Janvier 1784* (in JTS). This decree was registered by the *Conseil Souverain d'Alsace* on January 17, 1784, and by the *parlement* of Metz on March 8, 1784.

[5] Scheid, *Juifs d'Alsace*, pp. 253–56; Weiss, *Geschichte*, pp. 9–10; Loeb, "Les Juifs à Strasbourg depius 1349 jusqu'à la révolution," *ASEJ*, II, 137–98. The prohibition against the residence of Jews in Strasbourg dated back to 1349, when they were accused of responsibility for the Black Death and the entire Jewish community was murdered. On June 16, 1784, the city of Strasbourg was given a *rente* of 2,400 livres a year as indemnity. It refused to accept this as adequate (its *péage* revenues were 10,000 livres a year at that point). Strasbourg then tried to "indemnify" itself by doubling the toll for Jews, in specific, on the bridge over the Rhine. This was sternly forbidden by the royal intendant in a decree that was published in Strasbourg on December 3, 1786.

of the *péage* was part of a royal policy to make an end to hindrances to commerce. Such a declaration evoked memories of the recent attempts of the Jews to enter the guilds in several places in France; of the on-going battle between Strasbourg and Cerf Berr for his right to live there and of the illegal trade that the Jews were managing to conduct in that city despite the most careful policing; and of the continuing pressure by the Jews to obtain the right to enter all economic pursuits in Alsace. In the second place the royal rhetoric had come to a climax by announcing that the king was extending his grace to the Jews of Alsace, whom he here called part of "all our subjects." This is the *only* act in all the jurisprudence of the *ancien régime* in which the Jews of eastern France were accepted as, in law, subjects of the French crown and not aliens who were, at least in theory, subject to expulsion at any moment. That the significance of this phrase did not escape notice is clear from the preamble to the later, more general decree of July 10, 1784, in which Louis XVI spoke of the "Jews of Our province of Alsace." Having weighed the pros and cons, he proposed in this new code to conciliate "to the degree that it seems possible to Us, their interests with those of Our subjects." The crucial phrase was thus reversed.[6]

This second *lettres patentes* was the most comprehensive decree about Jews ever issued by the French crown. It was a retrograde act. The few increased opportunities that were now afforded were available only to the rich; but the essence of the Jewish problem in Alsace was the poor masses, and their lot was now being made harder. Every liberalization in the decree was counter-balanced by a new and severe restriction. In the area of personal status, the question had often been litigated throughout the eighteenth century whether a nobleman or the authorities of a town could exclude a Jew at will, after having once admitted him. The new law agreed with the Jewish contention that such reception was irrevocable, except for a cause that could be proved in a court of law. On the other hand, all the Jews residing in Alsace were now forbidden to contract any marriage whatsoever without express royal permission, and any rabbi who performed such a marriage was subject to the most

[6] *Lettres patentes du Roi portant Règlement concernant les Juifs d'Alsace du 10 Juillet 1784* (in JTS).

severe penalties. In effect, no new Jewish family could henceforth be started in Alsace until an older one ceased to exist.

Despite an appearance of some liberalization, the economic regulations in the new act were less than helpful. The Jews of Alsace were now permitted to rent farms, to cultivate vineyards, and to engage in any other kind of physical labor. However, in no case could any non-Jewish help be employed. Even if Jews turned to farming and physical labor, they would not be given permission to live wherever they did not already have that right. Under no circumstances could any Jew acquire real estate, not even the farmland that he might himself be cultivating. The only real property Jews could own was their homes and the grounds surrounding them, provided that such real estate was no more elaborate than was proper for the station of the individual concerned. The traditional major Jewish pursuits in Alsace, the trade in cattle and grain and in moneylending, were surrounded by new restrictions. Contracts for all such transactions would henceforth have to be executed either before a notary or before two *préposés* (*parnassim*) of the Jewish community. Receipts and contracts must be signed in French or German, if at all possible. On the other hand the few Jews in Alsace who had that kind of capital were now permitted to engage in banking and in every kind of large-scale business or commerce, subject to the restrictions which usually governed such pursuits. They were also authorized to open factories, especially in textiles, as well as to establish works in iron, glass, and pottery on an equal basis with the king's Christian subjects.

Jewish internal autonomy in Alsace was confirmed, but with some significant changes. The rabbis who were officially appointed either by the king or by those *seigneurs* who possessed the right to make such appointments were confirmed in their exercise of judicial power in all matters, both civil and religious, which involved only Jews. For all other purposes the Jews in Alsace were subject to the general judiciary. The previously existing *préposés généraux* were renamed syndics, but their powers were kept intact. As previously, they were elected by the Jews themselves. It was their duty to assess their individual share of the royal impositions upon each of the Jews of the province and to collect the sums involved. The *préposés* who were elected to lead each individual Jewish community were to supervise the collection of royal and local taxes in each town and were to exercise supervision over the internal affairs of the Jewish community. There was in these *lettres patentes,* however, more than a hint of a desire to lessen the cohesiveness of the Jewish community, especially when read in the light of the draft documents that preceded them. Jews were forbidden to go to court except as individuals, unless they could clearly demonstrate that the case at issue involved them collectively. This was a clear warning to the *préposés* that their task, in the royal view, was to keep the Jewish community quiet, not to fight its battles. This decision was more than a bow to anti-Jewish opinion, which wanted to destroy the role of the organized Jewish community as a defender of the Jews.[7]

A crucial clause of the *lettres patentes* of July 10, 1784, was the ordering of a census of all the Jews in Alsace, in preparation for the expulsion of all those who could not prove their legal right to exist in the province. This census produced a total of 3,910 families or 19,624 souls.[8] It is almost beyond doubt that this last figure was an understatement and that the size of the Jewish population in Alsace in the years immediately before the Revolution was more than 4,000 families, approaching the number of 25,000 individuals. Quite apart

[7] A favorable view of the *lettres patentes* of July 10, 1784, was maintained by a Catholic apologist for the *ancien régime,* the Abbé Joseph Lémann (*L'entrée des israélites dans la société française,* pp. 42–89). Even he criticized the limitation of Jewish marriages. On this point Louis XVI was following the recent example of Joseph II. In the various versions of his *Toleranzpatent* he had decreed the strictest limitation on Jewish population and freedom of marriage in all his domains, except for Galicia and Hungary. Substantially negative views of these *lettres patentes* are to be found in Anchel, *Les Juifs de France,* pp. 213–33, and Szajkowski, "The Jewish Problem in Alsace," *JQR,* XLIV, 223–27.

[8] The census of 1784 of the Jews in Alsace was published in 1785 as a book (*Dénombrement général des Juifs d'Alsace*), in Colmar, the seat of *Conseil Souverain* of the province. It is a prime source. Its summary of places and their Jewish population was re-published by Scheid, *Juifs d'Alsace,* pp. 248–51. This census was also studied by Hemerdinger, "Le Dénombrement des Israélites d'Alsace (1784)," *REJ,* XLII, 253–64. The most recent study of the whole question is by Szajkowski, "The Growth of the Jewish Population of France," *JSS,* VIII, 180–81. The estimate of 25,000 Jews in Alsace is somewhat higher than the figure given by Szajkowski (22,570 to 23,800) based on contemporary birth and death rates (*Economic Status,* p. 25) but it agrees with the highest guess of Anchel, *Napoléon et les Juifs,* p. 1. The evidence for the presence of many Jews without fixed habitation is too great to permit a lower estimate. For the constant complaints of non-resident Jewish poor in Alsace, see Hoffman, *L'Alsace,* IV, 480–88, and Chapter VII.

from those not recorded, who were protected by the Alsatian Jews against the threat of expulsion, there must be added an unknown but noticeable number of the most miserable of all, Jews with no domicile whatsoever, who wandered in the province with their families in search of alms or some temporary means of support. After the census was printed a decree was issued on May 6, 1786, announcing that all Jews whose names did not figure in the book would be given one month to leave France, after a date to be designated by the *Conseil Souverain* of Alsace. Under intense Jewish pressure the expulsion was not decreed until more than two years later, in November, 1788. It was then further delayed until May, 1789, on the grounds that it was inhumane to expel Jews in the middle of a very cold winter. By the spring of 1789 the whole question had become academic; events were marching towards the Revolution.[9]

Jewish leaders in Alsace had more to worry about after the middle of 1784, however, than these threats to even those of the poor whom they wanted to protect. They had engaged a lawyer, Mirbeck, to petition against the decree as a whole, and they themselves continued to lobby for changes. The pressure on the government became all the more intense to do something about the question of the Jews in November, 1787, when, under the leadership of Malesherbes, the act of toleration that he and Turgot had failed to effect in 1775 now became law. The royal government issued an edict in November, 1787, giving Protestants an *état civil* of their own. This meant that for the first time since the revocation of the Edict of Nantes in 1685 Protestant marriages were now legally recognized in France. They would be recorded on separate marriage registers that were to be kept by the various local jurisdictions. This decree had spoken not of Protestants but of "non-Catholics," and Jews made immediate attempts in several places to get broader rights for themselves on the basis of this language. These efforts were, however, minimal, for it was soon ruled everywhere in which the matter

[9] The decree of expulsion that was enacted on May 6, 1786, was not actually issued by the *Conseil Souverain* of Alsace until November, 1788. The second decree of December 13, 1788, gave June 1, 1789, as the final date for non-registered Jews to leave the province. Printed copies of both these acts are in JTS: *Extrait des registres du Conseil souverain d'Alsace, du 6 mai 1786; Extrait des registres du Conseil souverain d'Alsace, du 31 decembre, 1788.*

was tested that this act did not apply to Jews. Nonetheless, this decree did make a substantial change in the "Jewish question." Citizenship in France now no longer depended upon being a Catholic; the door was thus opened for more effective action by the Jews on their own behalf.[10]

Malesherbes, the author of this act of toleration, was very much aware that some such connection existed between this decree and the whole question of the Jews. He was known at that time to be collecting much information and opinion about the Jews. He evidently never did write the work he projected, but we do possess a statement of his point of view in 1787. Malesherbes has enjoyed a "good press," both in his own time and among later writers, as a pro-Jewish "enlightener." On the evidence of what he wrote, however, this judgment needs to be qualified. His main reason for wanting some reform and kinder treatment of the Jews was that it would lead to their conversion; he was utterly opposed to the organized Jewish community. In his view, the Jews could not be allowed to remain in France or anywhere else as an *imperium in imperio*. One of the obnoxious results of the legally established Jewish community, he said, was that Jewish individuals were not free to convert, because they were tied so closely to the whole body of Jewry. "The Jewish nation," Malesherbes added, in language that is reminiscent of the views of Hell, "is a powerful body which often uses its power in a way which is prejudicial to society." He therefore proposed an edict which would permit the Jews to use public legal registers for their personal status and other matters and would thus abstract them from their ties to the Jewish community. The Jews would be brought closer to society; the majority would ultimately rid itself of its prejudices against them and the Jewish minority would ultimately convert to the Christian faith.[11]

In the spring of 1788 Malesherbes undertook to study the Jewish

[10] Szajkowski, "The Reform of the *Etat-Civil,*" *JQR*, XLIX, 63; *idem*, "Protestants and Jews," *PAAJR*, XXV, 119–35.

[11] The "conversionist" remarks by Malesherbes are in his *Sécond mémoire sur le mariage des Protestans*, p. 71. On this point see Szajkowski, "Protestants and Jews," pp. 120–21. The most recent biography of Malesherbes depicted his views on Jews as parallel to those of Grégoire, but the conversionist theme, which was also common to both, was overlooked (Grosclaude, *Malesherbes*, pp. 631–49).

question for the Council of State. He never organized a formal commission but he did co-opt a number of men with some record of involvement in the Jews to advise him. No new decrees emerged from these deliberations. Such matters always moved slowly during the *ancien régime* and in a few months all attention was on the events that were leading to the Revolution. Malesherbes had defined his task in the broadest terms. The attempt at a new policy that was made in the decree of July 10, 1784, had been a failure, but only a fundamentally new policy, and not some piecemeal tinkering, could now be envisaged. Such a policy was hard to define, not least because there were great differences in point of view among the men who were helping Malesherbes. Each of the participating figures was proceeding from quite different premises. Malesherbes was a Christian and, even at his most liberal, he·remained a man of the *ancien régime*. In 1792 he was to make the heroic gesture of volunteering to defend Louis XVI in the trial in which the monarch was condemned to death. Malesherbes himself died on the guillotine a year later. Nicholas Dupré de Saint-Maur, who is known to have been greatly involved in these reconsiderations of the question of the Jews, was a new member of the Council of State who had recently been intendant in Bordeaux. His views were based mostly on the premise that free trade was good for the economy and he thus was heir to the most liberal royal administrators of the preceding century. Lacretelle was also involved (it will be recalled that he defended two Jews in 1775 in one of the battles over admission to the guilds); he was a *philosophe* and not a Christian. Pierre Louis Roederer, the central figure in organizing and carrying through the famous Metz essay contest on the Jewish question, was the most remote in outlook from Malesherbes. Indeed, as we shall see later, his opinions were, at least in part, radically different from almost all the others that were held by both Jews and gentiles in those critical years.[12]

[12] The views of Pierre-Louis Lacretelle have been discussed in Chapter IV; he was a close friend of Malesherbes, who had him appointed in 1787 as a member of a commission to reform the penal code (Lacretelle had won first prize in a Metz essay contest in 1784 on the subject of degrading punishments; the second had been won by Robespierre). Dupré de Saint-Maur's opinion in 1781 on the Jewish question is also quoted in Chapter IV. In 1788, after the

# THE REVOLUTION 325

The royal government thus entered the year of preparation for the *Etats Généraux*, the deliberative body that it was calling into session in 1789 to consider the state of France, without any new policy concerning the Jews. The representatives of the several Jewish communities, in their negotiating and lobbying in Paris in the spring of 1788, also had no new policy to suggest. The Ashkenazim were continuing to plead for the broadest kind of economic equality; they argued again that this was the only means of enabling the mass of Jews in Alsace to leave usury and become self-supporting in less dangerous and more normal occupations. Cerf Berr and his several associates who had come to Paris in the spring of 1788 wanted rights for the Ashkenazim as large as those that the Sephardim had already attained. Despite the growing attacks on all sides on the organized Jewish community, and Malesherbes' own unfriendliness on this point, the leaders of the Ashkenazim kept insisting that the communal autonomy of the Jews should be maintained and that the power of the *parnassim* within such a structure should even be strengthened.[13] The leaders of the Jews of eastern France entered the Revolutionary era holding to this position; they were to surrender it with the greatest reluctance.

The Sephardim of Bordeaux sent Solomon Lopes Dubec, who had long been a leader in the affairs of their community, and a

delegation from Bordeaux came to Paris, he wrote to Malesherbes that "things ought not to be done by halves," and that in order to increase the population of France with some thousands of rich and industrious citizens one "ought to tolerate the practice of the Jewish religion and allow the Jews to work on Sundays and holidays" (Grosclaude, *Malesherbes*, pp. 635–39). On Roederer, see below in this chapter.

13 Mirbeck's *mémoire* for the Jews of Alsace, pleading against the *lettres patentes* of July 10, 1784, was the last important formal statement of the Jewish position. It was devoted mostly to asking for larger economic rights, and it was presumed almost without question that the autonomous Jewish community should be maintained. In the light of the remarks made earlier in Chapter IX about Montesquieu as a main source of pro-Jewish arguments at that time, it is of interest that Mirbeck quoted large excerpts from Montesquieu in the first chapter of his *mémoire*, where he was defending the character of the Jews (see Anchel, *Juifs de France*, pp. 226–31). At the end of April, 1788, Cerf Berr was supposedly working on a new statement of the Ashkenazi position for Malesherbes but there is no record that such a *mémoire* was ever completed. That this was being contemplated is recorded in the diary of the Bordeaux delegation to Malesherbes printed in Szajkowski, "The Delegation of the Jews of Bordeaux to the Malesherbes Commission," *Zion*, XVIII, 56.

younger man, Abraham Furtado, who was later to be the central
personality in Napoleon's Sanhedrin, to confer with Malesherbes.
Lopes Dubec and Furtado had a quite complicated position to
defend. The Jewish oligarchs in Bordeaux would have much preferred that there be no new consideration of the Jewish question.
They feared that any new legislation about the Jews would lump
the Sephardim together with the Ashkenazim, with the result that
the far larger rights that the Sephardim had already attained would
be reduced. In the one encounter that Furtado and Lopes Dubec
had directly with Malesherbes, they spent three hours convincing
him that a certain legal and religious separatism should be allowed
to the Portuguese Jews, even if the rights of the Ashkenazim were
substantially increased. Early in their mission to Paris, Furtado and
Lopes Dubec even foresaw the possibility that all Jews might be
given rights equal to those of all other citizens of the same economic
station and that the government would abolish all the Jewish communities, both Sephardi and Ashkenazi, as autonomous corporations.
In that case the Sephardim hoped to be able to get authorization
to recreate by free choice their own Sephardi communities, in order
to maintain their separation from all other Jews in religion and in
the care of their own poor.[14]

This was precisely what the Sephardim of Bordeaux did do three
years later, immediately after the Revolutionary *Assemblée* gave
them full citizenship on January 28, 1790. Lopes Dubec and Furtado
were then in Paris again, along with several other leaders of the
Sephardim of Bordeaux, to represent the interests of their community. When four members of this delegation returned to Bordeaux
on February 17, a meeting was called the very next day of the
Sephardi *nation*. In the minute book, in which the activities of the
days of glory of the "Jewish nation" had been recorded, the elders
now entered the final lines: "Since the Jews of Bordeaux can no
longer be considered as a national community, the body of the
elders who represent them has now dissolved itself, and they have

[14] There are two accounts of the Sephardi delegation to Malesherbes, a contemporary one by Furtado and one written much later by Lopes Dubec. Both
documents are in the archives of the Israel Historical Society in Jerusalem and
they have been published by Szajkowski in the article cited in the previous
footnote, pp. 49–61. On the Sephardi position, see especially pp. 56, 57, and 59.

immediately concerned themselves with the formation of a welfare society." [15] This "welfare society" continued to perform all the customary religious functions. It fought during the Terror to safeguard the synagogues and cemetery of the Sephardim of Bordeaux.[16]

The most sensitive issue for the Sephardim before Malesherbes, and later, was the question that had already troubled Pinto and Péreire two decades before: what effect the Sephardi efforts on their own behalf would have on the cause of the Ashkenazim. In 1788 the instructions to the two delegates from Bordeaux followed the line that Pinto and Péreire had once defined; it was their task to do whatever was in their power for the Sephardim "without any prejudice to other Jews." In answer to a set of general questions that Malesherbes asked the delegates from Bordeaux, Furtado and Lopes Dubec formulated a *mémoire* (it was largely written by Furtado). The Sephardi representatives maintained quite forthrightly that the *lettres patentes* of July 10, 1784, would make no positive change of the status of Alsatian Jews. Its provisions "are applied against the Jews only because they are Jews"; the prohibition of marriage without permission from the government "is a revolting barbarism." This discussion came to a climax by blaming all the faults of the Jews of Alsace, especially in the economic realm, on the regime of persecution and exclusion by which "one pretends to govern them." [17] The Sephardim thus joined with the Ashkenazi leaders themselves and with the mainstream of contemporary pro-Jewish statesmen and intellectuals in the proposition that the conduct of the Alsatian Jews could be regenerated not by decreasing their opportunities but rather by broadening them. This was the argument that was repeated most often in all the agitation that led to the decree of September 27, 1791, emancipating the Ashkenazim.

In pure logic this argument could be made in an utterly pro-Jewish way: the Jews have no inherent faults; what is wrong with them is created by persecution. Nonetheless, psychologically this

[15] *Répertoire des délibérations de la nation juive depuis 1710 jusqu'au février 1790* (MS in *Archive de la Gironde*, V 5).

[16] Szajkowski, "Jewish Autonomy," *HJ*, XX, 43.

[17] The substance of Furtado's *mémoire* to Malesherbes has been published (this text probably represents a first draft) by Mossé, *Mémoire d'Abraham Furtado*; see especially pp. 37, 45–46.

rhetoric had a rancid and hostile side. If the economic conduct of the Jews was indeed so wicked and baleful, were they entirely blameless? Were there not some predispositions in their religion and culture towards usury and away from honest work? The Sephardim contributed to this negative estimate of the Ashkenazim, for the self-proclaimed hidalgos of Bordeaux kept insisting on their cultural superiority and on the greater reasonableness of their religious views. Inevitably this called the orthodox pieties in eastern France severely into question. The Ashkenazi leaders were themselves not blameless. They were arguing that they, the most Westernized and financially upright element along the Jews in eastern France, should be given larger control of the mass of their brethren in order to retrain them for acceptability to the larger society. They presented their supposedly "enlightened" selves as the model for all the other Ashkenazim. On the eve of the Revolution there thus was general agreement, even among Jewish spokesmen and, a fortiori, among even the friendliest non-Jews, that the existing Jew was a negative phenomenon, for religious and cultural as well as economic reasons. He was an object for reform, who had to reorganize not only his commercial practices but also the whole of his own inner life. He had to give up some of the customs of his religion. The leaders of the Ashkenazim did defend Judaism against hurtful charges, such as the assertion that it taught usury. What they did not do was insist that the existing Jewish community was the valid heir of a distinguished tradition of its own.

## Pre-Revolutionary Debates

Many references have already been made to the Metz essay contest on the question "Are there means of making the Jews happy and more useful in France?" This was the central event in the battle of opinion in the last years before the Revolution. The Royal Society of Arts and Sciences in Metz announced this question in 1785 as a subject for a prize essay, the prize to be awarded in 1787. Neither the date nor the place is surprising. This decision was made by a group of intellectuals who were living in the city that contained the major Jewish community of eastern France; the subject was announced on the heels of the publication of the two decrees of 1784 about the Jews of Alsace. The members of the Metz Academy had a range of interests that was typical of their kind of person all over France. These were progressive, "enlightened" figures, who were concerned with social progress and who believed that men could be perfected by the right kind of effort. In 1785 the Academy had given a prize for the best invention of a new printing press. The subject in 1786 had been how to make illegitimate children more useful to the state, and for the next year the Academy was concerning itself with the Jews.[18]

There were eventually nine contestants for the prize, but the announcement of the contest evoked some immediate debate on both sides of the question. The pamphlet of "Foissac" (it was no secret at the time that this was a pseudonym for Aubert-Dubayet) appeared in Metz in 1786. As we have seen, his prescription was that the Jews should be removed entirely from Alsace to uncultivated land in the interior of France, where honest labor on the soil might just possibly regenerate them. Aubert-Dubayet borrowed all of his rhetoric and arguments from Voltaire, but in this pamphlet he went one step further on his own, towards overt racism. Voltaire had already said often, following after the Greeks and Romans, that the Jews were the implacable enemies of the human race. Aubert-Dubayet added that the physical characteristics of the Jews make them an ugly people "disgraced by nature." [19]

The Jews of Metz succeeded in having this pamphlet suppressed immediately after it appeared, but that decree did not really help the situation, for the incendiary content of Aubert-Dubayet's work was widely known. Isaiah Berr Bing, the leading "enlightened" Jew in Metz, felt constrained to answer this pamphlet in the next year.[20] Bing's rebuttal amounted to a defense of the Bible against the attacks of Voltaire and his young military disciple. Bing insisted that the Jews were commanded to love all men, and he denied in par-

[18] Broadsheet announcement by the Royal Society of Arts and Sciences in Metz (JTS).

[19] *Le cri du citoyen*, p. 19.

[20] Bing, *Lettre du S. I. B. B.* There were two editions, the original in 1787 and a second in 1805, after Bing's death, published by his son-in-law, Michel Berr. The citations that follow are from the second edition.

ticular that usury was commanded to Jews as proper practice in their relations with gentiles. He went on to make the already well-won point that whatever is wrong with the Jews had been created by persecution and not by their religion and, therefore, to plead for better conditions. Bing was himself aware that there was nothing new to be said on this subject. He praised the Metz Academy for interesting itself in the Jewish question, but he added that he did not believe "that there will be need of long dissertations to prove that there are means of making us more useful and happier."

Bing clearly felt the force of his adversary's attack on the Jews as strangers who were harmful to the national economy. He responded by agreeing that this was indeed true, but that the fault was not theirs. Their very exclusion from most pursuits has made the Jews "more the movers of commerce, the agents of circulation, rather than the real proprietors of capital." The labor of the Jews profits others more than themselves, and the economic subjection in which they are held is as harmful to the majority as it is to the Jews. Bing, nonetheless, avoided prescribing any means whatsoever for solving the Jewish problem, not even as an alternative to the harsh suggestions of his adversary. This avoidance possibly reflected his knowledge that his master Mendelssohn had wanted to end Jewish legal separatism and the power of the community, whereas the Jewish leadership of Metz was firmly committed to retaining this structure.[21]

Bing's most perceptive remarks were on the subject of the relationship of the most advanced contemporary opinion to the question of the Jews. In the Middle Ages, he cried out, we were persecuted for religious reasons and we were accused of such absurd crimes as using the blood of Christians for our religious rituals.

In more enlightened times these revolting absurdities do not make the required impression and so it is argued that we lack morality. . . . People are writing and arguing much in France about tolerance, but what people are thinking about are only the various Christian sects. We are ignored, for the *philosophes* look upon us as much too unim-

[21] Speaking directly to "Foissac," Bing writes: "You have literary pretensions. . . . Full of Voltaire, you have copied from the works of this genius those pages which are the least worthy of his pen" (*Lettre*, p. 5, and see also p. 19; on his avoidance of prescribing precisely for the future, see p. 33).

portant to have any pity for our sad estate. I do not know if in this philosophic century the prejudices against us are still believed, but I do know that we still feel their unrelenting effects.[22]

There was more than a hint of prophecy in these remarks. The first serious debate about the Jewish question to take place in the *Assemblée* during the Revolution ended on December 24, 1789. The next day Jean-Paul Marat, the famous leader of the extreme left, wrote in his journal *L'Ami du Peuple* that he could not be bothered "to make any observation about the childish questions with which the *Assemblée* is busying itself at this moment." Camille Desmoulins was more overtly Voltairian. He reacted that day to the prospect that the Jews would be admitted to citizenship by speculating ironically that circumcision might now become a precondition for the admission of any gentile to that status.[23]

The greatest single problem that Bing faced in his defense of the Jews was the question of the Jewish religion and culture. On the one hand he reacted with great dignity to the accusations that the Jews were a superstitious people. They were attached with inviolable bonds to their religion and "if that appears superstitious I admit openly that we are and it is my deepest hope that we will always remain so." As he was making this outcry Bing knew that he was defending his faith against its most serious contemporary adversary, "the progress of fashionable philosophy, with its aversion for ritual and for everything which it cannot touch physically and immediately." Nevertheless, Bing made serious concessions to precisely this philosophical attack. Persecution throughout the centuries had indeed made the Jews a cultural backwater, Bing admitted; it accounted for the deplorable materialism and cowardliness of the Jewish character. Perhaps worst of all, exclusion had condemned the Jews to conducting their inner life not in some Western language of general culture but in the debased jargon, Yiddish, which they used in their ghettos. This was an obstacle to culture, which even men of talent found almost impossible to overcome. The end of persecution, indeed even a breath of semi-equality, would make it possible for men like Mendelssohn to arise, whom Bing described as the

[22] *Lettre*, p. 26.
[23] Quoted in L. Kahn, *Les Juifs de Paris pendant la révolution*, pp. 44–45.

representative figure of a generation that had appeared in Berlin and Vienna to take an honored and creative place in the life of society.[24] In the light of these remarks Bing's defense of Judaism amounted to an assertion that an enlightened, dignified, Westernized version of the faith, as represented by a new generation, was worthy of respect and equality. This defense added little dignity to the existing Jew.

Was there indeed anything worth preserving in the existing Jewish culture and religion as they were exemplified by the Jews of Metz in the late 1780s? This question was raised in 1787 by Pierre Louis Roederer after he read the seven entries that had arrived to be judged by the Academy for its contest. Roederer and the committee of judges had found that none of these works, not even the two they liked best, by Grégoire and Thiéry, was as yet worthy of the prize. The Academy therefore prolonged the contest for another year, in order to give the contestants time to revise their works in the light of certain questions that Roederer put to them. The very first of these issues was whether "the changes which you propose can be harmonized with the religious and political laws of the Jews and with their prejudices; whether a revolution in their political constitution would not act to do harm to the praiseworthy elements which perhaps exist in their moral outlook." In a private *mémoire* that Roederer wrote at the time, analyzing all the issues for his own satisfaction, he was forthright. "Does not the Jew have within himself the seed of virtues which can make him more useful to society than we gentiles are ourselves? Will we not impose upon him our softness, our dissipation, our frivolity, our immorality, our impatience with evil, and will we not erase from his heart his domestic virtues, his frugality, his simplicity, and his patience?" These remarks were more than a recasting of the Jew for the role of the noble savage or the virtuous Oriental, in order to be able to criticize contemporary culture in the name of his supposed virtues. Roederer added that there were austere moralists among the Jewish people and not only a mass governed by superstition. "In calling an ancient and considerable people to the service of our society we cannot flatter ourselves that we are calling it to virtues which are superior

[24] Bing, *Lettre*, pp. 24–25.

to their own." Clearly, Roederer was praising some Jews of the old
school whom he knew. Such remarks would not be made, at least
not in public, by any of the figures who debated the Jewish question
before 1789 or by any of those who argued for the Emancipation of
the Jews between 1789 and 1791.

Roederer's question, in his instructions to the contestants in the
essay contest, was, as we shall soon see, either ignored or misunder-
stood. For that matter, Roederer himself did not see the implications
of these assertions, for his own suggestions contradicted them, at
least to some degree. He proposed that a distinction be made between religious and moral instruction; the latter ought to be the
same for all children of all the faiths and should therefore be imparted in a national school system that Jewish children too should
be required to attend. Jewish schools would then be limited to
strictly religious instruction and they should not be allowed to
teach religious or moral prejudices or the hatred of other people.
Even for Roederer, therefore, no reordering of the mass of Jewry
could be conceivable unless it were based on the assumption that
governmental authority ought to exercise the strictest supervision
over the content of all the education imparted to Jews. Their community was less than virtuous and it was a matter for the state to
reform its inner life.

It was this second theme, and not Roederer's more generous
estimate of the morality of the Jews, that dominated among the
contestants in the essay contest. By the time the prize was finally
awarded in 1788 nine authors had appeared. Their works ran the
gamut from a four-page letter from a judicial official in the French
islands in America, who declared simply that the Jews are men like
us and ought, therefore, to be given full citizenship, to an even
shorter letter by another judicial official at the *parlement* of Metz,
who proposed that all the Jews be exiled to the deserts of Guiana.
An otherwise unknown *curé* from eastern France wrote an essay of
some seventy pages in which he reasserted the standard medieval
Christian view that the Jews were the sworn enemy of Christianity
and deserved to be persecuted.[25] None of these views were pub-

[25] On Roederer's participation in the Metz essay contest see Cahen, "L'émancipation des Juifs devant la Société royale de Metz," *REJ*, I, 83–104, and es-

lished at the time, for all attention centered on the three essays
which were jointly given the prize. They were the works of Grégoire,
Thiéry, and Zalkind-Hourwitz, and all three of them were published
within the year. They thus played an important role in the battles
of opinion right before and during the Revolution.

All three of these writers agreed on the premise on which all
pro-Jewish argumentation at that time was based: persecution is the
major cause of what is wrong with the Jews and it must be ended
as the indispensable first step for reforming them. Their prescriptions were substantially the same. The Jews ought to be given
economic equality and access, even compulsory access, to Western
education and to the life of the larger society. On this point they
were carrying forward, with variations, the work of Dohm at the
beginning of the decade. Mirabeau's short book in 1787, *On Moses
Mendelssohn and the Political Reform of the Jews,* belonged to the
same outlook. It was in the name of this argument that during the
Revolution Mirabeau and Grégoire would soon be taking the lead
towards achieving the Emancipation of the Jews.

But was oppression the only cause of the inferiority of the Jews?
Mirabeau and Thiéry tended to think so. Neither of them respected
the traditional religion of the Jews and both regarded it as a prime
purpose of enlightened governmental policy to free the Jews from
the ridiculous laws of the Talmud, but both were sure that the Jews
would have freed themselves a long time ago if they had not been
forced into ghettos and excluded from the wider society.[26] However, the two winners of the Metz contest who were taken most
seriously by public opinion, Grégoire, because he was a priest, and
Zalkind-Hourwitz, because he was a Jew and an inveterate writer

---

pecially pp. 99 and 101, for the text of his report on the first batch of essays
and his own *mémoire.* The unpublished entries in this contest were summarized
by Cahen, pp. 86–90. We now know, on the evidence of a letter by Lacretelle
to Malesherbes, that Roederer suggested the subject and that *he knew the Jews
of Metz very well, at first hand* (Grosclaude, *Malesherbes,* p. 636).

[26] Thiéry began his book by saying that the intent of society ought to be
"to raise the Jews to the level of educated and civilized peoples." He added,
"Let us see whether we can hope to develop among them the germ of social
virtue" (*Dissertation,* pp. 3–4). Mirabeau's main reason for admiring Mendelssohn was that "humanity and truth seemed much dearer to Mendelssohn than
the dark phantoms of the Talmudists" (*Sur Moses Mendelssohn,* p. 28; see
also Chapter IX).

of letters to the newspapers in Paris, both held violently negative views of the inherited Jewish religion. Like Bing, Zalkind-Hourwitz equated the basic moral dogmas implicit in Judaism with the highest form of reasonable religion and he, too, invoked the existing circles of Westernized Jews as proof that Judaism could produce such an "enlightened" outlook. It did not yet occur to him, or to anyone else, that such figures were perhaps products of on-going Westernization and not at all of Judaism. Zalkind-Hourwitz thus defended a certain kind of Jewish modernity, but he was a bitter enemy of the Talmud and particularly of the rabbis. He asked that the rabbis be denied any authority to discipline those Jews who did not observe the traditional rituals. The Talmud had acted to cut Jews off from the world and the hold of its legislation upon them had to be broken. In his hatred of rabbis Zalkind-Hourwitz reached such fury that he even put into print an accusation that must be called a piece of overt "anti-Semitism." Commenting on the custom enjoined by the Talmud that Jewish dead are to be buried on the very day of death (this matter was then under considerable debate in various places in Europe), Zalkind-Hourwitz wrote that "it is quite probable that this homicidal custom was introduced by some rabbi who was a poisoner, in order to hide his crime from the law." [27] Those who read Zalkind-Hourwitz with any attention could only be confirmed in their worst prejudices: the existing Jews did not have to be corrupted by persecution; they had enough wickedness which they could derive directly from their own teachings. His readers did not have to agree with this Polish Jew (as Zalkind-Hourwitz always ostentatiously proclaimed to be) that these evils would disappear in an open society. On the contrary, unfriendly readers were given ground to fear that the Jews would, in freedom, only spread wider and infect France more seriously.

The cumulative effect of Zalkind-Hourwitz's book was to promise society that, in payment for equality, the Jew would give up his tradition and become an enlightened Deist. Grégoire, as we have seen in earlier discussion, was holding out, at least to himself, the hope that the regenerated Jew would ultimately turn Christian.

[27] Zalkind-Hourwitz, *Apologie*, pp. 66–67, 72. His positive suggestions for means of change were substantially the same as Grégoire's.

In the short run, however, Grégoire had no clear vision of how that Jew was to be fitted into society. More dangerously still, there were very pronounced elements in his thinking of the desire to protect society against the depredations of the Jews; he was just as caustic on the subject of their evils as the worst of their enemies.

Grégoire was himself slightly embarrassed by the vehemence with which he identified with the peasants who were in debt to the Jews. "What will become of the honest workmen who is ruined by the Jews? . . . Answer, unfortunate inhabitants of the Sundgau. . . . Your animals and your agricultural tools have been sold to gratify these vipers, and only a small part of the usurous interest which has accumulated has been paid." This was the language of Hell, and Grégoire knew it. He wrote a bit shamefacedly in a footnote that he did not want to join with Hell in blaming the Jews for direct participation in the death of Jesus, but Grégoire added that Hell could not be entirely wrong in all his accusations, and certainly not in those against Jewish usury. In this note Grégoire addressed himself directly to Bing (who was widely known to have helped him), but he did not apologize for these remarks and not even for the unnecessary nastiness of his rhetoric. Grégoire merely implied that he excepted such people as Bing and Mendelssohn from his attack.[28]

This was no isolated outburst. In his suggestions for the reordering of the economic rights of the Jews, Grégoire wanted to give them full liberty of commerce but with express prohibition against any credit transaction, because Jews could not be trusted to keep honest accounts. Grégoire added that Jews should be allowed some minor public offices but that they should be excluded from all those jobs which dealt with money, for "one should not lose sight of the character of the people that one is proposing to reform." In order to change this inherited character it was absolutely necessary that the organized Jewish community be broken up and that the Jews even be forbidden to live together in the same places. "It is essential to isolate them, to break to the degree to which this is possible all communication between them." Grégoire saw merit in continuing the medieval Christian custom of making the Jews listen to

[28] Grégoire, *Essai*, pp. 78–79, 219 (the note addressed to Bing).

conversionist sermons, for he had no doubt, of course, that Christianity was the best teacher of civic morality. "To make the Jews listen to some lectures does not seem to me to be contrary to human rights. Who can prove to me that the state cannot make its subjects acquire enlightenment?" Grégoire conceded that there were then, and there had been in the past, some intelligent men among the Jews but the mass "is sunk in the depths of grossest superstition and submerged in an ocean of the most stupid beliefs." The Talmud, he asserted, is a horrible chaos of anti-social opinions, and one must replace it with reason. Grégoire was even willing to believe that if the Jews had not regularly killed Christians for their own horrible religious reasons, this must as least have happened on some occasions.[29]

There were many very generous, humane, and deeply felt pages in Grégoire's essay and these, along with his labors during the Revolution, have justly made him famous as the crucial figure in the fight for the Emancipation of the Jews. He did feel for their misery and he did cry out against it. In the body of his book almost every section ended with the sentiment and rhetoric with which he closed the whole volume:

A new century is about to begin. . . . The Jews are members of the universal family which is in the process of creating fraternity among all the peoples. . . . Children of the same father, cast off every pretext for hating your brothers. . . . Provide them with shelter where they will be able to rest their heads in peace and dry their tears, so that the Jew, returning such love to the Christian, will embrace me as his fellow citizen and his friend.[30]

But how wicked, debased in his religion, and inimical to society was this Jew whom Grégoire had painted. At very best, as Grégoire imagined, kindness and movement towards equality would make

[29] *Ibid.*, pp. 146–147, 152, 156–60, 179–80, 183, 186–87. At least one Jewish leader reacted negatively in 1789 to Grégoire's work. In a private letter to Zalkind-Hourwitz, Lopes Dubec wrote that he disagreed with Grégoire and Thiéry on their suggestions to improve the Jews, for the proposed limitations on their activities would do harm. More important, "they have depicted the faults of the Jews as so blameworthy that this is more likely to increase rather than lessen the reigning prejudices against them, at least among the great mass of the readers" (Private letter dated September 15, 1789, in the possession of the family of the late Rabbi Joseph Cohen of Bordeaux).

[30] *Ibid.*, p. 194.

this Jew into a blank page on which society could write something acceptable to itself. Grégoire never contemplated the emancipation of the Jew; what he envisaged was the creation of some tens of thousands of enlightened Frenchmen who would soon forget that their ancestors had been disfigured both by persecution and by their own inner heritage. This was also the vision of Mirabeau and of Thiéry. Dohm, writing for Cerf Berr and under the influence of Mendelssohn, had more positive hopes for a reformed and enlightened Judaism; so did the Jewish pamphleteers, Bing and Zalkind-Hourwitz. These writers all agreed, however, that what was to be emancipated was some Jewish "new man" who had either just came into view or was not yet even born.

## The Emancipation

Why were the Jews emancipated by the French Revolution? This question was being asked amid the very events of the Revolution and it has been raised repeatedly to this very day. The main outlines of the answer have by now assumed the proportions of consensus. The majority of the *philosophes* sincerely believed that it was their moral duty to extend equality to all men and that even the Jews would be regenerated by the new order. Those who had their doubts or prejudices could, nonetheless, do no other, after they had taken part in the destruction of the old order of special status and privilege in the name of the doctrine of the rights of man. The economic thrust of the Revolution was towards the creation of a modern economy, and it was impossible to maintain regulations and exclusions from an earlier time and apply them only to Jews. Politically the essence of the meaning of the Revolution was that the state no longer dealt with hereditary groups but only with individuals. It was simply unthinkable, as the framers of the first French constitution had to remind themselves in the closing days of their deliberations, that they could extend this principle to all of France and leave only the Jews to be born into the status of exclusion.[31] The final act of emancipation of the vast majority of the

[31] The most important recent discussion of the reasons for the Emancipation is in the article by Baron cited in Chapter I, fn. 8.

Jews in France thus passed on September 27, 1791, because there was really no alternative for the makers of the Revolution.

The story of the battle for this decree in the years 1789–91 has been told many times, for this was the hinge on which Jewish history in Europe turned into the modern era. Nonetheless, these events need to be reexamined. The emphasis of almost all the analysts has consistently centered on the fact that the fight succeeded. Our rereading of the evidence, in the light of two preceding centuries of interaction between the Jews and the government and society of France, suggests a different emphasis and a different question. As a matter of fact, the battle for the Emancipation very nearly failed. At every moment during those two crucial years when the question of the Jews of eastern France was debated on its own merits and not, as it finally was, as a logical necessity for the Revolution itself, a majority could not be mustered to pass the decree in their favor. When the Declaration of the Rights of Man was voted into law on August 27, 1789, the delegates of the Sephardim in Paris and even those of the Ashkenazim wanted to believe that this action represented the automatic granting of equality to the Jews. Had not the Revolutionary parliament declared as the foundation of its new constitutional law that all men are born free and equal? It became clear immediately that this broad philosophical language, so consciously reminiscent of the opening lines of the American Declaration of Independence of 1776, did not yet include the Jews. The matter of the status of the Jews was first raised directly in a long debate that spread over three sessions, from December 21 to 24, 1789; the issue was finally tabled on the motion of one of the chief proponents of the emancipation of the Jews, Mirabeau. He knew that he did not have the votes with which to pass such a decree at that moment.[32] The debate on January 28, 1790, in which the Sephardim and the Jews from the Papal States were given equality, was the most scandalously unruly in the brief but tempestuous history of the Assemblée up to that time. After several hours of disorder the decree passed on a roll-call vote, 374

[32] This debate was recorded in the Moniteur, II, 439, 462, 463, 472. This report and most of the other accounts in the Moniteur of discussion of the Jews were reprinted by Halphen, Recueil des lois, pp. 179–226.

in favor to 280 opposed, at a moment when many prelates and curates who were known to be against the proposal had already gone from the hall.[33] There were repeated attempts to reraise the issue of emancipating the Jews of eastern France in the next two years, but nothing came of them. When the matter was again brought up on January 18, 1791, at a moment that had been chosen as especially propitious because Grégoire was in the chair as the president of the *Assemblée*, a large majority still voted to table the question.[34] The act of emancipation had fateful historic consequences, but so did the very nearly successful opposition to it. What were the roots of this near failure? What unresolved problems did it deed to the future?

In the hectic first two years of the Revolution the "Jewish question" was furiously debated, but no positions were changed by these arguments. All of the parties to the battle entered the post-emancipation era fixed in positions which had crystallized before 1789 and which had only hardened during the Revolution. Each accepted the decree of emancipation, whether willingly or grudgingly, having firmly in mind a set of standards to which the Jews had to conform. Both they and society knew that they had been given equality on the presumption that they would change radically. On the face of the legal documents there was, to be sure, no "social compact" which required the Jews to give up anything other than their separatist communal autonomy—but this was precisely the problem. It had already been decided for decades on all sides that the Jews did indeed have to change themselves, and the very absence of a formal "social compact" left them with no crystallized guidance as to the kind of change that was expected of them. This left the Jews to be attacked by clashing demands.

After 1789 the only group which made any substantial changes in its position was the Jews. The Sephardim began by treading their usual path of wanting no discussion. During the very days that the Declaration of the Rights of Man was being debated by the *Assemblée*, in the third week of August 1789, the Sephardim were aware that Grégoire was eager to raise the issue of Jewish rights. He was moved, in part, by the news of anti-Jewish outbreaks in

---

[33] *Moniteur*, II, 251–62, 255–56.      [34] *Moniteur*, VII, 167.

Alsace in those days, and he had arisen at the session of August 3 to ask the *Assemblée* to protect the Jews of Alsace against the threat of further violence. It is not too far-fetched to imagine that Grégoire had a more personal motive; he wanted to act because he had cast himself in the role of the regenerator of the Jews. The four delegates of the Jews of Bordeaux in Paris wrote him a public letter on August 14 in which they thanked him for his recent intervention on behalf of "some unfortunate inhabitants" (note that they did not call them Jews) who had recently been attacked in Alsace. On the other hand, they saw no need now for any special laws about the Jews. The Declaration of the Rights of Man, which was being debated at that moment, would be enough. The Sephardim informed Grégoire, and public opinion as a whole, that they were already in freedom in Bordeaux. The Jews had been admitted to the national militia there and some had even been elected captain. The four signatories to this open letter had formally represented the Jews at the meeting in Bordeaux at which the electors for representatives to the *Etats Généraux* had been chosen, and one of them, David Gradis, had even been voted in as one of the ninety electors. The Sephardim thus regarded themselves, with considerable justice, as one of the recognized political elements in their community.[35]

This policy of avoiding the issue of Jews could not last. It was soon clear that even the Protestants had not been given full equality by the Declaration of the Rights of Man. A separate decree was required to grant them the right to hold all civil and military offices. In this very debate, which came to an end on December 24, 1789, the question of the Jews occupied most of the attention and, as we have seen, they were then specifically excluded from the purview of this act. The Sephardim, and the Jews from Avignon who had formally joined with them, now had no choice. The issue of their status had to be raised directly. On January 28, 1790, Talleyrand brought in a report in their favor in the name of the committee on the constitution. His basic arguments were two: the Sephardim and the Avignonnais were in a different situation from all other Jews, so that a decision in their favor would have no effect on the

[35] *Lettre addressée à M. Grégoire* (in JTS).

desire of the *Assemblée* to delay the question of the Ashkenazim. Talleyrand's most important proof that the Sephardim were different was that they were behaving and were currently being treated in Bordeaux as a quite normal *corps*. They had never had separatist Jewish laws or tribunals and they were at present fully part of the political life of Bordeaux. In the second place, Talleyrand maintained that the *lettres patentes* of 1776 and a comparable decree in 1780 on behalf of the Avignonnais had already made these Jews into citizens, as these matters were defined by the pre-Revolutionary government. A decree of equality would only confirm the rights that they were already enjoying. As a matter of fact, both of these arguments were only partially true, as the enemies of the Emancipation pointed out in the debate. Nevertheless, these immediate petitioners were sufficiently "French" and were held to be sufficiently different from the mass of the Ashkenazim for the decree to pass. Its language was a legal fiction: "In consequence of the rights" that the Sephardim had already held for two centuries in the *lettres patentes* in their favor, they could now take the oath of active citizenship.

The need for the Sephardim to have their case argued directly at the *Assemblée* represented some degree of failure of their hopes, but in largest measure the policy that they had followed after 1776 was successful even in the midst of this debate. One of their crucial proponents was de Sèze, a representative from Bordeaux who maintained that the Jews were an indigenous element in his city and even part of his own electorate.[36] More important, the bitterest enemies of the emancipation of the Jews, such as Rewbell and Maury, were concerned almost entirely with the effects that a precedent involving the Sephardim might have on the issue of the Ashkenazim. No one raised the question of the nature of the religion, business practices, or patriotism of the Sephardim. There was more than an implication that a community like theirs was acceptable to the makers of the Revolution, provided that it was decorously inconspicuous. Popular anti-Semitism was not so ac-

[36] Talleyrand's and de Sèze's arguments were summarized in *Moniteur*, II, 251. Raymond de Sèze was, along with Malesherbes and François Denis Franchet, a lawyer for Louis XVI in his trial before the Convention.

THE REVOLUTION                                              343

cepting even of the Sephardim, for there was a near-riot in Bordeaux when the news of their emancipation arrived from Paris, but the civic authorities and the national guard intervened immediately. In the nineteenth century *faites-vous oublier* (make yourself inconspicuous) was the oft-repeated slogan of the highest socio-economic element among the Jews of France. The ancestors of this policy were the Sephardim of Bordeaux; this was the implicit "social compact" with which they entered the era of the Emancipation.

The situation was very much more complicated for the Ashkenazim. During the months of preparation for the *Etats Généraux* they too had attempted to be included directly in the electorate for the choosing of the delegates. They had failed, but the royal government had permitted them to have elections of their own and to have their representatives prepare petitions (*cahiers*) of their own.[37] The representatives of the major Jewish communities in eastern France came to Paris in 1789 with no new ideas. All of them asked that their tax burdens be equalized with that of all other subjects of the crown; that they should be given full commercial equality; and that they should be allowed to conserve their autonomous communities, with full internal power over individual Jews. The delegates from Metz wanted also to be freed of the burden of the Brancas tax of 20,000 livres a year and the Alsatians complained against the recent decision in the *lettres patentes* of July 10, 1784, forbidding them to marry without special permission.[38] Because these petitions were official documents, having been produced as

[37] In Lorraine there were elections in each community, by vote of all the heads of families, of deputies to a central meeting in Nancy (Godchot, "Comment les Juifs de Lorraine élurent leurs députés in 1789," *REJ*, LXXXI, 48–54). All of the Jews of eastern France had first attempted, together, to convince the royal government in the spring of 1789 that they should be represented directly by delegates of their own at the *Etats Généraux*. The result of this request, which Cerf Berr probably inspired and is known to have pushed in Paris, was permission for meetings for the Jews to write their own *cahiers* (Liber, "Les Juifs et la convocation des Etats Généraux," *REJ*, LXIV, 261–77).

[38] These Jewish *cahiers* were summarized in the fall of 1789 by Grégoire in his *Motion en faveur des Juifs;* this pamphlet contained the text of what Grégoire had intended to say on October 14, 1789, when a deputation from the Jews of eastern France had appeared before the *Assemblée* but the Jewish question was not debated then. Liber has written an extended commentary on this summary by Grégoire, putting the requests of the Jews in their immediate context ("Les Juifs et la convocation des Etats Généraux," *REJ*, LXV, 96–133).

formal addresses to the *Etats Généraux* through a process parallel
to that out of which the mass of *cahiers* from all over France arose,
the content of their argument is profoundly important. The one
from Metz was written by Isaiah Berr Bing. In it he restated the
views that he had advanced in his ow name in 1787. The Metz
Jews were now formally telling all of France that they agreed that
the mass of Jews were vegetating, without arts, science, or manners.
This could be changed only by increasing their rights. In the short
run the Jewish community was asking for the opportunity to establish schools in which to train the poor as artisans, in the hope
that within a generation Jews would be admitted to all fields of
endeavor. The Jews from Metz said openly that they would not
change their habits immediately after the passage of new laws in
their favor. Their climactic argument for such legislation was that
a new generation would arise to replace the present one, which
was "despised and regarded as useless." [39]

In the wake of the passage of the Declaration of the Rights of
Man Ashkenazi policy had to change, but it changed reluctantly.
Four days after the final passage of the basic first act of the new
constitution the delegates from all the communities in eastern
France presented a joint address to the *Assemblée*. They now asked
for full citizenship; the difference between Frenchmen and Jews
should be abolished entirely, leaving only the difference of religion.
Nevertheless, the leaders of the Ashkenazim tried desperately to
retain the right to Jewish communal organization. They argued
that it could not be the intention of the government to give them the
benefit of equality while at the same time demeaning them by
taking away their autonomy. Their inherited practices had been
their consolation in adversity and they wanted to preserve them
in happier times. It was to the interest of France that the Jews
remained faithful to their religion, because this would guarantee
the morality of their conduct in society. As legal bodies the Jewish
communities owed large debts and their abolition would bankrupt
their creditors. [40]

This document was conservative and it was already out of date

[39] *Mémoire particulier des Juifs établis à Metz.*
[40] *Adresse . . . le 31 août 1789 . . . des Juifs établis à Metz, dans les Trois Evêchés, en Alsace, en Lorraine.*

when it was published. The Jews of Paris had approached the *Assemblée* five days before with a plea for complete equality. They confronted the issue of Jewish separatism head-on: "We request that we be subject, like all Frenchmen, to the same laws, the same police, the same courts; we, therefore, renounce, for the public good and for our own advantage, always subordinate to the general good, the right which we have been given to have our own leaders, chosen among us and appointed by the government." [41] It was easy for the Jews of Paris to do this because there never had been a legally recognized Jewish community in that city in the eighteenth century. They were renouncing nothing that they had ever had. A comparable and more serious renunciation came from two smaller Jewish communities in Lorraine, from Lunéville and Sarreguemines. The men who wrote this petition knew that not all the Jews in France would agree with them, but they asked that those who did not want full integration into the larger society should not be allowed to stand in the way of those who did. Commenting on the position that had been taken on August 31 on behalf of "all the Jews of eastern France," those from Lunéville and Sarreguemines insisted that these leaders did not speak for them. Their two communities wanted to be freed from the dominance over them of the syndics of the Jews in Nancy who, they claimed, were overtaxing them without allowing them any representation. They therefore asked the *Assemblée* to make an end of all distinctions between Jews and gentiles and especially to dissolve the Jewish communal bodies. In a later *mémoire* dated February 26, 1790, these two Jewish communities associated themselves directly and fully with the Jewish inhabitants of Paris, who were continuing to ask for full freedom and the end of all Jewish separatism. [42]

On October 14, 1789, the official leaders of the Ashkenazim, the men who had written the *mémoire* of August 31, were formally presented to the *Assemblée* by the deputies from Lorraine. Berr Isaac Berr, of the family of bankers in Nancy, spoke for the entire group. His remarks were brief and they were couched in generali-

[41] *Adresse . . . le 26 août 1789, par les Juifs résidans à Paris.*

[42] *Mémoire pour les Juifs de Lunéville et de Sarguemines* (undated, but in the fall of 1789) and *Nouveau mémoire*, which was presented to the *Assemblée* on February 26, 1790.

# THE REVOLUTION

ties. He asked in the name of God, "Who by giving each man the same rights has ordained for all men the same duties," and "in the name of outraged humanity" that the *Assemblée* should not ignore the unfortunate lot of the Jews. He did not specifically ask for equality. The Jews wanted "a less sad existence"; they hoped that "men should regard them as brothers" and that "an absolute reform should take place of the ignominious institutions to which they are in bondage." [43]

This vagueness did not last. Many bitter things had been said about the Alsatian Jews in the debate towards the end of December and inevitably there had to be some immediate response. On December 24, the very date that debate ended with the postponement of the Jewish question, the representatives of the Jews of eastern France issued a short unsigned pamphlet. Without defining a program they pleaded for equality. The very increase in liberty in society as a whole was making the Jews all the more conscious of their unchanged servitude, and the *Assemblée* itself ought not to contradict all its acts of wisdom and justice by ignoring the Jews. The whole issue of Jewish communal separatism was ignored in those few short pages. An entirely new theme was now introduced into the discussion of the Jewish question. These Jews of eastern France insisted that they were loyal partisans of the Revolution and that they therefore deserved to participate in its benefits. They tried in a new way to deny the standard argument that they had vices which made them unworthy of citizenship. They no longer merely promised that equality would make them better; they pointed to some changes that had already taken place in the conduct of the Jews. Jews had been admitted to the national guard in some places in eastern France and they were fulfilling their military duties even on the days of Jewish festivals. Here was the first token of the kind of change that society expected of them as a corollary of their equality.[44]

[43] Berr Isaac Berr's speech and the response of the president of the *Assemblée* were printed immediately in an eight-page pamphlet (*Discours des députés des Juifs*) as part of the effort to influence opinion. The chair had promised the delegation that the *Assemblée* would consider its request in the spirit of the desire "to recall your brothers to tranquility and happiness."

[44] This was a pamphlet of four pages entitled *Nouvelle adresse des Juifs à l'Assemblée Nationale, 24 décembre 1789.*

The formal turns by the Ashkenazim away from any insistence on the maintenance of their communal autonomy took place a month later. They joined hands with the Jews from Paris in an elaborate petition in which they gave up all their previous programs in favor of the simple demand for immediate equality. This document was written for the Jews by Godard, their lawyer, who was a leader of liberal opinion in Paris, and more than a little of his outlook is to be found in its text. The Jewish leaders themselves were still clearly hoping to retain some kind of organized Jewish community, for the author of this petition pointed out very early that the wishes of Jews were really now irrelevant to the question of their emancipation, because "the immutable source of reason and justice" from which the legislators were drawing their inspiration demanded such an act. The *Assemblée* had the duty of forcing even the men who wanted to remain debased to become better. By keeping the Jews separate, society could only hurt itself, for the Jews would forever remain angry and vengeful. A more immediate threat was uttered in this document. France was at war with Austria and a few Jews had already become *émigrés* to the country of the enemy. To continue to keep the Jews in subjection in France would mean that more would consider joining the emigration. The American Constitution, which had just been adopted by the new nation across the sea, was invoked to help make the point that the Jews in France were asking for the same rights that had been granted in America: not tolerance but absolute equality before the law of all the religious sects. At the very core of this petition there stood, however, the oft-repeated argument that the existing inferior status of the Jews had in truth made their majority into debased people and that the Jews deserved freedom much more for what they promised to become than for what they were.[45]

[45] *Pétition des Juifs établis en France . . . sur l'ajournement du 24 décembre 1789*, pp. 5–6, 15–17, 21–22, 38. A highly laudatory summary of this *Pétition* appeared in the issue of *Moniteur* of February 15, 1790. This article was signed with the initial G, and it is at least possible that the author was Godard himself. Jacques Godard was then twenty-eight years old, a lawyer at the *parlement* of Paris, and a figure of some consequence in the commune of Paris. As we shall see below, that commune was very busy at the moment pleading for the Jews and Godard was a prime mover in that effort there. He died in December, 1791.

The last gasp of the attempt by the Jewish leadership in eastern France to maintain the autonomous Jewish community occurred in the spring of 1790. Berr Isaac Berr, who had been the spokesman at the bar of the *Assemblée* in October of the year before, published a pamphlet on April 22, 1790, in which he answered the anti-Jewish speech that had been given by the Bishop of Nancy, de la Fare, in the debate in December. That speech was being reprinted all over Lorraine and Berr felt impelled to answer it, especially because de la Fare had excepted him by name from his attack on the Jews. Berr turned the compliment to himself by saying that if he, who had been born and raised in exclusion, had been found praiseworthy by such a critic as de la Fare, how much more would French society like his successors, who would be raised amidst freedom. Berr made an "offer" to de la Fare. It was clear, Berr insisted, that the *Assemblée* could not now exclude the Jews of eastern France from the rights of man, especially after it had given them to the Sephardim and Avignonnais three months before. If men such as de la Fare continued to object to complete political equality for the Ashkenazim, let a bargain be struck; let the *Assemblée* give the Ashkenazim all rights with the exception of the right to hold public office and let the Jews in eastern France, in return, keep their full internal autonomy, including civil jurisdiction in cases involving only Jews. This "offer" outraged Jacob Berr, the nephew of its author, who published a pamphlet three days later denouncing any thought of maintaining such separatism.[46]

The re-publication of de la Fare's anti-Jewish views in the early months of 1790 was not accidental. As Maury and Rewbell had predicted in that debate, the granting of equality to the Sephardim in January did arouse further the rampant and endemic anti-Jewish passions in eastern France. The Jews of Alsace, therefore, addressed themselves directly to the gentile majority of the province. They stated with great clarity the promises that they were willing to make in order to achieve their equality. Their essential assertion was: "Do not judge what we will become one day by whatever we have

---

[46] Berr-Isaac Berr's pamphlet was entitled *Lettre du Sr. Berr-Isaac Berr . . . à monseigneur l'évêque de Nancy*. The reply by Jacob Berr (he was a surgeon in Nancy) appeared as *Lettre à monseigneur l'évêque de Nancy . . . pour servir de réfutation de quelques erreurs (du) Sr. Berr-Isaac Berr*.

been up to the present. This would be a great mistake and you are too wise to be guilty of it." The Jews of Alsace promised that they would become like the members of the majority, if they would be given the same status and rights. A decree of equality would, "by making us citizens, compel us to be useful to the homeland." On the most painful of concrete issues, the Alsatian Jews promised to accept without any thought of further appeal the decree which had ended the battle over the "false receipts" (their debtors had been given long terms in which to pay).[47] This last promise was to be redeemed by the *Assemblée* on September 28, 1791, the day after the Jews of eastern France were given their equality. A decree was passed instructing the Jews to register with the local authorities all the debts that were owed them, so that the central government, on the basis of this information, could make a new disposition of the question. The Jews of Alsace refused to obey. They maintained that, since they were now equal citizens, it was against the Constitution to name them as a group in such an act. Nevertheless, in actual fact, the majority of these debts were never collected. The authorities were not eager to enforce them on the peasants and the Jews largely preferred not to stir up passions by insisting.[48]

In the course of the six opening months of the Revolution the Jews of eastern France had repeatedly assented to the proposition that in their mass they were inferior to the level of honesty and culture of the majority; that they had to abandon at least some aspects of their religion; and that they needed to become more like all other Frenchmen. The question remained: Which Frenchmen? Who was willing to accept them, and on what terms?

[47] *Adresse des Juifs alsaciens au peuple d'Alsace.* The last of many decrees dealing with the "false receipts" had been enacted on August 28, 1787, by the *Conseil Souverain* of Alsace. Debtors were given two years to pay debts of under 100 livres and as much as ten years for debts of more than 1,200 livres (Szajkowski, *Economic Status,* p. 139).

[48] Szajkowski, "The Law of September 28, 1791," *Zion,* XVII, 84–100; the debate at the *Assemblée* that day is recorded in *Moniteur,* IX, 794–95. Rewbell said that the Jews themselves know that they can have no peace in Alsace unless the question of debts is settled. He estimated that of the perhaps fifteen million livres now owed to Jews in Alsace, only three million would represent capital, for that was what all the debtors were worth corporately, and "the Jews could not have lent money without security." Rewbell told the *Assemblée* that the Jews themselves had informed him that they would accept four million in settlement, to make peace.

### French Opinion, 1789–91

During the preparation for the *Etats Généraux* many of those who had written the *cahiers* in eastern France had been much concerned with the question of the Jews. In Metz the nobility had asked that "all people who were indigenous to France, regardless of their religious faith, should enjoy the right of citizenship in the kingdom." The third estate had used the language of the Metz essay contest in asking that "counsel should be taken regarding the means of making the Jews into useful people." The nobility of Toul, in the region of Metz, stated that the people of their locality were suffering more than those in any other part of France under the oppression of usury; they therefore asked that Jews be given the right to enter all the arts and professions. Such statements were, however, very much in the minority. The *cahiers* in Alsace were bitterly anti-Jewish, and they were little less so in Lorraine. Hell was busy circulating a draft of an anti-Jewish *cahier*, but his activities were hardly necessary. The preliminary *cahiers* from various places in Lorraine, where his influence was not as direct as in Alsace, were just as hostile to the Jews as the statements from Alsace which used his language. From almost all the villages of Lorraine there came suggestions such as forcing the Jews to engage in physical labor, to forbidding usury or any business on credit, or even simply expelling them entirely from France. Opinion was unanimous, wherever the matter was mentioned, that Jewish communal organization had to be forbidden.[49]

In the battles of the pamphlets and in the speeches at the *Assem-*

[49] The *cahiers* from eastern France which deal with the Jewish question have been studied by Liber, "Les Juifs et la convocation des Etats Généraux," *REJ*, LXIII, 185–210; LXIV, 89–108. The *cahiers* from Alsace were influenced by the negative views not only of Hell but of a committee to study the Jewish question that he headed in 1788–89; this group was appointed by the *Commission intermédiaire* of the Alsatian provincial administration. Among its members were de Broglie, Pflieger, and Schwendt, all of whom figure in the years 1789–91 as opponents of the emancipation of the Jews. The report of this committee, rendered in September, 1788, favored the abolition of Jewish immigration; some move towards making the Jews become artisans, without admitting them to the guilds; and the forcing of the Jews to observe their Sabbath on Sunday. For the work of this committee, see Szajkowski, "The Jewish Problem in Alsace," *JQR*, XLIV, 234–43; for the activities of many of its members during the Revolution, see below in this chapter.

*blée* by the Alsatian representatives this matter of Jewish autonomy did not even come up. The enemies of the Jews, who had long been dedicated to the destruction of the organized Jewish community, presumed even earlier than the Jewish leaders themselves that the Jewish representative bodies would be swept away by the new regime. The two leading clerical adversaries of the Jews, Anne-Louis Henry de la Fare and the Abbé Jean Sieflein Maury, centered on a more fundamental point. Each insisted that by the very nature of their religion the Jews were an alien nation which could not possibly have any attachment to the land of France and to its society. If the Jew is faithful to his law, de la Fare and Maury argued, he cannot bear arms on the Sabbath; his obedience to his own dietary laws cuts him off from social intercourse with gentiles; the calendar of his faith with all its many holidays makes it impossible for him to be an artisan or a farmer and therefore any decrees that might offer such possibilities to the Jews would be irrelevant rhetoric, constructed to make a sham case for granting them civic equality. Whatever might have been done to the Jews by their exclusion by the majority, the real root of their apartness in society was the nature of their religion. Maury went even further than de la Fare. He insisted that it was the innate character of the Jews, even more than their religion, which was the cause of their continuing bad conduct throughout the centuries and which had rightly evoked most, if not all, of the punishment that had been meted out to them. On this point Maury, the most articulate of clerical reactionaries, quoted Voltaire in proof. Both Maury and de la Fare suggested that the Jews should be given the status of protected foreigners and that they should be treated with reasonable decency, but that France could on no account admit these aliens to citizenship. The clerical right, at its most literate, was thus saying that only the Jew who had ceased entirely to be one, no doubt by formal conversion to the Catholic culture and religion of the mass of Frenchmen, could be admitted to civic equality.[50]

[50] Maury came from a community where there were no Jews; he represented the clergy of the *bailliage* of Peronne near Lyons. He survived the Revolution to serve as Napoleon's cardinal of Paris. De la Fare had preached the sermon at the formal mass which opened the *Etats Généraux* on May 4, 1789. He, too, survived the Revolution and he played a role in the Bourbon restoration. De la Fare's speech was printed as *Opinion . . . sur l'admissibilité des Juifs;* Maury's remarks at the debate were summarized in *Moniteur,* II,

The commune of Strasbourg in 1790 did not represent clerical influence; it spoke for the economic interests of the bourgeois of the city. The *Société des Amis de la Constitution* of Strasbourg, a group of liberal intellectuals, had pronounced themselves at the end of February, 1790, in favor of the Jews. The commune of the city tried to kill the effect of this statement by sending an address to the *Assemblée*. The commune announced that every one of its sections had been unanimous against the admission of Jews to citizenship and that this unanimity was itself a devastating argument against the Jews. The reason for such total agreement was to be found in the fact that everyone knew the inherent bad character of the Jews and no one doubted that they were foreigners. Let the "enlighteners" stop defaming the gentiles by blaming them for what was wrong with Jews; their conduct was their own fault. Perhaps the Jews might eventually give up every aspect of their separatism and all the characteristics of their nature. Let us sit and wait until that happens; we might then judge them to be worthy of equality.[51]

This pro-Jewish stand by the *Société des Amis de la Constitution* evoked two other counter-attacks. Pflieger, one of the deputies to the *Assemblée* from Alsace, counter-attacked the *Société* in substantially the same manner as the commune of Strasbourg.[52] A local figure, Ginzrot, was even more hostile; his rhetoric is disturbing be-

---

455–56. Among other canards, he repeated the tale that the doctor Sedecias poisoned Charles the Bald (see Chapter IV for Hénault's use of this same story). Maury's speech was answered in a letter by Berr Isaac Berr, which evoked an answer in which Maury took back nothing. Both of these letters appeared in the second edition of Berr Isaac Berr's translation of Weisel's *Divrei Shalom ve-Emet*, which was published early in 1790, to help make the case that the Jews could change towards "enlightened" ways and "productive" occupations (see end of Chapter VI).

[51] *Très-humble . . . adresse qui présente . . . la commune . . . de la ville de Strasbourg;* on the genesis of this action see Hildenfinger, "L'adresse de la commune de Strasbourg," *REJ*, LXVIII, 112–28. In the last pages of this petition the authorities of the Revolutionary local government in Strasbourg asked for the expulsion of Cerf Berr and his family, thus repeating the consistent demand of the city in the fifteen years before. The enemies of Cerf Berr now had a new reason. His son Marx Berr had just been admitted, on February 20, 1790, as the first Jewish member of the *Société des Amis de la Constitution*. On that day it had appointed a commission to study the Jewish question and a week later it had accepted its favorable report (Hildenfinger, p. 113).

[52] Jean Adam Pflieger was deputy of the Third Estate from Altkirch. His pamphlet was entitled *Réflexions sur les Juifs d'Alsace*. It appeared also in a German edition.

cause of its "modern" ring. "Even if we recognize the Jews as our unhappy brothers, we cannot be moved by emotion to offer up our health to their perhaps incurable disease." They infect society. Their real character was "usury and cheating." All the present claims about their wanting to learn trades and the arts, Ginzrot maintained, were "craftily contrived phantoms with which Jews are trying to fool us." Society must protect itself against the Jews until such time as they may perhaps become totally assimilated to the ways and outlook of all other Frenchmen. In the petition by the commune of Strasbourg, as well as in the pamphlets by Pflieger and Ginzrot, there was more than a hint that none of these writers believed that the Jew would or could change. At the very least, these authors left themselves the possibility of maintaining always that, no matter how much the Jew might transform himself, such changes were not yet adequate to qualify him for admission to society.[53]

The most anti-Jewish views of all occurred among some of the members of the extreme left. As we have seen, Desmoulins ironized and Marat was impatient and disdainful. Lesser figures occupied themselves with the Jewish question more seriously. On the morrow of the debate of January 28, 1790, in which the Sephardim and Avignonnais had been given their equality, a left-wing pamphleteer, de Laissac, who was then serving in the army, addressed a public letter to one of the proponents of that decree. De Laissac's basic thesis was that the Revolution represented an attempt to create, by man's own effort, the best human community in all of history. France dared not risk this great hope by adding to its polity "the vilest people in the world." The Jews would poison the new spirit; they were and would remain strangers, and the presence of strangers within a nation would hurt the body politic. Treason and espionage flourished most readily among aliens. A nation was in danger of falling apart when its population became mixed, as Rome moved towards decline after it admitted Jews and all kinds of Orientals.

De Laissac made three other observations of some importance. The first was an almost flat statement of racism. In arguing that the

[53] I have been able to find no information about Ginzrot. He appears on the title page as Ginzrot, Sohn. The long title of the pamphlet begins: *Antwort über eine Schrift.*

Jews were irrevocably alien, he added, "I will admit, if you will, that
the Jews are born like us." He did not let it go at that, however;
he added in a note on the same page: "One could argue against this
view. The same law of nature which ordains that animals transmit
their characteristics from generation to generation is also assuredly
true of the human species, even though here it may be less obvious."
In the second place, de Laissac admonished the representatives to
the *Assemblée* that they must remember that they are "the deputies
of France and not of all mankind." He was willing to contemplate,
in a vague and general way, the possibility that mankind as a whole
had to deal with the Jews and to find a place for them, but within
the specific purview of France the Jews had to be contained and
held separate, as a source of infection. In the third place, de Laissac
was aware of the American Constitution, but he argued that the
freedom of religion that it was guaranteeing to all was proper to a
new country which needed to attract population but that it was not
a sound policy for France, which already had the largest population
in Europe.

Towards the very end of his pamphlet de Laissac addressed himself to the makers of the Revolution on the larger issue of what their
future policy ought to be. "You must now unite all your zeal and
your efforts to restrain or to exterminate all the disturbers of public
peace." [54] The kind of man who wrote this sentence in 1790 was
perhaps on his way to being one of the makers of the Terror, but in
its immediate context this remark meant that the issue of the Jews
was troubling public order as a whole and that repressive measures
had to be taken both against the Jews and their friends who had
raised the question of their rights.

This was essentially the premise on which the more famous figure, Rewbell, the Jacobin deputy from Alsace, based his view of the
Jewish question. Rewbell fought the emancipation of the Jews
bitterly. He either spoke or intervened at almost every one of the
sessions at which any aspect of the Jewish question was raised in the

[54] De Laissac, *Lettre à M. Le Chapellier;* the author is probably identical
with the de Laissac who published a book on military tactics in 1783. The
notion that the Jews are totally alien and physically repulsive and that they
must therefore be expelled entirely was also expressed by an anonymous Alsatian pamphleteer in 1790: *Ueber die Vertreibung der Juden* (in JTS).

*Assemblée.* At the very end of the battle, on September 27, 1791, he was the only delegate who still fought the decree of emancipation. On the next day, when the final version of that decree was presented by Duport for adoption, he was the author of the abortive decree that required the Jews to register the debts owed them.

Rewbell's first appearance was on December 24, 1789, when he made the opening statement for the anti-Jewish side in the first great debate at the *Assemblée* on the question of the Emancipation. In his account of this debate Desmoulins had not only joked about the Jews; he had also not spared Rewbell. On January 5, 1790, Rewbell answered Desmoulins in a letter. After acknowledging that Desmoulins' ironic remark about circumcision had given him pleasure, Rewbell went on to explain his reasons for being opposed to citizenship for the Jews. He announced that he regarded himself as perhaps the most tolerant member of the *Assemblée;* "religion can undoubtedly not be a reason for excluding anyone from equality." Nevertheless, it was a different problem if a religion was intertwined with civil and political principles that were incompatible with the society into which its believers wanted admission. Rewbell attacked the desire of the Jews of eastern France, as announced in their joint petition of August 31, 1789, to maintain their autonomous communal structure and the internal jurisdiction of Jewish law; this, Rewbell insisted, was incompatible with the request of the Jews for citizenship. "What do you think of individuals who want to become French and who want nonetheless to keep Jewish administrators, Jewish judges, Jewish notaries and all of this within their own confines." Rewbell went further, to argue that Jewish religious practice, which forbade Jews to eat or drink with Frenchmen or to marry them, in itself represented a set of devices by which the Jews separated themselves from the rest of society. "You will see that it is not I who excludes the Jews, they exclude themselves." The Jew will perhaps be admissible to society when, on leaving the synagogue, he will say: "I am joining the crowd and I will follow the same customs as my neighbors." He will then have ceased practicing his hatred for other men. For the present we must exclude the Jew and we can review this question only when a moment of radical change and renunciation on his part does come.

These views were not at all different from those of Maury or de la Fare or of the various pamphleteers in Strasbourg, but there were other elements as well in Rewbell's thinking. He concluded this letter by insisting that the proper employ of Desmoulins' talents would not be in any labors in behalf of the Jews. He should rather concern himself with the Alsatians whom they were despoiling. If Desmoulins were to know the Jews of Alsace and the entire situation in the province at first hand, as Rewbell did, he would come to the same conclusions. At the climax of his letter Rewbell added a racist slur: "After just a few hours of visiting Alsace your humanity would certainly move you to use all your talents in defense of a numerous, industrious, and honest class of my unfortunate compatriots who are oppressed and ground down by these cruel hordes of Africans who have infested my region." [55]

Where did Rewbell get the idea that the Jews were Africans? The source was probably Voltaire. The high priest of the Enlightenment had been brought to mind in this opening debate about the Jews, for Maury had quoted him directly to establish their bad character. Voltaire had been the most prominent of the contemporary authors who suggested, on occasion, that the Jews were not ignorant Arabs from the desert, which was his favorite description of them, but rather that they were lepers who had been expelled from Egypt. Whatever may have been the immediate source of Rewbell's slur,[56] it is inconceivable that he did not know his Vol-

[55] Rewbell's letter was not printed by Desmoulins. It was written in response to a remark in his *Révolutions de France et de Brabant* (No. 5; December 28, 1789) that Rewbell's attack on the Jews had been "too harsh." The text was printed by Hoffman, *L'Alsace*, IV, 518–19; Jean-Francois Rewbell represented the Third Estate of Colmar and Schelestadt at the *Assemblée*. He was a republican from the very beginning of the Revolution and the principal author of the decree of May 15, 1791, admitting Negro freedmen to citizenship in the French Antilles. Though the proponents of the Negro cause were mostly identical with the friends of the Jews (Grégoire, Martineau, Mirabeau, and the commune of Paris), Rewbell saw no connection between the two causes. In the period after the fall of Robespierre he became a member of the Directorate. On Rewbell, see Guyot, *Documents biographiques sur J. F. Rewbell;* on the Negro question, see McCloy, "The Race Question in Late Eighteenth Century France," *South Atlantic Quarterly*, L, 348–60.

[56] This charge was an ancient one, which had been repeated by many Greek and Latin authors from Manetho to Tacitus. Voltaire repeated it in his article *Dieu* (see *Oeuvres*, XXVIII, 158–60, and Emmrich, *Das Judentum bei Voltaire*, pp. 22–23).

taire very well, for the works of the sage of Ferney were the staple reading of that generation. The premises on which Rewbell was basing his position on the Jews were, in any case, precisely those of Voltaire. Rewbell asserted that he had no intolerance of religion but that Judaism was a special case, for it taught separatism and contempt for others; it had created a lasting character that was both alien and obnoxious; these dangerous differences could be explained by the foreign origins of the Jews in a different continent, outside of Europe.

A few weeks later Rewbell added a new, economic nuance to this secular theory of Jew-hatred. In the debate of January 28, 1790, he reported that Alsace was being flooded with counter-Revolutionary rumors (which was true) and he added that the possibility of citizenship for the Jews would simply allow the enemies of the Revolution to say that "there is an alliance of Jews and speculators to seize all property." Rewbell maintained that the only class in Alsace that could be trusted to be Revolutionary were the peasants. To threaten the peasants with any increase in the rights of the Jews meant to endanger the Revolution itself. The Jews were the alien despoilers of the peasants, and they would turn against the Revolution if they were abandoned to their oppressors.[57]

The possibility was thus sketched out by these men of the left that, for the sake of its regeneration, France had to exclude the Jews. What Voltaire and d'Holbach had said or hinted at in theory had become a political program. Ginzrot and de Laissac had come near to defining a racist outlook and Rewbell had outlined, at least dimly, an economic theory which posited lasting and inevitable conflict between the Jews and the most oppressed class, the peasants. Most of the time the pamphleteers who belonged to this outlook apologized for attacks on the Jews or proposed their expulsion; sometimes they suggested that the Jews ought to go off to some uninhabited place and form their own society. The new secular anti-Semitism of the left had taken its first step towards "solving" the Jewish problem by isolation or pogroms.

The answer to this economic theory in the name of which the Jews of Alsace were being attacked was given very early in the

[57] *Moniteur*, III, 251–52.

Revolution by no less a figure than Clermont-Tonnerre. The Jews of Metz had sent to the *Assemblée* an urgent plea for protection, for the riots against Jews in eastern France had not yet quieted down. Clermont-Tonnerre agreed that Jews did merit the hatred against them in eastern France but he ascribed it, as was usual among pro-Jewish figures, to the effects oᶜ oppression. He then added that the people of Alsace did not know and was not subtle enough to know that the men who victimized it were themselves victims of others; that Jews were as much trapped and oppressed by those who gained from them as were the peasants by the Jews who took petty usury from them (there was a broad hint here of a slur against the Brancas family, which got 20,000 livres a year from the Jews of Metz for "protecting" them). Clearly both the Jews and their Alsatian enemies needed the regenerating power of liberty.[58]

The only other attempt, evidently, to answer the economic attack on the Jews of Alsace was made in a more serious and thorough way by the authors of the report to the *Société des Amis de la Constitution* in Strasbourg, which, as we have just seen, aroused the ire of the commune of Strasbourg and of at least two individual pamphleteers. The authors of this report met head-on the objections to any greater rights for the Jews that were common coin in Alsace and which were then being voiced in Paris by Rewbell, de Broglie, and all the other Alsatian deputies: the Jews would be in greater danger if they were given civic equality because the people would attack them; in two or three generations the Jews would own the whole province and the people would be miserable. Both of these points were denied, and very shrewdly so: the peasants do not have a real stake in opposing the Jews. Sentiment is being whipped up against them by the nobility, which wants to keep its financial gains from the Jews, and by the Church, which is helping to enflame anti-Semitism as a tool for scaring off all capitalists from buying any of the recently nationalized church property. The peasants will even-

[58] Clermont-Tonnerre was a count who was elected in 1789 as first deputy of the nobility of Paris. He led the seceders among the nobility who united with the Third Estate, the act which transformed the *Etats Généraux* into the *Assemblée Nationale*. He was thus a major figure in its affairs. The account of the debate of September 28, 1789, regarding the protection of the Jews of Metz is in *Moniteur*, I, 526; his speech was printed as a pamphlet: *Opinion relativement aux persécutions qui ménacent les Juifs d'Alsace.*

tually understand that they are being used and misled, for the nationalized lands belong to the entire nation of which the peasants are the backbone. It is calumny to accuse the peasant of being as ferociously hostile to anybody as they are supposed to be to the Jews. The ultimate economic interest of the peasants is for the Jews to become equal citizens, because they will then help pay the common burden of taxation. Economic opportunity which will allow the Jews to enter productive occupations will be an economic boon to Alsace as a whole. Five times the number of its present Jewish population engaged in productive work will cost the province as a whole less than the cost to it of the Jews who are there right now, living in misery and financing themselves by usury and dishonesty. Such a new regime of light and philosophy will purify the Jews themselves. They will learn to distinguish between the true precepts of their law, the moral commandments which are common to all mankind, "which we know as well as they, and the obnoxious superstitions which the extravagant zeal of the ancient rabbis has imposed on them." They will thus come closer to Christian society and be part of a regenerated mankind.[59]

These last lines represent, of course, the mainstream of pro-Jewish opinion in the speeches and the pamphlets of the years 1789–91. Such views are the best known and the most frequently quoted; there is almost nothing to be found in any such pamphlet or speech, even in nuance, that is not in another, or in some essay written before 1789 by some of the same people.

Mirabeau, for example, closed the debate of December 24, 1789, by making again the essential point that he had made two years before in his book in their defense: the Jew is more of a man (*homme*) than he is a Jew. On this premise Mirabeau denied the assertion of Rewbell that "they do not regard themselves as citizens." Mirabeau adduced the very fact that the Jews were requesting equality as proof of their desire to cease being Jewish in any separatist way. Having said this, it was possible for Mirabeau to

[59] *Rapport lu à l'assemblée de la société des amis de la constitution.* The influence of the Cerf Berr family on this action is directly evident at the end of the report, where the national guard of Strasbourg was castigated for not admitting members of this family, thus disregarding the example of Paris, where Jews had been accepted into these military formations.

add that the new society that the Revolution was creating should banish those who did not want to be *hommes*. This was the meaning, as well, of Clermont-Tonnerre's famous and oft-quoted remarks in the same debate. He, too, was responding to Rewbell. Clermont-Tonnerre was associating himself with Mirabeau to deny the allegation that the Jews did not want to become citizens. On the contrary, Clermont-Tonnerre asserted, the Jews had participated in the elections in Bordeaux; they joined various military bodies and they gave much proof of their patriotism; therefore it is a slur to pretend that they do not want to be citizens. To be sure, were they to say such a thing, one should rightly banish them, for "there cannot be a nation within a nation," but Clermont-Tonnerre's point was that this was not happening and that it was almost inconceivable that it should. In his own mind, he was taking no risks when he said, "One must refuse everything to the Jews as a nation but one must give them everything as individuals; they must become citizens." In context this was less of a demand than a description of an on-going process which the grant of equality would assuredly hasten.[60]

At the core of Clermont-Tonnerre's outlook there were two definitions: his understanding of religion and his view of man. On both these matters of the greatest importance he spoke for the mainstream of the enlightened intelligentsia who fought the battle for the emancipation of the Jew. For all of these minds there was a fundamental distinction between the moral laws, which defined human conduct in society, and sectarian religion. Morality was the common possession of all men. Society had the duty to make laws about human conduct and God himself had accorded this right to the legislators. How men acted was therefore properly the domain in which other men could constrain and judge them, in the name of universal reason. There was, however, freedom of conscience. This meant, for Clermont-Tonnerre and men of his viewpoint, that individuals had a right to differ in their dogmas and in their ways of addressing themselves to heaven. Clermont-Tonnerre did not involve himself at all in the question of how the various traditions expressed their differing dogmas in varying rituals. His silence on this point indicates that he did not consider ritual a matter of any con-

[60] *Moniteur*, II, 455–56, 462–63.

sequence, on the presumption that the Jews would assuredly surrender their specific rituals if the new order would allow them to
keep a non-Trinitarian set of dogmas. Behind this view there were,
obviously, ideas about religion which came from Christianity, from
the doctrine of natural law, and most directly from Deism. In the
context of these ideas the term *homme* meant an individual who had
abandoned superstitions and prejudices for reason and light; he
had become the *philosophe* that Voltaire, on one rare occasion, had
called on Isaac de Pinto to be.

The major political body that was consistently pro-Jewish during
the Revolution was the commune of Paris. With the exception of
one of its sections, which dragged its feet because it was concerned
that the Jews supposedly wanted to remain a nation within a nation,
the commune was unanimous in its support of complete equality for
the Jews. Its influence made a large difference at the *Assemblée*.[61]
On January 28, 1790, the very day that the decree on behalf of the
Sephardim and the Avignonnais was being passed at the *Assemblée*,
Godard appeared before the commune to plead the cause of all
other Jews. He was speaking for a deputation of the Jews of Paris;
the essential argument was that equality for all men was a principle
that conformed "to the laws of reason and humanity" and that such
a decision would help remake the Jews so that they as individuals
would reflect the virtues which reason and love of all mankind
taught.[62] Two days later someone who was not professionally involved in pleading the cause of the Jews, Debourge, addressed the
commune. He admitted that the *cahiers* that had come from Paris
had pleaded for the emancipation of the Negroes but they had been
entirely silent on the subject of the Jews. Debourge maintained that
this had happened because these *cahiers* had been done in haste.
He himself had wanted to introduce the question of the Jews but
he had been absent from the crucial meeting at which these petitions were put in final form. On the basis of this explanation Debourge was able to maintain that Paris did care about the emancipa-

[61] On the pro-Jewish activities of the commune of Paris see Kahn, *Les Juifs
de Paris pendant la révolution*, pp. 83–112; see also *Moniteur*, III, 319, 443,
488–89, for the commune's pressure on the *Assemblée* in February, 1790.
[62] This speech was published by the commune: *Discours prononcé le 28
janvier 1790*.

tion of the Jews and that, being in the forefront of the Revolution, it was the duty of Paris to take the lead here as it had in all other great matters. Like Godard and especially Clermont-Tonnerre, Debourge presumed that two propositions were beyond any question: the state had a right to ask of a citizen that he should obey its laws and that he should conform in his outward conduct to the norms that it expected of everybody; religion was a matter of private belief, without any relevance to public conduct in society. Debourge added that the Jews were proving by their patriotism and zeal that they were in the vanguard of the new men whom the Revolution was fashioning.[63]

These definitions were made most explicit of all during those days by an anonymous abbé (he announced himself with some pride as a former teacher of Grégoire) who wrote an elaborate answer to Maury's attack on the Jews. In the opinion of this abbé the Jews differed from the rest of society only in incidental attributes which would utterly disappear when they would be given "the rights which belonged to human nature." Any analysis of the character, customs, and habits of the Jews would therefore be useless and irrelevant, for equality would change the whole of their system of behavior. Indeed, even now the veneration for the Sabbath and for all of their other rituals "comes less from religious ardor than from profound and tender filial piety." Maury had said that the Jews were a foreign nation; this writer answered that "Jews are no longer a nation; they are only the remains and the debris of a destroyed nation." Having no territory, sovereignty, or government of their own, they are the stones of a building that has fallen. These stones could and must be incorporated into the new structure that the Revolution was erecting.

As men (*hommes*), therefore, the Jews were as much candidates for regeneration by justice and reason as were all other men, and the talents of the Jews would be as useful to the new order as those of all other people. The anonymous abbé insisted that the essential question was, however, not any calculus as to the usefulness to the state of a decree emancipating the Jews. This issue could not be

[63] Debourge was a representative to the commune. His speech appeared in print: *Discours prononcé le 30 janvier.*

determined by such considerations as whether the Jews would represent a profit or loss to society or whether they would become good farmers, soldiers, artists, or artisans. The only issue before the *Assemblée* was to consider the Jews in the manner in which it was considering all other issues, in the light of "the decrees of nature and the eternal order of things." There could be no perspective on any questions except that which was provided by the regenerating thrust of the Revolution, which was changing the entire face of France. The Jews alone could not be excluded from the moral triumph of the *Assemblée* in reordering all of society. The emancipation of the Jews was thus envisaged as the completion of the task of the Revolution, as it addressed itself to perhaps the most difficult problem with which it was confronted. True revolutionaries had to forget their petty complaints against the Jews and even the fears that they might not become better, for "your mission is not to use men as you find them but to make of them what you require them to be." [64]

When Duport arose on September 27, 1791, to insist that the Jews had to be emancipated in order to complete the Revolution, he himself was probably making an assertion about constitutional logic; those who finally voted for the decree were, we can be sure, hearing an appeal to the moral pathos of the era. The anonymous abbé who had argued with Maury had expressed it well when he said that the purpose of the Revolution was to take men and make them what they ought to be. This is the kind of assertion that has been cited by Jacob L. Talmon to help him maintain the thesis that the main thrust of the Revolution was "totalitarian democracy." [65] Whatever may be the merits of Talmon's views in general (they have occasioned a large and still unfinished debate), it is strange that he did not even mention the Jewish question during the Revolution as a case in point. Here there can be no doubt whatsoever that the Revolution was "totalitarian." Almost all of those who helped to emancipate the Jews, from Grégoire through Robespierre, had in mind some vision of what they ought to be

---

[64] *Observations sur l'état civil des Juifs;* the author has been identified by Szajkowski as the Abbé Antoine Adrien Lamourette ("The Emancipation of Jews during the French Revolution," *SBB,* III, 89).
[65] Talmon, *The Origins of Totalitarian Democracy.*

made to become. Talmon's critics may be correct in maintaining that the main body of the revolutionaries, the political center, were willing to leave men to be themselves within the new political order. It was these very people, however, who made demands not only on the public behavior but also on the inner spirit and religion of the Jews. Here the Revolution appeared at its most doctrinaire.

Some of the revolutionaries were even aware of the problem. In the opening debate in December, 1789, Duport himself maintained that it was enough for the Jews to accept whatever duties the French state might impose upon them as citizens. He added: What if the Jews are faithful to their own laws? For France as a whole it should be enough that they accept their obligations under the civil code of the state. There are, certainly, prejudices against the Jews and they have their own separatist tendencies, but the law can take no notice of either; it must simply give them citizenship in return for their agreement to perform their civic duty.[66] These remarks would have spoken for the dominant view among the authors of the American Constitution, but what Duport said in France in 1789 was not repeated by anyone, not even by Jews, in the course of the French Revolution. Here is the ideological seed of the difference between Jewish experience in America and in Europe in the modern era. For Jews, if for no one else, their right to participate in the new order in France was made conditional on their becoming "new men."

But the insistent question remained, in 1791 and beyond, what kind of "new men"? Those who emancipated the Jews in the hopes of regenerating them did not themselves act consistently. The favorite target of even the most pro-Jewish forces had been the organized Jewish community. In all logic, when the Revolution abolished all the corporations of the *ancien régime* and assumed their debts, and especially when it nationalized the property of the Church in France, it should have added the Jews to these regenerating acts. It did not. Here the makers of the Revolution, for all their passion for the end of Jewish separatism, made one exception to their general rule. The debts of the older Jewish communities were not assumed by the state; the Jewish communal bodies were kept in existence in order to pay off the debts that had been contracted

[66] This was Duport's direct response to Maury; see *Moniteur*, II, 462–63.

during the *ancien régime*.[67] In less tangible fashion, the makers of the Revolution presumed that a special kind of Jewish communal cohesion would continue, at least with respect to the Jewish poor. They assumed that the Jewish rich would continue to exercise direct concern for their own poor. The presence of this concern was used by pro-Jewish forces as an argument for the proposition that equal citizenship for the Jews would not create any new burdens for society.

The anonymous abbé who had argued with Maury had, indeed, said in the most doctrinaire and logical way that the Revolution could ask no question of economic utility of the Jews, but such questions were as much on the minds of the friends of the Jews as of their enemies. How should the new Jew make his living? As a banker or industrialist? As an artisan or farmer? As a peddler or shopkeeper? Whatever the Jew did, there was someone to say that the Revolution had intended for him to do something else that was more regenerative of his nature and more useful to society.

The question of the changes that the Jew was supposed to make in his religion was equally problematic. Everyone had agreed that such change was required and that it was even a condition of the Emancipation, but what changes were necessary? Did the Jews need to prove to the most left-wing of revolutionaries that they were the quickest to abandon all their ancient traditions and adopt the cult of civic virtue? Was it enough to be decently inconspicuous in public by removing all marks of Jewish ritual distinctiveness outside the home? Who, for that matter, was to be the judge as to whether the Jews had, indeed, made adequate changes in their religion, economic conduct, and communal cohesion?

Two roads led from the Revolution. One was paved by the decrees of emancipation. In their ultimate effect in Europe as a whole, they allowed the Jews to enter into society as equal citizens before the law and as participants in the general culture. On this road there appeared a great galaxy of creative spirits who were among the makers of the nineteenth and twentieth centuries. Nonetheless, a certain discomfort was inherent in their situation; it caused pain in the souls of many. This "new Jew" had been born into a society

[67] Szajkowski, *Autonomy and Communal Jewish Debts*, pp. 45–46.

which asked him to keep proving that he was worthy of belonging
to it. Unfortunately, this "new Jew" was never quite told exactly
what he had to prove and before which tribunal. Franz Kafka has
described this phenomenon in his novel *The Trial*. The hero, and
the victim, of this tale is K., who feels burdened by crimes which
he wished he knew how to define and who keeps hoping to find the
judges who would read him the charges, or at least accept his pleas
of guilt.

One wing of the Revolutionary left, represented primarily by the
commune of Paris, had, as we have seen, adopted the cause of the
Jews, but its leaders knew that this attitude was unpopular with the
masses. Godard himself admitted that this was so in a letter to
*Mercure*. He argued that a decree emancipating the Jews should
be passed at that very moment, because it would then be accepted
together with other changes that the masses found more to their
interest: "Decrees which might at this moment be contrary, to a
degree, to the will of the people will not arouse its discontent if
these acts are offered together with other actions which are calculated to assure its well-being." [68] The commune of Paris did not,
however, have to deal directly with any serious local passions against
the Jews, for they were only a handful in Paris at the time. In
eastern France, where the "Jewish problem" really existed, the
leaders of the Revolutionary left were mostly anti-Jewish, even after
September 27, 1791. During the Terror, for example, the administrators of the region of Bas-Rhin were outraged to discover that a Jew
who had died in Strasbourg was being brought to Rosenweiler "in
order to be buried there according to the idiotic laws of rabbinism."
These Jacobins stated very clearly, in a circular letter that they
wrote to all the districts under their jurisdiction, that they were
angry for more than religious reasons: "We are less concerned in
this case about their religious system than about their criminal
antipathy to all citizens who do not belong to their ridiculous cult.
It is to this that you and we ought to pay particular attention."
This desire of a Jewish family to bury one of its members in a
Jewish cemetery then became the occasion for a further outburst:
"Citizens, redouble your watchfulness and your severity! Make the

[68] *Moniteur*, III, 663–64.

Jews give up their swindles and extortions . . . and work with their hands in the workshops and fields . . . We will put them under the supervision of the National Convention and under its authority; we will institute the most severe measures against the detested remnants of a people which has always been both hated and despised." [69]

This was the language of the extreme Jacobins in eastern France; [70] it was to be the post-Christian secularized rhetoric of at least one wing of the revolutionary left in France and all over Europe in the nineteenth and twentieth centuries. The idea that the Jew was irretrievably alien and that any new order for all of society had to defend its purity against him was to recur many times, and in ever more dangerous forms, in the next age.

The debate about the Jewish question on the way to the Revolution, during it, and after it happened, thus produced not only new, modern Jewish intellectuals and an intelligentsia that was willing to accept them. This has been obvious and well known, though our analysis has qualified these conventional assertions with a description of the many ambiguities that surrounded the Emancipation. What has not been noticed is that an anti-Jewish, left-wing intelligentsia arose at the same time. The liberal age in Europe was, indeed, made by the new intellectuals who first appeared in power in the French Revolution. It was to be devastated by the heirs and

[69] Reuss, "L'antisémitisme dans le Bas-Rhin," *REJ*, LXVIII, 263. On the question of Jacobin anti-Semitism Szajkowski has maintained in numerous places in his writings that "the synagogue suffered during the Revolution," but that this was merely a part of a general policy against religion (see, for example, his article "Synagogues during the French Revolution," *JSS*, XX, 215–29). The most Marxist of Jewish historians in this generation, Raphael Mahler, is willing to admit that Jacobin anti-Semitism did exist, but he ascribes it to the "petty bourgeoisie" of eastern France and ignores the hatreds by the peasants (*History of the Jews in the Modern Age*, II, 164–65). My own view is that the left-wing intelligentsia was the crucial force, for it provided a new way in which to express all the older conflicts, both religio-cultural and economic (on *several* class levels).

[70] That the ideas of French anti-Semitism in the nineteenth century bore relation to Voltaire's work was mentioned by Byrnes. who also saw Voltaire as a prime source of Karl Marx's outlook (*Anti-Semitism in Modern France*, pp. 77, 115–18). The question of the anti-Semitism of parts of the European left in the nineteenth century has been studied by Silberner, *Western Socialism and the Jewish Question*, but with no attention to its roots in the eighteenth century and the French Revolution. The subject needs to be looked at again in the light of the suggestions made here.

successors to the anti-Jewish intelligentsia that appeared in the very midst of these events.

The outline of all the modern versions of the "Jewish question," as it was to be defined in the future by both Jews and gentiles, existed in 1791. The glories and the tragedies to come had already been conceived.

# Bibliography

## Manuscript Sources

Archive de la Gironde, Bordeaux, Box V 13.

———— *Registre des délibérations de la Nation Portugaise depuis le II May 1710, tiré des anciens livres pour servir au besoin, lequel registre servira pour y coucher toutes celles qui seront passées de l'avenir dans le corps, commencé du sindicat de sieur David Lameyra à Bordeaux le premier Juin 1753. Le présent registre a été continué jusqu'au 22 Mars 1787, époque de la nomination de Ab. Furtado l'ainé pour syndic, les fonctions duquel ont duré jusqu'au mois de Mars 1788* (in Spanish and French), 138 leaves.

———— *Répertoire des délibérations de la nation juive depuis 1710 jusqu'au février 1790* (index to *Registre*, with additional entries covering the period 1787 to 1790).

Archives Nationales de France, Paris, *Dénombrement de la population juive*, 1808, F19-11023.

———— *Mémoire pour la nation juive établie en Alsace, sur son état actuel et la necessité d'y apporter un remède*, F12 854B.

Bibliothèque Municipal de Bayonne, Box GG 229.

———— Minutes of the hôtel de ville, Folio BB 60.

British Museum, Haguenau collection, MS Oriental 01233.

Cohen Family, Letter of September 15, 1789, from Solomon Lopes Dubec to Zalkind-Hourwitz.

Ecole Rabbinque, Paris, MS No. 64, *Novellae* by Abraham Broda, Jonathan Eibschütz, Samuel Hillman, and others, 135 pp.

———— No. 68, *Novellae* by Tevele Scheuer and Meyer Charleville.

———— No. 72, *Commentaries on the Pentateuch*, by Jonathan Eibeschütz and Jacob Joshua (Falk), 74 pp.

———— No. 73, *Novellae and sermons*, by Eibeschütz, Broda, and others.

———— No. 82, *Novellae*, by Hillman, Eibeschütz, and Wolf Pousweiler, 35 pp.

———— No. 148, *Novellae*, by Charleville, 194 pp.

Jewish Theological Seminary, New York, MS 01679, *Pinkas* of Metz (in Hebrew and Yiddish), 1749–89, 144 leaves, folio.

―――― MS uncatalogued, Decrees of the rabbinic court in Niedernai, for 1775–81 and 1781–83, 2 vols., folio.

―――― MS 01922, 1 leaf, in re tax assessments for the *pays messin* for 1777.

―――― MS 01565, Tax list of the Jews of Metz, 1792–93.

―――― MS uncatalogued, Decree by the *parlement* of the Provence, September 20, 1683.

―――― MS uncatalogued box, Business papers of Alexander Hess (in Yiddish and French), mid-eighteenth century.

―――― MS uncatalogued, Business journal of Jacob Marig (?), "Garçon Juif," for 1751–55, 51 leaves.

―――― MS uncatalogued, Two tax rolls for Jews of *pays messin*, 1756–58 and 1772.

―――― MS uncatalogued, Tax roll for the *pays messin* for 1772.

―――― MS uncatalogued, Tax roll for the *pays messin* for 1785.

―――― MS uncatalogued, Six leaves of accounts of the Jewish Charity of Metz (in Hebrew), mid-eighteenth century (n.d.).

―――― MS uncatalogued, Anonymous complaint against the Jews of Metz, 1745.

―――― MS uncatalogued, dated September 30, 1790, report from Colmar to *Assemblée Nationale* on the Jews of eastern France, 16 pp.

Schlamme Collection, Mulhouse, No. 1, *Novellae and sermons*, by Raphael Cohen of Bischheim, 120 pp.

Strasbourg University, No. 12, *Novellae*, by Eibeschütz, Broda, Hillman, and others, 97 pp.

―――― No. 13, *Novellae*, by Eibeschütz, Hillman, and others.

―――― No. 57, *Novellae*, by Wolf of Pousweiler, 41 pp.

―――― No. 79, *Novellae*, by Eibeschütz, Hillman, and others, 102 pp.

―――― No. 99, *Catalogue* of the books of Jacob Meyer.

Yiddish Scientific Institute (YIVO), Decisions of the rabbinic court in Metz, 2 folio vols., uncatalogued; some 1,500 decisions, 1771–89.

### Printed Primary Sources

*Adresse des Juifs alsaciens au peuple d'Alsace*, 6 pp., n.p. [1790].

*Adresse présentée à l'Assemblée Nationale le 26 Août 1789, par les Juifs résidans à Paris*, 10 pp. [Paris, 1789].

*Adresse présentée à l'Assemblée Nationale, le 31 Août 1789, par les députés réunis des Juifs établis à Metz, dans les Trois Evêchés, en Alsace et en Lorraine*, 18 pp., n.p. [1789].

D'Alembert, Jean le Rond, *Oeuvres philosophiques, historiques et littéraires*, Vol. X, Paris, an XIII [1805].

*L'Ami du peuple ou le publiciste parisien*, No. 77, December 25, 1789.

Annet, Peter, *David, the History of the Man after God's Own Heart*, London, 1761.

Anonymous, *Essais historiques et critiques sur les Juifs anciens et modernes: ou supplément aux moeurs des Israélites de M. l'Abbé Fleuri*, 4 vols., Lyon, 1771.

—————— *L'intolerance éclairée ou lettres critiques d'un vicaire à l'auteur de la brochure intitulée "les Protestans déboutés de leurs prétentions,"* n.p., 1777.

—————— *Lettres Juives du Célèbre Mendels-Sohn, philosophe de Berlin; avec les remarques et réponses de Monsieur le Docteur Kölble et autres savants hommes, recueil mémorable concernant le Judaisme*, Frankfurt and La Haye, 1771.

—————— *Réflexions critiques sur l'Apologie pour la nation juive, par un Vénitien*, London, 1768.

—————— *Sefat Emet ve-Lashon Zehurit* [Amsterdam], 1752.

—————— *Ueber die Vertreibung der Juden*, 16 pp., n.p., 1790.

*A nosseigneurs de parlement, supplient humblement les syndics de la communauté de Juifs de cette ville*, Metz, 1765,

[D'Argens, Jean Baptiste de Boyer], *Lettres Juives, ou correspondance philosophique, historique et critique, entre un Juif voyageur à Paris et ses correspondans en divers endroits*, 6 vols., La Haye, 1736–37.

—————— *Lettres cabalistiques, ou correspondance philosophique, historique et critique entre deux cabalistes, divers esprits élementaires et le seigneur Astaroth*, La Haye, 1737.

—————— *Mémoires du Comte Vaxere, ou le Faux Rabbin*, 2d ed., Amsterdam, 1749.

*Arrest du conseil du roy, du 20 février 1731, qui casse deux arrets rendus au parlement de Dijon, le 22 juin 1724 et 29 juillet 1730*, 4 pp., Dijon, 1731.

Ashkenazi, Gershon, *Hiddushei ha-Gershuni*, Frankfurt am Main, 1710.

Azulai, Hayyim Joseph David, *Maagal Tov ha-Shalem*, ed. Aaron Freimann, Jerusalem, 1934.

Basnage de Beauval, Henri, *Tolérance des religions*, Rotterdam, 1684.

Basnage de Beauval, Jacques, *Histoire des Juifs depuis Jésus-Christ jusqu'à présent*, 2d ed., 15 vols., La Haye, 1716.

Bayle, Pierre, *Dictionnaire historique et critique*, 5 vols., Paris, 1820.

Berr, Berr-Isaac, *Lettre du sr. Berr-Isaac Berr, négociant à Nancy . . . à monseigneur l'évêque de Nancy député à l'Assemblée Nationale*, 20 pp. n.p., 1790.

Berr, Jacob, *Lettre du sr. Jacob Berr, juif, maître en chirurgie à Nancy, à monseigneur l'évêque de Nancy, député à l'Assemblée Nationale, pour servir de réfutation de quelques erreurs qui se trouvent dans celle adressée à ce prélat par le Sr. Berr-Isaac Berr* [Nancy], 1790.

Bing, Isaiah Berr, *Lettre du Sr. I. B. B. Juif de Metz, à l'auteur anonyme d'un écrit intitulé: "Le cri du citoyen contre les Juifs de Metz,"* Metz, 1787; 2d ed., n.p., 1805.

*Bibliothèque des Sciences et des Beaux Arts,* Vol. XVIII, La Haye, 1762.

Bodin, Jean, *Joannis Bodini Colloquium Heptaplomeres de rerum sublimium arcanis abditis,* ed. Ludwig Noack, Schwerin, 1857.

────── *Les six livres de la république,* Paris, 1576.

Boissi, Louis Michel de, *Dissertations critiques pour servir à d'éclaircissemens à l'histoire des Juifs . . . et de supplément à l'histoire de M. Basnage,* 2 vols., Paris, 1785.

Bossuet, Jacques Benigne, *Discours,* ed. Armand Gasté, 2 vols., n.p., 1885.

Cahen, Oury Phoebus, *Halakhah Berurah,* Metz, 1792.

Calmet, Augustin, *Dictionnaire historique, critique, chronologique, géographique et littéral de la Bible,* 2 vols., Paris, 1722.

────── *Histoire de l'Ancien et du Nouveau Testament et des Juifs pour servir d'introduction à l'histoire écclésiastique de M. l'Abbé Fleury,* "new and corrected edition" in 3 vols., Paris, 1737.

*Certificats que rapportent les Srs. Dalpuget, beau-père et gendre, justificatifs de leur ancienne résidence à Bordeaux, de la regularité et probité de leur commerce, de l'exactitude à leur paymens et engagements, de la satisfaction des seigneurs, communautés et particuliers qui se sont pourvus chez eux de différentes étoffes et marchandises, et enfin de l'avantage qu'il y auroit pour la province et habitans de Bordeaux qu'ils y fussent rétablis,* Bordeaux, 1737. (JTS copy was signed by 42 names.)

Chandler, Samuel, *A Critical History of the Life of David,* London, 1766.

Charron, Pierre, *De la sagesse,* Paris, 1657.

Chavanettes, Pernin des, *Discours sur l'histoire moderne pour servir de suite aux discours sur l'histoire des Juifs et sur l'histoire ancienne,* Paris, 1769.

Clermont-Tonnerre, Cte. Stanislas de, *Opinion relativement aux persécutions qui menacent les Juifs d'Alsace,* 4 pp., Versailles [1789].

Colbert, Jean Baptiste, *Lettres, instructions et de Colbert* (7 vols. in 9), ed. Pierre Clément, Paris, 1863–73.

Collins, Anthony, *Discourse on Freethinking,* London, 1713.

────── *Examen des prophéties qui servent de fondement á la religion chrétienne,* tr. d'Holbach, London, 1768.

[Cordova, Joshua Hezekiah de], *Emet ve-Emunah, Reason and Faith, or Philosophical Absurdities and the Necessity of Revelation, intended to promote faith among the infidels and the unbounded exercise of humanity among all religious men, by one of the sons of Abraham to his brethren,* Philadelphia, 1791.

Debourge, Jean Claude Antoine, *Discours prononcé le 30 Janvier* [1790] *dans l'assemblée générale des représentans de la commune par M. Debourge l'un des représentans de la commune à l'occasion dé la demande faite, le 27, par les Juifs de Paris*, 15 pp. [Paris, 1790].

*Dénombrement général des Juifs d'Alsace*, Colmar, 1785.

Diderot, Denis, *Oeuvres complètes*, ed. Assézat, 20 vols., Paris, 1875 ff.

*Discours des députés des Juifs des provinces des Evêchés, d'Alsace et de Lorraine, prononcé à la barre de l'Assemblée Nationale par le Sieur Berr-Isaac-Berr, l'un des députés de la Lorraine, et l'extrait du procès-verbal de l'Assemblée Nationale y relatif*, 8 pp., Paris, 1789.

Dohm, Christian Wilhelm, *Ueber die buergerliche Verbesserung der Juden*, Berlin and Stettin, 1781.

———— *De la réforme politique des Juifs*, Dessau, 1782.

[Dubayet, Jean Baptiste Annibal Aubert ?], *Le cri du citoyen contre les Juifs de Metz. par un capitaine d'infanterie*, Lausanne (Metz), 1786.

*Edit du roi portant l'exemption des droits de péage corporel sur les Juifs*, 4 pp., Colmar, 1784.

Eibeschütz, Jonathan, *Luchot Edut*, Altona, 1755.

———— *Sefer Yaarot Devash*, 2 vols., Karlsruhe, 1779–82.

*Encyclopédie*, 1st ed., 18 vols., Paris, 1751–65; second ed., 36 vols., Lausanne and Berne, 1781.

Ensheim, Moses, *Shalosh Hiddot*, Metz, 1787.

*Extract from the minutes of the province (Alsace), of the meeting of the representatives of the communites on Iyyar 21, 5537* (in Hebrew and Yiddish), 8 pp.

*Extrait des registres du Conseil souverain d'Alsace*, du 6 mai 1786, Colmar, 1788 (in JTS).

*Extrait des registres du Conseil souverain d'Alsace*, du 13 décembre, 1788, Colmar, 1788 (in JTS).

[Fare, Anne-Louis Henry de la], *Opinion de M. l'évêque de Nancy, député de Lorraine, sur l'admissibilité des Juifs à la plenitude de l'état civil et des droits de citoyens actifs*, 14 pp., Paris, 1790.

Fleury, Claude, *Les moeurs des Israélites*, Paris, 1681.

———— *Les moeurs des Israélites et des Chrétiens*, Paris, 1766.

[Francia de Beaufleury, Louis], M. L. F. D. B., *Projets de bienfaisance et de patriotisme pour la ville de Bordeaux, et pour toutes les villes et gros bourgs du royaume*, Paris and Bordeaux, 1783.

———— *Supplément au projets de bienfaisance et de patriotisme*, Paris, 1785.

Fresnay, Nicholas Lenglet du, *Plan de l'histoire générale et particulière de la monarchie française*, Vol. II, Paris, 1753.

Gayot de Pitaval, François, *Causes célèbres et intéressantes*, Vol. XX, La Haye, 1745.

Ginzrot, Sohn, *Antwort über eine Schrift betitelt: Bericht welcher in der Gesellschaft der Freunde der Constitution über die Frage vorgelesen wurde: "Können die Juden in Elsass des Bürgerrechts theilhaftig werden?" und zur widerlegung der darinn vorkommenden Stellen eine, Biedermanns unwürdig, den der edle Name Bürgerfreund zieren sollte,* 15 pp. [Strasbourg], 1790.

Godard, Jacques, *Discours prononcé le 28 janvier 1790 par M. Godard, avocat au parlement, l'un des représentans de la commune, en présentant à l'assemblée générale de la commune une députation des Juifs de Paris,* 12 pp., Paris, 1790.

Goudar, Ange, *Les intérêts de la France mal entendus,* 2 vols., Amsterdam, 1756.

Grégoire, Henri, *Essai sur la régéneration physique, morale et politique des Juifs,* Metz, 1789.

——— *Histoire de sectes religieuses,* 2 vols., Paris, 1810.

——— *Mémoires de Grégoire,* ed. M. H. Carnot, 2 vols., Paris, 1837.

——— *Motion en faveur des Juifs par M. Grégoire, curé d'Embermenil, député de Nancy, précédée d'une notice historique sur les persécutions qu'ils viennent d'essuyer en divers lieux, notamment en Alsace, et sur l'admission de leurs députés à la barre de l'Assemblée Nationale,* xvi, 47 pp., Paris, 1789.

[Gradis, David], *Courte dissertation sur l'origine du monde ou refutation du système de la création,* Bordeaux, an VI (1797).

D. G. [David Gradis], *Discussions philosophiques sur la préexistence de la matière, sur la providence divine, et accessoirement contre l'athéisme,* Paris and Bordeaux an VIII (1799).

——— *Discussions philosophiques sur l'athéisme,* Paris and Bordeaux, an XII (1803).

——— *Essai de philosophie rationelle sur l'origine des choses et sur leur éternité future,* Paris and Bordeaux, an X (1801).

Gravelle, Charles, *Politiques royales,* Lyon, 1596.

[Guénée, Antoine], *Lettres de quelques Juifs portugais et allemands à M. de Voltaire,* 2d ed., Paris, 1769.

Hell, François J. A., *Observations d'un alsacien sur l'affaire présente des Juifs d'Alsace,* Frankfurt, 1779.

Hénault, Charles Jean François, *Nouvel abrégé chronologique de l'histoire de France jusqu'à la mort de Louis XIV,* 2 vols., Paris, 1768.

[D'Holbach, Paul Henri Dietrich, tr.], *David, ou l'histoire de l'homme selon le coeur de Dieu,* London, 1768.

[D'Holbach?], "Abbé Bernier," *Théologie portative,* London, 1767.

——— *L'Esprit du Judaisme,* London, 1770.

Hume, David, *Essays,* Oxford, 1963.

Lacretelle, Pierre Louis, *Plaidoyer pour deux Juifs de Metz contre l'hôtel de ville et le corps de marchands de Thionville.* Textes de 1777 et de 1823, ed. André Spire, Paris, 1928.

Laissac, de, capitaine au régiment de Limousin, *Lettre à M. Le Chapellier, membre de l'Assemblée Nationale,* 48 pp., Paris, 1790.

L., Abbé [Lomourette, Antoine Adrien], *Observations sur l'état civil des des Juifs, adressées à l'Assemblée Nationale*, 20 pp., Paris, 1790.

Lançon, Nicolas François, *Recueil des lois, coûtumes et usages observés par les Juifs de Metz*, Metz, 1786.

*Lettre adressée à M. Grégoire, curé d'Embermeénil, député de Nancy, par les députés de la nation juive portugaise de Bordeaux*, 4 pp., Versailles [1789].

*Lettres patentes et autres pièces en faveur des Juifs Portugais* [perhaps edited by J. R. Péreire], 46 pp., Paris, 1753.

*Lettres patentes du Roy en faveur des Juifs ou nouveaux Chrétiens avignonois, établis à Bordeaux. données à Versailles en moi de mai 1759*, Bordeaux, n.d.

*Lettres-patentes du Roi, confirmatives de privilèges, dont les Juifs Portugais jouissent en France depuis 1550; données à Versailles, au mois de juin 1776*, Bordeaux, 1781.

*Lettres patentes du Roi, portant règlement concernant les Juifs d'Alsace, du 10 Juillet 1784*, Colmar, 1786.

Limborch, Philipp van, *De veritate religionis Christianae, amica collatio cum eriditio Judaeo*, Gauda, 1687.

Lion, Asser, *Turei Even*, Metz, 1781.

A. M. J. M. D. [Liron, Jean], *Dissertation sur le temps de l'établissement des Juifs en France, où on examine ce que M. Basnage a écrit sur cette matière* . . . Paris, 1708.

Lisle de Sales, Jean Baptiste Nicolas de, *De la philosophie de la nature*, Amsterdam, 1770.

Locke, John, *The Second Treatise of Civil Government and a Letter Concerning Toleration*, ed. J. W. Gough, London, 1946.

Mably, Joseph de, *Oeuvres*, Vol. 8, Paris, 1795.

[Malesherbes, Chrétien-Guillaume Lamoignon de], *Second mémoire sur le mariage des Protestans*, 2d ed., London, 1787.

[Malot, François], *Dissertation sur l'époque du rappel des Juifs*, Avignon(?), 1776.

——— *Dissertation sur l'époque du rappel des Juifs*, "second edition," Paris, 1779.

——— *Suite et défense de la dissertation sur l'époque du rappel des Juifs*, Paris(?) [1782].

*ha-Meassef*, Vols. 1–3, Königsberg, 1784–86; Vol. 4, Berlin, 1788; Vol. 5, Berlin, 1789; Vol. 6, Berlin, 1790.

Meldola, David, *Divrei David*, Amsterdam, 1753.

Meldola, Raphael, *Mayyim Rabbim*, 4 vols., Amsterdam, 1737.

——— *Parshat ha-Ibbur*, 24 pp., Amsterdam, 1734.

*Mémoire justificatif pour le Sieur Cerf Beer, entrepeneur général des fourrages, pour le service des troupes, dans les provinces des Trois-Evêchés, Lorraine, Alsace et Franche-Comté*, 79 pp., Metz, 1783.

*Mémoire des marchands boutiquiers de Bordeaux*, n.d. [but in the 1730s].

*Mémoire particulier pour la communauté des Juifs établis à Metz redigé par Isaac Beer Bing, l'un des membres de cette communauté*, n.p. [1789].

*Mémoire pour les Juifs de Lunéville et de Sarguemines, à nosseigneurs de l'Assemblée Nationale*, 8 pp., n.p. [1789].

Mendelssohn, Moses, *Gesammelte Schriften*, ed. G. B. Mendelssohn, 7 vols., Leipzig, 1843–45.

———— *Phédon;* Berlin, 1772 (tr. Burja); Paris and Bayeux, 1772 (tr. Junker).

———— *Phédon*, tr. into Hebrew by Isaiah Berr Bing, Berlin, 1786.

———— *Small Writings on Jews and Judaism* (in Hebrew), Tel Aviv, 1947.

Mirabaud, Jean Baptiste de, *Opinions des anciens sur les Juifs . . . réflexions impartiales sur l'Evangile*, London, 1769.

Mirabeau, Honore Gabriel Riquetti, Marquis de, *De la monarchie Prussienne sous Frédéric le grand*, 4 vols., London, 1788.

———— *Sur Moses Mendelssohn, sur la réforme politique des Juifs. Et en particulier sur la révolution tentée en leur faveur en 1753 dans la Grande Bretagne*, London, 1787.

[Mirabeau, Victor de Riquetti, Marquis de], *Théorie de l'impôt*, n.p., 1760.

————and François Quesnay], *Philosophie rurale*, 1 vol. ed., Amsterdam, 1763.

Modène, Léon de, *Cérémonies et coustumes qui s'exercent aujourd'hui parmi les Juifs*, traduites de l'italien de Léon de Modène . . . par Don Recared Scimeon (Richard Simon), Paris, 1674.

*Moniteur universel, Réimpression de l'ancien Moniteur, seule histoire authentique et inaltérée de la révolution française depuis la réunion des Etats-Généraux jusqu'au Consulat (mai 1789–novembre 1799) avec des notes explicatives*, Vols. I–IX (first series), Paris, 1847–50.

Montesquieu, Charles-Louis de Secondat, *Oeuvres complètes*, ed. Roger Caillois, 2 vols., Paris, 1949.

*The Monthly Review*, Vol. XXVIII, London, 1763.

*Nouveau mémoire pour les Juifs de Lunéville et de Sarguemines, présenté à l'Assemblée Nationale, le 26 février, 1790*, 8 pp., Paris [1790].

*Nouvelle adresse des Juifs à l'Assemblée Nationale, 24 décembre 1789*, 4 pp., Paris, [1789].

Orobio de Castro, Isaac, *Certamen philosophicum propugnatum veritatis divinae ac naturalis adversus Jo. Bredemburgh*, Amsterdam, 1689.

———— *Israel vengé où exposition naturelle des prophéties hébraiques que les Chrétiens appliquent à Jésus, leur prétendu messie*, London, 1770.

———— *La observancia de la divina ley de Mosseh*, ed. Moses Bensabat Amzalek, Coimbra, 1925.

Pascal, Blaise, *Pensées*, ed. Victor Girand, Paris, n.d.

Pastoret, Emile Claude de, *Moyse considéré comme législateur et comme moraliste*, Paris, 1788.

—— *Zoroastre, Confucius et Mahomet comparés comme sectaires, législateurs et moralistes*, 2d ed., Paris, 1788.

Péreire, Jacob Rodrigues, *Lettre Circulaire*, 2 pp., Paris, 1767.

—— *Mémoire que M. J. R. Péreire a lu dans la séance de l'Académie royale des sciences du 11 Juin 1749 et dans lequel, en présentant à cette compagnie un jeune sourd et muet de naissance, il expose avec quel succès il lui a appris à parler.*

—— *Observations sur treize des principales langues de l'Europe*, 1st part of 1st vol. (no more appeared), Paris, 1779.

—— *Séconde lettre circulaire en défense des Juifs Portugais*, signed: Péreire, September 30, 1767, Paris.

*Pétition des Juifs établis en France, adressée à l'Assemblée Nationale, le 28 janvier 1790 sur l'ajournement du 24 décembre 1789*, iv, 107 pp., Paris, 1790.

Peyrère, Isaac de la, *Du rappel des Juifs*, n.p., 1643.

—— *Systema, theologicum ex praeadamitarum hypothesi*, n.p., 1655.

Pflieger, Jean Adam, *Réflexions sur les Juifs d'Alsace*, 20 pp., Paris, 1790.

[Pinto, Isaac de], *Apologie pour la nation juive, où reflexions critiques sur le premier chapitre du VIIᵉ tome des oeuvres de M. de Voltaire au sujet des Juifs. Par l'auteur de "l'Essai sur le luxe,"* Amsterdam, 1762.

—— *Essay on Luxury* (anonymous tr.), London, 1766.

—— *Letters on the American Troubles* (anonymous tr. from French), London, 1776.

—— *Précis des arguments contre les matérialistes*, Amsterdam, 1774.

—— *Réflexions critique sur le premier chapitre du VIIᵉ tome des oeuvres de monsieur de Voltaire, au sujet des Juifs*, Paris, n.d. [but 1762].

—— *Réponse de Pinto aux observations d'un homme impartial*, La Haye, 1776.

—— *Réponses à deux critiques qui ont été faits de l'apologie de la nation juive dans le Monthly Review et dans la Bibliothèque des Sciences et des Arts*, La Haye, 1766.

—— *Traité de la circulation et du credit*, Amsterdam, 1771. This volume contains also *Lettre sur la jalousie du commerce*, pp. 277–88; *Table ou exposé de ce qu'on appelle le commerce, ou plutôt le jeu d'actions, en Hollande*, pp. 291–312; *Méthode dont on se sert en Hollande pour faire la perception des taxes, et des impôts sur les biens fonds*, pp. 313–20; *Essai sur le luxe*, pp. 323–42.

*Plaidoyer pour la demoiselle Sara Mendes d'Acosta, épouse du sieur Peixotto, contre le sieur Peixotto, son mari* [Paris], 1779.

*Pour les Juifs établis en Alsace*, 4 pp., 1716.

Rabinowitz, A. Z., *Zichronot Glückel* (in Hebrew), Tel Aviv, 1929.

Rapport lu à l'assemblée de la société des amis de la constitution, le 27 février 1790, sur la question de l'état civil des juifs d'Alsace, 32 pp. [Strasbourg, 1790].

Recueil de lettres patentes, et autres pièces en faveur des Juifs portugais contenant leurs privilèges en France [anonymous but ed. J. R. Péreire], 19 pp., Paris, 1765.

Reischer, Jacob, Shevut Yaacov, Vol. 3, Metz, 1789.

Requête des marchands et négocians de Paris, contre l'admission des Juifs, Paris, 1767.

Requête au roi pour les Juifs de Sarrelouis, 28 pp., Paris, 1777.

Révolutions de France et de Brabant, No. 5, December 28, 1789.

Richard, C. L., ed., Bibliothèque sacrée, Vols. I–V, Paris, 1762; Vol. VI, Paris, 1765.

———— Lettre du rabbin de la synagogue des Juifs de Metz au sieur Liefman Calmer (pamphlet), 10 pp., Paris, 1777.

———— Les Protestants déboutés le leurs prétentions, 2d ed., Paris, 1776.

———— Recueil des pièces intéressantes sur les deux questions célèbres, savoir si un Juif converti au christianisme peut épousé une fille chrétienne et si un Juif endourci devenu baron peut nommer aux cononicats d'une collégiale de sa baronie, Paris, 1779.

———— Voltaire parmi les ombres, Paris, 1775; 2d ed., Paris, 1776.

Rondet, Laurent Etienne, Dissertation sur le rappel des Juifs, Paris, 1777.

———— Seconde lettre de l'Auteur de la Dissertation sur l'epoque du rappel des Juifs, Paris (?), 1782.

———— Supplément à la dissertation sur le rappel des Juifs, Paris, 1780.

Rousseau, Jean-Jacques, Emile, ed. P. T. Masson, Freibourg, 1914.

Royal Society of Metz, broadsheet announcement of essay contests for 1786 and 1787, 2 pp., Metz, 1785.

Saint-Pierre, Charles Irénée Castel, Abbé de, Projet pour rendre la paix perpétuelle en Europe, 2 vols., Utrecht, 1713.

Salachli, Jean, Apologie de l'histoire du peuple Juif suivant les auteurs sacrés, Geneva and Lausanne, 1770.

Schmoll, J. C., ed., Sammlung von Aufsatzen verschiedener Verfasser besonders für Freunde der Kameralwissenschaften und der Staatswirtschaft, Leipzig, 1781.

Senger, M., L'Esprit des lois mosaiques, Bordeaux, 1785.

Simon, Richard, Histoire critique du vieux testament, Rotterdam, 1685.

———— Juifs de Metz, Paris, 1670.

———— Lettres choisies, 4 vols., Amsterdam, 1730.

Spinoza, Benedict de, The Chief Works of Benedict de Spinoza, tr. R. H. M. Elwes, Vol. I, New York, 1955.

Takkanot ha-Kehillah, Amsterdam, 1736.

Takkanot li-Seudah, Amsterdam, 1722.

Thiéry, Adolphe, Dissertation sur cette question: est-il des moyens de *rendre les Juifs plus heureux et plus utiles en France?* . . . Paris, 1788.

Tindal, Matthew, *Christianity as Old as Creation*, London, 1730.

Treni, Akiba, *Mayyan Ganim*, Metz, 1767.

*Très humble et très respectueuse adresse qui présente à l'Assemblée Nationale la commune toute entière de la ville de Strasbourg*, 20 pp., Paris [1790].

Turgot, Anne-Robert Jacques, *Oeuvres de Turgot et documents le concernant*, ed. Gustave Schelle, 5 vols., Paris, 1913–23.

[Valabrègue, Israel Bernard de], *Lettre ou réflexions d'un milord à son correspondant à Paris, au sujet de la requête des marchands des six-corps, contre l'admission des Juifs aux brevets*. London [Paris?], 1767.

Venture, Mordecai, *Patshegen Ketav*, Amsterdam, 1770.

—— *Prières*, 4 vols., Nice, 1772–83.

Voltaire, François Marie Arouet de, *Correspondence*, ed. Theodore Besterman, Geneva, 1953 ff.

—— *Oeuvres complètes*, 52 vols., ed. Louis Moland, Paris, 1877–85.

—— *Philosophical Dictionary*, 2 vols., ed. and tr. Peter Gay, New York, 1962.

Weisel, N. H., *Instruction salutaire adressée aux communautés juives de l'empire, par le célèbre Hartwic Wessely, Juif de Berlin*, 2d ed., Paris, 1790 (1st ed., Paris, 1782), tr. Berr Isaac Berr.

Worms, Jacob, *Meorei Or*, Vols. 1–3, Metz, 1789–92.

Young, Arthur, *Letters Concerning the Present State of the French Nation*, London, 1769.

Zalkind-Hourwitz, *Apologie des Juifs*, Paris, 1789.

## Secondary Sources

Anchel, Robert, "The Early History of the Jewish Quarters in Paris," *JSS*, II (1940), 45–60.

—— *Les Juifs de France*, Paris, 1946.

—— "Les Juifs à Paris au XVIIIᵉ siècle," *Bulletin de la société de l'histoire de Paris et de l'île de France*, LVIII (1931), 76–78; LIX (1932), 9–23.

—— *Napoléon et les Juifs*, Paris, 1928.

Anonymous, "Bossuet et les Juifs de Metz," *AIF*, XCII (1931), 178–79.

—— *Ha-Sifrut ha-Yaffah be-Ivrit*, Jerusalem, 1927.

—— "Juifs Tudesques et Allemands à Bordeaux, 1762–1763," *Archive de la Gironde*, XLVIII (1913), 583–88.

Arendt, Hannah, *The Origins of Totalitarianism*, New York, 1951.

Aron, Maurice, "Le duc de Lorraine Léopold et les Juifs," *REJ*, XXXIV (1897), 107–16.

Aubery, Pierre, "Voltaire et les Juifs, ironie et demystification," *Studies on Voltaire and the Eighteenth Century*, XXIV (1963), 67–79.

Bachelier, M. L., *Histoire du commerce de Bordeaux*, Bordeaux, 1862.

Baer, Fritz, *Das Protokollbuch der Landjudenschaft des Herzogtums Kleve*, Berlin, 1922.

Baron, Salo W., *The Jewish Community*, 3 vols., Philadelphia, 1943.

————— "Newer Approaches to Jewish Emancipation," *Diogenes*, No. 29 (Spring, 1960), pp. 56–81.

————— *A Social and Religious History of the Jews*, 2d ed., Vol. X, New York, 1965.

Bégin, F. A., "Voyage de Louis XV à Metz en 1744," *AIF*, IV (1843), 734–36.

Beik, Paul H., *A Judgment of the Old Regime*, New York, 1944.

Ben Lévi, G., *Mémoires d'un colporteur juif en Lorraine*, *AIF*, II (1841), 686–91; III (1842), 459–65.

Bergasse, Louis, *Histoire du commerce de Marseilles*, Vol. IV, part I, Marseilles, 1954.

Bethencourt, Cardozo de, "Le trésor des Juifs Stephardim; notes sur les familles françaises israélites du rite portugais," *REJ*, XX (1890), 278–300; XXV (1892), 97–110, 235–45; XXVI (1893), 240–56.

Betting de Lancastel, *Considérations sur l'état des Juifs dans la société chrétienne*, Strasbourg, 1824.

Bloch, Camille, "Un épisode de l'histoire commerciale des Juifs (comtadins) en Languedoc (1738)," *REJ*, XXIV (1892), 272–80.

————— "L'opinion publique et les Juifs au XVIIIᵉ siècle en France," *REJ*, XXXV (1897), 112–14.

Bloch, Joseph, "Le cimetière juif de Haguenau," *REJ*, CXI (1951–52), 142–86.

Bloom, Herbert T., *The Economic Activities of the Jews in Amsterdam in the Seventeenth and Eighteenth Centuries*, Williamsport, 1937.

Blumenkranz, Bernhard, *Bibliographie des Juifs en France*, Paris, 1961.

Braude, Azriel Meier, *The Broda Family* (in Hebrew), Warsaw, 1938.

Brav, Stanley R., "Jews and Judaism in *The Jewish Spy*," *SBB*, IV (1960), 133–41.

Brummer, Rudolph, *Studien zur Französischen Aufklärungsliteratur, in Anschlusz an J. A. Naigeon*, Breslau, 1932.

Brunschvicg, Léon, "Les Juifs en Bretagne au XVIIIᵉ siècle," *REJ*, XXXIII (1896), 88–121.

————— "Les Juifs de Nantes et du pays nantais," *REJ*, XIV (1887), 80–91; XVII (1888), 123–42; XIX (1889), 294–305.

Bush, N. R., *The Marquis d'Argens and his Philosophical Correspondence*, Ann Arbor, 1953.

Byrnes, Robert F., *Antisemitism in Modern France*, Vol. 1, New Brunswick, 1950.

Cahen, Abraham, "L'émancipation des Juifs devant la Société royale des sciences et des arts de Metz en 1787 et M. Roederer," *REJ*, I (1880), 83–104.

—— "Enseignement obligatoire edicté par la communauté israélite de Metz (1689)," *REJ*, II (1881)), 303–305.

—— "Les Juifs dans les colonies françaises au XVIIIᵉ siècle," *REJ*, IV (1882), 127–45, 236–48; V (1882), 68–92, 258–72.

—— "Le rabbinat de Metz pendant la période française, 1567–1871," *REJ*, VII (1883), 103–15, 204–26; VIII (1884), 255–74; XII (1886), 283–97; XIII (1886), 105–26.

—— "Règlements somptuaires de la communauté juive de Metz à la fin du XVIIᵉ siècle, 1690–1697," *Annuaire de la société des études juives*, I (1881), 75–121.

Cahen, Samuel, "De la littérature hébraique et juive en France," *AIF*, I (1840), 33–52.

Carmoly, E., "Bemerkungen zur Geschichte der Metzer Rabbinat von Tsarfati," *Israelitische Annalen*, II (1840), 61–62, 80–81, 96, 185–86.

—— *Biographies des Israélites de France*, Frankfurt, 1868.

—— *La France Israélite, mémoires pour servir à l'histoire de notre littérature*, Frankfurt, 1858.

—— *Toledot: Gedolei Yisrael*, Metz, 1828.

—— "De la typographie hébraique à Metz," *Revue orientale*, III (1843/4), 209–15, 282–89.

Cassirer, Ernst, *The Philosophy of the Enlightenment*, Princeton, 1951.

Charpentier, Genevieve, *Les relations économiques entre Bordeaux et les Antilles au XVIIIᵉ siècle*, Bordeaux, 1937.

Chatelat, Paul, *Etude sur Du Guet*, Paris, 1899.

Cirot, Georges, "Les Juifs de Bordeaux, leur situation morale et sociale de 1550 à la Révolution," *RHB*, II (1909), 368–82; IV (1911), 145–67; VII (1914), 353–70; VIII (1915), 22–38, 169–85, 267–75; IX (1916), 23–36, 203–20; XI (1918), 129–42, 200–207; XII (1919), 14–28; XXIX (1936), 209–19; XXXI (1938), 63–75, 119–27, 162–71; XXXII (1939), 15–21, 60–66.

—— *Recherches sur les Juifs espagnols et portugais à Bordeaux*, Bordeaux, 1920.

Clément, Roger, *La condition des Juifs de Metz dans l'ancien régime*, Paris, 1903.

Clough, Shepard B., *France, A History of National Economics, 1789–1939*, New York, 1939.

—— and Charles W. Cole, *Economic History of Europe*, 3d ed., Boston, 1952.

Cobban, Alfred, *In Search of Humanity*, New York, 1960.

Cole, Charles W., *Colbert and a Century of French Mercantilism*, 2 vols., New York, 1939.

Cole, Charles W., *French Mercantilist Doctrines before Colbert*, New York, 1931.

Cole, Hubert, *First Gentleman of the Bedchamber; the Life of Louis François-Arnaud, maréchal duc de Richelieu*, New York, 1965.

Cremieux, Ad., "Pour contribuer à l'histoire de l'accession des Juifs à la qualité de citoyen francais," *REJ*, XCV (1933), 44–53.

Dakin, Douglas, *Turgot and the Ancien Régime in France*, London, 1939.

Darlow, H., and N. F. Moule, *Historical Catalogue of Printed Editions of Holy Scriptures*, London, 1903.

Davidson, Philip, *Propaganda and the American Revolution, 1763–1783*, Chapel Hill, 1941.

Detcheverry, Arnaud, *Histoire des Israélites de Bordeaux*, Bordeaux, 1850.

Dianous, Jean de, "Les communautés juives du Comtat Venaissin et de l'état d'Avignon d'après leurs statuts (1490–1790)," *Ecole nationale des chartes, Positions des thèses*, 1938, pp. 31–36.

—— "Les Juifs d'Avignon et du Comtat Venaissin de 1490 à 1790," *Ecole nationale des chartes, Positions des thèses*, 1939, pp. 53–59.

Drach, P. L. B., *De l'harmonie entre l'église et la synagogue*, Vol. I, Paris, 1844.

Emmrich, Hanna, *Das Judentum bei Voltaire*, Breslau, 1930.

Ettinger, S., "Jews and Judaism as seen by the English Deists of the 18th Century" (in Hebrew), *Zion*, XXIX (1964), 182–207.

Finkelstein, Louis, *Jewish Self-Government in the Middle Ages*, New York, 1924.

Francia de Beaufleury, Louis, *Histoire de l'établissement des Juifs à Bordeaux et à Bayonne depuis 1550*, Bordeaux, an 8 (1799–1800).

Francisque-Michel, M., *Histoire du commerce et de la navigation à Bordeaux*, Bordeaux, 1870.

Frankel, Zecharias, "Eine historische Notiz," *MGWJ*, XXI (1872), 44–47.

Franklin, Julian H., *Jean Bodin and the Sixteenth Century Revolution in the Methodology of Law and History*, New York, 1963.

Friedberg, Benjamin, *Bet Eked Sepharim*, 4 vols., 2d ed., Tel Aviv, 1951–56.

—— *Toldot ha-Defus ha-Ivri*, Antwerp, 1937.

Friedenwald, Harry, *The Jews and Medicine*, 2 vols., Baltimore, 1944.

—— "Montaigne's Relation to Judaism and Jews," *JQR*, XXXI (1940), 141–48.

Gay, Peter, *The Party of Humanity*, New York, 1964.

—— *Voltaire's Politics*, Princeton, 1959.

Ginsburger, E., *Le comité de surveillance de Jean-Jacques Rousseau*, Paris, 1934.

—— *Les Juifs de Belgique au XVIIIe Siècle*, Paris, 1932.

———— "Les Juifs de Peyrehorade," *REJ*, CIII (1938), 35–69.

———— "Les Juifs et la révolution française," *REJ*, CIV (1938), 35–69.

———— *Les statuts juridiques de la communauté Israélite de Bayonne, 1550–1941* (mimeographed), 28 pp., Paris, n.d.

Ginsburger, M., "Les anciens cimetières israélites de Metz," *REJ*, LII (1906), 272–83.

———— *Cerfberr et son epoque*, Gebweiler, 1908.

———— *Cerf Berr et son temps*, Strasbourg, 1936.

———— "Elie Schwab, rabbin de Haguenau (1721–1747)," *REJ*, XLIV (1902), 104–21, 260–82; XLV (1902), 255–84.

———— "Les familles Lehmann et Cerf Berr (de Bischheim)," *REJ*, LIX (1910), 106–30.

———— "Une fondation de Cerf Berr," *REJ*, LXXVI (1923), 47–51.

———— "Hatten," *Souvenir et Science*, III (1932), 6–8.

———— *Histoire de la communauté israélite de Bischheim au Saum*, Strasbourg, 1937.

———— *Der israelitische Friedhof in Jungholz*, Gebweiler, 1904.

———— "Jacob Jeqil Meyer, premier grand rabbin de Strasbourg, 1739–1830," *AIF*, XCIV (1933), 154–55.

———— *Les Juifs à Ribeauvillé et à Bergheim* (a pamphlet), Strasbourg, 1939.

———— "Mutzig," *Souvenir et Science*, IV (1933), 5, 10, 12.

———— "Nancy et Strasbourg," *REJ*, LXXXIX (1930), 83–97.

———— "Samuel Lévi, rabbin et financier," *REJ*, LXV (1913), 274–300; LXVI (1903), 111–33, 263–84; LXVII (1914), 82–117, 262–87; LXVIII (1914), 84–109.

———— "Samuel Sanvil Weil, rabbin de la haute et basse-Alsace (1711–1753)," *REJ*, XCVI (1933), 54–75, 179–98.

———— "Strasbourg et les Juifs (1530–1781)," *REJ*, LXXIX (1924), 61–78, 170–86; LXXX (1925), 88–94.

———— "Zwei unveröffentliche Briefe von Abbé Grégoire," *Festschrift zu Simon Dubnows siebzigsten Geburtstag*, ed. Ismar Elbogen, Berlin, 1930, 201–206.

Glaser, Alfred, *Geschichte der Juden in Strassburg von der Zeit Karls des Grossen bis auf die Gegenwart*, Strasbourg, 1894.

Godchot, Jacques, "Comment les Juifs de Lorraine élurent leurs députés en 1789," *REJ*, LXXXI (1925), 48–54.

———— "Deux procès de sorcellerie et de sacrilège à Nancy au XVIIIᵉ siècle," *REJ*, LXXXIX (1930), 86–97.

———— "Les Juifs de Nancy de 1789 à 1797," *REJ*, LXXXVI (1928), 1–35.

Gradis, Henry, *Notice sur la famille Gradis et sur la maison Gradis et fils de Bordeaux*, Bordeaux, 1875.

Graetz, Heinrich, "Don Balthasar Isaak Orobio de Castro: eine biographische Skizze," *MGWJ*, XVI (1867), 321–30.
—— "Die Familie Gradis," *MGWJ*, XXIV (1875), 447–59; XXV (1876), 78–85.
—— "Einige handschriftliche Briefe von Jonathan Eibeschütz," *MGWJ*, XVI (1867), 421–30.
—— *Geschichte der Juden*, Vol. XI, Leipzig, 1876.
—— "Voltaire und die Juden," *MGWJ*, XVII (1868), 161–74, 201–23.
Grosclaude, Pierre, *Malesherbes, témoin et intreprète de son temps*, Paris, 1961.
Gruenebaum-Ballin, P., "Grégoire convertisseur? ou la croyance de retour d'Israel," *REJ*, CXXI (1962), 383–98.
Guttman, Jacob, "Über Jean Bodin in seinen Beziehungen zum Judentum," *MGWJ*, XLIX (1905), 315–48, 459–89.
Guyot, Raymond, *Documents biographiques sur J. F. Reubell (1747–1807)*, Tours, 1911.
Halgouet, H. du, *Nantes, ses relations commerciales avec des îles d'Amerique au XVIIIᵉ siècle*, Rennes, 1939.
Halphen, Achille Edmond, *Recueil des lois, décrets ordonnances, avis du Conseil d'Etat, arrêtés et règlements concernant les Israélites depuis la révolution de 1789*, Paris, 1851.
Hay, Malcolm, *The Prejudices of Pascal*, London, 1962.
Hazard, Paul, *The European Mind: The Critical Years (1680–1715)*, New Haven, 1953.
Heckscher, Eli F., *Mercantilism*, rev. ed., 2 vols., New York, 1955.
Hemerdinger, Gabriel, "Le Dénombrement des Israélites d'Alsace," *REJ*, XLII (1901), 253–64.
Hemleben, Sylvester John, *Plans for World Peace through Six Centuries*, Chicago, 1943.
Hertzberg, Arthur, *The Zionist Idea*, Garden City, 1959.
Hildenfinger, Paul, "L'adresse de la commune de Strasbourg à l'Assemblée Nationale contre les Juifs (avril 1790)," *REJ*, LXVIII (1909), 112–28.
—— *Documents sur les Juifs à Paris au XVIIIᵉ siècle, actes d'inhumation et scellés*, Paris, 1913.
Hoffman, Charles, *L'Alsace*, 4 vols., Colmar, 1906–1907.
Horkheimer, Max and Samuel H. Flowerman, eds., *Studies in Prejudice*, 5 vols., New York, 1949–50.
Hyamson, Albert M., *The Sephardim of England*, London, 1951.
Jager, François, *De la transmission héréditaire des biens d'après la coutume de Metz et pays messin*, Paris, 1911.
Jardeni, Miriam, "The Attitude to the Jews in the Literary Polemics during the Religious Wars in France" (in Hebrew), *Zion*, XXVIII (1963), 70–85.

Jaupart, F., *L'activité commerciale et maritime de Bayonne au XVIII<sup>e</sup> siècle*, unpublished typescript, n.d. [but 1963], in the Bibliothèque Municipale de Bayonne.

Kahn, Daniel, "Le ghetto de Nancy," *Revue juive de Lorraine*, VIII (1932), 253–56.

Kahn, Léon, *Les Juifs de Paris au dix-huitième siècle*, Paris, 1894.

———— *Les Juifs de Paris sous Louis XV (1721–1760)*, Paris, 1892.

———— *Les Juifs de Paris pendant la révolution*, Paris, 1898.

Kahn, S., "Les Juifs de Montpellier au XVIII<sup>e</sup> Siècle," *REJ*, XXXIII (1896), 283–303.

Katz, Jacob, "To Whom was Mendelssohn Responding in his *Jerusalem*" (in Hebrew), *Zion*, XXIX (1964), 112–32.

Kaufmann, David, "Extraits de l'ancien livre de la communauté de Metz," *REJ*, XIX (1889), 115–30.

Kayserling, M., *Biblioteca española*, Strasbourg, 1890.

———— *Moses Mendelssohn, sein Leben und seine Werke*, Leipzig, 1862.

Kellenbenz, Hermann, *Sephardim an der unteren Elbe*, Wiesbaden, 1958.

Klausner, Joseph, *Historiah shel ha-Sifrut ha-Ivrit he-Hadashah*, Vol. I, Jerusalem, 1952.

Korn, Bertram W., "The Haham de Cordova of Jamaica," *American Jewish Archives*, XVIII (1966), 141–54.

Lagarde, Georges de, *La naissance de l'esprit laique au déclin du moyen age*, Vol. I, Louvain and Paris, 1956.

Lamphecht, S. P., *The Moral and Political Philosophy of John Locke*, New York, 1962.

La Rochelle, Ernest, *Jacob Rodrigues Péreire*, Paris, 1882.

Lataulade, Joseph de, *Les Juifs sous l'ancien régime*, Bordeaux, 1906.

Lehrmann, Charles, *L'elément Juif dans la littèrature française, des origines à la révolution*, Paris, 1960.

Lémann, Joseph, *L'entrée des Israélites dans la société française*, Paris, 1886.

Léon, Jacob Henry, *Histoire des Juifs de Bayonne*, Paris, 1893.

Leroux, Alfred, "Histoire externe de la communauté des religionnaires de Bordeaux de 1758 à 1789," *Bulletin de la société de l'histoire du Protestantisme français*, LXVIII (1919), 35–62.

Lévi, Israel, "L'affaire bourgeois (1652)," *REJ*, XXVII (1893), 180–206.

Levy, Alphonse, "Jean Jacques Rousseau und das Judentum," *MGWJ*, LVI (1912), 641–63.

[Levylier, Roger], *Notes et documents concernant la famille Cerf Berr*, 4 vols., Paris, 1902–1906.

Lheritier, Michel, *L'intendant Tourny*, 2 vols., Paris, 1920.

———— "La Révolution à Bordeaux de 1789; la transition de l'ancien au nouveau régime," *RHB*, VIII (1915), 130–45.

Liber, Maurice, "Les Juifs et la convocation des Etats Généraux," *REJ*, LXIII (1912), 185–210; LXIV (1912), 89–108, 244–77; LXV (1913), 89–133; LXVI (1913), 161–212.

Livet, Georges, *L'intendance d'Alsace sous Louis XIV, 1648–1715*, Strasbourg, 1956.

Lodge, Eleanor C., *Sully, Colbert and Turgot*, London, 1931.

Loeb, Isidore, "Un baron juif français," *AIF*, XLVI (1885), 188–90, 196–98.

—— "Les Juifs à Strasbourg depuis 1349 jusqu'à la révolution," *ASEJ*, II (1882), 137–98.

Lucien-Brun, Henry, *La Condition des Juifs en France depuis 1789*, Paris and Lyon, 1901.

Mahler, Raphael, *History of the Jewish People in Modern Times* (in Hebrew), Vol. I, bk. 1, Merhavia, 1955.

Maignial, M., *La question juive en France en 1789*, Paris, 1903.

Malvezin, Théophile, *Histoire des Juifs à Bordeaux*, Bordeaux, 1875.

Marcus, Jacob R., *American Jewry*, Cincinnati, 1959.

Martin, Germain, *La grande industrie en France sous le règne de Louis XV*, Paris, 1900.

Mathorez, J., *Les étrangers en France sous l'ancien régime*, 2 vols., Paris, 1919.

Maupassant, Jean de, "Un grand armateur de Bordeaux, Abraham Gradis," *RHB*, VI (1913), 175–96, 276–97, 344–67, 423–48; VII (1914), 53–67, 118–39, 272–89, 329–45.

McCloy, Shelby T., "The Race Question in Late Eighteenth Century France," *South Atlantic Quarterly*, L (1951), 348–60.

Meinecke, Friedrich, *Machiavellism, the doctrine of raison d'état and its place in modern history*, New Haven, 1957.

Meiss, Hone, *A travers le ghetto*, Coup d'oeil retrospectif sur l'Université israélite de Nice (1648–1860), Nice, 1923.

Merlin, M., *Répertoire universel et raisonné de jurisprudence*, 5th ed., Vol. VI, Brussels, 1826.

Meyer, Paul A., "The Attitude of the Enlightenment towards the Jew," *Studies on Voltaire and the Eighteenth Century*, XXVI (1963), 1161–1205.

Mevorah, B., "Jewish Diplomatic Activities to Prevent the Expulsion of Jews from Bohemia and Moravia in 1744–45" (in Hebrew), *Zion*, XXVIII (1963), 125–69.

Monin, H., "Les Juifs de Paris à la fin de l'ancien régime," *REJ*, XXIII (1891), 85–98.

Mornet, Daniel, "Bibliographie d'un certain nombre d'ouvrages philosophiques du XVIIIe siècle," *Revue d'histoire littéraire de la France*, XL (1933), 259–81.

—————— *Les origines intellectuelles de la révolution française*, Paris, 1934.

Mossé, Armand, *Histoire des Juifs d'Avignon et du Comtat Venaissin*, Paris, 1934.

Mossé, Gabriel, ed., *Mémoire d'Abraham Furtado sur l'état des Juifs en France jusqu'à la Révolution*, Paris, 1930.

Moulaert, B. C. B., *Vie et oeuvres du R. P. Richard*, Louvain, 1867.

Nahon, Gerard, "Contribution à l'histoire des Juifs en France sous Philippe le Bel," *REJ*, CXXI (1962), 58–82.

Nasatir, A. P., and Leo Shpall, "The Texel Affair," *PAJHS*, LIII (1963), 3–43.

Naville, Pierre, *Paul Thiry d'Holbach*, Paris, 1943.

Netter, Nathan, "Les anciens cimitières israélites de Metz situés près de la porte chambière," *REJ*, LI (1906), 280–302; LII (1906), 98–113.

—————— *Vingt siècles d'histoire d'une communauté juive; Metz et son grand passé*, Paris, 1938.

Pansier, P., "Une comédie en argot hébraico-provençal de la fin du XVIIIe siècle," *REJ*, LXXXI (1925), 113–45.

Pedro II D'Alcantare, *Poésies hébraico-provençales du rituel israélite comtadin*, Avignon, 1891.

Perey, Lucien, *Le président Henault et Madame du Deffand*, Paris, n.d.

Pfister, Christian, "Les Juifs d'Alsace sous le régime français (1648–1791)," *Pages Alsaciennes*, Fasc. 40 (1927), 197–217.

Poisson, Charles, *Les Fournisseurs aux armées sous la révolution française*, Paris, 1932.

Poliakov, Léon, *Histoire de l'antisémitisme, du Christ aux Juifs de cour*, Paris, 1955.

Posener, S., "A Bibliography of French Works on Jews in the Second Half of the 18th Century," *The Jews in France*, ed. Tcherikower, New York, 1942, II, 56–74.

—————— "French Sources to Jewish History in France" (in Yiddish), *ibid.*, I, 33–77.

—————— "Les Juifs sous le premier empire, les statistiques générals," *REJ*, XCIII (1932), 192–214; XCIV (1933), 157–66.

—————— "The Social Life of the Jewish Communities in France in the 18th Century," *JSS*, VII (1945), 195–232.

Rapoport, M.W., *Christian Wilhelm Dohm, der Gegner der Physiocratie, und seine Thesen*, Berlin, 1908.

Reinach, Solomon, "De l'origine des prières pour les morts," *REJ*, IV (1882), 161–73.

Reinach, Theodore, "Les Juifs dans l'opinion chrétienne aux XVIIe et XVIIIe siècles: Peuchet et Diderot," *REJ*, VIII (1884), 138–44.

—————— *Textes d'auteurs grecs et romains relatifs au Judaisme*, Paris, 1895.

Reiszner, Hans, "Mirabeaus Judenpolitik," *Morgen*, VIII (1932), 122–30.

Renouard, A. A., *Annales de l'imprimerie des Estienne*, Paris, 1843.

Reuss, Rodolphe, "L'antisémitisme dans le Bas-Rhin pendant la révolution (1790–1793)," *REJ*, LXVIII (1914), 246–63.

———— "Quelques documents nouveaux sur l'antisémitisme dans le Bas-Rhin, de 1794 à 1799," *REJ*, LIX (1910), 248–76.

Revah, I. S., "Un pamphlet contre l'Inquisition d'Antonio Enriquez Gomez: La seconde partie de la 'Politica Angelica' (Rouen 1647)," *REJ*, CXXI (1962), 81–168.

Rochette, Jacqueline, *La Condition des Juifs en Alsace jusqu'au décret du 28 septembre 1791*, Paris, 1938.

———— *Histoire des Juifs d'Alsace*, Paris, 1939.

Rostenberg, Leona, "The Printing of Hebrew Textbooks in Strasbourg, 1544–1549," *Journal of Jewish Bibliography*, II (1940), 47–50, 92.

Roth, Cecil, "Elie Montalto et sa consultation sur le sabbat," *REJ*, XCIV, 113–36.

———— *A History of the Jews in England*, Oxford, 1949.

———— *The History of the Jews of Italy*, Philadelphia, 1946.

———— *A History of the Marranos*, Philadelphia, 1947.

———— "Les marranes à Rouen; un chapitre ignoré de l'histoire des Juifs en France," *REJ*, LXXXVIII (1929), 113–55.

———— "Sumptuary Laws of the Community of Carpentras," *JQR*, XVIII (1927–28), 353–83.

Roubin, H., "La vie commerciale des Juifs comtadins en Languedoc au XVIIIᵉ siècle," *REJ*, XXXIV (1897), 276–93; XXXV (1897), 91–105; XXXVI (1898), 75–100.

Sagnac, P., "Les Juifs et la révolution Française," *Revue d'histoire moderne et contemporaine*, I (1899), 5-23, 209–34.

Sänger, Hermann, *Juden und Altes Testament bei Diderot*, Wertheim am Main, 1933.

Scheid, Elie, *Histoire des Juifs d'Alsace*, Paris, 1882.

———— *Histoire des Juifs de Haguenau*, Paris, 1885.

———— "Histoire des Juifs de Haguenau pendant la période française," *REJ*, VIII (1884), 243–54; X (1885), 204–31.

Schoeps, Hans Joachim, *The Jewish-Christian Argument*, New York, 1963.

———— *Philosemitismus im Barock*, Tübingen, 1952.

Scholem, Gershom, *Shabbetai Zvi* (in Hebrew), 2 vols., paged as one, Jerusalem, 1957.

Schwab, Moise, "Documents pour servir à l'histoire des Juifs de France," *REJ*, XI (1885), 141–49.

Sée, Henri, *Economic and Social Conditions in France during the Eighteenth Century*, New York, 1931.

———— *L'evolution de la pensée politique en France au XVIIIᵉ siècle*, Paris, 1925.

—— *Histoire économique de la France, le moyen age et l'ancien régime*, Paris, 1948.

—— *Les idées politiques en France au XVII<sup>e</sup> siècle*, Paris, 1923.

—— "Note sur le commerce des Juifs en Bretagne au XVIII<sup>e</sup> siècle," *REJ*, LXXX (1925), 170–78.

Shackleton, Robert, *Montesquieu*, Oxford, 1961.

Silberner, Edmund, *Western Socialism and the Jewish Question* (in Hebrew), Jerusalem, 1955.

Soboul, Albert, *La France à la veille de la révolution*, Paris, 1960.

Solow, Herbert, "Voltaire and Some Jews," *Menorah Journal*, XIII (1927), 186–97.

Sombart, Werner, *Die Juden und das Wirtschaftsleben*, Leipzig, 1911.

—— *Das Wirtschaftsleben im Zeitalter des Hochkapitalismus*, Munich and Leipzig, 1928.

Soria, Isaac, "Incidents in the life of Mr. Aaron Soria, furnished by his son, Mr. Isaac Soria, in April, 1871," *PAJHS*, XXVII (1920), 457–79.

Stillschweig, Kurt, "Die Judenemanzipation im Lichte des französischen Nationsbegriffs," *MGWJ*, LXXXI (1937), 457–58.

Strauss, Leo, *Spinoza's Critique of Religion*, New York, 1965.

Szajkowski, Zosa, "The Attitude of French Jacobins toward Jewish Religion," *HJ*, XVIII (1956), 107–20.

—— *Autonomy and Jewish Communal Debts during the French Revolution of 1789*, New York, 1959.

—— "The Delegation of the Jews of Bordeaux to the Malesherbes Commission (1788) and to the *Assemblée Nationale* (1790)" (in Hebrew), *Zion*, XVIII (1953), 31–79.

—— "The Demographical Aspects of Jewish Emancipation in France during the French Revolution," *HJ*, XXI (1959), 7–36.

—— "Documents dealing with the 'Four Communities' in the 18th century" (in Yiddish), *The Jews in France*, ed. Tcherikower, New York, 1942, II, 304–309.

—— *The Economic Status of the Jews in Alsace, Metz and Lorraine (1648–1789)*, New York, 1954.

—— "The Emancipation of Jews During the French Revolution: a Bibliography of Books, Pamphlets and Printed Documents 1789–1800," *SBB*, III (1957–58), 55–68, 87–114; IV (1959), 21–48.

—— *Franco-Judaica, An Analytical Bibliography of Books, Pamphlets, Decrees, Briefs and Other Printed Documents Pertaining to the Jews in France 1500–1788*, New York, 1962.

—— "French Notices of Jews in Poland and Russia from the 15th to the beginning of the 19th century" (in Yiddish), *Jews in France*, ed. Tcherikower, New York, 1942, I, 16–32.

—— "The Growth of the Jewish Population of France," *JSS*, VIII (1946), 179–96, 297–318.

Szajkowski, Zosa, "Internal Conflicts within the Eighteenth Century Jewish Community," *HUCA*, XXXI (1960), 167–80.

—— "Jewish Autonomy Debated and Attacked during the French Revolution," *HJ*, XX (1958), 31–46.

—— "The Jewish Community of Marseilles at the End of the Eighteenth Century," *REJ*, CXXI (1962), 367–82.

—— "Jewish Emigration from Bordeaux during the Eighteenth and Nineteenth Centuries," *JSS*, XVIII (1956), 118–24.

—— "The Jewish Problem in Alsace, Metz and Lorraine on the Eve of the Revolution of 1789," *JQR*, XLIV (1954), 205–43.

—— "The Jewish Status in Eighteenth Century France and the *Droit d'Aubaine*," *HJ*, XIX (1957), 147–61.

—— *The Language of the Jews in the Four Communities of the Comtat Venaissin* (in Yiddish), New York, 1948.

—— "The Law of September 28, 1791 regarding Debts Owed to Jews in France" (in Hebrew), *Zion*, XVII (1952), 84–100.

—— "Notes on the Demography of the Sephardim in France," *HUCA*, XXX (1959), 217–32.

—— "Occupational Problem of Jewish Emancipation in France 1789–1800," *HJ*, XXI (1959), 109–32.

—— "Population Problems of the Marranos and Sephardim in France, from the Sixteenth to the Twentieth Centuries," *PAAJR*, XXVII (1958), 83–105.

—— *Poverty and Social Welfare among French Jews (1800–1880)*, New York, 1954.

—— "Protestants and Jews of France in Fight for Emancipation, 1789–1791," *PAAJR*, XXV (1956), 119–35.

—— "Quarrels between the Orthodox and the Reformed in France" (in Hebrew), *Horeb*, XIV–XV (1960), 253–92.

—— "Relations among Sephardim, Ashkenazim and Avignonese Jews in France from the 16th to the 20th Centuries," *YIVO Annual*, X (1955), 165–96.

—— "Religious Propaganda against Jews during the French Revolution of 1789," *PAAJR*, XXIV (1955), 137–64.

—— "Secular Private Libraries Among French Jews in the Eighteenth Century" (in Hebrew), *Kirjath Sefer*, XXXV (1960), 495–98.

—— "Synagogues during the French Revolution of 1789–1800," *JSS*, XX (1958), 215–29.

—— "Trade Relations of Marranos in France with the Iberian Peninsula in the Sixteenth and Seventeenth Centuries," *JQR*, I (1959–60), 69–78.

—— "La vita intellettuale profana fra gli Ebrei nella Francia del XVIII secolo," *La rassegna mensile di Israel*, XXVII (1961), 122–29, 179–91.

Tcherikower, E., ed., *The Jews in France* (in Yiddish), 2 vols., New York, 1942.

[Terquem, Olry], "Rabbins de Metz depuis le commencement du XVIIᵉ siècle jusqu'à nos jours," *AIF*, I (1840), 25–31.

Torrey, N. L., *Voltaire and the English Deists*, New Haven, 1930.

Vernière, Paul, *Spinoza et la pensée française avant la révolution* (1 vol., 2 parts), Paris, 1954.

Vigouroux, F., *Les livres saints et la critique rationaliste*, 5th ed., 2 vols., Paris, 1901.

Waxman, Meyer, *A History of Jewish Literature*, Vol. 3., New York, 1945.

Weill, Julien, "Une texte de Montesquieu sur le Judaisme," *REJ*, XXXXIX (1904), 117–19.

Weinryb, B. D., "Enlightenment and German-Jewish Haskalah," *Studies in Voltaire and the Eighteenth Century*, XXVII (1963), 1817–47.

Weiss, Carl T., *Geschichte und Rechtliche Stellung der Juden im Fürstbistum Strassburg*, Bonn, 1894.

Weulersse, George, *Le mouvement physiocratique en France de 1756 à 1770*, 2 vols., Paris, 1910.

Weyl, Jonas, "La résidence des Juifs à Marseilles," *REJ*, XVII (1888), 96–110.

Wijler, Jacob Samuel, *Isaac de Pinto, sa vie et ses oeuvres*, Apeldoorn, 1923.

Wilson, Arthur M., *Diderot, the Testing Years*, New York, 1957.

Wolfson, David, "Le Bureau de commerce et les réclamations contre les commerçants Juifs (1726–46)," *REJ*, LX (1910), 93–97; LXI (1911), 88–101, 255–78; LXII (1911), 93–106.

Wright, Dudley, "Le prêtre qui réfuta Voltaire et son antijudaisme," *Bulletin catholique*, XVII (1939), 743–47.

Zeitlin, Wilhelm, *Bibliotheca Hebraica Post-Mendelssohniana*, Leipzig, 1891–95.

# Index

Abbatoirs, 197-99, 201, 215*n*, 219*n*
Abraham, 303
*Abrégé chronologique* (Hénault), 60*n*,
  61*n*
Academy of Bordeaux, 155
Academy at Caen, 141
Academy of Chalons-sur-Marne, 155
Academy of Rome, 155
Acculturation: Zionist view of, 4-5;
  Emancipation premises of, 8, 11,
  246-47, 275, 286, 292, 293-94, 298-
  99, 307-8, 323, 328, 331-33, 334,
  340, 344, 346, 348-49, 350-68; public avowal of Judaism and, 25-28,
  182, 185-87, 275-76; the Diaspora
  and, 31, 309; of Spinoza, 38, 159;
  Sephardim, 61, 62*n*, 71, 138, 140,
  160-61, 162, 178, 179, 181, 182,
  183, 184, 191-92, 203, 206, 208-9,
  290-91, 342-43; wealth and, 113*n*,
  140, 178, 181, 183, 278, 291, 328;
  language and, 138-39, 140, 142,
  177-78, 331; religious skepticism
  and, 160-65, 178, 182, 208-9, 211,
  258, 278, 279, 282, 291, 298-99,
  312-13, 331, 334-38; environment
  and, 276, 292
Addison, Joseph, 145
*Adresse des Juifs alsaciens au peuple
  d'Alsace*, 349*n*
Africa, 92, 151, 356-57
Agriculture, 24, 42, 53, 65; physiocratic view of, 72-73, 74, 75, 77;
  Polish, 76-77; peasants and, 83;
  Bordeaux, 84, 86; Peyrehorade,
  99*n*; farm animals, 103, 118; Metz,

121, 132*n*; Pinto on, 145, 153;
  Foissac on, 290, 329; decree of
  1874 on, 320; holidays and, 351
Aix, France, 23
Alcan, Moses, 124*n*
Alcohol, 88*n*, 89
Alembert, Jean d', 64, 252, 306, 313
Aleppo, 101
Alexander the Great, 303
Alexandria, Egypt, 303
Algeria, 101
Alsace, 1, 10, 99, 137, 263; conquered
  status of, 18, 114-15; trade limitations in, 20-21, 28, 52-54, 56, 66,
  76, 238, 286, 316, 317, 319, 320;
  Jewish Code of 1781, 71; decree of
  1784 and, 73, 317-22, 324, 325*n*,
  327, 329, 343; guilds, 113*n*, 286,
  319; Jewish loans to, 115-16, 349*n*;
  Jewish education in, 166, 168, 174,
  204, 206, 220; rabbinic appointments in, 167-68, 170, 211, 238-39,
  243, 246; languages in, 172; civil
  rights struggle (1776-89), 180,
  184, 191, 227-28, 236, 270-71, 286-
  87, 292-93, 314-28, 339, 341-49,
  350, 351-53; Jewish provincial organization of, 190, 235-36, 238,
  244, 320-21, 325; cemeteries in,
  196-97; abbatoirs in, 198-99; synagogues, 201-2, 203*n*; marriage regulations, 208, 319-20; regulation of
  social conduct in, 212, 236; tax burden, 219-21, 224, 236, 317, 318-19,
  343; expulsion threats, 224, 321-22,
  329, 354*n*, 356, 357; Hirtzel Lévy

Crown, The (*Continued*)
271, 316; American Revolution and, 150, 151, 153; royal tax collection, 216, 217, 219, 220-21, 223, 232, 320-21; mediation of intendants, 229; rabbi appointments and, 238, 239, 243; on community civil jurisdiction, 242; the Enlightenment and, 315-16; *péage* abolition, 318-19. See also *individual rulers*

Crusades, The, 281

Culture, 138-87, 275, 285, 328, 365; the Diaspora and, 1, 31, 309; Asian influences, 43, 262, 300, 306, 310, 312; climate and, 276, 292, 295; secular anti-Semitism in, 286, 287, 313, 331-32, 350-68; Greco-Roman influences in, 299-308, 310, 329. See also Acculturation; *and see specific cultural fields, e.g.,* Education

DaCosta, Anthony Mendez, London banker, 283
DaCosta, Isaac, 163n, 229n
Dacosta, Sara Mendes, 207-8
Dalpuget, Emanuel, 96n, 97
Dalpuget, Jacob, 96n, 97
Dalpuget, Israel, 104
Dalpuget, Salon, 97
Dalpuget family, 95, 96, 97, 101
Damiens, Robert François, 203n
*Daniel*, 262
David, King, 38, 45
*David, the History of the Man after God's Own Heart* (Annet), 38n
Deaf-mutes, 134, 141, 142
Debourge, Jean Claude Antoine, 361-62
Declaration of Independence (American), 339
Declaration of the Rights of Man, 2, 175n, 339; Alsatian persecution and, 340-41; Ashkenazi acculturation and, 344, 348
*Défense de mon oncle, La* (Voltaire), 303
Defoe, Daniel, 172
Deism, 34, 282; Bodin and, 22, 31; English, 38, 39, 45, 309, 312-13; Judaism and, 43, 192, 206; Pinto and, 150, 182; Cerf Berr and, 178-

79; Richard and, 255; conversionism and, 335, 361
Delgado, Moses Pinto, 269
*Demonstratio evangelica* (Huet), 40
*Dénombrement général des Juifs d'Alsace*, 321n
Deschamps, Jules, Abbé, 261n
Desmoulins, Camille, 331, 353, 355, 356
Dessau, Germany, 292
Deutsch, Emmanuel, 166
*Dialogue* (Justin Martyr), 255
Diaspora, 1, 31, 309; as "punishment," 35, 42n, 250, 258; Inquisition and, 268-69
*Dictionnaire historique et critique* (Bayle), 45-46
*Dictionnaire historique, critique, chronologique, géographique et littéral de la Bible* (Calmet), 252-53
Diderot, Dénis, 64, 271, 285; Pinto and, 145-46; on the Jews, 281-82, 286, 299, 310-12
Dietary laws: public provision for, 27, 87, 197-99, 201, 205, 206; Fleury on, 42; Azulai and, 161, 162; Metz, 164, 165; prison and, 201; anti-Semitic stereotypes and, 305, 351, 355
*Dieu et les hommes* (Voltaire), 303, 356n
Dijon, France, 100
Directory, The, 289, 356n
*Discourse* (Collins), 310n
*Discours prononcé le 30 janvier* (1791), (Debourge), 362n
*Discussions philosophiques sur l'athéisme*, (Gradis), 160n
*Dissertation sur le rappel des Juifs* (Rondet), 261
Divorce, 207-8
*Divrei David* (Meldola), 163n
*Divrei Shalom ve-Emet* (Weisel), 185, 351n
Dohm, Christian Wilhelm, 120, 236; economic principles of, 75, 292; Mirabeau and, 76, 287, 294, 334, 338; on persecution, 185, 265; community autonomy issue and, 188, 189n, 316; on America, 272n
Dorlisheim, Alsace, 224n
Douin, M., 215n66
Drach, Paul, 166

127-28, 129, 133, 134n, 201; debtor's prison, 125; Calmer and, 136, 137; margin speculation, 143; community budgeting, 217, 218-19, 220; Grégoire on, 336. *See also* Poverty; Wealth

Fish, 109, 115, 148

Fleury, Claude, abbé, 41-43, 252, 256, 257; Bossuet and, 41, 258; on persecution, 263

Flour, 89

Foissac (Jean Baptiste Annibal Aubert Dubayet), 76, 289-90, 329, 330n

Fonseca, scholar in Constantinople, 273n

Fonsecqua, 109

Fontaine, Countess of, 218

Fontenelle, Bernard le Bouvier de, 149

Fourier, Charles, 11

France, 6, 8, 29, 30; Jewish readmission (1500), 9, 12-28, 60, 79; American possessions, 24, 25, 54, 84, 88-93, 151, 333; Austrian War, 347. *See also* French Revolution; *and see specific place names*

Franchet, François Denis, 342n

Francia family, 90, 140n8, 155

Francia de Beaufleury, Louis, 25n, 155-58, 160, 276n

Frankfurt, Germany, 85n18, 124n, 244

Frederick the Great, King of Prussia, 113n, 273n, 283

Free trade movement, 65, 68, 78-137, 324; guild abolition efforts, 9, 69-70; production and, 66-67, 72-73; Avignonnais and, 96-98, 102-6, 112; Pinto and, 145, 152-53; Dohm and, 292; Ashkenazim request (1780), 317

French language, 138-40, 142; Pinto and, 143; Mendelssohn and, 154; Francia de Beaufleury and, 155; Hebrew printing in, 171n, 176; Hebrew translation into, 177-78, 185, 186; patriotic services in, 203; school study of, 205; community leadership and, 237

French Revolution, 19, 24, 48, 314-68; emancipation issue in, 1-2, 248-49, 264-65, 315, 331, 334, 337, 338-68; anti-Semitism in, 5, 7-8, 9-10, 11, 244, 287, 290, 297-99, 356n, 357, 366-68; Jewish immigration af-

ter, 14; Jewish community government after, 27, 222; economic changes and, 49, 64, 82n, 131-32, 135, 136-37, 338; physiocrats and, 71-72; acculturation and, 137, 165, 334, 350-68; Burke on, 151n; Gradis and, 158; Cremieu (Carmi) and, 171; egalitarianism and, 192-93, 337-38, 346, 360, 361, 362; civil registers and, 196; patriotic services, 203; rabbinical authority after, 245n; Pastoret and, 295n, 296; the Terror, 327, 354, 366; counterrevolution and, 357

Fresnay, Nicholas Lenglet du, 61n

Frois, Isaac, 111

Furtado, Abraham, 326, 327

*Gabbai* functions, 235n

Galicia, 321n

Galigai, Leonora, 12n

Galileo Galilei, 149

Gallican church, 21

Gambling, 212, 213, 242. *See also* Card-playing

Gay, Peter, 285; quoted, 283-84

Gayot de Pitaval, François, quoted, 34n

*Gazette littéraire* (periodical), 301

German Jews, *see* Ashkenazim

German language, 139, 142, 179n, 292

Germans, in Bordeaux, 79-80, 85n18, 228

Germany, 2, 21, 79, 113, 133, 298; Jewish persecution in, 6, 182, 183; Alsace-Lorraine and, 18, 114, 123; Jewish community organization in, 239; Richard's false "letter" to, 252; Voltaire in, 272, 283

Ghettoes, 76, 84, 107, 122, 211. *See also* Residential restrictions

Ginsburger, E., 17n

Ginzrot, Sohn, 352-53, 357

Glückel of Hamelm, 124n, 133, 139, 167n; on Samuel Lévy, 246

Gobineau, Joseph Arthur, 78, 276

Godard, Jacques, 347, 361, 362, 366

Gold trade, 107, 118; metalwork and, 122-23; American mines, 148

Gomez, Antonio Enriquez, 269

Goudar, Ange, 66-67

Gouguenheim, Joseph, 170n

Progressivism, 149
*Projet pour rendre la paix perpetuelle
en Europe* (St. Pierre), 152n
Proletariat, 83
Proops brothers, 174
Protestants, 6, 15, 25n, 255, 264; persecution of, 13, 22, 28, 34, 46, 103, 263, 274, 287, 293; in Holland, 43, 45, 46; civil status (1787), 68-69, 322; middle class and, 80; Bordeaux colony, 85, 87n; crypto-Protestants, 85n18; in Alsace, 227n; marriages, 251; rationalism and, 256; Jewish Emancipation and, 293, 296, 298, 322-23; Declaration of the Rights of Man and, 341
Proudhon, Pierre Joseph, 4, 10
Provençal dialect, 138-39, 171, 176
Provence, France, 14, 72-73
Prussia, 115, 293-94
Psalms, 177
Psychosis, 6
"Public Credit, Of," (Hume), 147n
Public office, 26, 336, 341, 348
Pudeffer, Bordeaux sergeant-major, 97
*Pugio fidei* (Martin), 35
Purim, 139

Quakers, 46n
Québec, Canada, 89
*Queen Esther*, 138-39
Quesnay, François, 67, 72, 74, 75, 77
Quiros (dancing master), 110

Raba family, 86n, 89n
Rabalho, Aaron Gomes, 111
Racist theory, 276, 300, 307, 312, 329, 353-54, 356, 357
*Rappel futur des Juifs* (Deschamps), 261n
*Rappel des Juifs, Du* (Peyrère), 32
Rashi, 159n
Rationalism: Biblical criticism and, 29-47, 159, 256, 257, 282, 283; law and, 58, 63, 360-61; intolerance and, 70, 279-80, 291, 300-1, 331; education and, 149; the soul and, 150; Talmudic criticism and, 257-58, 279, 311-12, 334n, 337; Christianity and, 277, 278, 279, 307, 309, 310, 311, 361; literary style and, 301, 311-12; social values and, 362-63
Real estate, *see* Housing; Land

*Reason and Faith* (Cordova), 301n, 92
*Recueil de lettres patentes* (Péreire), 60n
*Recueil des lois* (Lançon, ed.), 139n4, 240-41
*Réflexions sur la formation et la distribution des richesses* (Turgot), 75
*Réflexions sur les Juifs d'Alsace* (Pflieger), 352n
Reformation, The, 21, 259
*Réforme politique des Juifs, De la* (Dohm), 272n, 292
Regency, The, 133, 218
Régnicole status, 55, 56, 57, 110, 316, 351
Reims, France, 97
Reinach, Theodor, 145n
Reis, Isaac, 219n
Reischer, Jacob, 173, 246
Reischer, Nehemiah, 209-10
Religion: freedom of, 2, 12n, 14, 22, 24, 56, 68-69, 70-71, 85n18, 86, 125, 152, 185, 189, 272-73, 274, 275, 276, 278, 280, 293, 313, 354, 355, 357, 360; rationalism and, 149, 150, 159-60, 162n64, 182, 192, 206, 211, 256, 257-58, 279-80, 282, 283-84, 291, 300-1, 307, 309, 310-11, 312, 328, 331, 360-61 (*see also* Deism); monarchy and, 151n. See *also* specific faiths
Rennes, France, 104
Residential restrictions, 76, 107; Papal States, 84; Bayonne, 107, 108-9, 112; Strasbourg, 118, 121, 124, 131n162, 271, 318n, 319; Lorraine, 125; Paris, 133, 134, 135-36, 162, 189, 201, 345; Metz, 197, 218, 219, 233, 234, 237; Alsace, 221, 224, 290, 317, 320, 321-22; Jewish community regulations on, 129-30, 189, 193, 208, 224, 229, 317; Austria, 315n; community scattering proposal, 336
Revelations, Book of, 260, 261, 262
*Révolutions de France et de Brabant* (Desmoulins), 356n
Rewbell, Jean François, 10, 115n, 342, 348; Emancipation and, 354-57, 358, 359, 360
Rhine River, 318n
Ribeauvillé, France, 173, 174, 238